The
HISTORY
of the
OLYMPICS

The
HISTORY
of the
OLYMPICS

NIGEL BLUNDELL
&
DUNCAN MACKAY

PARKGATE
BOOKS

The publisher gratefully
acknowledges the assistance of
Allsport in supplying all the
photography for this book.
Individual photographers or
sources have been
credited in the relevant
captions throughout.

First published in 1999 by
PRC Publishing Ltd,
Kiln House, 210 New Kings Road, London SW6 4NZ

This edition published in 1999 by
London House,
Great Eastern Wharf,
Parkgate Road, London
SW11 4NQ
Great Britain

British Library Cataloguing in Publication Data:
A catalogue record for this book is available from the British Library.

ISBN 1-902616-61-8

Printed and bound in China

c o n t e n t s

THE HISTORY OF THE GAMES 8

1936   BERLIN 34

1948   LONDON 62

1952   HELSINKI 98

1956   MELBOURNE 120

1960   ROME 142

1964   TOKYO 168

1968   MEXICO CITY 196

1972   MUNICH 220

1976   MONTREAL 254

1980   MOSCOW 278

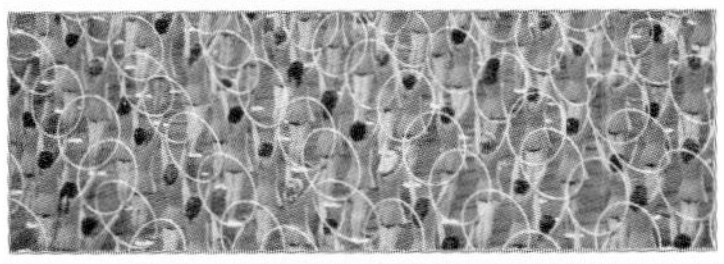

1984   LOS ANGELES 298

1988   SEOUL 322

1992   BARCELONA 390

1996   ATLANTA 442

2000   SYDNEY 490

LIST OF ABBREVIATIONS 512

1936
1948
1952
1956
1960
1964
1968
1972
1976
1980
1984
1988
1992
1996
2000

foreword

BY RAYMOND HECHT

I was born in Gardelgen, a little town in Germany, 200 kilometers west of Berlin, and from the age of three I was preparing myself for a future in sport, making my body strong and flexible. The first sports that I was involved with were gymnastics and soccer, both of which helped develop a will to win. At the age of ten, however, I was more interested in running, jumping and throwing whatever I could — nothing was safe, especially the neighbors' windows (though being able to run fast helped to keep me out of trouble). My first trainer saw me practicing and took me to the Magdeburg sportsclub where, at thirteen, I started to throw the javelin. Today, I think I can say that I am one of the best javelin throwers in the world — my personal best (92.60 meters) is a German record and the third best throw ever in the world. I have won seven medals in national championships, have dozens of wins in Grand Prixs and a third place in the '98 European Championships.

But all these are just small steps toward the major championships. The Olympic Games is the most important sporting event in history. As an athlete, everything you do, everything you learn in training, leads to this one day.

One cycle of the Olympic Games to the next takes four years. During these years each athlete prepares and perhaps allows themself a few dreams of victory. But if they want these dreams to come true they must train; not only bringing their body to a peak of fitness but also learning the perfect technique as well as how to compete at international level and how to keep their nerves in line. After all, it is only one day in four years, and they must muster every ounce of strength and remain calmly focused on their goal.

The Olympics are incredibly emotional. Before competing your mind goes crazy — you are thinking "have I done everything right." But all the competitors have the same problems; it doesn't matter which event they compete in, every athlete feels the same and knowing this helps, it makes you stronger. However, any comradeship or friendship you might feel stops the moment that the referee calls your name. Your mind shuts down and your eyes empty, but your body is full of power.

For an athlete who gains a place on the pedestal, this is probably the happiest moment of their life. But those who don't make it often have broken hearts, and even the strongest will be in tears while thinking to themselves, never again. Their training over the last four years has been so hard, they have sweated, injured muscles, had no holidays and fixed one moment in their minds.

Everybody expects so much at Sydney, but there can be only one winner in each event and I don't know anybody who doesn't want to be the the Olympic Champion — king or queen of their event. I wish every athlete all the best, all the luck they need for that important point, second or centimeter.

The HISTORY *of the*
GAMES

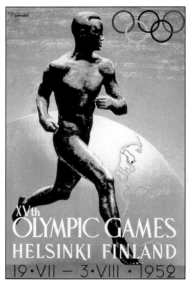

The HISTORY of the GAMES

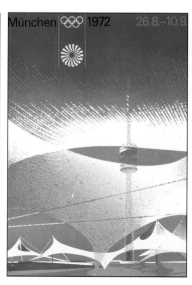

"In the name of all the competitors, I promise that we shall take part in these Olympic Games, respecting and abiding by the rules which govern them in the true spirit of sportsmanship, for the glory of sport and the honour of our teams."

— the Olympic Oath, taken publicly by athletes for the first time in 1920

Today the Olympic Games is a global business of mind-boggling proportions. Hundreds of millions of dollars change hands in negotiations for TV rights, merchandise sales, athletes' sponsorship, advertising contracts, corporate entertainment and package tourism. Successful competitors discover they have a market value fixed by an army of number-crunching middle-men — a value determined as much by their performance on TV and radio as their ability on track or field. The Olympic dream, complain the cynics, now amounts to little more than a plump bank balance.

There is no better illustration of the games' financial muscle than Sydney, where the XXVII Olympiad will be held between September 15 and October 1, 2000. When the chief executive of the organizing committee, Sandy Holloway, sat down with his aides to work out TV revenue estimates, they concluded that total income would amount to US$664 million. As it turned out, the American broadcasters NBC paid $51 million more than this solely for the exclusive US rights. With a predicted global audience of four billion, the world rights ended up raising a staggering $1.245 billion. On top of this, the IOC's marketing program is expected to rake in a further $500 million through sponsorship from leading companies. Given that the 2002 Winter Olympics are due to be staged on US soil, in Salt Lake City, it looks like corporate America can be counted upon to ensure yet another bidding bonanza.

In many ways, the media "spectacle culture" which now enmeshes the Olympics is inevitable. Sports administrators have long realized that to survive in a commercial age obsessed with leisure time and individual choice, they have to present a product which both hooks

BELOW RIGHT: Alfred Schwarzmann shows winning form on the horse during the 1936 Olympics in Berlin. Allsport

The games on show

The Olympic Museum was officially opened in 1993 — appropriately on the IOC's June 23 founding day. It is based at Ouchy, Lausanne, and deploys state-of-the-art technology to illustrate the history of the games together with artifacts assembled over the past century.

public interest and is self-financing. That means finding heroes (and the occasional villain), nurturing marketable personalities, promoting good role models and engineering excitement. Yet for all this backstage wheeling and dealing, the public relations stunts, the Byzantine organization and the ever-more spectacular special effects which dominate opening ceremonies, the modern games has somehow remained a unique piece of theater. Athletes on the blocks at the start of a 100-meter sprint final have no thought for hyperbole or the ephemeral trappings of fame. They just want to show they're

faster than the rest. The truth is, they would probably race for a packet of stale peanuts if it proved the point.

In that sense at least, things have not changed so much since the Ancient Greeks first came up with the idea of a sporting championships. The Olympian Games were the most famous of the four ancient games (the others being the Isthmian, Pythian and Nemean gatherings) and were held in tribute to Zeus at Olympia, the god's most important shrine. They were officially founded in 776 BC — the year names of winners were first recorded — and a full list of champions between then and

AD 217 was meticulously compiled by the historian Eusebius of Caesarea, the Ancient World's equivalent of today's media sports pundit! In those days, the games were a strictly male-only affair and female spectators were banned. It was felt to be immoral for women to watch men competing naked or wearing only a thong (although an exception was apparently made for the priestess of Demeter, presumably because she was unshockable and able to cast aside carnal thoughts).

The games were held every Olympiad, a four-year period used in the Greek calender, and during the spring of the chosen year messengers were despatched to all the principal city-states urging them to send their finest athletes — provided that they were of Greek descent and proven to be honorable men. Those who returned successful with an olive-wreath prize could expect to be fêted for the rest of their days, eulogized by poets and offered an allowance from state coffers. However, the stakes were high. Losers disgraced their city and were treated with contempt.

During the first 300 years of its history, the Olympian meeting was held on a single day. But in 472 BC it was expanded into a five-day event

ABOVE RIGHT: Jesse Owens of the USA sprinting to victory in 1936. IOC

Pace-setting presidents

There have been seven IOC presidents, not counting De Blonay whose position was temporary. The early constitution of the IOC required new presidents to come from the nation next hosting the games. Over the years, the choice of potential candidates has grown considerably; the IOC now has a membership of 96 from more than 80 countries.

beginning with a full day of sacrificial worship to Zeus. The program of events which followed is unclear but it seems the foot race was considered the main event, with boxing, wrestling and a fighting discipline called the *pancratium* taking place in an oblong-shaped stadium. Boxing was challenging enough; the pugilists progressing from gloves of wound soft leather strips to others made of tough hide weighted with lead. But the *pancratium* proved still more demanding. Here the fight was never stopped until one or other contestant publicly accepted defeat.

Other events included horse-racing (entrants had to supply their own horse), the pentathlon (sprinting, wrestling, javelin-throwing, discus-hurling and the long jump) and a climactic finale in which athletes raced in body armor. The discus was oval-shaped and made of bronze, while the standard javelin technique involved a strap wound around the shaft which was ripped downwards at the moment of delivery to impart greater distance and accuracy.

Even in those early days, there was a political dimension to the games. Quite apart from inter-city rivalries, the later Roman emperors

BELOW LEFT: The Olympic flame is passed from one torch bearer to another at the 1948 games in London. Hulton Deutsch

Waving the flag

The Olympic flag comprises five interlocking rings (representing the five continents) colored blue, yellow, black, green and red on a white background. De Coubertin discovered this emblem at Delphi, Greece, in 1913. The flag, made of embroidered satin, flew for the first time at the 1920 Antwerp games when it was formally presented by the Belgian Olympic committee. It was a feature of every subsequent meeting until 1988, when a replica made of Korean silk was raised as a replacement. A tradition at every closing ceremony is for the flag to be handed on from the mayor of the host city to the mayor of the next Olympic venue. The IOC president then "calls on the youth of the world to come together in four years time" to join the games of the next Olympiad.

BELOW: King George VI of Great Britain at the opening ceremony of the London games, 1948.
Hulton Deutsch

frowned upon overt acts of pagan worship. In AD 391 the emperor Theodosius I banned all such gatherings and the Olympian ideal rapidly faded. With the coming of the Dark Ages interest in sport declined and by medieval times it was all but forgotten. It was not until the early 19th century that European aristocrats, schooled in the classics and enticed by the Greek notion of developing one's mind and body in harmony, began to indulge in sports such as boxing, golf, cricket, tennis and soccer. Clubs and associations were formed, scientists hailed the importance of physical exercise (especially among adolescents) and soon Europe was in the midst of a sporting renaissance. Into this background, on January 1, 1863, was born the father of the modern Olympic Games: Baron Pierre de Coubertin.

De Coubertin was a member of an old aristocratic French family and from his teenage years he embraced the ideals of the Classical Age. His interest in the origins of competitive sport was heightened when between 1875 and 1881 the German archaeologist Ernst Curtius painstakingly laid bare the remains of Olympia and triggered a new wave of public interest in Ancient Greece.

BELOW: The graceful form of American Samuel Lee in the diving event at the 1952 Olympic Games in Helsinki. IOC

De Coubertin wasn't the first European to consider reviving the games — Curtius himself had suggested the same thing — and there had already been limited attempts to stage replicas in the form of Britain's Much Wenlock Games, started in rural Shropshire in 1852, and Greece's popular Pan-Hellenic Games, launched in 1859. But De Coubertin emerged as the driving force behind a truly global event, convinced that physical exercise and healthy competition were crucial to a rounded education. Moreover, he felt that his own country needed to regain some national pride following the humiliation of defeat by Germany in the 1870–71 war. His first attempt to float the idea in 1892 was greeted with confusion and misunderstanding. Refusing to be disheartened he began what was in effect a one-man public relations campaign in support of the Olympic ideal — traveling, writing articles and addressing meetings. In 1894, at an international congress convened to ratify the rules of amateur sporting competition, de Coubertin again presented his revival plan. With a masterly piece of audience manipulation, he played the *Hyme d'Apollon* to 2,000 people seated in the Grande Amphitheatre at the Sorbonne in Paris. Charmed by his Hellenist vision, de Coubertin won the unanimous support of all 79 official delegates and the 12 countries present agreed to reconvene the games in Athens in 1896. The conference ended on June 23 — a date still commemorated by the worldwide Olympic "family" as its founding day.

In his memoirs of 1920, de Coubertin later recalled: "I re-established the Olympic Games to ennoble and strengthen sports and to assure their independence and durability and, moreover, to allow them better to fulfil an educational

role which was their duty in the modern world. For the glorification of the individual athlete, whose existence is necessary for the physical activities of the multitude, and whose prowess is essential to continuing general emulation." Soon afterward, he declared: "I shall burnish a flabby and cramped youth, its body and its character, by sport, its risks even its excesses... all this is to be for everyone with no discrimination on account of birth, caste, financial standing or occupation."

In the run up to the 1896 games, however, it was obvious that de Coubertin still had plenty of work

BELOW LEFT: The 800 m final in Helsinki, 1952. The gold medalist was Malvin Whitfield of the USA. Hulton Deutsch

Lighting the flame

The Olympic flame was originally a sacred torch lit at the god Zeus's shrine during the ancient games at Olympia. The practice was revived in 1928 in Amsterdam when a torch was ignited in the main stadium. But it was not until 1936 in Berlin that the ritual of lighting the torch at Olympia, and relaying it to the host city, was introduced. In the case of Sydney, the flame will be flown from Greece and carried through Australia's neighboring Oceanic islands of American Samoa, the Cook Islands, Micronesia, Fiji, Guam, Nauru, New Zealand, Papua New Guinea, the Solomon Islands, Tonga, Vanuatu and Samoa. Once on the Australian mainland, the torch will be carried for 100 days before being placed in the cauldron at Sydney's Olympic Stadium during the evening of Friday, September 15.

to do. There was concern about financing and but for the intervention of Crown Prince Constantine of Greece, who established a fund-raising committee, and George Averoff, the Greek benefactor who paid for the new stadium, the first contest could easily have degenerated into shambles. As it was, the games were voted a success by all who participated. Winners received silver medals; runners-up bronze and there were no awards for third place.

In the aftermath of the Athens meeting, de Coubertin decided to create a sound administrative structure for the newly-formed International Olympic Committee. He wanted people who could decide policy while upholding the spirit and concept of the games and this meant ensuring true independence. De Coubertin selected the original committee members personally and stipulated that each was regarded as an ambassador from the IOC to his respective country, rather than the reverse.

These men, chosen for their knowledge of and commitment to sport, included Lord Arthur O. Ampthill (Great Britain), Viktor Balck (Sweden), Dimitrios Vikelas (Greece), Aleksei Butovsky (Russia), Ernest Callot (France), Leonard A.

BELOW LEFT: Competitors blaze around Montreal's cycle track during the 1976 games. Tony Duffy

Swifter, Higher, Stronger

The motto *Citius, Altius, Fortius* (Swifter, Higher, Stronger), which was adopted by the IOC for the 1920 Olympics, came from a Domincan monk called Father Henri Didon who greatly influenced De Coubertin. Some equally revered lines, first uttered by Bishop Ethelbert Talbot of Pennsylvania in his sermon at an Olympic service in St Paul's Cathedral, London, on July 19, 1908, read: "The most important thing in the Olympic Games is not to win but to take part, just as the most important thing in life is not the triumph but the struggle. The essential thing is not to have conquered but to have fought well."

18

BELOW: Lasse Viren wins the 5000 m event at the 1976 games. Tony Duffy

Cuff (New Zealand), Jiri Guth (Bohemia), Charles Herbert (Great Britain), Ferenc Kemeny (Hungary), Ferdinando Lucchesi-Palli (Italy), William M. Sloane (USA) and José Zubiaur (Argentina). De Coubertin himself, who initially acted as the committee's secretary general, held the IOC's presidency from 1896 until 1925.

The committee's constitution was based heavily on that of the Henley Royal Regatta — the celebrated UK summer rowing festival — and proved flexible enough to accommodate the workings of other bodies such as National Olympic Committees and International Federations. The idea was that these three pillars of world athletics would meet at a regular Olympic congress to discuss rule changes or other contentious issues.

One of the earliest moves for reform came from Greece, which wanted to build a permanent venue for the games on its own soil; this was rejected as being against the principles of global partnership. There then followed an uncertain start to the century in which the 1900 games (the first in which women were permitted to compete) went to Paris and the 1904 games to St Louis, USA.

BELOW: Carl Lewis takes a run-up to a gold medal for the USA in the long jump during the 1984 games in Los Angeles. David Cannon

Both events were linked to international expositions or fairs and were marked by unsatisfactory organization and over-bureaucratic officials.

In 1906, an unofficial "intercalateda" games took place in Greece, which proved popular and helped restore kudos. But when, two years later, London staged the games at short notice following Rome's withdrawal, there were again political disputes and accusations of home bias from five countries, most notably the United States. It was not until Stockholm in 1912 that the Olympics notched up an acclaimed success. The American Jim Thorpe won both the pentathlon and decathlon and became one of the first true superstars of the modern games.

Stockholm proved to be a brief calm before a very long storm. From this moment on, almost every games became enmeshed in high politics or grandstanding between rival countries. With preparations well advanced for the 1916 games in Berlin, Europe lurched into the Great War and the Olympics became an immediate casualty. Sadly, many of the young men who helped turn Stockholm into such a superb festival of sport lost their lives on the killing fields of France and Belgium.

Until now, De Coubertin had shouldered much of the administrative burden from his Paris home. But when war broke out, he enlisted in the army and passed the IOC Presidency to a Swiss, Baron Godefroy de Blonay. This, coupled with de Coubertin's ambition to house the IOC in a neutral state, prompted a move to the Swiss city of Lausanne, where in 1922 the IOC established its headquarters in a manor called "Mon Repos." The organization remained there until 1968, when the need for more space required a further move to the Chateau de Vidy, on the shore of Lake Geneva, where it remains today.

Despite the ravages of war, the Olympic movement remained intact and the IOC promptly handed the first post-World War I games to Antwerp, Belgium, a nation which had taken the brunt of the fighting. Although Berlin had been a non-event, its designation as the VI Olympiad was not passed on to Antwerp. The 1920 games were therefore titled the VII Olympiad.

The Belgians proved adept at organizing the games, even though they had little notice. The defeated powers of World War I — Germany, Austria, Hungary, Bulgaria and Turkey — were excluded by the IOC,

BELOW LEFT: American Evelyn Ashford, winner of the 100 m in 1984, takes the baton in the 4x100 m relay. Steve Powell

Music to inspire

The Olympic hymn, sung during each opening and closing ceremony, was written in 1896 by the Greek Spyros Samaras and his colleague Costis Palamas. In the 1950s calls to replace it were over-ruled.

and the event was marked by a requiem Mass for the war dead. However, it seemed that the public was still too traumatized by the aftermath of conflict to embrace the Olympics wholeheartedly. A specially-built 30,000-seat stadium was rarely more than half full and rock-bottom ticket prices failed to ignite enthusiasm. But Antwerp did at least donate one powerful symbolic legacy to the movement: a large white banner bearing the five Olympic rings fringed in gold. It is still handed on to each host city today.

Until the 1920s, there had been no talk of a Winter Olympics. True,

figure skating had been incorporated into London's 1908 games, and featured together with ice hockey in the Antwerp program, but the general view was that winter sports belonged outside the Olympic movement. This curiously illogical position could not be sustained and after intensive lobbying the IOC finally agreed to allow an "International Winter Sports Week" at Chamonix, France, in 1923. It was voted a success and a year later the IOC opted to stage the first proper Winter Olympic Games, again at Chamonix. They were planned for the same year as the Paris-based Summer Games but would be

BELOW LEFT: Athletes in the 4x400 m relay, Seoul, 1988. Tony Duffy

For the glory...

In 1920 athletes publicly took the Olympic oath for the first time and since then it has been repeated at every Olympiad by a representative from the host country. A judge also affirms that: "In the name of all the judges and officials, I promise that we shall officiate in these Olympic Games with complete impartiality, respecting and abiding by the rules which govern them in the true spirit of sportsmanship."

BELOW: British decathlete Daley Thompson shows his form at the pole vault in 1988. Gerard Vandystadt

organized separately. By now, the Scandinavian countries, which had feared that winter sports events established in their own countries would be jeopardized by a Winter Olympics, withdrew their objections.

The Paris games attracted more than 3,000 athletes from 44 countries and were so popular that the first Olympic ticket touts were able to make their black market debut. Paris produced a number of great competitors, among them Johnny Weismuller of "Tarzan" fame. However, the meeting was dominated by an unfolding drama between the 100 meters sprint challengers. The American Charley Paddock was believed to be the fastest man on Earth but it soon became clear that two British athletes, Harold Abrahams and Eric Liddell, were worthy candidates for his crown. Liddell, a devout Christian, refused to run in the final because it was held on a Sunday and instead went to preach at a church in Paris. Abrahams won the 100 meters gold in a time of 10.6 seconds and the drama of those two weeks were later characterized in the award-winning film *Chariots Of Fire*.

In 1925, Henri de Baillet-Latour, a Belgian, took over from

de Coubertin as IOC president. Like his colleague, de Baillet-Latour wanted to stop the increasing involvement of women in the Olympics but a tide of public opinion was flowing against him. The number of women participants had been increasing steadily with each successive games and in 1928 the IOC finally bowed to the principle of women entering track and field competitions. Nevertheless, these Amsterdam games prohibited women from competing in races further than 200 meters — a ruling that, amazingly, lasted until 1960.

The Los Angeles games of 1932 fell victim to another major world crisis: the Great Depression. IOC officials had hoped that LA would trigger a big expansion in sporting investment and the overall profile of the Olympics but, with the world economy heading for meltdown and the still-rumbling shockwaves of the 1929 Wall Street crash, sports budgets were seen as a low priority among governments. One innovation of LA '32, however, was a male athletes' village — following up an idea first tried at Athens in 1906.

The last games before World War II were held in Berlin in 1936. They provided a platform for one of the most loathsome events in 20th

BELOW LEFT: The impressive Olympic stadium in Barcelona, where the games were held in 1992. Mike Powell

BELOW RIGHT: Mike Conley of the USA, triple jump gold medalist at the 1992 games in Barcelona. Gary Mortimore

century sporting history: the moment when an angry Adolf Hitler refused to celebrate the awarding of four gold medals to US athlete Jesse Owens four gold medals on the grounds that he was black. This was to be a defining moment in the light of subsequent events... the first unequivocal demonstration by Hitler to the rest of the world that a culture of inherent racism was stamped across the Third Reich. To the Führer, architect of a white master race, Owens' performance must have been an infuriating rebuff. There can be no doubt that Jesse Owens ranks among the true greats of track and field. At Berlin he won the 100 meters sprint in 10.3 seconds, matching the Olympic record, set a new 200 meters sprint world and Olympic record of 20.7 seconds, won a new Olympic record with a long-jump of 8.05 meters (8cm short of his own world record) and was a member of the world-record beating US 100 meters relay team.

A touching footnote to the Owens-Hitler saga came in 1951 when the athlete made a special guest appearance during an exhibition match by the Harlem Globetrotters basketball team in the Berlin Olympic stadium. At half time, Owens, cheered by an 80,000 crowd,

Wings of peace

Doves or pigeons were first released at the 1896 opening ceremony as a symbol of world peace. They next appeared in the 1920 post-World War I games and have been part of the Olympic tradition ever since.

completed a steady lap of honor around the 400-meter track and made his way up to a VIP box situated directly below the verandah that 15 years earlier had been Hitler's vantage point. He was greeted by the mayor of West Berlin, Ernst Reuter, who immediately raised an arm to quieten the crowd. Picking up a microphone, Mayor Reuter said: "Jesse Owens, fifteen years ago Hitler refused to shake your hand. I will try to make up for it today by taking both of them." The two men embraced before Owens jogged out of the stadium to the sound of the crowd chanting his name.

The outbreak of the Sino-Japanese war in 1938 meant that the XII Olympic Games, due to be staged in Japan in 1940, were transferred to Helsinki. The Winter Games, also awarded to Japan, were shifted first to St. Moritz and later to Garmisch Partenkirchen. However, the Soviet invasion of Finland in 1939 and the declaration of war between the Allies and Germany that same year prevented either from taking place. The 1944 games, planned for Cortina d'Ampezzo and London, were also shelved and a ceremony marking the 50th anniversary of the Olympic revival, held in Lausanne in 1944,

BELOW LEFT: Gymnast Alina Stoica of Romania competes in the Rhythmic Individuals at the Atlanta games in 1996. David Cannon

Dogged tradition

Olympic mascots, often animal characters, have been popular since the 1972 Munich games when the dachshund "Waldi" made his debut. Sydney is offering three animals named Syd, Millie and Olly — a platypus, echidna and kookaburra.

BELOW: American Amy Van Dyken proudly displays her four gold medals, won in swimming events at Atlanta in 1996. Ross Kinnaird

was attended by only a handful of IOC members.

Yet the war did not entirely extinguish the Olympic flame. In the US, coaches and athletes decided to organize California's own mini-Olympics in aid of the Finnish Relief Fund, a charity dedicated to helping displaced Finns driven from their country following the Soviet Union's attack in 1939. The so-called "Champions of 1940" track and field meeting had the Finn Taisto Maki, the world's foremost two-miler, as its star name. It also roped in showbusiness figures like Stan Laurel and Oliver Hardy, who performed a skit

for the 18,000-strong crowd, Mary Martin, Dennis Day and Bill "Bojangles" Robinson. Robinson delighted spectators with a dance routine; then showed his track skills with a 75-yard backward dash in 10.7 seconds.

In the competitive programme, the big shock came when Maki was beaten in the two miles. In 1940, nine minutes in the two miles got roughly the same attention as a four-minute mile would 20 years later. At the time, only two Americans had broken the nine-minute barrier. Whereas Maki held the world record of 8min 53.2sec, the next two Finns in the race had

both clocked under 8min 58sec Maki lined up that night with Wisconsin star Walter Mehl and Notre Dame's Greg Rice and there was an air of expectancy in the stadium because it was thought anyone staying close to the fast finishing Maki could push him to a new world record. As it turned out, Mehl took the lead from Maki at the gun lap and though the Finn tried to fight back with 220 yards left he was eventually beaten into second place by Rice. Mehl's time was a creditable 9min 1sec.

In 1948, in the presence of the IOC's newly-elected Swedish president Sigfrid Edstrom, the Olympics resumed as normal, once more in London. However, as the post-war period progressed, top-class performances couldn't hide the inevitable conclusion that so-called amicable meetings of the world's sporting youth were being manipulated as part of a battle for international prestige. The Cold War began to dominate competition in the stadiums, while the notion of global fellowship became severely strained through ideological dogma and a political determination to prevent contact between the athletes. With the brutal suppression of the Hungarian uprising, the

On the rostrum

Gold medals are actually silver-gilt — the silver base metal being heavily gilded with at least six grams of solid gold. Ribbons and chains first appeared in the 1960 games. Host nations are not required to follow any standard design.

Anglo-French involvement in Suez, the use of apartheid in South Africa and Rhodesia (later Zimbabwe), and the Soviet invasion of Afghanistan, boycotts and exclusions came to be almost an expected part of the games from 1956 onward.

In 1952, the IOC made the American Avery Brundage its new president, a position he held with distinction until 1972. He was a vociferous defender of amateurism and ensured that breaches of the official code were ruthlessly punished. (The Austrian alpine skier Karl Schranz was among those penalized.) The closing years of Brundage's

term, however, involved a far more serious crisis: the 1972 attack on the Israeli team in the Munich Olympic village, carried out by members of the Black September terrorist movement. In the president's eyes, this confirmed his view that the larger and more high-profile the games became, the more they would suffer at the hands of politicians, fanatics and marketing men with fat wallets.

Outside political pressures reached their peak in the boycotts of 1980, when the US refused to go to Moscow in protest at the invasion of Afghanistan, and of 1984, when the Soviets hit back with a boycott of the

Los Angeles games (poor security arrangements was the official reason given). But for all these problems, the 1984 games produced a sea-change in attitude and helped shape the future of the movement for the 21st century. Brundage's fear of professionalism had to be cast aside in the face of overwhelming evidence that the Olympics were no longer affordable without aggressive marketing, sponsorship deals and revenue from television rights. A sign of the growing influence of television was evident in the way more popular events were scheduled to coincide with peak times for advertising revenue.

This new spirit of Olympic free enterprise was largely down to the diplomatic manoeuvrings of Spain's Juan Antonio Samaranch, who assumed the IOC presidency in 1980. The following year, the games became partly accessible to professional sportsmen, ending the long-standing and controversial Clause 26 of the IOC statute which specified the exclusive admission of amateurs. Despite this, Olympic competitors have been quickly disabused of any notion that their mere presence is a licence to print money. The public is interested only in champions, and so sponsors want champions to promote

BELOW LEFT: Television crews (bottom left in photograph) are now as common a sight at the games as the athletes themselves! Gerard Vandystadt

TV times

The 1936 Berlin meeting was first to be televised — relayed via closed circuit to the city's main cinemas. Twelve years later, the London games were broadcast to 80,000 television sets within a 50-mile radius of the capital while Helsinki (1952) and Melbourne (1956) each flew footage to countries around the world for transmission. The first live broadcast was made at the 1960 Rome games and the following Olympiad at Tokyo sent TV signals by satellite. Mexico in 1968 boasted the first live color coverage. All this attention from the new media meant that track athletes were required to wear lane numbers on their sides for easier identification.

BELOW: Olympic opening ceremonies have become increasingly elaborate affairs over the years. David Taylor

their goods. Being second-best, however valiantly, doesn't make good advertising.

It is largely this pressure to succeed that has spawned one of the most challenging issues in the history of the Olympic movement — the use of performance-enhancing drugs to cheat. Even though the IOC fired warning shots in 1988 by naming, shaming and banning the Canadian sprinter Ben Johnson (he was unceremoniously stripped of his gold medal and had his world record struck off), officials have found it difficult to implement an effective system of random drug testing. Since Johnson,

a succession of leading athletes have been publicly exposed in an uncertain game of increasingly high stakes.

Drug or "dope" testing at the Olympics is administered by the IOC's Medical Commission which was formed in 1967. Early tests concentrated on amphetamines and it was not until the Montreal games of 1976 that a reliable system of analysis for anabolic steroids was introduced. Since 1968, female athletes have been compelled to undergo so-called "sex tests" to make sure that they are not biologically male and therefore deemed to possess an unfair physical advantage. Unsurprisingly, there

BELOW: Olympic opening ceremonies have become increasingly elaborate affairs over the years. David Taylor

continues to be a robust debate about the methods, validity and ethics of this process.

In tackling performance-enhancing drugs, the IOC knows that an athlete with a knowledgeable coach can deploy several cunning techniques to beat the system. Steroids, for instance, can't magically make a person run faster or jump further. What they can do is drastically reduce the recovery time between gruelling training sessions — allowing a crooked athlete to build muscle much faster than his honest opponent. With the right training program, perhaps in some far-flung corner of the earth away from the risk of random blood sampling, an athlete can develop muscle with the use of steroids or growth hormones and still come off the drug in good time to test "clean" at a major event.

Cheats have been further aided by advances in the use of masking agents — specially developed drugs which conceal the presence of an illegal substance in the bloodstream. Another weapon is the propitious use of lawyers waving libel writs to frighten budget-conscious sport administrators. Some commentators have even argued for the free use of all performance drugs, under strict

Close finish

Electronic time-keeping devices and photo-finish cameras were first used officially to determine results in Tokyo in 1964. Until then, they had acted only as an aide to judges.

medical supervision, on the grounds that it would at least ensure a level playing field and cut the hugely expensive program of constant monitoring. The obverse of this argument is that detection techniques are improving all the time, driven by the all-powerful god of commercialism. No major sponsor wants to invest millions in a star athlete, only to find sales nosedive when he or she is exposed as a charlatan.

The IOC in general — and Juan Antonio Samaranch in particular — is acutely aware of the dangers that lie ahead. The games could ultimately become a battleground for biological science rather than true athleticism. And with so many ambitious human guinea pigs available, what risk do untested new drugs pose to competitors who care more for winning than the manner of winning.

Samaranch himself succinctly summed up the massive challenge facing the Olympic movement as it enters the new millennium. "The priority now," he said, "is to lay stress on Olympic ethics and education, the basic elements of which are tolerance, generosity, solidarity, friendship, non-discrimination and respect for others. Olympic ethics must be global in this sense, including the fight against doping, drug abuse and the evils that endanger the health of athletes and young people in general. The equality of opportunity between players, the impartial refereeing of competitions and the fair play of winners and losers alike are elements which encourage the virtues of justice. Sports activities must constantly rediscover their truly character-forming ideal, imbued with tolerance and promoting brotherhood between peoples."

ABOVE LEFT: The forthcoming games in Sydney promise to be a truly spectacular event. Nick Wilson

BERLIN 1936

INTRODUCTION

Berlin 1936

ABOVE: *The Berlin games commemorative pin.* Allsport

BELOW: *The Berlin Olympic torch.* Allsport

PREVIOUS PAGE: *The Berlin Olympics begin.* Hulton Deutsch

129 EVENTS

49 COUNTRIES

4,066 ATHLETES

	Gold	Silver	Bronze
GER	33	26	30
USA	24	20	12
HUN	10	1	5
ITA	8	9	5
FIN	7	6	6
FRA	7	6	6
SWE	6	5	9
NED	6	4	7
JPN	5	4	7
GBR	4	7	3
AUT	4	6	3
CZE	3	5	
ARG	2	2	3
EST	2	2	3
EGY	2	1	2
SUI	1	9	5
CAN	1	3	5
NOR	1	3	2
KOR	1		1
TUR	1		1
IND	1		
NZE	1		
POL		3	3
DEN		2	3
LAT		1	1
ROM		1	
SAF		1	
YUG		1	
MEX			3
BEL			2
AUS			1
PHI			1
POR			1

It was not until 1936 in Berlin that the symbolic and uplifting ritual was introduced of lighting the Olympic torch at Olympia and relaying it from Greece to the host city. It was also the first time the games were televised, relayed via closed circuit to the city's main cinemas. But there was another first that condemned the Berlin Olympics to infamy. It was the first time that politics — and a perverted philosophy at that — wholly hijacked the world's greatest sporting event.

Ironically, Berlin had been scheduled as a games venue once before. Indeed, preparations were well advanced for the 1916 games in the city until Europe lurched into the Great War and they became an immediate casualty, along with many of the young men who would have taken part in them. So when the games were again awarded to the German capital, it was a time of rejoicing.

The euphoria did not last long, however. The Olympics were awarded to the Germany before Adolf Hitler came to power. Despite demands to switch them, the plans were considered immutable — and the Third Reich leapt at the opportunity to use the event as a platform for the advancement of the "master race."

In the United States, Jewish groups in particular called for a boycott. US Olympic officials almost bowed to the storm of protest. But Avery Brundage, chairman of the US National Olympic Committee and future IOC president, argued that

RIGHT, BELOW RIGHT: The official poster. Allsport

the Germans had proved themselves by their smooth organizing of the previous winter games at Garmisch-Partenkirchen. Finally, the Americans voted by 58-56 to send a team.

Thus the Olympic torch, sparked alight by the sun in Greece, was relayed by 3,075 torchbearers to the German capital. There, 3,956 athletes from 49 countries paraded around Berlin's impressive new 100,000-seat stadium.

The home team was overall winner of the games, with 32 golds, ahead of America's 24. But it was as well that the US team came to Berlin — because it allowed one man's achievement to make a mockery of the Nazi creed of Aryan superiority.

That hero was, of course, Jesse Owens. The son of a cotton picker and the grandson of slaves, ran faster and jumped further than anyone else. He won the long jump, 100 and 200 meters, and led the US 400-meter relay team to victory as Hitler looked on.

He made his feats look "like water flowing downhill," according to one rival. And, to Hitler's chagrin, his achievements were celebrated by ordinary Germans who bombarded him with gifts and even invaded the Olympic Village at night to seek his autograph.

Owens was the greatest athlete of his age or perhaps of any age. Yet at Berlin in 1936, another lesser-known name also stands for the triumph of the Olympic ideal over politics and prejudice. Owens's long-jump opponent Luz Long,

RIGHT: A torchbearer at the Berlin games' opening ceremony. IOC

a fair-haired, blue-eyed German, befriended his black opponent and encouraged him when he was in danger of going out through fouls during in the qualifying round.

Owens said of the friend who was the first to congratulate him after his win: "You can melt down all my medals and cups and they would be just a plating on the 22-carat friendship I felt for Luz Long at that moment."

So, after all the Nazi propaganda, the enduring image of the Berlin games is of one black hero and one white rival eclipsing the politics of hatred beneath the swirling Swastika banners which almost — but not quite — obliterated the five rings of the Olympic flag.

The commemorative pins and commemorative medals. Allsport

OPPOSITE PAGE: *This was the first games to bring the symbolic flame from Greece.* Allsport

JESSE OWENS

ABOVE: Jesse Owens, USA.
Hulton Getty

RIGHT: Jesse Owens signs autographs. Hulton Deutsch

OPPOSITE PAGE
ABOVE: Jesse Owens' running was described as "like water flowing downhill." IOC

BELOW RIGHT: Jesse Owens winning easily. Hulton Getty

BELOW LEFT: Jesse Owens (4th from the right) with some of his team mates. Allsport

Jesse Owens won four gold medals at the 1936 Berlin Olympics but his achievement the previous year, when he broke five world records and equaled a sixth in the space of 45 minutes during a meeting in Ann Arbor, Michigan, was probably even greater.

In Berlin, the American triumphed in the 100 meters, 200 meters, long jump, and 4x100 meters relay. Thirty-seven years later a panel of major sportswriters would call Owens' Olympic triumph the most important sports story of the century. But this story, which will be told as long as men and women celebrate grace and courage, was more than a sports story. It was politics, history even, played out on an international stage with big stakes riding on every contest.

Owens, the son of sharecroppers and the grandson of slaves from Alabama, became the emblem of opposition to Nazi ideology. But he was also so unappreciated in his own country that the "Ebony Antelope" ended his career sprinting against racehorses, dogs and motorcycles.

The myth has grown that Adolf Hitler snubbed Owens by refusing to meet him after his 100 meters victory. "I was not invited to shake hands with Hitler — but I was not invited to the White House to shake hands with the president either," Owens said: "This was the social stigma we lived under."

Indeed, elaborate plans were made to celebrate the homecoming from Berlin of America's newest heroes, especially Owens. Yet on the day Owens arrived in New York, his mother, father and wife — all invited to participate in the celebrations — were refused admission to the first four hotels they tried because they were black.

Owens had grown up with racial bigotry. He was barred from living on campus at Ohio State University because he was black. He was also barred from the local restaurants and all but one of Columbus's cinemas. Years later, he said: "I came back to my native country and I couldn't ride in the front of the bus. I had to go to the back door. I couldn't live where I wanted." The hero of Berlin did not receive the official thanks of his country until 1976, when President Gerald Ford awarded him the Medal of Freedom. By that time he was a successful public relations executive and the international symbol of the Olympic movement.

After 35 years of pack-a-day cigarette smoking, Owens died in Arizona in March 1980. Toward the end of his life, he told a reporter that the four gold medals of Berlin had kept him alive "over the years," adding: "Time has stood still for me. That golden moment dies hard."

One little-known fact is that Owens' real name was not Jesse. He was christened James Cleveland Owens and known as J.C. until, when he was nine, his family moved to Cleveland. There, on his first day at school, he was asked his name and responded "J.C." in a thick drawl unfamiliar to his teacher, who put him down as Jesse. It stuck.

KITEI SON

BELOW: Korean marathon runner, Kitei Son, ran begrudgingly for the Japanese at the Berlin Olympics. Allsport

Berlin 1936

Just as Jesse Owens came to symbolize the struggle against Nazi idealism in Berlin, Kitei Son's victory in the 1936 marathon came to embody Korea's opposition to Japan's occupation of their country.

His only hope of running the Olympics after setting a world record of 2hr 26min 42sec in 1935 was to represent the land of the rising sun. He was also forced to endure the insult of adopting the Japanese name Kee Chung Sohn.

The defending champion, Juan Carlos Zabala of Argentina, had been preparing in Berlin for months and it was no surprise when he led for the first 25 kilometers. But Son, who ran a more patient race, passed him three kilometers later and went on to win from Britain's Ernie Harper by more than two minutes.

Son used his victory to denounce "Japanese imperialism" but few reporters were interested.

In 1988, when the games were held in Seoul, Son lit the Olympic flame. "It was the proudest moment of my life," he said afterward. "I was never really able to celebrate my victory in 1936 because I was running for a country I hated. I did not want to be seen to be to glad to push the propaganda of a country which had caused me and my people so many problems. Seeing the Japanese flag going up the pole and having to listen to their national anthem was a moment I hated."

HELEN STEPHENS

Berlin 1936

Unbeaten in her brief sprinting career, Helen Stephens won the 1936 Olympic 100 meters title in Berlin, beating her more famous rival Stella Walsh.

The six-foot Missouri schoolgirl was first discovered after running 50 yards in 5.8sec, equaling the world's best time. Two years later she beat Walsh for the AAU title over 100 meters (running two 11.5sec times that year) as well for the distance. In an extraordinary handicap race in Toronto in 1935, Stephens apparently ran 10.4sec for 100 yards (the official world record was 11.0) and 23.2sec for 220 yards (straight), the official time being 23.6 by Walsh. However, there is some doubt as the accuracy of the timing.

In Berlin she powered her way to the gold, ahead of Walsh, running 11.4sec in the heats and 11.5sec in the final, both wind-assisted.

She collected a second gold in the 4x100 meters relay, running a fine anchor leg. Bigger and stronger than any of her American rivals she also set US records with 13.61 meters and 13.70 meters indoors at the 8lb shot, and had a discus best of 40.70 meters.

Afterward she turned professional as a runner and basketball player. After a career at the Defense Mapping Agency Aerospace center in St. Louis, she coached at her old school in Missouri.

Her physical abilities remained strong for many years and she took seven gold medals at the 1981 Senior Olympics.

JACK LOVELOCK

Winner of the Olympic 1,500 meters title in 1936, Jack Lovelock was called the greatest runner of his era by, among others, American middle-distance world record holders Glen Cunningham and Bill Bonthron.

Bonthron lost to him when the New Zealander set a new world mile record in 1933. Cunningham was defeated when Lovelock won the 1,500 metres title in Berlin in a world record time of 3min 47.8sec. "It was the most perfectly executed race of my career," said Lovelock afterward.

Lovelock boxed and ran at school, and by the time he went to Oxford University as a Rhodes Scholar in 1931, he was capable of a 4min 22sec mile. Chosen for the 1932 Olympics in Los Angeles, Lovelock finished seventh, unable to respond to the fast pace set by the Canadian Phil Edwards and maintained by the Italian Luigi Beccali who won in a new world record time.

Lovelock raced well after Los Angeles and made the conscious decision to do just as much work for his medical studies as was needed to pass and to concentrate on winning the gold medal in Berlin.

He completed his medical studies in 1937 and practiced as a doctor in London before moving to the United States in 1949. It was there, late that year on his way home from work as assistant director of physical medicine and director of rehabilitation at the Manhattan Hospital of Special Surgery in New York, he fell to his death beneath a subway car.

RIGHT: Jack Lovelock broke the 1,500 m world record.
Hulton Deutsch

Above: Medalists in the women's springboard diving competition. Hulton Deutsch

Above left: Gold medalist Alfred Schwarzmann performing the scissors. Allsport

Left: Germany's Ernst Krebs won gold for kayaking. Hulton

ABOVE: *America's Consetta Anne Caruccio, a gymnastics competitor. Allsport*

LEFT: *The Japanese male swim team line the pool.* Hulton Deutsch

BELOW: *Tickets for the Berlin Olympics.* Allsport

46

ABOVE LEFT: *The Berlin Olympic bell.* Hulton Deutsch

ABOVE: *As the torchbearer approaches, German officials give the Nazi salute at the opening ceremony.* Allsport UK

LEFT: *Nazi flags and trailers outside the games.* Allsport UK

ABOVE: The three medalists in the women's highboard diving event. Allsport.
OPPOSITE PAGE
TOP LEFT: Glenn Morris of America won the gold in the decathlon. Allsport UK.
RIGHT: Harold Whitlock of Great Britain, winner of the 50 km walk. Allsport
LOWER LEFT: America's Kenneth Carpenter captured gold in the discus. Hulton Deutsch

ABOVE AND TOP RIGHT: Germans pay tribute to their coaches and athletes by taking to the streets of Berlin during the Olympics.
Hulton Deutsch

ABOVE RIGHT: Alfred Schwarzmann helped Germany to a team gold in gymnastics. Hulton Deutsch

OVERLEAF: Rowers give the Nazi salute. Hulton Deutsch

BERLIN 1936 AUGUST 1 -AUGUST 16

PARTICIPANTS: 4,066

MEN: 3,738

WOMEN: 328

COUNTRIES: 49

SPORTS: 19

EVENTS: 129

FINAL TORCHBEARER: FRITZ SCHILGEN

MEDALS TABLE

PLACE	COUNTRY	GOLD	SILVER	BRONZE
1	Germany	33	26	30
2	USA	24	20	12
3	Hungary	10	1	5
4	Italy	8	9	5
5	Finland	7	6	6

OUTSTANDING ATHLETES

PLACE	NAME (NATIONALITY)	DISCIPLINE	GOLD	SILVER	BRONZE
1	Jesse Owens (USA)	Athletics	4		
2	Konrad Frey (GER)	Gymnastics	3	1	2
3	Hendrika Mastenbroek (HOL)	Swimming	3	1	
4	Alfred Schwarzmann (GER)	Gymnastics	3		2
5	Robert Charpentier (FRA)	Cycling	3		

ATHLETICS — MEN

EVENT	GOLD		SILVER		BRONZE	
100 m	Jesse Owens (USA)	10.3	Ralph Metcalfe (USA)	10.4	Martinus Osendarp (HOL)	10.5
200 m	Jesse Owens (USA)	20.7	Matthew Robinson (USA)	21.1	Maranus Osendarp (HOL)	21.3
400 m	Archie Williams (USA)	46.5	Godrey Brown (GBR)	46.7	James LuValle (USA)	46.8
800 m	John Woodruff (USA)	1:52.9	Mario Lanzi (ITA)	1:53.3	Philip Edwards (CAN)	1:53.6
1,500 m	John Lovelock (NZL)	3:47.8	Glenn Cunningham (USA)	3:48.4	Luigi Beccali (ITA)	3:49.2
5,000 m	Gunnar Hoeckert (FIN)	14:22.2	Lauri Lehtinen (FIN)	14:25.8	Henry Jonsson (SWE)	14:29.0
10,000 m	Ilmari Salminen (FIN)	30:15.4	Arvo Askola (FIN)	30:15.6	Volmari Iso-Hollo (FIN)	30:20.2
Marathon	Kitei Son (JPN)	2:29:19.2	Ernest Harper (GBR)	2:31:23.2	Shoryu Nan (JPN)	2:31:42.0
110 m Hurdles	Forrest Towns (USA)	14.2	Donald Finlay (GBR)	14.4	Frederick Pollard (USA)	14.4
400 m Hurdles	Glenn Hardin (USA)	52.4	John Loaring (CAN)	52.7	Miguel White (PHI)	52.8
3000 m Steeplechase	Volmari Iso-Hollo (FIN)	9:03.8	KaarloTuominen (FIN)	9:06.8	Alfred Dompert (GER)	9:07.2
4x100 m	USA	39.8	Italy	41.1	Germany	41.2
4x400 m	Great Britain	3:09.0	USA	3:11.0	Germany	3:11.8
50 km Walk	Harold Whitlock (GBR)	4:30:41.1	Arthur Schwab (SUI)	4:32:09.2	Adalbert Bubenko (LAT)	4:32:42.2
High Jump	Cornelius Johnson (USA)	6'7.75"	David Albritton (USA)	6'6.75"	Delos Thurber (USA)	6'6.75"
Pole Vault	Earle Meadows (USA)	14'3.25"	Shuhei Nishida (JPN)	14'0"	Sueo Oe (JPN)	13'11.25"
Long Jump	Jesse Owens (USA)	26'5.25"	Luz Long (GER)	25'9.75"	Naoto Tajima (JPN)	25'4.5"
Triple Jump	Naoto Tajima (JPN)	52'5.75"	Masao Harada (JPN)	51'4.5"	John P Metcalfe (AUS)	50'10"
Shot	Hans Woellke (GER)	53'1.75"	Sulo Bärlund (FIN)	52'10"	Gerhard Stock (GER)	51'4.25"
Discus	Kenneth Carpenter (USA)	165'7"	Gordon Dunn (USA)	161'11"	Giorgio Oberweger (ITA)	161'6"
Hammer	Karl Hein (GER)	185'4"	Erwin Blask (GER)	180'6.5"	Fred Warngard (SWE)	179'10.5"
Javelin	Gerhard Stöck (GER)	235'8"	Yrjö Nikkanen (FIN)	232'2"	Kalervo Toivonen (FIN)	232'0"
Decathlon	Glenn Morris (USA)	7900	Robert Clark (USA)	7601	Jack Parker (USA)	7275

ATHLETICS — WOMEN

EVENT	GOLD		SILVER		BRONZE	
100 m	Helen Stephens (USA)	11.5	Stanislawa Walasiewicz (POL)	11.7	Käthe Krauß (GER)	11.9
80 m Hurdles	Trebisonda Valla (ITA)	11.7	Ann Steuer (GER)	11.7	Elizabeth Taylor (CAN)	11.7
4x100 m	USA	46.9	Great Britain	47.6	Canada	47.8
High Jump	Ibolya Csák (HUN)	5'3"	Dorothy Odam (GBR)	5'3"	Elfriede Kaun (GER)	5'3"
Discus	Gisela Mauermayer (GER)	156'3"	Jadwiga Wajswna (POL)	151'7.5"	Paula Mollenhauer (GER)	130'6.5"
Javelin	Tilly Fleischer (GER)	148'2.5"	Luise Krüger (GER)	142'0"	Maria Kwasniewska (POL)	137'1.5"

SWIMMING — MEN

EVENT	GOLD		SILVER		BRONZE	
100 m Freestyle	Ferenc Csik (HUN)	57.6	Masanori Yusa (JPN)	57.9	Shiego Arai (JPN)	58.0
400 m Freestyle	Jack Medica (USA)	4:44.5	Shumpei Uto (JPN)	4:45.6	Shozo Makino (JPN)	4:48.1
1500 m Freestyle	Noboru Terada (JPN)	19:13.7	Jack Medica (USA)	19:34.0	Shumpei Uto (JPN)	19:34.5
100 m Backstroke	Adolf Kiefer (USA)	1:05.9	Albert van de Weghe (USA)	1:07.7	Masaji Kiyokawa (JPN)	1:08.4
200 m Breaststroke	Tetsuo Hamuro (JPN)	2:42.5	Erwin Sietas (GER)	2:42.9	Reizo Koike (JPN)	2:44.2
4x200 m Freestyle	Japan	8:51.5	USA	9:03.0	Hungary	9:12.3
Springboard Diving	Richard Degener (USA)	163.57	Marshall Wayne (USA)	159.56	Albert Greene (USA)	146.29
Highboard Diving	Marshall Wayne (USA)	113.58	Elbert Root (USA)	110.60	Hermann Stork (GER)	110.31
Water Polo	Hungary		Germany		Belgium	

SWIMMING — WOMEN

EVENT	GOLD		SILVER		BRONZE	
100 m Freestyle	Hendrika Mastenbroek (HOL)	1:05.9	Jeanette Campbell (ARG)	1:06.4	Gisela Arendt (GER)	1:06.6
400 m Freestyle	Hendrika Mastenbroek (HOL)	5:26.4	Ragnhild Hveger (DEN)	5:27.5	Lenore Wingard-Kight (USA)	5:29.0
200 m Breaststroke	Hideko Maehata aPN)	3:03.6	Martha Genenger (GER)	3:04.2	Inge Sörensen (DEN)	3:07.8
100 m Backstroke	Dina W. Senff (HOL)	1:18.9	Hendrika Mastenbroek (HOL)	1:19.2	Alice Bridges (USA)	1:19.4
4x100 Freestyle	Netherlands	4:36.0	Germany	4:36.8	USA	4:40.2
Springboard Diving	Marjorie Gestring (USA)	89.27	Katherine Rawls (USA)	88.35	Dorothy Poynton-Hill (USA)	82.36
Highboard Diving	Dorothy Poynton-Hill (USA)	33.93	Velma Dunn (USA)	33.63	Käthe Köhler (GER)	33.43

BOXING

EVENT	GOLD	SILVER	BRONZE
Flyweight (-112 lb)	Willy Kaiser (GER)	Gavino Matta (ITA)	Louis D. Laurie (USA)
Bantamweight (-118 lb)	Ulderico Sergo (ITA)	Jack Wilson (USA)	Fidel Ortiz (MEX)
Featherweight (-126 lb)	Oscar Casanovas (ARG)	Charles Catterall (SAF)	Josef Miner (GER
Lightweight (-135 lb)	Imre Harangi (HUN)	Nikolai Stepulov (EST)	Erik Agren (SWE)
Welterweight (-147 lb)	Sten Suvio (FIN)	Michael Murach (GER)	Gerhard Petersen (DEN)
Middleweight (-160 lb)	Jean Despeaux (FRA)	Henry Tiller (NOR)	Raul Villareal (ARG)
Light-Heavyweight (-175 lb)	Roger Michelot (FRA)	Richard Vogt (GER)	Francisco Risiglione (ARG)
Heavyweight (+ 175 lb)	Herbert Runge (GER)	Guillermo Lovell (ARG)	Erling Nilsen (NOR)

WEIGHTLIFTING

EVENT	GOLD		SILVER		BRONZE	
Featherweights	Anthony Terlazzo (USA)	312.5	Saleh Mohammed Soliman (EGY)	305.0	Ibraham Shams (EGY)	300.0
Lightweight	Anwar Mesbah (EGY)	342.5			Karl Jansen (GER)	327.5
	Robert Fein (AUT)	342.5				
Middleweight	Khadr Sayed El Touni (EGY)	387.5	Rudolf Ismayr (GER)	352.5	Adolf Wagner (GER)	352.5
Light-Heavyweight	Louis Hostin (FRA)	372.5	Eugen Deutsch (GER)	365.0	Ibrahim Wasif (EGY)	360.0
Heavyweight	Josef Manger (GER)	410.0	Václav Psenicka (TCH))	402.5	Arnold Luhaäär (EST)	400.0

WEIGHTLIFTING WEIGHTS

FEATHERWEIGHT -132.25 lb	LIGHTWEIGHT -148.75 lb	MIDDLEWEIGHT -165.5 lb	
LIGHT-HEAVYWEIGHT -182 lb	HEAVYWEIGHT +182 lb		

GRECO-ROMAN WRESTLING

EVENT	GOLD	SILVER	BRONZE
Bantam Weight (-123.25 lb)	Márton Lorincz (HUN)	Egon Svensson (SWE)	Jakob Brendel (GER)
Featherweight (-134.25 lb)	Yasar Erkan (TUR)	Aarne Reini (FIN)	Einar Karlsson (SWE)
Lightweight (-l45.5 lb)	Lauri Koskela (FIN)	Josef Herda (TCH)	Voldemar Väli (EST)
Welterweight(-158.5 lb)	Rudolf Svedburg (SWE)	Fritz Schäfer (GER)	EinoVirtanen (FIN)
Middleweight (-174 lb)	Ivar Johansson (SWE)	Ludwig Schweickert (GER)	Jósef Palotás (HUN)
Light-Heavyweight (-194.75 lb)	Axel Cadier (SWE)	Edwin Bietags (LAT)	August Neo (EST)
Heavyweight (+191.75 lb)	Kristjan Palusalu (EST)	John Nyman (SWE)	Kurt Hornfischer (GER)

FREESTYLE WRESTLING

EVENT	GOLD	SILVER	BRONZE
Bantamweight (-123.25 lb)	Ödön Zormbori (HUN)	Ross Flood (USA)	Johannes Herbert (GER)
Featherweight (-134.25 lb)	Kustaa Pihlajamäki (FIN)	Francis Millard (USA)	Gösta Jönsson (SWE)
Lightweight (-145.5 lb)	Károly Kárpáty (HUN)	Wolfgang Ehrl (GER)	Hermanni Pihlajamäki (FIN)
Welterweight (-158.5 lb)	Frank Lewis (USA)	Ture Andersson (SWE)	Joseph Schleimer (CAN)
Middleweight (-174 lb)	Emile Poilvé (FRA)	Richard Voliva (USA)	Ahmet Kirecci (TUR)
Light-Heavyweight (-191.75 lb)	Knut Fridell (SWE)	August Neo (EST)	Erich Siebert (GER)
Heavyweight (+194.75 lb)	Kristjan Palusalu (EST)	Josef Klapuch (TCH)	Hjalmar Nyström (FIN)

FENCING

EVENT	GOLD		SILVER		BRONZE	
Individual Foil–Men	Guilio Gaudini (ITA)	7	Edward Gardière (FRA)	6	Giorgio Bocchino (ITA)	4
Team Foil	Italy		France		Germany	
Individual Épée	Franco Riccardi (ITA)	5	Saverio Ragno (ITA)	6	Giancarlo Cornaggia-Medici (ITA)	6
Team Épée	Italy		Sweden		France	
Individual Sabre	Endre Kabos (HUN)	7	Gustavo Marzi (ITA)	6	Aladír Gerevich (HUN)	6
Team Sabre	Hungary		Italy		Germany	
Individual Foil–Women	Ilona Elek (HUN)	6	Helene Mayer (GER)	5	Ellen Preis (AUT)	5

MODERN PENTATHLON

EVENT	GOLD		SILVER		BRONZE	
Individual	Gotthard Handrick (GER)	31.5	Charles Leonard (USA)	39.5	Silvano Abba (ITA)	45.5

CANOEING

EVENT	GOLD		SILVER		BRONZE	
1,000 m Kayak Singles K1	Gregor Hradetsky (AUT)	4:22.9	Helmut Cämmerer (GER)	4:25.6	Jacob Kraaier (HOL)	4:35.1
10,000 m Kayak Singles K1	Ernst Krebs (GER)	46:01.6	Fritz Landertinger (AUT)	46:14.7	Ernest Riedel (USA)	47:23.9
1,000 m Kayak Pairs K2	Austria	4:03 8	Germany	4:08.9	Netherlands	4:12.2
10,000 m Kayak Pairs K2	Germany	41:45.0	Austria	42:05.4	Sweden	43:06.1
1000 m Canadian Singles C2	Francis Amyot (CAN)	5:32.1	Bohuslav Karlik (TCH)	5:36.9	Erich Koschik (GER)	5:39.0
1000 m Canadian Pairs C2	Czechoslovakia	4:50.1	Austria	4:53.8	Canada	4:56.7
10,000 m Canadian Pairs C2	Czechoslovakia	50:33.5	Canada	51:15.8	Austria	51:28.0
10,000 m Folding Kayak Singles F1	Gregor Hradetzky (AUT)	50:01.2	Henri Eberhardt (FRA)	50:04.2	Xaver Hörmann (GER)	50:06.5
10,000 m Folding Kayak Pairs	Sweden	45:48.9	Germany	45:49.2	Netherlands	46:12.4

ROWING

EVENT	GOLD		SILVER		BRONZE	
Single Sculls	Gustav Schäfer (GER)	8:21.5	Josef Hasenöhrl (AUT)	8:25.8	Daniel Barrow (USA)	8:28.0
Double Sculls	Great Britain	7:20.8	Germany	7:26.2	Poland	7:36.2
Coxless Pairs	Germany	8:16.1	Denmark	8:19.2	Argentina	8:23.0
Coxed Pairs	Germany	8:36.9	Italy	8:49.7	France	8:54.0
Coxless Fours	Germany	7:01.8	Great Britain	7:06.5	Switzerland	7:10.6
Coxed Fours	Germany	7:16.2	Switzerland	7:24.3	France	7:33.3
Coxed Eights	USA	6:25.4	Italy	6:26.0	Germany	6:26.4

YACHTING

EVENT	GOLD		SILVER		BRONZE	
Olympic Monotype	Daniel Kagchelland (HOL)	163	Werner Krogmann (GER)	150	Peter Scctt (GBR)	131
International Star	Germany	80	Sweden	64	Netherlands	63
6 m	Great Britain	67	Norway	66	Sweden	62
8 m	Italy	55	Norway	53	Germany	53

CYCLING

EVENT	GOLD		SILVER		BRONZE	
Individual Road Race (62 miles)	Robert Charpentier (FRA)	2:33:05.0	Guy Lapebie (FRA)	2:33:05.2	Ernst Nievergelt (SUI)	2:33:05.8
Team Road Race	France	7:39:16.2	Switzerland	7:39:20.4	Belgium	7:39:21.0
1,000 m Time Trial	Arie van Vliet (HOL)	1:12.0	Pierre Georget (FRA)	1:12.8	Rudolf Karsch (GER)	1:13.2
1,000 m Sprint	Toni Merkens (GER)	11.8	Arie van Vliet (HOL)	NA	Louis Chaillot (FRA)	NA
2,000 m Tandem	Germany	11.8	Netherlands	NA	France	NA
4,000 m Team Pursuit	France	4:45.0	Italy	4:51.0	Great Britain	4:52.6

EQUESTRIANISM

EVENT	GOLD		SILVER		BRONZE	
Three-Day Event	Ludwig Stubbendorf (GER)	-37.70	Earl Thomson (USA)	-99.90	Hans Mathiesen-Lunding (DEN)	-102.20
Three-Day Event-Team	Germany	-676.65	Poland	-991.70	Great Britain	-995.50
Grand Prix (Dressage)	Heinz Pollay (GER)	1760.0	Friedrich Gerhard (GER)	1745.5	Alois Podhajsky (AUT)	1721.5
Grand Prix (Dressage)-Team	Germany	5074.0	France	4846.0	Sweden	4660.5
Grand Prix (Jumping)	Kurt Hasse (GER)	4	Henri Rang (ROM)	4	Jozsef von Platthy (HUN)	8
Grand Prix (Jumping)-Team	Germany	-44.00	Netherlands	-51.50	Portugal	-56.00

SHOOTING

EVENT	GOLD		SILVER		BRONZE	
Small-Bore Rifle (Prone)	Willy Rögeberg (NOR)	300	Ralf Berzseny (HUN)	296	Wladyslaw Karas (POL)	296
Rapid-Fire Pistol	Cornelius van Oyen (GER)	36	Heinz Hax (GER)	35	Torsten Ullman (SWE)	34
Free Pistol (50 m)	Torsten Ullmann (SWE)	559	Erich Krempel (GER)	544	Charles des Jammonières (FRA)	540

GYMNASTICS — MEN

EVENT	GOLD		SILVER		BRONZE	
Individual Combined Exercises	Alfred Schwarzmann (GER)	113.100	Eugen Mack (SUI)	112.334	Konrad Frey (GER)	111.532
Team	Germany	657.430	Switzerland	654.802	Finland	638.468
Parallel Bars	Konrad Frey (GER)	19.067	Michael Reusch (SUI)	19.034	Alfred Schwarzmann (GER)	18.967
Floor	Georges Miez (SUI)	18.666	Josef Walter (SUI)	18.500	Eugen Mack (SUI)	18.466
					Konrad Frey (GER)	18.466
Horse Vault	Alfred Schwarzmann (GER)	19.200	Eugen Mack (SUI)	18.967	Matthias Volz (GER)	18.467
Horizontal Bar	Aleksanteri Saarvala (FIN)	19.367	Konrad Frey (GER)	19.267	Alfred Schwarzmann (GER)	19.233
Rings	Alois Hudec (TCH)	19.433	Leon Stukelji (YUG)	18.867	Matthias Volz (GER)	18.667
Pommel Horse	Konrad Frey (GER)	19.333	Eugen Mack (SUI)	19.167	Albert Bachmann (SUI)	19.067

GYMNASTICS — WOMEN

EVENT	GOLD		SILVER		BRONZE	
Team	Germany	506.50	Czechoslovakia	503.60	Hungary	499.00

BASKETBALL

GOLD	SILVER	BRONZE
USA	Canada	Mexico

SOCCER

GOLD	SILVER	BRONZE
Italy	Austria	Norway

HANDBALL

GOLD	SILVER	BRONZE
Germany	Austria	Switzerland

HOCKEY

GOLD	SILVER	BRONZE
India	Germany	Netherlands

POLO

GOLD	SILVER	BRONZE
Argentina	Great Britain	Mexico

THE IMPORTANT THING
THE OLYMPIC GAMES IS
WINNING BUT TAKING PART
THE ESSENTIAL THING
LIFE IS NOT CONQUERING
BUT FIGHTING WELL

BBC
TELEVISION

INTRODUCTION

London 1948

ABOVE: A detail of the official poster. Allsport

PREVIOUS PAGE: King George VI salutes the athletes as they arrive at the opening ceremony of the 1948 London summer games. Hulton Deutsch.

136
EVENTS

59
COUNTRIES

4,099
ATHLETES

	Gold	Silver	Bronze
USA	38	27	19
SWE	16	11	17
FRA	10	6	13
HUN	10	5	12
ITA	8	12	9
FIN	8	7	5
TUR	6	4	2
CZE	6	2	3
SUI	5	10	5
DEN	5	7	8
NED	5	2	9
GBR	3	14	6
ARG	3	3	1
AUS	2	6	5
BEL	2	2	3
EGY	2	2	1
MEX	2	1	2
SAF	2	1	1
NOR	1	3	3
JAM	1	2	
AUT	1		3
IND	1		
PER	1		
YUG		2	
CAN		1	2
POR		1	1
URU		1	1
CUB		1	
ESP		1	
TRI		1	
SRL		1	
KOR			2
PAN			2
BRA			1
IRN			1
POL			1
PUR			1

The first post-war Olympic Games, held in and around London's famed Wembley Stadium, was a triumph of every kind — a celebration of peace and a symbol of how sport could reunite a world torn apart by war.

The Second World War had wiped out two Olympic years, 1940 and 1944. London had been the original choice for the cancelled '44 games, so happily it was first to be offered the '48 games. But the truth was that the Olympics could not have taken place anywhere else in Europe.

The Americans had considered bidding to stage the games, but everyone recognized it would be virtually impossible for the impoverished European nations to travel across the Atlantic at such a critical time. No one else was willing to make the necessary arrangements to host such a monumental undertaking in less than two years. London did.

Britain still had wartime rationing, with food, fuel and building materials in short supply. So the notion of an Olympic Village for these so-called "Austerity Games" was abandoned, the athletes instead being housed in schools, military camps and private homes.

World-famous Wembley Stadium rose to the challenge of creating a modern facility suitable for the optimism of the post-war period. A special Act of Parliament was required to make structural changes, build modern dressing rooms, recondition

the terraces, widen corridors, improve car parking facilities and build a new road to the stadium.

Down at pitch level, there was also much work to be done. The running track, first laid in 1923, had long been buried beneath a greyhound course so, with only three weeks to go before the opening ceremony, 100 workmen began the awesome task of recreating a world-class running surface. They dug down to the foundations, laid 800 tons of specially prepared cinders and used the latest scientific measuring equipment to set the levels and distances. The excellence of their work resulted in 17 world and Olympic records being broken on that brand new track.

A giant scoreboard, the size of a three-storey house, was constructed from timber specially imported from Finland and Sweden, and a concrete platform was laid to house the Olympic flame. When the games officially opened on July 29, in the presence of the IOC's newly-elected Swedish president, Sigfrid Edstrom, London had prepared for the arrival of 59 nations and more than 4,000 competitors. The stadium itself would see 33 track and field events being contested by 815 athletes from 53 of those countries.

King George VI, Queen Elizabeth, Queen Mary, Princess Margaret, the Duke and Duchess of Gloucester, the Duchess of Kent and Lord and Lady Mountbatten watched the magnificent opening ceremony of the XIVth Olympiad, serenaded by the massed bands of the Brigade of Guards. Seven

ABOVE RIGHT: *The official poster for the 1948 London summer games.* Allsport

TOP RIGHT: *The commemorative pin.* Allsport

ABOVE AND RIGHT: Details of the London 1948 commemorative pin. Allsport

thousand pigeons, symbolizing doves of peace, were released, and a 21-gun salute was followed by the arrival of the Olympic flame, borne aloft by Cambridge Blue John Mark.

The games were celebrated in a fantastic, honest, sporting spirit. The era of semi-professionalism — and worse — had not yet dawned. When they closed on August 14, American broadcaster Siegmund Smith told the world: "I record my genuine admiration for the achievements of the British people, not only in staging the games but in staging them the way they did. I liked the crowd's behavior at every event and I admired their sportsmanship."

The only hint of politics was the fact that Germany and Japan had not been invited to the games — and that they included the first entries by countries under Communist governments.

One figure stands out above all those who took part in the 1948 games: 30-year-old Dutch housewife Fanny Blankers-Koen, who picked up four athletics gold medals and set a new world and Olympic record in the 80 meters hurdles. Pundits reckon she could easily have carried off *six* golds but she didn't compete in the long jump or high jump — both disciplines in which she was the current world record holder.

Recently she recalled: "With the war so soon over, we were surprised but happy that Britain was organizing an Olympic Games, but I had no great expectations of it — or myself, because I had had two babies during the war. I remember the track had been made only weeks before the event. It was cinder and there had been quite a lot of rain, but we were just very happy to be able to run and compete again.

"There was no Olympic Village and we girls were housed in a school, six to a room, about half an hour's journey by train from the stadium. We used to walk to the station, wait for a train and then make our own way to Wembley.

"Now athletes are very well looked after. It is a great commercial business enterprise these days. Back then there was much more in the way of friendship and we were all happy just to be taking part."

Total expenditure on the 1948 Olympics amounted to just £600,000 and final accounts showed profits of £10,000. Small sums by present standards but it had nevertheless been a remarkable achievement.

For the millennium, Wembley Stadium is being demolished and rebuilt. But two mementos of the XIVth Olympiad remain... Flanking Wembley's main entrance since 1948 have stood the plaques honoring the various event winners. And high on a balcony, positioned appropriately between Wembley's landmark twin towers, is the pedestal that once held the Olympic flame.

LEFT: The official Olympic torch used in the London games. Allsport

FANNY BLANKERS-KOEN

ABOVE: *Holland's Fanny Blankers-Koen.* Allsport

BELOW RIGHT: *Blankers-Koen leading the field in the 80 m hurdles.* Allsport

OPPOSITE PAGE
ABOVE: *After winning the 80 m hurdles Blankers-Koen congratulates silver medalist Maureen Gardner of Great Britain.* Hulton Deutsch

BELOW: *Blankers-Koen crosses the 100 m finish line.* Hulton Deutsch

Fanny Blankers-Koen — The "Flying Dutchwoman" — was the heroine of the 1948 "Austerity Games" in London. Twelve years after finishing sixth in the high jump at the Berlin Olympics as a teenager and asking Jesse Owens for an autograph, she (by then a mother of two) matched the great man's achievement.

Blankers-Koen won gold medals in the 100 meters, 200 meters, 80 meters hurdles, and 4x100 meters relay. That means she won four of the nine events women could enter.

If she had contested the long jump, Blankers-Koen would have won that as well — because the winning mark was long short of her personal best. Incredibly, however, her chances had been dismissed beforehand by Jack Crump, the secretary of the Amateur Athletics Association, who wrote that she was too old at 30 and with two children to do anything other than hope for a medal.

Blankers-Koen's acclaim has matured with her, and she is still in great demand in Holland. "When I got home after London I thought people would soon forget," she says, "but I don't think they are going to, are they?"

Her 5 foot 6 inch figure hasn't stooped in the following years and barely more than a few pounds have thickened a frame which weighed 117 punds in her prime. Energy radiates from her ("I still walk to the shops — I must keep fit").

She is a calm, gentle woman, proud not so much of her athletic achievement but of a family which has grown up. She takes pride, too, in being an Olympian.

"The Olympics are the greatest uniting competition in the world," she says. "Every four years people come together from all over the world to compete against each other, meet one another, and share their experiences. They don't speak each other's languages; but, for a few weeks, they can live together peacefully. How different my life might have been if others had learned that lesson earlier."

Blankers-Koen already held the world record for the 100 yards when Germany invaded Holland in 1940, forcing her and her country to live under the Nazi jackboot. She continued to train and compete when the opportunity allowed, but by the time London rolled round in 1948, Crump was not alone in giving her little chance of success.

Blankers-Koen arrived home to a rapturous welcome — and in those days of modest rewards, the city of Amsterdam presented her with a new bicycle.

"I remember thinking how strange that I had made so many people happy," she says. "But times were harsh and I think people were just glad of the opportunity to celebrate anything. It made me very proud to know I had been able to bring joy into people's lives."

The closest any woman has come to matching Blankers-Koen's feat was in 1988 when Florence Griffith Joyner raced to three golds and a silver in Seoul. After the games, she continued running all the way to millionaires' row. But Blankers-Koen refuses to play the nostalgia game of translating her achievements into modern terms.

"I competed then and this is now," she says. "In 1948 no one ever thought it would be possible to make money from doing something you enjoyed. We were happy to have the opportunity to travel, see interesting places, and meet nice people.

"If people can make lots of money from doing something they are good at, then I am pleased for them. But it doesn't mean they are having any more fun than I did when I competed. I think money often brings only pressure, not happiness.

"I have no regrets because I have my memories and they are worth all the money in the world as far as I'm concerned. Anyway, that bicycle was very good — it lasted me for many years."

BOB MATHIAS

ABOVE AND RIGHT: Young Bob Mathias, gold medalist in the decathlon. Allsport

Bob Mathias wrote himself a special place in Olympic history when in 1948, aged only 17, he became the youngest male medalist in any track and field event by winning the decathlon.

Even more remarkably, he had only taken up the event earlier that year when his high school coach suggested he might be good at it. In fact, at London, he was the winner in only one out of the ten disciplines: the discus, which remained his strongest event.

When news of his victory reached his hometown of Tulare, California, the local telegraph office had to stay open all night so his family and friends could wire their congratulations.

He retained his title in Helsinki four years later with a world record score of 7,592 points and he won all 11 decathlons he contested between 1948 and 1956.

Remarkably Mathias had injured himself during the long jump on the first day in Helsinki and looked unlikely to win until, in the penultimate discipline, he hurled the javelin well over 194 feet to leave himself the relatively simple task of beating 4min 55.3sec in the 1,500 metres, the final event. In almost complete darkness on the track, he ran 4min 50.8sec.

In 1961, he starred with Jayne Mansfield in a spoof movie of the 1896 games, *It Happened in Athens.* He was a US congressman as a Republican for California's 18th district between 1966 and 1974. In 1973, he introduced legislation to amend the US Olympic Charter, creating a "Bill of Rights" for amateur athletes.

WILLIE GRUT

A captain in the Swedish artillery, the 33-year-old Willie Grut scored the most decisive victory in the history of modern pentathlon in London in 1948 when he finished first in three of the five disciplines — horse riding, fencing, and swimming. He was fifth in the pistol shooting and eighth in the 4,000 meters cross-country running.

The same year he had finished second in a demonstration pentathlon at the Winter Olympics in St. Moritz which consisted of downhill skiing, cross country skiing, fencing and an equestrian course.

He was rightly voted Sweden's sportsman of the year for 1948.

He later became Sweden's national team manager and was general secretary of the sport's international governing body in 1960.

His father, Torben Grut, was a finalist in the Swedish tennis championships and a distinguished architect who designed Stockholm's 1912 Olympic Stadium. Grut had planned to study medicine but after his father had lost much of his money opted instead to become a soldier.

At the age of 16, Willie Grut was Swedish schoolboy champion and record holder at 100 meters freestyle swimming. A year later, in 1932, he was Swedish champion at 100 meters, 400 meters and 1,500 meters.

In 1936, as a second lieutenant in the artillery he was a reserve on the Swedish Olympic swimming team, and started his pentathlon training. In 1938, he won the first of five Swedish titles at the five-day event discipline and had a brilliant victory against Germany.

MICHELINE OSTERMEYER

While the achievements of Fanny Blankers-Koen in the 1948 Olympics have been well documented, the story of Frenchwoman Micheline Ostermeyer is less well known.

Three months before the London games, this pianist graduated from the Paris Conservatory of Music with high honors. At Wembley, she used these same hands that so delicately played the piano to win gold medals in both the shot and discus. She also took the bronze at the high jump.

Ostermeyer was also the first African born woman to win an Olympic gold (she originated from Tunisia). She started her athletics career with Orientale Tunis before moving to compete for Stade Français.

A talented all round athlete, Ostermeyer won 12 French titles, including two at the pentathlon. Two years after the London Olympics, at the European Championships in Brussels, she once again showed her versatility. She was placed third in the shot, fourth in the discus and won the bronze in the 80 meters hurdles.

She would obviously have benefited from multi-event competition, but the pentathlon was not added to the Olympic program until many years later.

Her athletic success actually harmed her reputation as a concert pianist and for a long time she was afraid to play Liszt because he was "sportif." However, she overcame this prejudice and remains among the world's foremost concert pianists. She always said that going to the Olympics never matched the thrill she got from playing the piano.

RIGHT: Micheline Ostermeyer of France won two golds in discus and shot. Allsport UK

TOP: *The start of the 100 m final.* Allsport UK
ABOVE: *Duncan White of Ceylon fixes his starting blocks.* Hulton Deutsch
LEFT: *Athletes gather for the opening ceremony.* Hulton Deutsch

ABOVE: *Torchbearers for the opening ceremony.* Hulton Deutsch

*Emil Zátopek of
Czecholslovakia approaches
the 10,000 m finish line.*
Allsport

ABOVE: Crowded seats at the London games. Allsport UK

LEFT: Italy versus Hungary in fencing. Hulton Deutsch

ABOVE: A gymnast on the beam. Allsport UK

OPPOSITE PAGE
TOP: French cyclists win gold in the 4,000 m team pursuit Allsport UK

BELOW: Frank Henry, a silver medalist in the three-day equestrian event. Allsport

77

ABOVE: King George VI opens the London games. Hulton Deutsch

ABOVE RIGHT: Henry Eriksson of Sweden won gold in the 1,500 m. Hulton Deutsch

ABOVE: Gazanfer Bilge of Turkey takes gold in the featherweight wrestling division. Allsport UK

TOP: South African athletes take some shade before the opening procession. Hulton Deutsch

PREVIOUS PAGE: Athletes enter the stadium during the opening ceremony. Hulton Deutsch

ABOVE: Great Britain's male gymnastics team. Allsport UK

Left: Herma Bauma of Austria won gold in the javelin. Allsport UK

ABOVE: *India versus Great Britain in the hockey final. India won 4–0.* Allsport UK

LEFT: *Melvin Patton of the United States comes first in the 200 m final.* Allsport UK

ABOVE: A lightweight boxing bout between Joseph Vissers of Belgrade and Wallace Smith of the United States. Allsport

ABOVE: *The 100 m sprint won by American Harrison Dillard.* Allsport

LONDON 1948 JULY 29 - AUGUST 14

PARTICIPANTS: 4,099

MEN: 3,714

WOMEN: 385

COUNTRIES: 59

SPORTS: 17

EVENTS: 136

FINAL TORCHBEARER: JOHN MARK

MEDALS TABLE

PLACE	COUNTRY	GOLD	SILVER	BRONZE
1	USA	38	27	19
2	Sweden	16	11	17
3	France	10	6	13
4	Hungary	10	5	12
5	Italy	8	12	9

OUTSTANDING ATHLETES

PLACE	NAME (NATIONALITY)	DISCIPLINE	GOLD	SILVER	BRONZE
1	Fanny Blankers-Koen (HOL)	Athletics	4		
2	Veikko Huhtanen (FIN)	Gymnastics	3	1	1
3	Paavo Aaltonen (FIN)	Gymnastics	3		1
4	James McLane (USA)	Swimming	2	1	
	Anne Curtis (USA)	Swimming	2	1	

RIGHT: *The British male gymnastic team.*

ATHLETICS — MEN

EVENT	GOLD		SILVER		BRONZE	
100 m	Harrison Dillard (USA)	10.3	Norwood Ewell (USA)	10.4	Lloyd LaBeach (PAN)	10.4
200 m	Melvin Patton (USA)	21.1	Norwood Ewell (USA)	21.1	Lloyd LaBeach (PAN)	21.2
400 m	Arthur Wint (JAM)	46.2	Herbert McKenley JAM)	46.4	Malvin Whitfield (USA)	46.9
800 m	Malvin Whitfield (USA)	1:49.2	Arthur Wint (JAM)	1:49.5	Marcel Hansenne (FRA)	1:49.8
1,500 m	Henry Eriksson (SWE)	3:49.8	Lennart Strand (SWE)	3:50.4	Willem Slijkhuis (HOL)	3:50.4
5,000 m	Gaston Reiff (BEL)	14:17.6	Emil Zátopek (TCH)	14:17.8	Willem Slijkhuis (HOL)	14:26.8
10,000 m	Emil Zátopek (TCH)	29:59.6	Alain Mimoun (FRA)	30:47.4	Bertil Albertsson (SWE)	30:53.6
Marathon	Delfo Cabrera (ARG)	2:34:51.6	Thomas Richards (GBR)	2:35:07.6	Etienne Gailly (BEL)	2:35:33.6
110 m Hurdles	William Porter (USA)	13.9	Clyde Scott (USA)	14.1	Craig Dixon (USA)	14.1
400 m Hurdles	Leroy Cochran (USA)	51.1	Duncan White (CEY)	51.8	Rune Larsson (SWE)	52.2
3,000 m Steeplechase	Thore Sjostrand (SWE)	9:04.6	Erik Elmsater (SWE)	9:08.2	Gosta Hagstrom (SWE)	9:11.8
4x100 m	USA	40.6	Great Britain	41.3	Italy	41.5
4x400 m	USA	3:10.4	France	3:14.8	Sweden	3:16.0
10 km Walk	John Mikaelsson (SWE)	45:13.2	Ingemar Johansson (SWE)	45:43.8	Fritz Schwab (SUI)	46:00.2
50 km Walk	John Ljunggren (SWE)	4:41:52	Gaston Godel (SUI)	4:48:17	Tebbs Lloyd-Johnson (GBR)	4:48:31
High Jump	John Winter (AUS)	6'6"	Björn Paulson (NOR)	6'4.75"	Georpe Stanich (USA)	6'4.75"
Pole Vault	Guinn Smith (USA)	14'1.25"	Erkki Kataja (FIN)	13'9.25"	Robert Richards (USA)	13'9.25"
Long Jump	Willie Steele (USA)	25'7.75"	Thomas Bruce (AUS)	24'9"	Herbert Douglas (USA)	24'8.75"
Triple Jump	Arne Ahman (SWE)	50'6.25"	George Avery (AUS)	50'4.75"	Ruhi Sarialp (TUR)	49'3.5"
Shot	Wilbur Thomson (USA)	56'2"	Fancis Delaney (USA)	54'8.5"	James Fuchs (USA)	53'10.25"
Discus	Adolfo Consolini (IRA)	173'1.5"	Giuseppe Tosi (ITA)	169'10.5"	Fortune Gordien (USA)	166'6.5"
Hammer	Imre Németh (HUN)	183'11"	Ivan Gubijan (YUG)	178'0.5"	Robert Bennett (USA)	176'3"
Javelin	Tapio Rautavaara (FIN)	228'10.5"	Steve Seymour (USA)	221'7.5"	József Várszegi (HUN)	219'10.5"
Decathlon	Robert Mathias (USA)	7139	Ignace Heinrich (FRA)	6974	Floyd Simmons (USA)	6950

ATHLETICS — WOMEN

EVENT	GOLD		SILVER		BRONZE	
100 m	Fanny Blankers-Koen (HOL)	11.9	Dorothy Manley (GBR)	12.2	Shirley Strickland (AUS)	12.2
200 m	Fanny Blankers-Koen (HOL)	24.4	Audrey Williamson (GBR)	25.1	Audrey Patterson (USA)	25.2
80 m Hurdles	Fanny Blankers-Koen (HOL)	11.2	Maureen Gardner (GBR)	11.2	Shirley Strickland (AUS)	11.4
4x100 m	Netherlands	47.5	Australia	47.6	Canada	47.8
High Jump	Alice Coachman (USA)	5'6"	Dorothy Tyler-Odam (GBR)	5'6"	Micheline Ostermeyer (FRA)	5'3"
Long Jump	Olga Gyarmati (HUN)	18'8"	Noëmi Simonetto De Portela (ARG)	18'4.75"	Ann-Britt Leyman (SWE)	18'3.25"
Shot	Micheline Ostermeyer (FRA)	45'1.25"	Amelia Piccinini (ITA)	42'11.5"	Ine Schaffer (AUT)	42'10.75"
Discus	Micheline Ostermeyer (FRA)	137'6"	Edera Gentile-Cordiale (ITA)	35'0.5"	Jacqueline Mazeas (FRA)	132'9"
Javelin	Herma Bauma (AUT)	149'6"	Kaisa Parviainen (FIN)	143'8"	Lily Carlstedt (DEN)	140'6.5"

SWIMMING — MEN

EVENT	GOLD		SILVER		BRONZE	
100 m Freestyle	Walter Ris (USA)	57.3	Alan Ford (USA)	57.8	Géza Kádas (HUN)	58.1
400 m Freestyle	William Smith (USA)	4:41.0	James McLane (USA)	4:43.4	John Marshall (AUS)	4:47.7
1,500 m Freestyle	James McLane (USA)	19:18.5	John Marshall (AUS)	19:31.3	György Mitró (HUN)	19:43.2
100 m Backstroke	Allen Stack (USA)	1:06.4	Robert Cowell (USA)	1:06.5	Georges Vallerey (FRA)	1:07.8
200 m Breaststroke	Joseph Verdeur (USA)	2:39.3	Keith Carter (USA)	2:40.2	Robert Sohl (USA)	2:43.9
4x200 m Freestyle	USA	8:46.0	Hungary	8:48.4	France	9:08.0
Springboard Diving	Bruce Harlan (USA)	163.64	Miller Anderson (USA)	157.29	Samuel Lee (USA)	145.52
Highboard Diving	Samuel Lee (USA)	130.05	Bruce Harlan (USA)	122.30	Joaquin Caprilla Pérez (MEX)	113.52
Water Polo	Italy		Hungary		Netherlands	

SWIMMING — WOMEN

EVENT	GOLD		SILVER		BRONZE	
100 m Freestyle	Greta Andersen (DEN)	1:06.3	Ann Curtis (USA)	1:06.5	Marie-Louise Vaessen (HOL)	1:07.6
400 m Freestyle	Ann Curtis (USA)	5:17.8	Karen-Margrete Harup (DEN)	5:21.2	Catherine Gibson (GBR)	5:22.5
100 m Backstroke	Karen-Margrete Harup (DEN)	1:14.4	Suzanne Zimmermann (USA)	1:16.0	Judy Davies (AUS)	1:16.7
200 m Breaststroke	Petronella van Vliet (HOL)	2:57.2	Beatrice Lyons (AUS)	2:57.7	Evá Novák (HUN)	3:00.2
4x100 m Freestyle	USA	4:29.2	Denmark	4:29.6	Netherlands	4:31.6
Springboard Diving	Victoria Draves (USA)	108.74	Zoe Ann Olsen (USA)	108.23	Patricia Elsener (USA)	101.30
Highboard Diving	Victoria Draves (USA)	68.87	Patricia Elsner (USA)	66.28	Birte Christofferson (DEN)	66.04

BOXING

EVENT	GOLD	SILVER	BRONZE
Flyweight (-112.5 lb)	Pascual Perez (ARG)	Spartaco Bandinelli (ITA)	Soo-Ann Han (KOR)
Bantamweight (-119 lb)	Tibor Csik (HUN)	Giovanni Battista Zuddas (ITA)	Juan Venegas (PUR)
Featherweight (-127.75 lb)	Ernesto Formenti (ITA)	Dennis Shepherd (SAF)	Aleksy Antkiewicz (POL)
Lightweight (-136.5 lb)	Gerald Dreyer (SAF)	JosephVissers (BEL)	Sven Wad (DEN)
Welterweight (-148 lb)	Julius Torma (TCH)	Horace Herring (USA)	Alessandro D'Ottavio (ITA)
Middleweight (-161 lb)	László Papp (HUN)	John Wright (GBR)	Ivano Fontana (ITA)
Light-Heavyweight (-176.25 lb)	George Hunter (SAF)	Donald Scott (GBR)	Maurio Cia (ARG)
Heavyweight (+176.25 lb)	Rafael Iglesias (ARG)	Gunnar Nilsson (SWE)	John Arthur (SAF)

WEIGHTLIFTING

EVENT	GOLD		SILVER		BRONZE	
Bantamweight	Joseph Di Pietro (USA)	307.5	Julian Creus (GBR)	297.5	Richard Tom (USA)	295.0
Featherweight	Mahmoud Fayad (EGY)	332.5	Rodney Wilkes (TRI)	317.5	Jaffar Salmassi (IRN)	312.5
Lightweight	Ibrahim Shams (EGY)	360.0	Attia Hamouda (EGY)	360.0	James Halliday (GBR)	340.0
Middleweight	Frank Spellman (USA)	390.0	Peter George (USA)	382.5	Sung-Jip Kin (KOR)	380.0
Light-Heavyweight	Stanley Stanczyk (USA)	417.5	Harold Sakata (USA)	380.0	Gösta Magnusson (SWE)	375.0
Heavyweight	John Davis (USA)	452.5	Norbert Schemansky (USA)	425.0	Abraham Charité (HOL)	412.5

WEIGHTLIFTING WEIGHTS

BANTAMWEIGHT	-123.5 lb	FEATHERWEIGHT	-132.25 lb	LIGHTWEIGHT	-148.75 lb
MIDDLEWEIGHT	-165.5 lb	LIGHT-HEAVYWEIGHT	-182 lb	HEAVYWEIGHT	+182 lb

GRECO-ROMAN WRESTLING

EVENT	GOLD	SILVER	BRONZE
Flyweight (-114.5 lb)	Pietro Lombardi (ITA)	Kenan Olcay (TUR)	Reino Kangasmäki (FIN)
Bantamweight (-125.75 lb)	Kurt Pettersen (SWE)	Ali Mahmoud Hassan (EGY)	Halil Kaya (TUR)
Featherweight (-136.5 lb)	Mehmet Oktav (TUR)	Olle Anderberg (SWE)	Ferenc Tóth (HUN)
Lightweight (-147.5 lb)	Gustav Freij (SWE)	Aage Eriksen (NOR)	Károly Ferencz (HUN)
Welterweight (-160.75 lb)	Gosta Andersson (SWE)	Miklós Szilvási (HUN)	Henrik Hansen (DEN)
Middleweight (-174 lb)	Axel Grönberg (SWE)	Muhlis Tayfur (TUR)	Ercole Gallegati (ITA)
Light-Heavyweight (-191.75 lb)	Karl-Erik Nilsson (SWE)	Kaelpo Gröndahl (FIN)	Ibrahim Orabi (EGY)
Heavyweight (+191.75 lb)	Ahmet Kirecci (TUR)	Tor Nilsson (SWE)	Guido Fantoni (ITA)

FREESTYLE WRESTLING

EVENT	GOLD	SILVER	BRONZE
Flyweight (-114.5 lb)	Lennart Viitala (FIN)	Halat Balamir (TUR)	Thure Johansson (SWE)
Bantamweight (-125.75 lb)	Nasuh Akar (TUR)	Gerald Leeman (USA)	Charles Kouyos (FRA)
Featherweight (-136.5 lb)	Gazanfer Bilge (TUR)	Ivar Sjölin (SWE)	Adolf Müller (SUI)
Lightweight (-147.5 lb)	Celal Atik (TUR)	Gösta Frändfors (SWE)	Herimann Baumann (SUI)
Welterweight (-160.75 lb)	Yasar Dogu (TUR)	Richard Garrard (AUS)	Leland Merrill (USA)
Middleweight (-174 lb)	Glen Brand (USA)	Adil Candemir (TUR)	Erik Linden (SWE)
Light-Heavyweight (-191.75 lb)	Henry Wittenberg (USA)	Fritz Stöckli (SUI)	Bengt Fahlkvist (SWE)
Heavyweight (+191.75 lb)	Gyula Bóbis (HUN)	Bertil Antonsson (SWE)	Joseph Armstrong (AUS)

FENCING

EVENT	GOLD		SILVER		BRONZE	
Individual Foil — Men	Jehan Buhan (FRA)	7	Christian d'Oriola (FRA)	5	Lajos Maszlay (HUN)	4
Team Foil — Men	France		Italy		Belgium	
Individual Épée	Luigi Cantone (ITA)	7	Oswald Zappelli (SUI)	5	Edoardo Mangiarotti (ITA)	5
Team Épée	France		Italy		Sweden	
Individual Sabre	Aladár Gerevich (HUN)	7	Vicenzo Pinton (ITA)	5	Pál Kovacs (HUN)	5
Team Sabre	Hungary		Italy		USA	
Individual Foil — Women	Ilona Elek (HUN)	6	Karen Lachmann (DEN)	5	Ellen Müller-Preis (AUT)	5

MODERN PENTATHLON

EVENT	GOLD		SILVER		BRONZE	
Individual	William Grut (SWE)	16	George Moore (USA)	47	Gösta Gärdin (SWE)	49

CANOEING — WOMEN

EVENT	GOLD		SILVER		BRONZE	
500 m Kayak Singles K1	Karell Hoff (DEN)	2:31.9	Alide vall der Anker-Doedans (HOL)	2:32.8	Fritzi Schwingl (AUT)	2:32.9

CANOEING — MEN

EVENT	GOLD		SILVER		BRONZE	
1,000 m Kayak Singles K1	Gert Fredriksson (SWE)	4:33.2	Johan Kobberup (DEN)	4:39.9	Henri Eberhardt	4:41.4
10,000 m Kayak Singles K1	Gert Fredriksson (SWE)	50:47.7	Kurt Wires (FIN)	51:18.2	Ejvind Skabo (NOR)	51:35.4
1,000 m Kayak Pairs K2	Sweden	4:07.3	Denmark	4:07 S	Finland	4:08.7
10,000 m Kayak Pairs K2	Sweden	46:09.4	Norway	46:44.8	Finland	46:48.2
1,000 m Canadian Singles C1	Josef Holecek (TCH)	5:42.0	Douglas Bennett (CAN)	5:53.3	Robert Boutigny (FRA)	5:55.9
10,000 m Canadian Singles C1	Frantisek Capek (TCH)	1:02.05	Frank Havens (USA)	1:02.40	Norman Lane (CAN)	1:04.35
1,000 m Canadian Pairs C2	Czechoslovakia	5:07.1	USA	5:08.2	France	5:15.2
10,000 m Canadian Pairs C2	USA	55:55.4	Czechoslovakia	57:38.5	France	58:00.8

ROWING

EVENT	GOLD		SILVER		BRONZE	
Single Sculls	Mervyn Wood (AUS)	7:24.4	Eduardo Risso (URU)	7:38.2	Romolo Catasta (ITA)	7:51.4
Double Sculls	Great Britain	6:51.3	Denmark	6:55.3	Uruguay	7:12.4
Coxless Pairs	Great Britain	7:21.1	Switzerland	7:23.9	Italy	7:31.5
Coxed Pairs	Denmark	8:00.5	Italy	8:12.2	Hungary	8:25.2
Coxless Fours	Italy	6:39.0	Denmark	6:43.5	USA	6:47.7
Coxed Fours	USA	6:50.3	Switzerland	6:53.3	Denmark	6:58.6
Coxed Eights	USA	5:56.7	Great Britain	6:06.9	Norway	6:10.3

YACHTING

EVENT	GOLD		SILVER		BRONZE	
Olympic Monotype	Paul Elvström (DEN)	5543	Ralph Evans jun. (USA)	5408	Jacobus de Jong (HOL)	5204
International Star	USA	5828	Cuba	4949	Netherlands	4731
Swallow	Great Britain	5625	Portugal	5579	USA	4352
Dragon	Norway	4746	Sweden	4621	Denmark	4223
6 m	USA	5472	Argentina	5120	Sweden	4033

CYCLING

EVENT	GOLD		SILVER		BRONZE	
Individual Road Race (121 miles)	José Beyaert (FRA)	5:18:12.6	Gerardus Voorting (HOL)	5:18:16.2	Lode Wouters (BEL)	5:18:16.2
Team Road Race	Belgium	15:58:17.4	Great Britain	16:03:31.6	France	16:08:19.4
1,000 m Time-Trial	Jacques Dupont (FRA)	1:13.5	Pierre Nihant (BEL)	1:14.5	Thomas Godwin (GBR)	1:15.0
1,000 m Sprint	Mario Ghella (ITA)		Reginald Harris (GBR)		Axel Schandorff (DEN)	
2,000 m Tandem	Italy		Great Britain		France	
4,000 m Team Pursuit	France	4:57.8	Italy	5:36.7	Great Britain	5:55.8

EQUESTRIANISM

EVENT	GOLD		SILVER		BRONZE	
Three-Day Event	Bernard Chevallier (FRA)	+4	Frank Henry (USA)	-21	Robert Selfelt (SWE)	-25
Three-Day Event (Team)	USA	-161.50	Sweden	-165.00	Mexico	-305.25
Grand Prix (Dressage)	Hans Moser (SUI)	492.5	André Jousseaume (FRA)	480.0	Gustav-Adolf Boltenstern Jr (SWE)	477.5
Grand Prix (Dressage) Team	France	1269.0	USA	1256.0	Portugal	1182.0
Grand Prix (Jumping)	Humberto Marileo Cortés (MEX)	6.25	Rubén Uriza (MEX)	8	Jean François d'Orgeix (FRA)	8
Grand Prix ((Jumping) Team	Mexico	-34.25	Spain	-56.50	Great Britain	-67.00

SHOOTING

EVENT	GOLD		SILVER		BRONZE	
Free Rifle (3 Positions)	Emil Grunig (SUI)	1120	Pauli Janhonen (FIN)	1114	Willy Rögeberg (NOR)	1112
Small-Bore Rifle (Prone)	Arthur Cook (USA)	599	Walter Tomsen (USA)	599	Jonas Jonsson (SWE)	597
Rapid-Fire Pistol	Károly Takács (HUN)	580	Carlos E. Diaz Sáenz Valiente (ARG)	571	Sven Lundqvist (SWE)	569
Free Pistol (50 m)	Edwin Vasquez Cam (PER)	545	Rudolf Schnyder (SUI)	539	Torsten Ullman (SWE)	539

GYMNASTICS — MEN

EVENT	GOLD		SILVER		BRONZE	
Individual Combined Exercises	Veikko Huhtanen (FIN)	229.70	Walter Lehmann (SUI)	229.00	Paavo Aaltonen (FIN)	228.80
Team	Finland	1358.30	Switzerland	1356.70	Hungary	1330.85
Parallel Bars	Michael Reusch (SUI)	39.50	Veikko Huhtanen (FIN)	39.30	Christian Kipfer (SUI)	39.10
					Josef Stalder (SUI)	39.10
Floor	Ferenc Pataki (HUN)	38.70	János Mogyorósi-Klencs (HUN)	38.40	Zdenek Ruzicka (TCH)	38.10
Horse Vault	Paavo Aaltonen (FIN)	39.10	Olavi Rove (FIN)	39.00	János Mogyorósi-Klencs (HUN)	38.50
					Ferenc Pataki (HUN)	38.50
					Leo Sotornik (TCH)	38.50
Horizontal Bar	Josef Stalder (SUI)	39.70	Walter Lehmann (SUI)	39.40	Veikko Huhtanen (FIN)	39.20
Rings	Karl Frei (SUI)	39.60	Michael Reusch (SUI)	39.10	Zdenek Ru zi cka (TCH)	38.50
Pommel Horse	Veikko Huhtanen (FIN)	38.70	Luigi Zanetti (ITA)	38.30	Guido Figone (ITA)	38.20
	Paavo Aaltonen (FIN)	38.70				
	Heikki Savolaien (FIN)	38.70				

95

GYMNASTICS — WOMEN

EVENT	GOLD		SILVER		BRONZE	
Team	Czechoslovakia	445.45	Hungary	440.55	USA	422.63

BASKETBALL

GOLD	SILVER	BRONZE
USA	France	Brazil

SOCCER

GOLD	SILVER	BRONZE
Sweden	Yugoslavia	Denmark

HOCKEY

GOLD	SILVER	BRONZE
India	Great Britain	Netherlands

RIGHT: USA versus France in basketball. Allsport UK

HELSINKI 1952

INTRODUCTION

ABOVE: The Olympic rings. Hulton Deutsch

PREVIOUS PAGE: Rusaek Nielsen of Denmark takes a tumble after his horse, Saharas *failed to jump a fence during the endurance/speed cross-country event at the 1952 Helsinki summer games.* Hulton Deutsch

149
EVENTS

69
COUNTRIES

4,925
ATHLETES

	Gold	Silver	Bronze
USA	40	19	17
URS	22	30	19
HUN	16	10	16
SWE	12	12	10
ITA	8	9	4
CZE	7	3	3
FRA	6	6	6
FIN	6	3	13
AUS	6	2	3
NOR	3	2	
SUI	2	6	6
SAF	2	4	4
JAM	2	3	
BEL	2	2	
DEN	2	1	3
TUR	2		1
JPN	1	6	2
GBR	1	2	8
ARG	1	2	2
POL	1	2	1
CAN	1	2	
YUG	1	2	
ROM	1	1	2
BRA	1		2
NZE	1		2
IND	1		1
LUX	1		
GER		7	17
NED		5	
IRN		3	4
CHI		2	
AUT		1	1
LEB		1	1
IRL		1	
MEX		1	
ESP		1	
KOR			2
URU			2
TRI			2
BUL			1
EGY			1
POR			1
VEN			1

Helsinki 1952

The Soviet Union ended their 40-year self-imposed exile from the Olympics — and for the next 40 years the games would be the main battleground of the cold war.

The Soviets refused to mix with the rest of the world and they and their satellites were allowed to set up their own Olympic Village at Otaniemi, while everybody else was at Kapyla. At their secluded camp, the Soviet team erected a big scoreboard to highlight the competition between themselves and US athletes. Their determination seemed to pay off because, with strong showings in track, wrestling and gymnastics, the Soviet Union led the medal chart through the early stages.

Its scoreboard was wiped clear, however, when American athletes, helped by five gold medals from the boxing team, passed the Soviets in the closing days. The Americans wound up with more medals (76 against the Soviets' 71) and more golds (40 against 22).

Never before had George Orwell's theory that sport was merely an extension of war without the guns seemed more accurate.

Away from the politicking, these were a wonderful games. Helsinki, with a population of only 367,000, was the smallest city ever to host the games but the knowledgeable fans ensured the country got behind the event.

The honor of completing the Olympic torch relay fell to 55-year-old Paavo Nurmi, arguably the greatest distance runner in history, who lit the flame in the stadium. He then passed the torch on to 62-year-old Hannes Kolehmainen, another of the famed "Flying Finns," who lit a second flame.

Appropriately, in a country renowned for its distance runners, it was Emil Zátopek who shone the brightest. The Czechoslovakian runner won an unprecedented triple of the 5,000 meters, 10,000 meters and the marathon. To complete a great week for Zátopek, his wife Dana, born on the same day as Emil, also won a gold medal in the javelin, within an hour of his 5,000 meters victory.

The most successful female athlete was Marjorie Jackson, an Australian who set world records winning the 100 and 200 meters but lost out on the chance of a third gold medal when she dropped the baton in the 4x100 meters relay.

The smaller countries enjoyed a successful games. Jamaican runners excelled over the 400 meters and there was a major sensation in the 1,500 metres, where Josy Barthel of Luxembourg raced to victory. So unexpected was his win, that the medal ceremony had to be delayed while the band tried to find the sheet music for the national anthem.

Among those left trailing by Barthel were Britain's Roger Bannister, who was so disappointed he returned home determined to become the first man to break four minutes for the mile. He succeeded two years later.

One of the most memorable images of the games came at the swimming where after the 400 meters freestyle the father of France's Jean Boiteux jumped into the pool fully clothed to congratulate his son!

In the boxing ring Sweden's Ingemar Johansson was disqualified in the heavyweight final for "not trying." His silver medal was withheld for 14 years. In 1959 he won the world heavyweight title from Floyd Paterson, the American who had won the middleweight gold medal in Helsinki.

At the end of the games, it was announced that Avery Brundage, a former Olympian from the US, would be the new president of the International Olympic Committee. His period of office was to coincide with some of the most controversial and saddest moments in Olympic history.

EMIL ZÁTOPEK

ABOVE: Emile Zátopek of Czechoslovakia leads the field in the 5000 m final. IOC

RIGHT: A close-up of Zátopek on the track. Allsport

FAR RIGHT: Zátopek nears the end of his run. Hulton Deutsch

Famed sportswriter Red Smith once described Emil Zátopek's style as "the most frightful horror spectacle since Frankenstein." Where other runners were graceful, like human gazelles, the Czech "seemed on the verge of strangulation; his hatchet face was crimson; his tongue lolled out."

But Zátopek's fierce function defeated silkier form. He won four Olympic gold medals, including a unique treble of 5,000 meters, 10,000 meters, and marathon golds at the Helsinki games of 1952. (He had won the 10,000 meters in London four years earlier.)

On the same day he won the 5,000 meters, his wife Dana took a gold medal in the javelin. When asked if it was true he was going for the marathon, Zátopek replied: "At present, the score in the Zátopek contest is 2–1. This is too close — I must try for the marathon."

He had never raced so far before and chose to follow the favorite, Jim Peters of Britain. He had never met Peters but knew his race number and said to him at the start: "Hello, I am Zátopek." Peters led for ten miles when Zátopek pulled up to him and wondered aloud: "The pace, is it too fast?" Peters responded: "It is too slow." Peters surged ahead — but the heat wore him down and he failed to finish.

After hanging up his spikes, Zátopek became a sought-after coach from Indonesia to Egypt and a hero everywhere except, suddenly, in the Communist politburo back home.

During the 1968 reform efforts that came to be known as the Prague Spring, Zátopek and Dana stood on the front lines supporting the fight for greater freedom and improved living standards. When Soviet tanks rolled into the capital that August, the Zátopeks and other protesters paid for their dissent.

Zátopek was stripped of his colonel's rank in the army and reduced to manual labor. He was not allowed to travel abroad until the 1972 games and was eventually assigned to translate foreign press reports. With the end of the Cold War, the Czech defence minister issued a public apology to Zátopek, and today he is on personal terms with a president he admires, Vaclav Havel.

Emil and Dana now live in a small but comfortable home on the outskirts of Prague. The couple, who never had children, met when Dana set a record in the javelin just before the London Olympics. Zátopek was asked to pose with her; two and a half months later, they were married. While he was still competing, she sometimes helped him build strength by riding on his shoulders as he ran.

Now, she supports him in other ways. A nerve condition in his left leg hinders his walking, and he relies on a cane. "I am lazy," he confesses. "In our family, Dana does all the work."

He notes that modern training techniques have shaved more than a full minute off his 13min 57 sec best in the 5,000 meters. He adds modestly: "Today I would never be Olympic champion."

MARJORIE JACKSON

Marjorie Jackson, known as the "Lithgow Flash," became Australia's first Olympic gold medalist when, in 1952, she succeeded the great Fanny Blankers-Koen as the world's fastest woman by winning the 100 meters and 200 meters sprint double.

Just 20 years old, she set a new world record of 11.5sec in her 100 meters heat and then equaled it in the final, easily beating Daphne Hasenjager of South Africa and fellow Australian Shirley Strickland.

Three days later she equaled the 17-year-old 200 meters world record of 23.6sec in winning her heat, before reducing it to 23.4 in the semi final. Her second gold medal of the games came with a 23.7sec run in the final.

Jackson anchored the Australian 4x100 meters relay team to a 46.1sec world record in the heats, but a fumbled last baton exchange in the final cost them a medal.

Jackson went to the Olympics as a double Commonwealth sprint champion after winning the 100 yards and 220 yards in Auckland in 1950, equaling the world record at both distances. She also won gold medals in the 4x220 and 660 yards relays. It made her the first woman to hold Olympic and Commonwealth titles at the same time.

She retained her Commonwealth sprint titles in 1954 in Vancouver, where she also won a 4x110 yards gold medal. Her seven gold medals are the most won in Commonwealth Games history.

In her career, Jackson set the greatest number of officially ratified world records by a woman. At 100 yards she set 10.8sec (twice) and 10.7 in 1950, 10.4 in 1952, and clocked a wind assisted 10.3 in 1953.

She married the Olympic cyclist Peter Nelson in 1954.

HORACE ASHENFELTER

Horace Ashenfelter's day job as an FBI agent made it difficult for him to train, so he used to run at night using park benches to practice his hurdling technique.

Nothing was expected of him when he arrived in Helsinki for the 1952 games but he caused a stir when he ran 8min 51.0sec in the preliminary heat of the 3,000-meter steeplechase, the fastest of the round. However, he was still not considered a serious threat to world record holder Vladimir Kazantsev of the Soviet Union. The Soviet waited until the last lap when he sprinted ahead, only to stumble at the final water jump and allow the American to claim victory in a world record 8min 45.4sec.

It was America's first win in a distance race since 1908 and the US press lapped it up — half-joking that it was the first time that an FBI man had allowed himself to be followed by a Soviet.

"Everyone was shocked," Ashenfelter admitted afterward. "Even I was shocked. It had been so long since an American had won a gold medal in a distance running event that I think some people had given up on it ever happening again."

After Helsinki, Ashenfelter returned to his duties as an FBI officer. Not surprisingly, no one ever managed to run away from him.

FLOYD PATTERSON

As much as Floyd Patterson's peekaboo style of boxing baffled opponents, his ruminations on such topics as friendship and responsibility intrigued sportswriters. Red Smith characterized Patterson as "a man of peace whose life has been devoted to beating men with his fists," while other writers described him as "a fighter who is a flower child" or "a quiet tiger."

Patterson was a fascinating study, one of the rare men in whom sport seemed to have effected the miraculous change we often claim it can, turning a teenage hooligan into a disciplined member of society.

Like Mike Tyson, Patterson escaped the tough streets of Brooklyn and was trained by the legendary Cus D'Amato. Patterson used boxing to vent, in his words, his "convict tendencies" and he became a superb fighter.

He turned pro after winning the middleweight gold medal at the 1952 Olympics in controversial fashion. His opponent, Sweden's Ingermar Johansson, was disqualified for "not trying." His silver medal was withheld for 14 years.

Patterson was small for a heavyweight — he usually fought at less than 200 pounds and often gave away as many as 15. But he became the youngest man to win the heavyweight title when, at age 21, he knocked out Archie Moore in November 1956.

Patterson was also the first man to regain the championship, when he knocked out Johansson in June 1960, a year after he had lost his title to him. But Patterson did not like what that fight did to him. "I was so filled with hate," he said later, "and I wouldn't ever want to be like that again."

Patterson has maintained a close friendship with Johansson and has even run marathons with his former foe. Still a trim 182 pounds, Patterson lives on a 17-acre farm in New Paltz, New York.

He no longer trains fighters, as he did for 23 years following his retirement from the ring in 1972, but he remains active. As a Eucharistic minister, he administers Communion every Sunday to residents of a nearby nursing home.

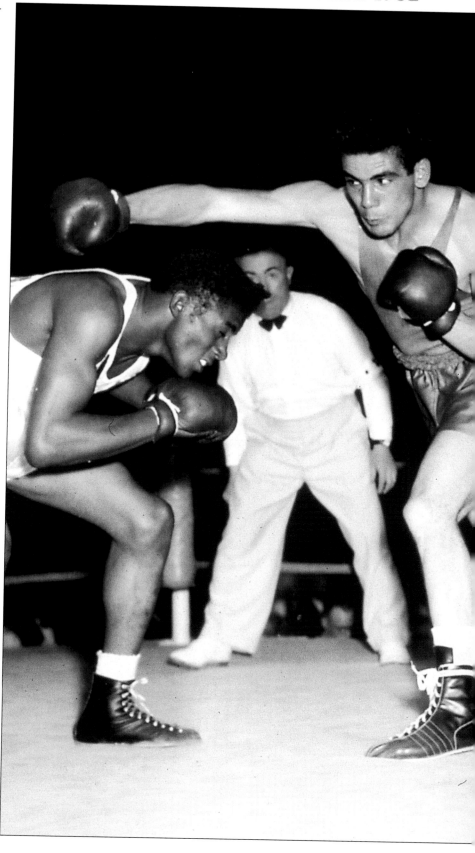

RIGHT: *Floyd Patterson (left) of the United States dodges a punch.* Hulton Deutsch

105

TOP: *American John Davis wins the heavyweight weightlifting division.* IOC

ABOVE: *Josy Barthel of Luxembourg smiles as he crosses the 1,500 m finish line.*
Allsport

ABOVE: *A high jumper clears the bar.* Hulton Deutsch

ABOVE: *America's Samuel Lee dives to gold in the highboard.* IOC

OPPOSITE PAGE:
TOP LEFT: *Soviet athlete Nina Romaschkova takes gold in the discus.* Hulton Deutsch
TOP RIGHT: *American Bob Richards in the pole vault.* Hulton Deutsch
BELOW: *The gold and silver medals in the 800 m final went to America and Jamaica respectively.* Hulton Deutsch

HELSINKI 1952 JULY 19 - AUGUST 3

PARTICIPANTS: 4,925

MEN: 4,407

WOMEN: 518

COUNTRIES: 69

SPORTS: 17

EVENTS: 149

FINAL TORCHBEARER: PAAVO NURMI

MEDALS TABLE

PLACE	COUNTRY	GOLD	SILVER	BRONZE
1	USA	40	19	17
2	USSR	22	30	19
3	Hungary	16	10	16
4	Sweden	12	12	10
5	Italy	8	9	4

OUTSTANDING ATHLETES

PLACE	NAME (NATIONALITY)	DISCIPLINE	GOLD	SILVER	BRONZE
1	Viktor Chukarin (URS)	Gymnastics	4	2	
2	Emil Zátopek (TCH)	Athletics	3		
3	Maria Gorochovskaya (URS)	Gymnastics	2	5	
4	Edoardo Mangiarotti (ITA)	Fencing	2	2	
	Grant Shaginyan (URS)	Gymnastics	2	2	
	Nina Bocharowa (URS)	Gymnastics	2	2	

RIGHT: Emile Zátopek takes an impressive lead. Allsport

110

ATHLETICS — MEN

EVENT	GOLD		SILVER		BRONZE	
100 m	Lindy Remigino (USA)	10.4	Herbert McKenley (JAM)	10.4	Emmanuel McDonald-Bailey (GBR)	10.4
200 m	Andrew Stanfield (USA)	20.7	Thane Baker (USA)	20.8	James Gathers (USA)	20.8
400 m	George Rhoden (JAM)	45.9	Herbert McKenley (JAM)	45.9	Ollie Matson (USA)	46 8
800 m	Malvin Whitfield (USA)	1:49.2	Arthur Wint (JAM)	1:49.4	Heinz Ulzheimer (GER)	1:49.7
1,500 m	Josy Barthel (LUX)	3:45.1	Bob McMillen (USA)	3:45.2	Werner Lueg (GER)	3:45.4
5,000 m	Emil Zátopek (TCH)	14:06.6	Alain Mimoun (FRA)	14:07.4	Herbert Schade (GER)	14:08.6
10,000 m	Emil Zátopek (TCH)	29:17.0	Alain Mimoun (FRA)	29:32.8	Alexander Anufriyev (URS)	29:48.2
Marathon	Emil Zátopek (TCH)	2:23.03.2	Reinaldo Gorno (ARG)	2:25.35.0	Gustaf Jansson (SWE)	2:26.07.0
110 m Hurdles	Harrison Dillard (USA)	13.7	Jack Davis (USA)	13.7	Arthur Barnard (USA)	14.1
400 m Hurdles	Charles Moore (USA)	50.8	Yuriy Lituyev (URS)	51.3	John Holland (NZL)	52.2
3,000 m Steeplechase	Horace Ashenfelter (USA)	8:45.4	Vladimir Kazantsev (URS)	8:51.6	John Disley (GBR)	8:51.8
4x100 m	USA	40.1	USSR	40.3	Hungary	40.5
4x400 m	Jamaica	3:03.9	USA	3:04.0	Germany	3:06.6
10 km Walk	John Mikaelsson (SWE)	45:02.8	Fritz Schwab (SUI)	45:41.0	Bruno Yunk (URS)	45:41.0
50 km Walk	Giuseppe Dordoni (ITA)	4:28:07.8	Josef Dolezal (TCH)	4:30:17.8	Antal Róka (HUN)	4:31:27.2
High Jump	Walter Davis (USA)	6'8.25"	Ken Wiesner (USA)	6'7"	J. Telles da Conceiceião (BRA)	6'6"
Pole Vault	Bob Richards (USA)	14'11"	Donald Laz (USA)	14'9"	Ragnar Lundberg (SWE)	14' 5"
Long Jump	Jerome Biffle (USA)	24'10"	Meredith Gourdine (USA)	24'8.25"	Ödön Földessy (HUN)	23'11.75"
Triple Jump	Adhemar Ferreira da Silva (BRA)	53'2.5"	Leonid Shcherbakov (URS)	52'5"	Arnoldo Devonish (VEN)	50'11"
Shot	Parry O'Brien (USA)	57'1.25"	Darrow Hooper (USA)	57'0.5"	Jim Fuchs (USA)	55'11.5"
Discus	Sim Iness (USA)	180'6.5"	Adolfo Consolini (ITA)	176'5"	James Dillion (USA)	174'9.5"
Hammer	József Csermák (HUN)	197'11.5"	Karl Storch (GER)	193'1"	Imre Németh (HUN)	189'5"
Javelin	Cyrus Young (USA)	242'0.5"	William Miller (USA)	237'8.5"	Toivo Hyytiäinen (FIN)	235'10"
Decathlon	Robert Mathias (USA)	7887	Milton Campbell (USA)	6975	Floyd Simmons (USA)	6788

ATHLETICS — WOMEN

EVENT	GOLD		SILVER		BRONZE	
100 m	Marjorie Jackson (AUS)	11.5	Daphne Hasenjager-Robb (SAF)	11.8	Shirley de la Hunty-Strickland (AUS)	11.9
200 m	Marjorie Jackson (AUS)	23.7	Bertha Brouwer (HOL)	24.2	Nadyezda Khnykhina (URS)	24.2
80 m Hurdles	Shirley de la Hunty-Strickland	10.9	Maria Golubnichaya (URS)	11.1	Maria Sander (GER)	11.1
4x100 m Relay	USA	45.9	Germany	45.9	Great Britain	46.2
High Jump	Esther Brand (SAF)	5'5.5"	Sheila Lerwill (GBR)	5'5"	Aleksandra Chudina (URS)	5'4"
Long Jump	Yvette Williams (NZL)	20'5.5"	Aleksandra Chudina (URS)	20'1.5"	Shirley Cawley (GBR)	19'5"
Shot	Galina Zybina (URS)	50'1.5"	Marianne Werner (GER)	47'9.5"	Klavdiya Tochenova (URS)	47'6.75"
Discus	Nina Romashkova (URS)	168'8"	Elizaveta Bagriantseva (URS)	154'5.5"	Nina Dumbadze (URS)	170'8"
Javelin	Dana Zátopková (TCH)	165'7"	Aleksandra Chudina (URS)	164'0.5"	Yelena Gorchakova (URS)	163'3"

SWIMMING — MEN

EVENT	GOLD		SILVER		BRONZE	
100 m Freestyle	Clarke Scholes (USA)	57.4	Hiroshi Suzuki (JPN)	57.4	Göran Larsson (SWE)	58.2
400 m Freestyle	Jean Boiteux (FRA)	4:30.7	Ford Konno (USA)	4:31.3	Per-Olof Östrand (SWE)	4:35.2
1,500 m Freestyle	Ford Konno (USA)	18:30.3	Shiro Hashizune (JPN)	18:41.4	Tetsuo Okamoto (BRA)	18:51.3
100 m Backstroke	Yoshinobu Oyakawa (JPN)	1:05.4	Gilbert Bozon (FRA)	1:06.2	Jack Taylor (USA)	1:06.5
200 m Breaststroke	John Davies (AUS)	2:34.4	Bowen Stassforth (USA)	2:34.7	Herbert Klein (GER)	2:35.9
4x200 m Freestyle	USA	8:31.1	Japan	8:33.5	France	8:45.9
Springboard Diving	David Browning (USA)	205.29	Miller Anderson (USA)	199.84	Robert Clotworthy (USA)	184.92
Highboard Diving	Samuel Lee (USA)	156.28	Joaquin Capilla Pérez	145.21	Günther Haase (GER)	141.31
Water Polo	Hungary		Yugoslavia		Italy	

SWIMMING — WOMEN

EVENT	GOLD		SILVER		BRONZE	
100 m Freestyle	Katalin Szöke (HUN)	1:06.8	JohannaTermeulen (HOL)	1:07.0	Judit Temes (HUN)	1:07.1
400 m Freestyle	Valeria Gyenge (HUN)	5:12.1	Eva Novák (HUN)	5:13.7	Evelyn Kawamoto (USA)	5:14.6
100 m Backstroke	Joan Harrison (SAF)	1:14.3	Geertje Wielema (HOL)	1:14.5	Jean Stewart (NZL)	1:15.8
200 m Breaststroke	Eva Székely (HUN)	2:51.7	Eva Novák (HUN)	2:54.4	Helen Gordon (GBR)	2:57.6
4x100 m Freestyle Relay	Hungary	4:24.4	Netherlands	4:29.0	USA	4:30.1
Springboard Diving	Patricia McCormick (USA)	147.30	Mady Moreau (FRA)	139.34	Zoe Ann Jensen-Olsen (USA)	127.57
Highboard Diving	Patricia McCormick (USA)	79.37	Paula Jean Myers (USA)	71.63	Juno Irwin-Stover (USA)	70.49

BOXING

EVENT	GOLD	SILVER	BRONZE
Flyweight (-112.5 lb)	Nathan Brooks (USA)	Edgar Basel (GER)	Anatoly Bulakov (URS)
			Bill Toweel (SAF)
Bantamweight (-119 lb)	Pentti Hämäläinen (FIN)	John McNally (IRL)	Gennadiy Garbusov (URS)
			Joon-Ho Kang (KOR)
Featherweight (-126 lb)	Jan Zachara (TCH)	Sergio Caprari (ITA)	Joseph Ventaja (FRA)
			Leonard Leisching (SAF)
Lightweight (-132 lb)	Aureliano Bolognesi (ITA)	Aleksy Antkiewicz (POL)	Erkki Pakkanen (FIN)
			Gheorge Fiat (ROM)
Light-Welterweight (-140 lb)	Charles Adkins (USA)	Viktor Mednov (URS)	Erkki Mallenius (FIN)
			Bruno Visintin (ITA)
Welterweight (-148 lb)	Zygmunt Chychla (POL)	Sergey Schtsherbakov (URS)	Victor Jörgensen (DEN)
			Günther Heidemann (GER)
Light-Middleweight (-157 lb)	László Papp (HUN)	Theunis van Schalkwyk (SAF)	BorisTishin (URS)
			Eladio Herrera (ARG)
Middleweight (-165 lb)	Floyd Patterson (USA)	Vasile Tita (ROM)	Stig Sjölin (SWE)
			Boris Nikolov (BUL)
Light-Heavy veight (-178.5 lb)	Norvel Lee (USA)	Antonio Pacenza (ARG)	Anatoly Perov (URS)
			Harri Siljander (FIN)
Heavyweight (+178.5 lb)	Hayes Edward Sanders (USA)	Ingemar Johansson (SWE)*	Andries Nieman (SAF)
			Jekka Koski (FIN)

*Disqualified - reinstated as silver medallist in 1982

WEIGHTLIFTING

EVENT	GOLD		SILVER		BRONZE	
Bantamweight	Ivan Udodov (URS)	315.0	Mahmoud Namdjou (IRN)	307.5	Ali Mirzai (IRN)	300.0
Featherweight	Rafael Chimishkyan (URS)	337.5	Nikolai Saksonov(URS)	332.5	Rodney Wilkes (TRI)	322.5
Lightweight	Thomas Kono (USA)	362.5	Yevgeniy Lopatin (URS)	350.0	Verne Barberis (AUS)	350.0
Middleweight	Peter George (USA)	400.0	Gerard Gratton (CAN)	390.0	Sung-Jip Kim (KOR)	382.5
Light-Heavyweight	Trofin Lomakin (URS)	417.5	Stanley Stanczyk (USA)	415.0	Arkady Vorobiev (URS)	407.5
Middle-Heavyweight	Norbert Schemansky (USA)	445.0	Grigory Nowak (URS)	410.0	Lennox Kilgour (TRI)	402.5
Heavyweight	John Davis (USA)	460.0	James Bradford (USA)	437.5	Humberto Selvetti (ARG)	432.5

WEIGHTLIFTING WEIGHTS

BANTAMWEIGHT	-123.5 lb	FEATHERWEIGHT	-132.25 lb	LIGHTWEIGHT	-148.75 lb
MIDDLEWEIGHT	-165.5 lb	LIGHT-HEAVYWEIGHT	-182 lb	MIDDLE-HEAVYWEIGHT	-198.5 lb
HEAVYWEIGHT	+198.5 lb				

GRECO-ROMAN WRESTLING

EVENT	GOLD	SILVER	BRONZE
Flyweight (-114.5 lb)	Boris Gurevich (URS)	Ignazio Fabra (ITA)	Leo Honkala (FIN)
Bantamweight (-125.75 lb)	Imre Hódos (HUN)	Zakaria Chihab (LIB)	Artem Teryan (URS)
Featherweight (-136.5 lb)	Yakov Punkin (URS)	Imre Polyak (HUN)	Abdel Rashed (EGY)
Lightweight (-147.5 lb)	Shazam Safin (URS)	Gustaf Freij (SWE)	Mikulás Athanasov (TCH)
Welterweight (-160.75 lb)	Miklós Szilvási (HUN)	Gösta Andersson (SWE)	Khalil Taha (LIB)
Middleweight (-174 lb)	Axel Grönberg (SWE)	Kalervo Ranhala (FIN)	Nikolai Belov (URS)
Light-Heavyweight (-191.75 lb)	Kaelpo Gröndahl (FIN)	Shalva Shikhladze (URS)	Karl-Erik Nilsson (SWE)
Heavyweight(+191.75 lb)	Johannes Kotkas (URS)	Josef Ruzicka (TCH)	Tauno Kovanen (FIN)

FREESTYLE WRESTLING

EVENT	GOLD	SILVER	BRONZE
Flyweight (-114.5 lb)	Hasan Germici (TUR)	Yushu Kitano (JPN)	Mahmoud Mollaghassemi (IRN)
Bantamweight (-125.75 lb)	Shohachi Ishii (JPN)	Rashid Mamedbekov (URS)	Kha-Shaba Jadav (IND)
Featherweight (-136.5 lb)	Bayram Sit (TUR)	Nasser Guivehtchi (IRN)	Josiah Henson (USA)
Lightweight (-147.5 lb)	Olle Anderberg (SWE)	Thomas Evans (USA)	Djanbakte Tovfighe (IRN)
Welterweight (-160.75)	William Smith (USA)	Per Berlin (SWE)	Abdullah Modjtabavi (IRN)
Middleweight (-174 lb)	David Tsimakuridze (URS)	Gholam Reza Takhti (IRN)	György Gurics (HUN)
Light-Heavyweight (-191.75 lb)	Wiking Palm (SWE)	Henry Wittenberg (USA)	Adil Atan (TUR)
Heavyweight (+191.75 lb)	Arsen Mekokishvili (URS)	Bertil Antonsson (SWE)	Kenneth Richmond (GBR)

FENCING

EVENT	GOLD		SILVER		BRONZE	
Individual Foil — Men	Christian d'Oriola (FRA)	8	Edoardo Mangiarotti (ITA)	6	Manlio Di Rosa (ITA)	5
Team Foil — Men	France		Italy		Hungary	
Individual Épée	Edoardo Mangiarotti (ITA)	7	Dario Mangiarotti (ITA)	6	Oswald Zappelli (SUI)	6
Team Épée	Italy		Sweden		Switzerland	
Individual Sabre	Pál Kovács (HUN)	8	Aladár Gerevich (HUN)	7	Tibor Berczelly (HUN)	5
Team Sabre	Hungary		Italy		France	
Individual Foil — Women	IreneCamber (ITA)	5+1	IlonaElek (HUN)	5	Karen Lachmam (DEN)	4

MODERN PENTATHLON

EVENT	GOLD		SILVER		BRONZE	
Individual	Lars Hall (SWE)	32	Gábor Benedek (HUN)	39	István Szondy (HUN)	41
Team	Hungary	166	Sweden	182	Finand	213

CANOEING — MEN

EVENT	GOLD		SILVER		BRONZE	
100 m Kayak Singles K1	Gert Fredriksson (SWE)	4:07.9	Thorvald Strömberg (FIN)	4:09.7	Luis Gantois (FRA)	4:20.1
10,000 m Kayak Singles K1	Thorvald Strömberg (FIN)	47:22.8	Gert Fredriksson (SWE)	47:34.1	Michael Scheuer (GER)	47:54.5
1,000 m Kayak Pairs K2	Finland	3:51.1	Sweden	3:51.1	Austria	3:51.4
10,000 m Kayak Pairs K2	Finland	44:21.3	Sweden	44:21.7	Hungary	44:26.6
1,000 m Canadian Singles C1	Josef Holecek (TCH)	4:56.3	János Parti (HUN)	5:03.3	Olavi Ojanpara (FIN)	5:08.5
10,000 m Canadian Singles C1	Frank Havens (USA)	57:41.1	Gábor Novák (HUN)	57:49.2	Alfred Jindra (TCH)	57:53.1
1,000 m Canadian Pairs C2	Denmark	4:38.3	Czechoslovakia	4:42.9	Germany	4:48.3
10,000 m Canadian Pairs C2	France	54:08.3	Canada	54:09.9	Germany	54:28.1

CANOEING — WOMEN

EVENT	GOLD		SILVER		BRONZE	
500 m Kayak Singles K1	Sylvi Saimo (FIN)	2:18.4	Gertrude Liebhart (AUT)	2:18.8	Nina Savina (URS)	2:21.6

115

ROWING

EVENT	GOLD		SILVER		BRONZE	
Single Sculls	Yury Tyukalov (URS)	8:12.8	Mervyn Wood (AUS)	8:14.5	Teodor Kocerka (POL)	8:19.4
Double Sculls	Argentina	7:32.2	USSR	7:38.3	Uruguay	7:43.7
Coxless Pairs	USA	8:20.7	Belgium	8:23.5	Switzerland	8:32.7
Coxed Pairs	France	8:28.6	Germany	8:32.1	Denmark	8:34.9
Coxless Fours	Yugoslavia	7:16.0	France	7:18.9	Finland	7:23.3
Coxed Fours	Czechoslovakia	7:33.4	Switzerland	7:36.5	USA	7:37.0
Coxed Eights	USA	6:25.9	USSR	6:31 2	Australia	6:33.1

SAILING

EVENT	GOLD		SILVER		BRONZE	
Finn Class	Paul Elvström (DEN)	8209	Charles Currey (GBR)	5449	Rickard Sarby (SWE)	5051
International Star	Italy	7635	USA	7216	Portugal	4903
Dragon	Norway	6130	Sweden	5556	Germany	5352
5.5 m	USA	5751	Norway	5325	Sweden	4554
6 m	USA	4870	Norway	4648	Finland	3944

CYCLING

EVENT	GOLD		SILVER		BRONZE	
Individual Road Race*	André Noyelle (BEL)	5:06:03.6	Robert Grondelaers (BEL)	5:06:51.2	Edi Ziegler (GER)	5:07:47.5
Team Road Race	Belgium	15:20:46.6	Italy	15:33:27.3	France	15:38:58.1
1,000 m Time Trial	Russel Mockridge (AUS)	1:11.1	Marino Morettini (ITA)	1:12.7	Raymond Robinson (SAF)	1:13.0
1,000 m Sprint	Enzo Sacchi (ITA)		Lionel Cox (AUS)		Werner Potzernheim (GER)	
2,000 m Tandem	Australia		South Africa		Italy	
4,000 m Team Pursuit	Italy	4:461	South Africa	4:53.6	Great Britain	4:51.5

*118.25 miles

EQUESTRIANISM

EVENT	GOLD		SILVER		BRONZE	
Three-Day Event	Hans v. Blixen-Finecke (SWE)	-28.33	Guy Lefrant (FRA)	-54.50	Wilhelm Büsing (GER)	-55.50
Three-Day Event (Team)	Sweden	-221.49	Germany	-235.49	USA	-587.16
Grand Prix (Dressage)	Henri Saint Cyr (SWE)	561.0	Lis Hartel (DEN)	541.5	André Jousseaume (FRA)	541.0
Grand Prix (Dressage) Team	Sweden	1597.5	Switzerland	1579.0	Germany	1501.0
Grand Prix (Jumping)	Pierre Jonquères d'Oriola (FRA)	-8/0	Oscar Cristi (CHI)	-8/4	Fritz Thiedemann (GER)	-8/8
Grand Prix (Jumping) Team	Great Britain	-40.75	Chile	-45.75	USA	-52.25

SHOOTING

EVENT	GOLD		SILVER		BRONZE	
Free Rifle (3 Positions)	Anatoliy Bogdanov (URS)	1123	Robert Bürchler (SUI)	1120	Lev Weinstein (URS)	1109
Small-Bore Rifle (Prone)	Josif Sarbu (ROM)	400/33	Boris Andreyev (URS)	400/28	Arthur Jackson (USA)	399
Small-Bore Rifles (3 Positions)	Erling Konshaug (NOR)	1164/53	Vilho Ylönen (FIN) 1164/49		Boris Andreyev(URS)	1163
Rapid-Fire Pistol	Károly Takács (HUN)	579	Szilárd Kun (HUN)	578	Gheorghe Lichiardopol (ROM)	578
Free Pistol (50 m)	Huelet Benner (USA)	553	Angel L. de Gozalo (ESP)	550	Ambrus Balogh (HUN)	549
Olympic Trap Shooting	George P. Généreux (CAN)	192	Knut Holmqvist (SWE)	191	Hans Liljedahl (SWE)	190
Running Deer Shooting	John Larsen (NOR)	413	Per Olof Sköldberg (SWE)	409	Tauno Mäki (FIN)	407

GYMNASTICS — MEN

EVENT	GOLD		SILVER		BRONZE	
Individual Combined Exercises	Viktor Chukarin (URS)	115.70	Grant Shaginyan (URS)	114.95	Josef Stalder(SUI)	114.75
Team	USSR	575.4	Switzerland	567.50	Finland	564.20
Parallel Bars	Hans Eugster (SUI)	19.65	Viktor Chukarin (URS)	19.60	Josef Stalder (SUI)	19.50
Floor	Karl William Thoresson (SWE)	19.25	Tadao Uesako (JPN)	19.15		
			Jerzy Jokiel (POL)	19.15		
Horse Vault	Viktor Chukarin (URS)	19.20	Masao Takemoto	19.15	Takashi Ono (JPN)	19.10
					Tadao Uesako (JPN))	19.10
Horizontal Bar	Jack Günthard (SUI)	19.55	Josef Stalder (SUI)	19.50		
			Alfred Schwarzmann (GER)	19.50		
Rings	Grant Shaginyan (URS)	19.75	Viktor Chukarin (URS)	19.55	Hans Eugster (SUI)	19.40
					Dimitri Leonkin (URS)	19.40
Pommel Horse	Viktor Chukarin (URS)	19.50	Yevgeniy Korolkov (URS)	19.40		
			Grant Shaginyan (URS)	19.40		

GYMNASTICS — WOMEN

EVENT	GOLD		SILVER		BRONZE	
Individual Combined Exercises	Maria Gorochovskaya (URS)	76.78	Nina Bocharova (URS)	75.94	Margit Korondi (HUN)	75.82
Team	USSR	527.03	Hungary	520.96	Czechoslovakia	503.32
Floor	Agnes Keleti (HUN)	19.36	Maria Gorochovskaya (URS)	19.20	Margit Korondi (HUN)	19.00
Horse Vault	Yekaterina Kalinchuk (URS)	19.20	Maria Gorochovskaya (URS)	19.19	Galina Minaitscheva (URS)	19.16
Beam	Nina Bocharowa (URS)	19.22	Maria Gorochovskaya (URS)	19.13	Margit Korondi (HUN)	19.02
Asymmetrical Bars	Margit Korondi (HUN)	19.40	Maria Gorochovskaya (URS)	19.26	Agnes Keleti (HUN)	19.16
Portable Apparatus	Sweden	74.20	USSR	73.00	Hungary	71.60

BASKETBALL

GOLD	SILVER	BRONZE
USA	USSR	Uruguay

SOCCER

GOLD	SILVER	BRONZE
Hungary	Yugoslavia	Sweden

HOCKEY

GOLD	SILVER	BRONZE
India	Netherlands	Great Britain

MELBOURNE 1956

INTRODUCTION

ABOVE: *A close-up of the Olympic rings.* Allsport

PREVIOUS PAGE: *Ron Clarke of Australia lights the Olympic torch to open the 1956 Melbourne games.* IOC

151 EVENTS

67 COUNTRIES

3,184 ATHLETES

	Gold	Silver	Bronze
URS	37	29	32
USA	32	25	17
AUS	13	8	14
HUN	9	10	7
ITA	8	8	9
SWE	8	5	6
GBR	6	7	11
GER*	6	13	8
ROM	5	3	5
JAP	4	10	5
FRA	4	4	6
TUR	3	2	2
FIN	3	1	11
IRN	2	2	1
CAN	2	1	3
NZE	2		
POL	1	4	4
CZE	1	4	1
BUL	1	3	1
DEN	1	2	1
IRL	1	1	3
NOR	1		2
MEX	1		1
BRA	1		
IND	1		
YUG		3	
CHI		2	2
BEL		2	
ARG		1	1
KOR		1	1
ICE		1	
PAK		1	
SAF			4
AUT			2
BAH			1
GRE			1
SUI			1
URU			1

*Represents a combined German team.

Melbourne 1956

For the first and only time in Olympic history, the games were staged in two countries. Australia's stringent animal quarantine laws kept foreign horses out and the equestrian events were staged in Stockholm, even though this was contrary to the Olympic Charter.

It did much to diminish the prestige of the games, the first and (until Sydney) only time they had been held in the Southern Hemisphere. To add to this unsatisfactory state of affairs, Sweden won three of the six titles on offer amid allegations they were benefiting from biased judging. Also, many riders criticized the state of the cross-country course, saying it was too dangerous.

Back in Melbourne, politics overshadowed sport. The Soviet invasion of Hungary and the Franco-British military intervention in the Suez Canal led to several countries boycotting the games. They included Spain, Switzerland, the Netherlands over the invasion of Hungary (although the Hungarians surprisingly chose to make the trip), and Egypt and Lebanon because of Suez. West and East Germany also managed to set aside their differences to enter a combined team, which they continued to do until after 1964 when the East realized the benefits of competing as a separate nation and went their own way.

With the situation so volatile, it was inevitable that Hungary would meet the Soviet Union somewhere. And when it happened in the water polo semi-final, the match erupted into little more than a brawl. The referee ended the match with the Hungarians leading 4–0 because it had degenerated into a boxing match under water.

RIGHT: The official poster. Allsport

There was great sympathy for the Hungarian team and at the end of the games more than half of them refused to travel back to Budapest, staying in Australia to seek political asylum. One who did return was the boxer Laszlo Papp who gained an unprecedented third gold medal.

The Soviet runner Vladimir Kuts was the star of the track, with record-breaking victories at 5,000 and 10,000 meters. Emil Zátopek, the Czech runner who had achieved the same feat four years earlier, confined himself to the marathon on this occasion and finished sixth behind France's Alain Mimoun.

Watching the games was Ron Clarke, a 19-year-old who was the final torch bearer at the opening ceremony. Clarke was later to become one of history's greatest ever distance runners. He never enjoyed much luck in the Olympic arena, however, and is generally considered to be the best runner never to win a gold medal.

Ireland had rare reason to celebrate when Ron Delany took the 1,500 meters, his country's first gold medal since 1932. America's Bobby-Joe Morrow and Australia's Betty Cuthbert each won three gold medals in the sprint, including the relay. A colleague of Cuthbert's in the relay was Shirley de la Hunty (née Strickland) who ended her Olympic career with a total of seven medals — three gold, one silver and three bronze. It is a record that has never been beaten.

There was a controversial finish to the 3,000

RIGHT: The commemorative pin. Allsport

123

meters steeplechase, in which Britain's Chris Brasher was disqualified after crossing the line first. He appealed and was reinstated. But he nearly missed his medal ceremony because he was in a local hotel at the time busy celebrating with members of the British press!

While some of the events had given the impression of being anything but friendly, a new Olympic tradition was started at the end of the games with all the competitors entering enmasse during the closing ceremony, signifying the friendship of the Olympics.

Commemorative medals of the 1956 Melbourne summer games. Allsport

The official Olympic torch.
Allsport

CHRIS BRASHER

Melbourne 1956

Chris Brasher of Great Britain on his way to winning the steeplechase.
Allsport

Perhaps best known in athletics terms as the man who, along with Chris Chataway, helped pace Roger Bannister to the first sub-four minute mile on May 6, 1954, and the driving force behind the London Marathon, Britain's Chris Brasher found his own place in the spotlight when he won the 3,000 meters steeplechase at the 1956 Olympic Games in Melbourne.

Brasher's part in Bannister's record was to make the pace for the opening two and a half laps, although he was a fair miler himself, recording 4min 9.0sec that year. But since 1950, realizing his limitations on the flat, he had been concentrating more and more on the steeplechase and made the Olympic team for Helsinki in 1952. He finished eleventh out of 12 in the final, but after regular training at Oxford University with Bannister and Chataway, improved his steeplechase time of 8min 49.2sec on the eve of the 1956 games.

While his team-mate John Disley, a bronze medalist in 1952, was more fancied, Brasher stormed to victory with a spectacular last lap in which he squeezed through a gap left by the two leaders to win in an Olympic record time.

He was initially disqualified for pushing his way through but both runners considered the incident insignificant and Brasher was reinstated as the winner, giving Britain its first athletics gold medal since 1936.

After a successful career in journalism, including sports editor of *The Observer*, it was with Disley that Brasher came up with the idea of a marathon through the streets of London after seeing the New York City Marathon in 1979.

At the first London Marathon in 1981, Brasher, then aged 52, set a personal best of 2hr 56min 56sec. He is now a life vice-president of the London Marathon, although he is now longer directly involved in organizing the race.

A millionaire, Brasher now lives in Newbury where he is one of Britain's most successful race horse owners.

1956 M

LÁSZLÓ PAPP

Laszlo Papp's record in the Olympic Games is matched only by the great Cuban heavyweight, Teofilo Stevenson. They both won three gold medals but the Hungarian was the first boxer to achieve the treble.

A former railway clerk, Papp beat Britain's John Wright to win the middleweight title in the 1948 games in London. Four years later he contested the new light-middleweight division in Helsinki and beat South Africa's Theunis van Schalkwyk in the final. Between the two games, Papp had won European titles at both middleweight and light middleweight.

He won his third Olympic gold medal, again at light middleweight, against the background of the Hungarian uprising of 1956. With Soviet tanks rumbling through the streets of Budapest, Papp and the Hungarian team were a picture of solidarity at the Melbourne games.

Papp's team-mates were at ringside to see the 30-year-old win the decision over American José Torres, who later went on to become world professional light-heavyweight champion and the trainer of Mike Tyson.

While many of those team-mates sought political asylum in Australia, Papp returned to Hungary where he was given permission by the government to become the first boxer from a Communist country to turn professional. It was not until the era of *glasnost* in the late eighties that other boxers were allowed to turn pro.

He won the European title and defended it six times before retiring to become national coach. For two decades between 1971 and 1992 he was just as successful as a coach as he was as a boxer.

BETTY CUTHBERT

Teenager Betty Cuthbert became the heroine of the 1956 games when, before her home crowd in Melbourne, she won the 100 meters and 200 meters and helped the Australian sprint relay squad set two world records.

Cuthbert was a natural sprinter, discovered by her high school physical education teacher June Ferguson, herself an international competitor at the 1948 London Olympics.

By the time she was 15, Cuthbert's best 100 yards time was 10.8sec. She reduced this to 10.6 at the beginning of 1956 at the New South Wales Championships, where she also clocked 24.2sec for 220 yards.

But the 18-year-old was unprepared for the magnitude of her achievement in the Melbourne games. Describing her 100 meters victory in her autobiography *Golden Girl*, she said: "There seemed nothing special about it. I couldn't realize then just what I had done and even later, when the telegrams,

letters, honors, victory functions and the like started, I was too shy and self conscious to fully appreciate it.

"However, at the time, Mum must have realized what I had done because I looked up in the crowd and she was crying her eyes out."

Injured four years later, Cuthbert returned in 1964 when she won the 400 meters in Tokyo. She was not the favorite, but a tremendous burst of speed from about 180 meters out brought her home in an Olympic record 52.0sec, ahead of Britain's Ann Packer in 52.2.

As she intended, Cuthbert retired after the 1964 Olympics, saying she wanted to be remembered for her 400 meters victory. "It was the only perfect race I ever ran," she says.

In 1979, it was revealed that she was suffering from multiple sclerosis. In 1998, she put her Olympic medals up for sale to help fund her medical treatment. But a series of fund raising dinners across Australia meant she was able to keep her treasured prizes.

VLADIMIR KUTS

Vladimir Kuts was a tough graduate of the Soviet navy who only started running when he was 23, after previously excelling at skiing. His searing displays of running, especially his classic duels with Britons Gordon Pirie and Chris Chataway at the White City Stadium, caught the imagination of the public.

Two months before the 1956 Melbourne Olympics, Kuts broke the world 10,000 meters record by more than 12 seconds.

The race in Melbourne turned into a titanic battle with Pirie refusing to lead while Kuts set the pace. With five laps remaining, Kuts slowed so much Pirie was forced to take over at the front. The Soviet took half a lap to gather himself and then sprinted away again, leaving Pirie a broken man. Five days later, Kuts beat Pirie again to win the 5,000 meters.

Kuts had experienced several arduous years during the Second World War, during which he was forced to work for the German occupying forces before escaping to fight against them. He then joined the Russian navy, where he discovered his talent for sports, particularly endurance events.

Kuts, who trained himself almost to complete exhaustion, fashioned a regime where he could maintain sustained speed against more more natural finishers like Pirie. Before the 10,000 meters in Melbourne, for example, in training he did 25 fast quarter miles, with only 30 seconds of jogging between each.

Unfortunately for Kuts, the experimental training techniques the Soviet coaches used on him took their toll, and he died of his fourth heart attack in 1975, at the age of 48.

Soviet athlete Vladimir Kuts won both the 10,000 m and 5,000 m gold. IOC

ABOVE: *A 1,500 m heat from the 1956 games.* Allsport

ABOVE: *American Bobby Morrow (no. 55) wins the 200 m final with a time of 28.6 seconds.* Allsport UK

LEFT: *American Bobby Morrow (no. 55), a winner again in the men's 100 m final.* Allsport UK

ABOVE: *Al Oerter of the United States — gold medalist in the discus.* Allsport

ABOVE: *America's Hal Connolly well on his way to capturing gold in the hammer.* Allsport

MELBOURNE 1956 NOVEMBER 22 -DECEMBER 8

PARTICIPANTS: 3,184
MEN: 2,813
WOMEN: 371
COUNTRIES: 67
SPORTS: 17
EVENTS: 151

EQUESTRIAN GAMES IN STOCKHOLM JUNE 10-17
PARTICIPANTS: 158
MEN: 145
WOMEN: 145
COUNTRIES: 29

FINAL TORCHBEARER:
RON CLARKE (MELBOURNE)
HANS WIKNE · KARIN LINDBURG · HENRI ERIKSON
(STOCKHOLM)

MEDALS TABLE

PLACE	COUNTRY	GOLD	SILVER	BRONZE
1	USSR	37	29	32
2	USA	32	25	17
3	Australia	13	8	14
4	Hungary	9	10	7
5	Italy	8	8	9

OUTSTANDING ATHLETES

PLACE	NAME (NATIONALITY)	DISCIPLINE	GOLD	SILVER	BRONZE
1	Larissa Latynina (URS)	Gymnastics	4	1	
2	Agnes Keleti (HUN)	Gymnastics	3	2	
3	Viktor Chukarin (URS)	Gymnastics	3	1	
4	Valentin Muratov (URS)	Gymnastics	3	1	
5	Betty Cuthbert (AUS)	Athletics	3		
	Robert Morrow (USA)	Athletics	3		
	Murray Rose (AUS)	Swimming	3		

ATHLETICS — MEN

EVENT	GOLD		SILVER		BRONZE	
100 m	Robert Morrow (USA)	10.5	Thane Baker (USA)	10 5	Hector Hogan (AUS)	10.6
200 m	Robert Morrow (USA)	20.6	Andrew Stanfield (USA)	20.7	Thane Baker (USA)	20.9
400 m	Charles Jenkins (USA)	46.7	Karl-Friedrich Haas (GER)*	46.8	Voitto Hellsten (FIN)	47.0
					Ardalion Ignanev	47.0
800 m	Tom Courtney (USA)	1:47.7	Derek Johnson (GBR)	1:47.8	Andun Boysen (NOR)	1:48.1
1,500 m	Ronald Delany (IRL)	3:41.2	Klaus Richtzenhain (GER)*	3:42.0	John Landy (AUS)	3:42.0
5,000 m	Vladimir Kuts (URS)	13:39.6	Gordon Pirie (GBR)	13:50.6	Derek Ibbotson (GBR)	13:54.4
10,000 m	Vladimir Kuts (URS)	28:45.6	József Kovács (HUN)	28:52.4	Allan Lawrence (AUS)	28:53.6
Marathon	Alain Mimoun (FRA)	2:25:00.0	Franjo Mihalic (YUG)	2:26:32.0	Veikko Karvonen (FIN)	2:27:47.0
110 m Hurdles	Lee Calhoun (USA)	13.5	Jack Davis (USA)	13.5	Joel Shankle (USA)	14.1
400 m Hurdles	Glenn Davis (USA)	50.1	Eddie Southern (USA)	50.8	Joshua Culbreath (USA)	51.6
3,000 m Steeplechase	Chris Brasher (GBR)	8:41.2	Sándor Rozsnyói (HUN)	8:43.6	Ernst Larsen (NOR)	8:44.0
4x100 m	USA	39 5	USSR	39 8	Germany*	40 3
4x400 m	USA	3:04 8	Australia	3:06.2	Great Britain	3:07.2
20 km Walk	Leonid Spirin (URS)	1:31:27.4	Antonas Mikenas (URS)	1:32:03.0	Bruno Yunk (URS)	1:32:12.0
50 km Walk	Norman Read (NZL)	4:30:42.8	Yevgeniy Maskinskov (URS)	4:32:57.0	John Lundgren (SWE)	4:35:02.0
High Jump	Charles Dumas (USA)	6'11.5"	Charles Porter (AUS)	6'10.5"	Igor Kashkarov (URS)	6'8.25"
Pole Vault	Bob Richards (USA)	14'11.5"	Bob Gutowski (USA)	14'10"	Georgios Roubanis (GRE)	4'5"
Long Jump	Greg Bell (USA)	25'8.25"	John Bennett (USA)	25'2.25"	Jorma Valkama (FIN)	24'7"
Triple Jump	Adhemar Ferreira da Silva (BRA)	53'7.5"	Vilhjámur Einarsson (ISL)	53'4"	Vitold Kreyer (URS)	53'14"
Shot	Parry O'Brien (USA)	60'11"	Bill Nieder (USA)	59'7.5.5"	Jiri Skobla (TCH)	57'9"
Discus	Al Oerter (USA)	184'10.5"	Fortune Gordien (USA)	179'9.5"	Desmond Koch (USA)	178'5"
Hammer	Harold Connolly (USA)	207'3"	Michail Krivonosov (URS)	206'9"	Anatoliy Samotsvetov (URS)	62 56
Javelin	Egil Danielsen (NOR)	281'2"	Janusz Sidlo (POL)	262'4"	Viktor Tsibulenko (URS)	79.50
Decathlon	Milton Campbell (USA)	7937	Rafer Johnson (USA)	7587	Vassily Kusnetsov (URS)	7465

* representing a combined German team (throughout tables)

ATHLETICS — WOMEN

EVENT	GOLD		SILVER		BRONZE	
100 m	Betty Cuthbert (AUS)	11.5	Christa Stubnick (GER)*	11.7	Marlene Matthews (AUS)	11.7
200 m	Betty Cuthbert (AUS)	23.4	Christa Stubnick (GER)*	23.7	Marlene Matthews (AUS)	23.8
80 m Hurdle	S. de la Hunty-Strickland (AUS)	10.7	Gisela Köhler (GER)*	10.9	Norma Thrower (AUS)	11.0
4x100 m	Australia	44.5	Great Britain	44.7	USA	44.9
High Jump	Mildred McDaniel (USA)	5'9.25"	Maria Pisaryeva (URS)	5'5.5"	Thelma Hopkins (GBR)	5'5.5"
Long Jump	Elzbieta Krzesinska (POL)	20'10"	Willye White (USA)	19'11.75"	Nadyezda Dhavalishvili (URS)	19'10.75"
Shot	Tamara Tyshkevich (URS)	54'5"	Gailna Zybina (URS)	54'2.25"	Marianne Werner (GER)*	51'2"
Discus	Olga Fikotová (TCH)	176'1.5"	Irina Beglyakova (URS)	172'4.5"	Nina Ponomaryeva (URS)	170'8"
Javelin	Inese Jaunzeme (URS)	176'8"	Marlene Ahrens (CHI)	165'3"	Nadyezda Konyayeva (URS)	164'11.5"

SWIMMING — MEN

EVENT	GOLD		SILVER		BRONZE	
100 m Freestyle	John Heinrichs (AUS)	55.4	John Devitt (AUS)	55.8	Gary Chapman (AUS)	56.7
400 m Freestyle	Murray Rose (AUS)	4:27.3	Tsuyoshi Yamanaka (JPN)	4:30.4	George Breen (USA)	4:32.5
1,500 m Freestyle	Murray Rose (AUS)	17:58.4	Tsuyoshi Yamanaka (JPN)	18:00.3	George Breen (USA)	18:08.2
100 m Backstoke	David Theile (AUS)	1:02.2	John Monckton (AUS)	1:03.2	Frank McKinney (USA)	1:04.5
200 m Breaststroke	Masaru Furukawa (JPN)	2:34 7	Masahiro Yoshimura (JPN)	2:36.7	Charis Yunitschev (URS)	2:36.8
200 m Butterfly	William Yorzik (USA)	2:19.3	Takashi Ishimoto (JPN)	2:23.8	György Tumpek (HUN)	2:23.9
4x200 m Freestyle Relay	Australia	8:23.6	USA	8:31.5	USSR	8:34.7
Springboard Diving	Robert Clotworthy (USA)	159.56	Donald Harper (USA)	156.23	Joaquin Capilla Pérez (MEX)	150.69
Highboard Diving	Joaquin Capilla Pérez (MEX)	152.44	Gary Tobian (USA)	152.41	Richard Connor (USA)	149.79
Water Polo	Hungary		Yugoslavia		USSR	

SWIMMING — WOMEN

EVENT	GOLD		SILVER		BRONZE	
100 m Freestyle	Dawn Fraser (AUS)	1:02.0	Lorraine Crapp (AUS)	1:02.3	Faith Leech (AUS)	1:05.1
400 m Freestyle	Lorraine Crapp (AUS)	4:54.6	Dawn Fraser (AUS)	5:02.5	Sylvia Ruuska (USA)	5:07.1
100 m Backstroke	Judith Grinham (GBR)	1:12.9	Carol Cone (USA)	1:12.9	Margaret Edwards (GBR)	1:13.1
200 m Breaststroke	Ursula Happe (GER)*	2:53.1	Eva Ezékely (HUN)	2:54.8	Eva-Maria ten Elsen (GER)*	2:55.1
100 m Butterfly	Shelley Mann (USA)	1:11.0	Nancy Ramey (USA)	1:11.9	Mary Sears (USA)	1:14.4
4x100 m Freestyle Relay	Australia	4:17.1	USA	4:19.2	South Africa	4:25.7
Springboard Diving	Patricia McCormick (USA)	142.36	Jeanne Stunyo (USA)	125.89	Irene MacDonald (CAN)	121.40
Highboard Diving	Patricia McCormick (USA)	84.85	Juno Irwin (USA)	81.64	Paula Jean Myers (USA)	81.58

WEIGHTLIFTING

EVENT	GOLD		SILVER		BRONZE	
Bantamweight	Charles Inci (USA)	342.5	Vladimir Stogov (URS)	337.5	Mahmoud Namdjou (IRN)	332.5
Featherweight	Isaac Berger (USA)	352.5	Yevgenyi Minayev (URS)	342.5	Marian Zielinski (POL)	335.0
Lightweight	Igor Rybak (URS)	380.0	Ravil Khabutdinov (URS)	372.5	Chang-Hee Kim (KOR)	370.0
Middleweight	Fyodor Bogdanovski (URS)	420.0	Peter George (USA)	412.5	Emanno Pignatti (ITA)	382.5
Light-Heavyweight	Thomas Kono (USA)	447.5	Vassiliy Stepanov (URS)	427.5	James George (USA)	417.5
Middle-Heavyweight	Arkadi Vorobyev (URS)	462.5	David Sheppard (USA)	442.5	Jean Debuf (FRA)	425.0
Heavyweight	Paul Anderson (USA)	500.0	Humberto Selvetti (ARG)	500.0	Alberto Pigiani (ITA)	452.5

WEIGHTLIFTING WEIGHTS

BANTAMWEIGHT	-123.5 lb	FEATHERWEIGHT	-132.25 lb	LIGHTWEIGHT	-148.75 lb
MIDDLEWEIGHT	-165.5 lb	LIGHT-HEAVYWEIGHT	-182 lb	MIDDLE-HEAVYWEIGHT	-192.5 lb
HEAVYWEIGHT	+198.5 lb				

BOXING

EVENT	GOLD	SILVER	BRONZE
Flyweight (-112.5 lb)	Terence Spinks (GER)	Mircea Dobrescu (ROM)	John Caldwell (IRL)
			René Libeer (FRA)
Bantamweight (-119 lb)	Wolfgang Behrendt (GER)*	Soon-Chung Song (KOR)	Frederick Gilroy (IRL)
			Claudio Barrientos (CHI)
Featherweight (-126 lb)	Vladimir Safronov (URS)	Thomas Nicholls (GBR)	Hendryk Niedzwiedzki (POL)
			Petti Hämäläinen (FIN)
Lightweight (-132 lb)	Richard McTaggart (GBR)	Harry Kurschat (GER)*	Anthony Byrne (IRL)
			Anatoli Lagetko (URS)
Light-Welterweight (-140 lb)	Vladimir Yengibaryan (URS)	Franco Nenci (ITA)	Henry Loubscher (SAF)
			Constanall Dumitrescu (ROM)
Welterweight (-148 lb)	Nicolae Lince (ROM)	Frederick Tiedt (IRL)	Kevin John Hogarth (AUS)
			Nicholas Gargano (GBR)
Light-Middleweight (-157 lb)	László Papp (HUN)	José Torres (USA)	John McCormack (GBR)
			Zbiegniew Pietrzykowski (POL)
Middlevweight (-165 lb)	Glennadiy Schatkov (URS)	Ramon Tapia (CHI)	Gilbert Chapron (FRA)
			Victor Zalazar (ARG)
Light-Heavyweight (-178.5 lb)	James Felton Boyd (USA)	Gherorghe Negrea (ROM)	Romuldas Murauskas (URS)
			Carlos Lucas (CHI)
Heavyweight (+178.5 lb)	Peter Rademacher (USA)	Lev Mukhin (URS)	Daniel Bekker (SAF)
			Giacomo Bozzano (ITA)

GRECO-ROMAN WRESTLING

EVENT	GOLD	SILVER	BRONZE
Flyweight (-114.5 lb)	Nikolai Solovyov (URS)	Ignazio Fabra (ITA)	Durum Ali Egribas (TUR)
Bantamweight (-125.75 lb)	Konstantin Vrupayev (URS)	Edwin Vesterby (SWE)	Francisco Horvat (ROM)
Featherweight (-136.5 lb)	Rauno Mäkinen (FIN)	Imre Polyák (HUN)	Roman Dzneladze (URS)
Lightweight (-147.5 lb)	Kyösti Lehtonen (FIN)	Riza Dogan (TUR)	Gyula Tóth (HUN)
Welterweight (-160.75 lb)	Mithat Bayrak (TUR)	Vladimir Maneyev (URS)	Per Berlin (SWE)
Middleweight (-174 lb)	Givy Kartoziya (URS)	Dimiter Dobrev (BUL)	Rune Jansson (SWE)
Light-Heavyweight (-191.75 lb)	Valentin Nikolayev (URS)	Petko Sirakov (BUL)	Kad-Erik Nilsson (SWE)
Heavyweight (+191.75 lb)	Anatoly Parfenov (URS)	Wilfried Dietrich (GER)*	Adelmo Bulgarelli (ITA)

FREESTYLE WRESTLING

EVENT	GOLD	SILVER	BRONZE
Flyweight (-114.5 lb)	Mirian Tsalkalamanidze (URS)	Mohamed Ali Khojastehpour (IRN)	Hüseyin Akbas (TUR)
Bantamweight (-125.75 lb)	Mustafa Dagistanli (TUR)	Mohamad Yaghoubi (IRN)	Michail Chachov (URS)
Featherweight (-136.5 lb)	Shozo Sasahara (JPN)	Joseph Mewis (BEL)	Erkki Penttilä (FIN)
Lightweight (-147.5 lb)	Emamali Habibi (IRN)	Shigeru Kasahara (JPN)	Alimberg Bestayev (URS)
Welterweight (-160.75 lb)	Mitsuo Ikeda (JPN)	Ibrahim Zengin (TUR)	Vakhtang Balavadze (URS)
Middleweight (-174 lb)	Nikola Stantschev (BUL)	Daniel Hodge (USA)	Georgiy Skhirtladze (URS)
Light-Heavyweight (-191.75 lb)	Gholam-Reza Takhti (IRN)	Boris Kulayev (URS)	Peter Steele Blair (USA)
Heavyweight (+191.75 lb)	Hamit Kaplan (TUR)	Hussein Mehmedov (BUL)	Taisto Kangasniemi (FIN)

FENCING

EVENT	GOLD		SILVER		BRONZE	
Individual Foil — Men	Christian d'Oriola (FRA)	6	Giancarlo Bergamini (ITA)	5	Antonio Spallino (ITA)	5
Team Foil — Men	Italy		France		Hungary	
Individual Épée	Carlo Pavesi (ITA)	5/1/2	Guiseppe Delfino (ITA)	5/1/1	Edoardo Mangiarotti (ITA)	5/1/10
Team Épée	Italy		Hungary		France	
Individual Sabre	Rudolf Kárpáti (HUN)	6	Jerzy Pawlowski (POL)	5	Lev Kuznetsov (URS)	4
Team Sabre	Hungary		Poland		USSR	
Individual Foil — Women	Gillian Sheen (GBR)	6+1	Olga Orban (ROM)	6	Renée Garilhe (FRA)	5

MODERN PENTATHLON

EVENT	GOLD		SILVER		BRONZE	
Individual	Lars Hall (SWE)	4833	Olavi Nannonen (FIN)	4774.5	Väinö Korhonen (FIN)	4750
Team	USSR	13,690.5	USA	13,482	Finland	13,185.5

CANOEING — MEN

EVENT	GOLD		SILVER		BRONZE	
1,000 m Kayak Singles K1	Gert Fredriksson (SWE)	4:12.8	Igor Pissaryev (URS)	4:15.3	Lajos Kiss (HUN)	4:16.2
10,000 m Kayak Singles K1	Gert Fredriksson (SWE)	47:43.4	Ferenc Halaczky (HUN)	47:53.3	Michael Scheuer (GER)*	48:00.3
1,000 m Kayak Pairs K2	Germany*	3:49.6	USSR	3:51.4	Austria	3:55.8
10,000 m Kayak Pairs K2	Hungary	43:37.0	Germany*	43:40.6	Australia	43:43.2
1,000 m Canadian Singles C1	Leon Rotman (ROM)	5:05.3	István Hernek (HUN)	5:06.2	Gennady Bukharin (URS)	5:12.7
10,000 m Canadian Singles C1	Leon Rotman (ROM)	56:41.0	János Parti (HUN)	57:11.0	Gennady Bukharin (URS)	57:14.5
1,000 m Canadian Pairs C2	Romania	4:47.4	USSR	4:48.6	Hungary	4:54.3
10,000 m Canadian Pairs C2	USSR	54:02.4	France	54:48.3	Hungary	55:15.6

CANOEING — WOMEN

EVENT	GOLD		SILVER		BRONZE	
500 m Kayak Singles K1	Elisaveta Dementyeva (URS)	2:18.9	Therese Zenz (GER)*	2:19.6	Tove Söby (DEN)	2:22.3

YACHTING

EVENT	GOLD		SILVER		BRONZE	
Finn Class	Paul Elvström (DEN)	7509	André Nelis (BEL)	6254	John Marvin (USA)	5953
International Star	USA	5876	Italy	5649	Bahamas	5223
Sharpie	New Zealand	6086	Australia	6068	Great Britain	4859
Dragon	Sweden	5723	Denmark	5723	Great Britain	4547
5.5 m	Sweden	5527	Great Britain	4050	Australia	4022

CYCLING

EVENT	GOLD		SILVER		BRONZE	
Individual Road Race (116.75 miles)	Ercole Baldini (ITA)	5:21:17.0	Arnaud Geyre (FRA)	5:23:16.0	Alan Jackson (GBR)	5:23:16.0
Team Road Race	France	22	Great Britain	23	Germany*	27
1,000 m Time Trial	Leandro Faggin (ITA)	1:09.8	Ladislav Foucek (TCH)	1:11.4	Alfred Swift (SAF)	1:11.6
1,000 m Sprint	Michel Rousseau (FRA)		Guglielmo Pesenti (ITA)		Richard Ploog (AUS)	
2,000 m Tandem	Australia		Czechoslovakia		Italy	
4,000 m Team Pursuit	Italy	4:37.4	France	4:39.4	Great Britain	4:42.2

EQUESTRIANISM

EVENT	GOLD		SILVER		BRONZE	
Three-Day Event	Petrus Kastennmann (SWE)	-66.53	August Lütke-Westhues (GER)*	-84.87	Frank Weldon (GBR)	-85.48
Three-Day Event (Team)	Great Britain	-355.48	Germany*	-475.91	Canada	-572.72
Grand Prix (Dressage)	Henri Saint Cyr (SWE)	860.0	Lis Hartel (DEN)	850.0	Liselott Linsenhoff (GER)*	832.0
Grand Prix (Dressage) Team	Sweden	2475	Germany*	2346	Switzerland	2346
Grand Prix (Jumping)	Hans Günter Winkler (GER)*	-4	Raimondo d'Inzeo (ITA)	-8	Piero d'Inzeo (ITA)	-11
Grand Prix (Jumping) Teams	Germany*	-40.00	Italy	-66.00	Great Britain	-69.00

SHOOTING

EVENT	GOLD		SILVER		BRONZE	
Free Rifle (3 Positions)	Vasiliy Borissov (URS)	1138	Allan Erdman (URS)	1137	Vilho Ylönen (FIN)	1128
Small-Bore Rifle (Prone)	Gerald R. Ouelette (CAN)	600	Vasiliy Borissov (URS)	599	Gilmour St. Boa (CAN)	598
Small-Bore Rifle (3 Positions)	Anatoliy Bogdanov (URS)	1172	Otakar Horinek (TCH)	1172	Nils Johan Sundberg (SWE)	1167
Rapid-Fire Pistol	Stefan Petrescu (ROM)	587	Evgeniy Schcherkasov (URS)	585	Gheorghe Lichiardopol (ROM)	581
Free Pistol (50 m)	Pentti Linnosvuo (FIN)	556 126	Makhmud Umarow (URS)	556 124	Offutt Pinion (USA)	551
Olympic Trap Shooting	Galliano Rossini (ITA)	195	Adam Smelczynski (POL)	190	Alessandro Ciceri (ITA)	188
Running Deer Shooting	Vitaly Romanenko (URS)	441	Per Olof Sköldberg (SWE)	432	Vladimir Sevrugin (URS)	429

GYMNASTICS — MEN

EVENT	GOLD		SILVER		BRONZE	
Individual Combined Exercises	Viktor Chukarin (URS)	114.25	Takashi Ono (JPN)	114.20	Yuri Titov (URS)	113.80
Team	USSR	568.25	Japan	566.40	Finland	555.95
Parallel Bars	Viktor Chukarin (URS)	19.20	Masami Kuboa (JPN)	19.15	Takashi Ono (JPN)	19.10
					MasaoTakemoto (JPN))	19.10
Floor	Valentin Muratov (URS)	19.20	Nobuyuki Aihara (JPN)	19.10		
			William Thoresson (SWE)	19.10		
			Viktor Chukarin (URS)	19.10		
Horse Vault	Helmut Bantz (GER)*	18.85			Yuri Titov (URS)	18.75
	Valetin Muratov (URS)	18.85				
Horizontal Bars	Takashi Ono (JPN)	19.60	Juri Titov (URS)	19.40	Masao Takemoto (JPN)	19.30
Rings	Albert Azaryan (URS)	19.35	Valentin Muratov (URS)	19.15	Masao Takemoto (JPN)	19.10
Pommel Horse	Boris Shaklin (URS)	19.25	Takashi Ono (JPN)	19.20	Viktor Chukarin (URS)	19.10

GYMNASTICS — WOMEN

EVENT	GOLD		SILVER		BRONZE	
Individual Combined Exercises	Larissa Latynina (URS)	74.933	Agnes Keleti (HUN)	74.633	Sofia Muratova (URS)	74.466
Team	USSR	444.80	Hungary	443.50	Romania	438.20
Floor	Agnes Keleti (HUN)	18.733	Elena Leustean (ROM)	18.700		
	Larissa Latynina (URS)	18.733				
Horse Vault	Larissa Latynina (URS)	18.833	Tamara Manina (URS)	18.800	Ann-Sofi Colling (SWE)	18.733
Beam	Agnes Keleti (HUN)	18.800	Tamara Manina (URS)	18.633		
			Eva Bésaková (TCH)	18.633		
Asymetrical Bars	Agnes Keleti (HUN)	18.966	Larissa Latynina (URS)	18.833	Sofia Muratova (URS)	18.800
Portable Apparatus Teams	Hungary	75.20	Sweden	74.20	Poland	74.00

BASKETBALL

GOLD	SILVER	BRONZE
USA	USSR	Uruguay

SOCCER

GOLD	SILVER	BRONZE
USSR	Yugoslavia	Bulgaria

HOCKEY

GOLD	SILVER	BRONZE
India	Pakistan	Germany*

ROME 1960

INTRODUCTION

Rome 1960

ABOVE: *Olympic poster detail. Allsport.*

PREVIOUS PAGE:
American Ralph Boston, broke Jesse Owens' long jump record — one of the games' longest standing records at the time.
Hulton Deusch

150 EVENTS

83 COUNTRIES

5,346 ATHLETES

	Gold	Silver	Bronze
URS	43	28	29
USA	34	21	16
ITA	13	10	13
GER*	12	19	11
AUS	8	8	6
TUR	7	2	
HUN	6	8	7
JPN	4	7	7
POL	4	6	11
CZE	3	2	3
ROM	3	1	6
GBR	2	6	12
DEN	2	3	1
NZE	2		1
BUL	1	3	3
SWE	1	2	3
FIN	1	1	3
AUT	1	1	
YUG	1	1	
PAK	1		1
ETH	1		
GRE	1		
NOR	1		
SUI		3	3
FRA		2	3
BEL		2	2
IRN		1	3
NED		1	2
SAF		1	2
ARG		1	1
UAR		1	1
CAN		1	
GHA		1	
IND		1	
MOR		1	
POR		1	
SIN		1	
TAI		1	
BRA			2
BWI			2
IRQ			1
MEX			1
ESP			1
VEN			1

*Represents a combined German team.

More than 1,500 years after the Roman Emperor Theodosius issued the decree which ended the ancient games, the modern version was awarded to the Eternal City of Rome. Fittingly, a number of old Roman sites were utilized, as well as a brand-new 100,000 capacity stadium. The Baths of Caracalla housed the gymnastics and the Basilica di Massenzio held the wrestling competitions.

The marathon began at the Capitol Hill and finished on the Appian Way, near the Arch of Constantine. It was the first time an Olympic marathon had not started or finished in the main stadium — and history was also made when Ethiopia's Abebe Bikila became the first black African to win an Olympic gold medal.

Bikila, unknown outside Ethiopia, padded barefoot through the streets of the ancient city to signal the entry of African runners onto the world distance running scene. It was a particularly sweet moment to triumph in Italy as many members of his family had been killed during the Italian invasion of his country in the thirties.

Bikila's victory emphasized that the spread of medals was growing wider with each passing games. By the end of Rome, a record 44 countries had shared in the medals.

The games were broadcast on worldwide television for the first time and people were able to share in the full glory and drama of the action. There were plenty of stars to cheer and dramatic stories to keep the TV producers happy.

Wilma Rudolph, a former polio victim, captivated the crowds in the Olympic Stadium with her three gold medals — winning the women's 100 and 200 meters and anchoring the US 400-meter relay team to victory. And Murray Halberg, a New Zealander handicapped by a withered arm, stormed to victory in the 5,000 meters.

It was a great games for Oceania as Australia's Herb Elliott produced one of the finest displays of middle-distance running ever seen to capture the 1,500 meters crown, winning by nearly three seconds as he broke his own world record.

But the games are mostly remembered for the emergence of an 18-year-old American boxer called Cassius Clay, who won the light-heavyweight title. As Muhammad Ali, he became the best known sportsman the world has ever seen and the greatest boxer in history.

The yachting was held in the Bay of Naples under the shadow of Mount Vesuvius, where Crown Prince Constantine (the heir to the throne of

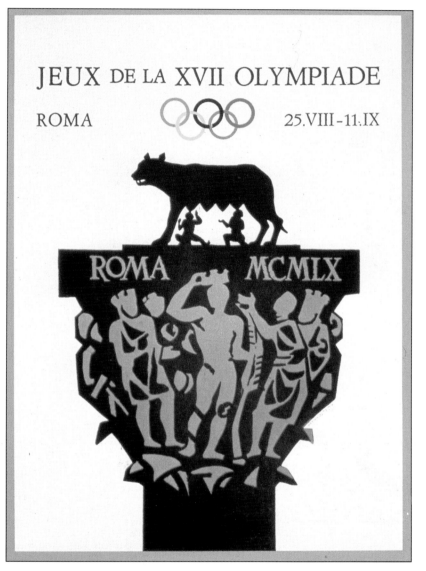

ABOVE RIGHT: Rome 1960's official poster. Allsport

ABOVE: A commemorative pin from the Rome Olympics 1960. Allsport

Greece) became only the second royal gold medalist in Olympic history when he triumphed in the Dragon class. An even more regal presence was reported at the canoeing on Lake Albano where the Pope was spied watching the action.

The games were not without controversy in the swimming pool, where America's Lance Larson was denied a gold medal in the 100 meters despite clearly finishing ahead of Australia's John Devitt. The incident led to the introduction of full electronic timing for future games.

Worryingly, two curses that continue to blight the games today also reared their ugly heads in 1960: politics and drugs.

ABOVE AND RIGHT: A commemorative medal from Rome 1960. Allsport

BELOW: Another commemorative pin from Rome 1960. Allsport

Nationalist China threatened to boycott the games after they were they told to appear under the name of Taiwan and not China.

More tragically, the Danish cyclist Knut Jensen became the first athlete to die in the games as a result of performance-enhancing drugs after collapsing during the road race.

The torch used at the 1960 Rome summer games.
Allsport

CASSIUS CLAY

Rome 1960

Cassius Clay won the light-heavyweight title at the Rome Olympics in 1960 — but discovered that where he came from, the color of his medal was less important than the color of his skin.

After showing off his medal at a reception given by the Mayor of Louisville, Clay and a friend, Ronnie King, stopped off to eat at a whites-only restaurant. Despite his protest that he was "Cassius Clay, Olympic champion," he was refused service.

The pair were chased by a gang of white motorcyclists who demanded Clay hand over the medal. After a fight on the Jefferson Country Bridge, Clay and King washed themselves in the Ohio River. By this time, the lead medal had lost its gold covering and, in his book *The Greatest*, Clay wrote: "For the first time, I saw it as it was. Ordinary, just an object."

On the bridge Clay took off the medal and threw it into the river.

After taking Sonny Liston's world title in 1964 Clay converted to Islam, adopted the name Muhammad Ali and became more than just a boxer.

In 1967 he defied the US draft, refusing to serve in Vietnam. "Why should I drop bombs and bullets on brown people in Vietnam while so-called Negro people in Louisville are treated like dogs?" he asked. He was stripped of his world heavyweight title, banned from boxing for three years, and reviled in the press.

Yet Ali's presence dominated heavyweight boxing in the sixties and seventies and he came back to regain the title. But much of the damage his body suffered was inflicted by former Olympic champions Joe Frazier, George Foreman and Leon Spinks. Long after he should have retired, Ali lost his title to the little-known Spinks only 18 months after he had won the Olympic light heavyweight gold medal in Montreal. Pride forced Ali to regain the Heavyweight Championship of the World for a record third time.

Despite suffering from Parkinson's Disease, Ali was named as Messenger of Peace by the United Nations, honored by Amnesty International with its Lifetime Achievement Award, and lauded in the press.

But Ali does not pay much heed to public opinion. His is an audience of one: "When God judges you, He will look at your good deeds and your bad deeds. Good deeds outweigh bad deeds in the hereafter. It pays off when you die."

Many people around the world were shocked when they saw his return to the Olympic arena in Atlanta in 1996 when he was chosen to raise the Olympic torch. The once animated face immobilized by disease, the once swift fists trembling, the onetime firebrand now a proud but humble patriot.

It would tire a young, well man to tackle Ali's schedule: Attend congressional hearing on Parkinson's disease, visit state capitol as advocate for new laws to protect children, hold press conference to raise funds for new track at hometown school, serve Thanksgiving dinners at local soup kitchen. These are just the events we know about.

"I do a lot of things I don't tell anyone," says Ali. "God knows."

Muhammad Ali is, without any question, one of the most famous people in the world. And what does Ali think about his fame? "Try not to think about it," he deadpans. "It'll make your head big."

American Cassius Clay (second from right) won gold in the light-heavyweight division before going onto an illustrious pro-boxing career, where he was better known by his Muslim name of Muhammad Ali. Hulton Deutsch

1960 ROME

ABEBE BIKILA

Abebe Bikila of Ethiopia during the 1960 Marathon. Hulton Deutsch

On the cobbled streets of Rome in 1960, Ethiopia's Abebe Bikila ran just as he had in practice he competed without shoes, and a legend was born. With bare feet and a silken stride, the 5 foot 9 inch, 128 pound Bikila personified the natural, unbound African runners who have come to dominate the endurance events in the last ten years.

It was somehow ironic and fitting that Bikila should choose Rome as the stage for his magnificent run. He was only three when his country was invaded by Mussolini's Italian troops. Now it was his turn to conquer.

The marathon was staged by moonlight and entirely outside the Olympic stadium, the runners passing one historic landmark after another. But Bikila, deep in concentration, noticed none of them as he broke the tape first in 2 hours 15min 17sec.

Originally from a family of shepherds, Bikila spent most of his adult life as a member of Emperor Haile Selassie's Imperial Bodyguard. His triumph earned him promotion to the rank of captain.

In the years after the 1960 Olympics, Bikila set out on a worldwide marathon tour, stimulating increased interest in the event. But his chances of retaining his title in Tokyo four years later seemed doomed when he had to undergo an emergency appendectomy just six weeks before the games. Incredibly, he defied the odds and his 2hr 12min 12sec was a world record by more than a minute.

Bikila suffered severe injuries in a car crash in 1969 which left him paralysed from the waist down and confined to a wheelchair. He spent several months at Britain's famed Stoke Mandeville Hospital, where he had a number of operations on his damaged spine. None was successful but he continued to display a remarkable strength of character. He took up archery from his wheelchair and competed in several Paraplegic Games.

"I was elated with my gold medals and I accepted these as part of life," Bikila said. "So I must accept the circumstances of my accident as part of life."

He had begun to carve out a new life for himself when he died from a brain haemorrhage in 1973 at the age of only 41. The news of his death saddened the world and he received a state funeral in Addis Ababa. But his legacy is the Africans running successfully in his footsteps.

HERB ELLIOTT

Few athletes have had such a short career at the top as Australia's Herb Elliott — nor one as successful. He retired undefeated at the age of 23 having never lost a race at 1,500 meters or the mile. His 44 race winning streak included victory in the 1,500 meters at Rome in 1960 when he set a world record of 3min 35.6secs.

Elliott's other great achievement during his career was improving Derek Ibbotson's 1957 world mile record from 3:57.2 to 3:54.5 in Dublin in 1958.

Following his racing successes in 1958, his low profile in 1959 was misinterpreted by some of his rivals as a case of the youngster having burned himself out. But Elliott proved them all wrong, producing a race in Rome that many experts still regard as the finest ever.

He took off at 950 meters like a "scared bunny." He was so afraid of being caught that he refused to look behind and just kept building his lead over Michel Jazy of France, eventually winning by nearly three seconds.

His most difficult task during these games was protecting his unique kangaroo hide spikes, which were almost stolen on three occasions.

In the month following his Olympic success, Elliott ran four further sub four minute miles before ending his career in London on May 13, 1961, with an easy mile victory, despite many tempting financial offers from promoters to continue running.

After studying at Cambridge University, he is now the managing director of the international sportswear company Puma.

Herb Elliot of Australia, a 1,500 m winner.
Hulton Deutsch

WILMA RUDOLPH

Wilma Rudolph matched Betty Cuthbert's 1956 feat by winning gold medals in the 100 meters, 200 meters, and 4x100 meters relay in Rome four years later. She was just 20. It was to be Rudolph's most glorious triumph. She was presented with the James E. Sullivan award in 1961 as America's finest amateur athlete and retired the following year, satisfied with her record.

Rudolph's life story, made into the TV movie *Wilma* in 1977, needed little dramatic embellishment. She was raised in Clarksville, Tennessee, the twentieth of 22 children reared by Eddie Rudolph, a railroad porter, and his second wife, Blanche, a domestic worker.

By four, Rudolph had been stricken with double pneumonia, scarlet fever and finally polio, leaving her left leg withered and paralysed. Doctors said she would never walk again but her mother and siblings would hear none of it. They massaged her leg four times a day and drove her each week to a Nashville hospital for special heat treatments.

"With all the love and care my family gave me, I couldn't help but get better," Rudolph said later.

Just how much better, few could have imagined. She was fitted with a leg brace which, several years later, she exchanged for a high-topped orthopaedic support shoe.

By the age of 13, Rudolph, fully recovered, was a star on the Burt High School basketball team, traveling to the state championships. One of the referees, Tennessee State University track coach Edward Temple, was so impressed by her that he invited her to his summer track camp.

Two years later, the scrawny 16-year-old won a spot on the 1956 US Olympic track and field team and returned home from Melbourne with a bronze medal in the 4x100 meters relay.

Rudolph enrolled at Tennessee State, where she joined the legendary Tigerbelles track team, which has produced 40 women Olympians. By 1962 Rudolph had won all there was to win. She earned a teaching degree at Tennessee State and, in the years that followed, worked as coach, teacher, co-host for an NBC radio show and goodwill ambassador to West Africa.

In 1981, Rudolph, who was married twice and had four children, founded the Wilma Rudolph Foundation, a non-profit group dedicated to helping disabled children. She died in 1994.

"All of us knew she was born to do more in the world than physically run on the track," said Tigerbelle and Olympic team-mate Isabelle Daniels Holston. "She was born to inspire, to love, and to give. She did, not only to the people of America but to the world."

American gold medalist Wilma Rudolph with Germany's Jutta Heine after the 200 m final.
Hulton Deutsch

TOP LEFT: *Al Oerter of the United States breaks the Olympic discus record.* Hulton Deutsch
TOP RIGHT: *Germany's Armin Hary winner of the 100 m gold.* Hulton Deutsch
ABOVE: *The marathon field passes the Rome Coliseum.* Hulton Deutsch

The Soviet Union's Polina Astakova in action during the Olympics gymnastics competition, in the compulsory exercises. Hulton Deutsch

The Soviet Union's Larissa Latynina won nine golds (three in Rome 1960), five silvers, and three bronzes during her entire Olympic career.
Allsport

TOP LEFT: *Dorothy Hyman of Great Britain (left) won a silver medal in the women's 100 m event. The race was won by Wilma Rudolph (USA) (center) and third went to Guiseppina Leone (Italy).* Allsport
TOP RIGHT: *Brian Phelps in action at the Olympic highboard event.* Hulton Deutsch
ABOVE: *Don Thompson of Great Britain came first in the 50 km walk.* Allsport

ABOVE: *American John Thomas won bronze in the high jump.* Hulton Deutsch

ABOVE RIGHT: *Ralph Boston in mid-air during the long jump.* Hulton Deutsch

ROME 1960 AUGUST 25 -SEPTEMBER 11

PARTICIPANTS: 5,346

MEN: 4,736

WOMEN: 610

COUNTRIES: 83

SPORTS: 17

EVENTS: 150

FINAL TORCHBEARER: GIANCARLO PERIS

MEDALS TABLE

PLACE	COUNTRY	GOLD	SILVER	BRONZE
1	USSR	42	28	29
2	USA	34	21	16
3	Italy	13	10	13
4	Germany*	12	19	11
5	Australia	8	8	6

OUTSTANDING ATHLETES

PLACE	NAME (NATIONALITY)	DISCIPLINE	GOLD	SILVER	BRONZE
1	Boris Schakhlin (URS)	Gymnastics	4	2	1
2	Larissa Latynina (URS)	Gymnastics	3	2	1
3	Takashi Ono (JPN)	Gymnastics	3	1	2
4	Chris von Saltza (USA)	Swimming	3	1	
5	Wilma Rudolph (USA)	Athletics	3		

* Represents a combined German team (throughout tables)

158

ATHLETICS — MEN

EVENT	GOLD		SILVER		BRONZE	
100 m	Armin Hary (GER)*	10.2	David Sime (USA)	10.2	Peter Radford (GBR)	10.3
200 m	Livio Berutti (ITA)	20.5	Lester Carney (USA)	20.6	Abdoulaye Seye (FRA)	20.7
400 m	Otis Davis (USA	44.9	Carl Kauffmann (GER)*	44.9	Malcolm Spence (SAF)	45 5
800 m	Peter Snell (NZL)	1:46.3	Roger Moens (BEL)	1:46 5	George Kerr (ANT)	1:47.1
1,500 m	Herbert Elliott (AUS)	3:35 6	Michel Jazy (FRA)	3:38.4	Istvan Rozsavölgyi (HUN)	3:39.2
5,000 m	Murray Halberg (NZL)	13:43.4	Hans Grodotzki (GER)*	13:44.6	Kasimierz Zimny (POL)	13:44.8
10,000 m	Pjotr Bolotnikov (URS)	28:32.2	Hans Grodotzki (GER)*	28:37.0	David Power (AUS)	28:38.2
Marathon	Abebe Bikila (ETH)	2:15:16.2	Rhadi Ben Abdesselam (MAR)	2:15:41.6	Barry Magee (NZL)	2:17:18.2
110 m Hurdles	Lee Calhoun (USA)	13. 8	Willie May (USA)	13.8	Hayes Jones (USA)	14.0
400 m Hurdles	Glenn Davis (USA)	49.3	Clifton Cushman (USA)	49.6	Richard Howard (USA)	49.7
3,000 m Steeplechase	Zdislaw Krzyszkowiak (POL)	8:34 2	Nikolai Sokolov (URS)	8:36.4	Semyon Rischtschin (URS)	8:42.2
4x100 m	Germany*	39.5	USSR	40.1	Great Britain	40.2
4x400 m	USA	3:02.2	Germany*	3:02.7	Antilles	3:04.0
20 km Walk	Vladimir Golubnitschky (URS)	1:34:07.2	Noel Freeman (AUS)	1:34:16.4	Stanley Vickers (GBR)	1:34:56.4
50 km Walk	Don Thompson (GBR)	4:25:30.0	John Ljunggren (SWE)	4:25:47.0	Abdon Panich (ITA)	4:27:55.4
High Jump	Robert Shavlakadze(URS)	7'1"	Valeriy Brumel (URS)	7'1"	John Thomas (USA)	7'0"
Pole Vault	Donald Bragg (USA)	15'5"	Ron Morris (USA)	15'1"	Eeles Landström (FIN)	14'11"
Long Jump	Ralph Boston (USA)	26'7.5"	Irvin Roberson (USA)	26'7.25"	Igor Ter-Ovanesian (URS)	26'4.5"
Triple Jump	Jozef Schmidt (POL)	55'1.75"	Vladimir Goryayev (URS)	54'6.25"	Vitold Kreyer (URS)	53'10.75"
Shot	Bill Nieder (USA)	64'6.75"	Parry O'Brien (USA)	62'8.25"	Dallas Long (USA)	62'4.25"
Discus	Al Oerter (USA)	194'1.5"	Richard Babka (USA)	190'4"	Dick Cochran (USA)	187'6"
Hammer	Vasiliy Rudenkov (URS)	220'1.5"	Gyula Zsivotzky (HUN)	215'10"	Tadeusz Rut (POL)	215'4"
Javelin	Viktor Tsibulenko (URS)	277'8"	Walter Kruger (GER)*	260'4"	Gergely Kulscsar (HUN)	257'9"
Decathlon	Rafer Johnson (USA)	8392	Chuan-Kwang Yang (TPE)	8334	Vassily Kusnetsov (URS)	7809

ATHLETICS — WOMEN

EVENT	GOLD		SILVER		BRONZE	
100 m	Wilma Rudolph (USA)	11.0	Dorothy Hyman (GBR)	11.3	Giuseppina Leone (ITA)	11.3
200 m	Wilma Rudolph (USA)	24.0	Jutta Heine (GER)*	24.4	Dorothy Hyman (GBR)	24.7
800 m	Ludmilla Schevtsova (URS)	2:04.3	Brenda Jones (AUS)	2:04.4	Ursula Donath (GER)*	2:05.6
80 m Hurdles	Irina Press (URS)	10.8	Carol Quinton (GBR)	10.9	Gisela Birkemeyer Köhler (GER)*	11.0
4x100 m	USA	44.5	Germany*	44.8	Poland	45.0
High Jump	Yolanda Balas (ROM)	6'0"	Jaroslawa Jozwiakowska (POL) Dorothy Shirley (GBR)	5'7.25" 5'7.25"		
Long Jump	Vera Krepkina (URS)	20'10.75"	Elzbieta Krzesinska (POL)	20'6.75"	Hildrun Claus (GER)*	20'4.25"
Shot	Tamara Press (URS)	56'9.75"	Johanna Lüttge (GER)*	54'5.75"	Earlene Brown (USA)	53'10.75"
Discus	Nina Ponomaryeva (URS)	180'9"	Tamara Press (URS)	172'6"	Lia Manoliu (ROM)	171'9"
Javelin	Elvira Ozolina (URS)	183'7.5"	Dana Zatopkova (TCH)	176'5"	Birute Kalediena (URS)	175'4"

SWIMMING — MEN

EVENT	GOLD		SILVER		BRONZE	
100 m Freestyle	John Devitt (AUS)	55.2	Lance Larson (USA)	55.2	Manuel Dos Santos (BRA)	55.4
400 m Freestyle	Murray Rose (AUS)	4:18.3	Tsuyoshi Yamanaka (JPN)	4:21.4	John Konrads (AUS)	4:21.8
1,500 m Freestyle	John Konrads (AUS)	17:19.6	Murray Rose (AUS)	17:21.7	George Breen (USA)	17:30.6
100 m Backstroke	David Theile (AUS)	1:01.9	Frank McKinney (USA)	1:02.1	Robert Bennet (USA)	1:02.3
200 m Breaststroke	Bill Mulliken (USA)	2:37.4	Yoshihiko Osaki (JPN)	2:38.0	Wilger Mensonides (HOL)	2:39.7
200 m Butterfly	Michael Troy (USA)	2:12.8	Neville Hayes (AUS)	2:14.6	David Gillanders (USA)	2:15.3
4x200 m Freestyle Relay	USA	8:10.2	Japan	8:13.2	Australia	8:13.8
4x100 m Medley Relay	USA	4:05.4	Australia	4:12.0	Japan	4:12.2
Springboard Diving	Gary Tobian (USA)	170.00	Samuel Hall (USA)	167.08	Juan Batello (MEX)	162.30
Highboard Diving	Robert Webster (USA)	165.56	Gary Tobian (USA)	165.25	Brian Phelps (GBR)	157.13
Water Polo	Italy		USSR		Hungary	

SWIMMING — WOMEN

EVENT	GOLD		SILVER		BRONZE	
100 m Freestyle	Dawn Fraser (AUS)	1:01.2	Chns von Saltza (USA)	1:02.8	Natalie Steward (GBR)	1:03.1
400 m Freestyle	Chris von Saltza (USA)	4:50.6	Jane Cederquist (SWE)	4:53.9	Caterina Lagerberg (HOL)	4:56.9
100 m Backstroke	Lynn Burke (USA)	1:09.3	Natalie Steward (GBR)	1:10.8	Satoko Tanaka (JPN)	1:11.4
200 m Breaststroke	Anita Lonsbrough (GBR)	2:49.5	Wiltrud Urselmann (GER)*	2:50.0	Barbara Gobel (GER)*	2:53.6
100 m Butterfly	Carolyn Schuler (USA)	1:09.5	Marianne Heemskerk (HOL)	1:10.4	Janice Andrew (AUS)	1:12.2
4x100 m Freestyle	USA	4:08.9	Australia	4:11.3	Germany	4:19.7
4x100 m Medley Relay	USA	4:41.1	Australia	4:45.9	Germany	4:47.6
Springboard Diving	Ingrid Krämer (GER)*	155.81	Paula J. Myers-Pope (USA)	141.24	Elizabeth Ferris (GBR)	139.09
Highboard Diving	Ingrid Krämer (GER)*	91.28	Paula J. Myers-Pope (USA)	88.94	Ninel Krutova (URS)	86.99

BOXING

EVENT	GOLD	SILVER	BRONZE
Flyweight (-112.5 lb)	GyulaTörök (HUN)	Sergey Sivko (URS)	Kiyoshi Tanabe (JPN)
			Abdel Elgiundi (VAR)
Bantamweight (-119 lb)	Oleg Grigoryev (URS)	Primo Zamparini (ITA)	Oliver Taylor (AUS)
			Brunon Bendig (POL)
Featherweight (-126 lb)	Francesco Musso (ITA)	Jerzy Adamski (POL)	Jorma Limmonen (FIN)
			William Meyers (SAF)
Lightweight (-132 lb)	Kasimierz Pazdzior (POL)	Sandro Lopopoli (ITA)	Richard McTaggart (GBR)
			Abel Laudonio (ARG)
Light-Welterwveight (-140 lb)	Bohumil Nemecek (TCH)	Clement Quartey (GHA)	Quincy Daniels (USA)
			Marian Kasprzyk (POL)
Welterweight (-148 lb)	Giovanni Benvenuti (ITA)	Yury Radonyak (URS)	Leszek Drogosz (POL)
			James Lloyd (GBR)
Light-Middleweight (-157.5 lb)	Wilbert McClure (USA)	Carmelo Bossi (ITA)	Boris Lagutin (URS)
			Bill Fisher (USA)
Middleweight (-165 lb)	Edward Crook (USA)	Tadeusz Walasek (POL)	Ion Monea (ROM)
			Yevgeniy Federanov (URS)
Light-Heavyweight (-178.5 lb)	Cassius Clay (USA)	Zbiegniew Pietrzykowski (POL)	Giulio Sarandi (ITA)
			Antony Madigan (AUS)
Heavyweight (+178 lb)	Franco De Piccoli (ITA)	Daniel Bekker (SAF)	Günter Siegmund (GER)*
			Josef Nemec (TCH)

WEIGHTLIFTING

EVENT	GOLD		SILVER		BRONZE	
Bantamweight	Charles Vinci (USA)	345.0	Yoshinobu Miyake (JPN)	337.5	Esmail Khan (IRN)	330.0
Featherweight	Yevginy Minayev (URS)	372.5	Isaac Berger (USA)	362.5	Sebastino Mannironi (ITA)	352.5
Lightweight	Viktor Bushuyev (URS)	397.5	Howe-Liang Tan (SIN)	380.0	Abdul Wahid Aziz (lRQ)	380.0
Middleweight	Alexander Kurynow (URS)	473.5	Thomas Kono (USA)	427.5	Gyözö Veres (HUN)	405.0
Light-Heavyweight	Ireneusz Palinski (POL)	442.5	James George (USA	430.0	Jan Bochenek (POL)	420.0
Middle-Heavyweight	Arkadiy Vorobyev (URS)	472.5	Trofim Lomakin (URS)	457.5	Louis Martin (GBR)	445.0
Heavyweight	Yury Vlassov (URS)	537.5	James Bradford (USA)	512.5	Norbert Schemansky (USA)	500.0

WEIGHTLIFTING WEIGHTS

BANTAMWEIGHT	-123.5 lb	FEATHERWEIGHT	-132.25 lb	LIGHTWEIGHT	-148.75 lb
MIDDLEWEIGHT	-165.5 lb	LIGHT-HEAVYWEIGHT	-182 lb	MIDDLE-HEAVYWEIGHT	--192.5 lb
HEAVYWEIGHT	+192 lb				

GRECO-ROMAN WRESTLING

EVENT	GOLD	SILVER	BRONZE
Flyweight (-114.5 lb)	Dumitru Pirvulescu (ROM)	Osman Sayed (UAE)	Mohamed Paziraye (IRN)
Bantamweight (-125.75 lb)	Oleg Karavayev (URS)	Ion Cernea (ROM)	Petrov Dinko (BUL)
Featherweight (-136.5 lb)	Müzahir Sille (TUR)	Imre Polyák (HUN)	Konstantin Vyrupayev (URS)
Lightweight (-147.5 lb)	Avtandil Koridze (URS)	Bronislav Martinovic (YUG)	Gustaf Freij (SWE)
Welterweight (-160.75 lb)	Mithat Bayrak (TUR)	Günther Maritschnigg (GER)*	René Schiermeyer (FRA)
Middleweight (-174 lb)	Dimiter Dobrev (BUL)	Lothar Metz (GER)*	Ion Taranu (EkOM)
Light-Heavyweight (-191.75 lb)	Tevfik Kis (TUR)	Krali Bimbalov (BUL)	Givi Kartoziya (URS)
Heavyweight (+191.75 lb)	Ivan Bogdan (URS)	Wilfried Dietrich (GER)*	Bohumil Kubát (TCH)

FREESTYLE WRESTLING

EVENT	GOLD	SILVER	BRONZE
Flyweight (- 114.5 lb)	Ahmet Bilek (TUR)	Masayuki Matsubara (JPN)	Mohamed Saifpour Saidabadi (IRN)
Bantamweight (-125.75 lb)	Terrence McCann (USA)	Nejdet Zalev (BUL)	Tadeusz Trojanowski (POL)
Featherweight (-136.5 lb)	Mustafa Dajistanli (TUR)	Stantcho Ivanov (BUL)	Vladimir Rubashvili (URS)
Lightweight (-147.5 lb)	Shelby Wilson (USA)	Vladimir Sinyavski (URS)	Enyu Dimov (BUL)
Welterweight (-160.75 lb)	Douglas Blubaugh (USA)	Ismail Ogan (TUR)	Muhammed Bashir (PAK)
Middleweight (-174.75 lb)	Hasan Güngör (TUR)	Georgiy Skhirtladze (URS)	Hans Y. Antonsson (SWE)
Light-Heavyweight (-191.75 lb)	Ismet Atli (TUR)	Cholham-R. Takhti (IRN)	Anatoliy Albul (URS)
Heavyweight (+191.75 lb)	Wilfried Dietrich (GER)	Hamit Kaplan (TUR)	Savkus Dzarassor (URS)

FENCING

EVENT	GOLD		SILVER		BRONZE	
Individual Foil — Men	Viktor Zhdanovich (URS)	7	Yury Sissikin (URS)	4	Albert Axelrod (USA)	3
Team Foil — Men	USSR		Italy		Germany*	
Individual Épée	Giuseppe Delfino (ITA)	5	Allan Jay (GBR)	5	Bruno Khabarov (URS)	4
Team Épée	Italy		Great Britain		USSR	
Individual Sabre	Rudolf Kárpáti (HUN)	5	Zoltan Horvath (HUN)	4	Wladimiro Calarese (ITA)	4
Team Sabre	Hungary		Poland		Italy	
Individual Foil — Women	Heidi Schmid (GER)*	6	Valentina Rastworowa (URS)	5	Maria Vicol (ROM)	4
Team Foil — Women	USSR		Hungary		Italy	

MODERN PENTATHLON

EVENT	GOLD		SILVER		BRONZE	
Individual	Ferenc Németh (HUN)	5024	Imre Nagy (HUN)	4988	Robert L. Beck (USA)	4981
Team	Hungary	14863	USSR	14309	USA	14192

CANOEING — MEN

EVENT	GOLD		SILVER		BRONZE	
1,000 m Kayak Singles K1	Erik Hansen (DEN)	3:53.00	Imre Szöllösi (HUN)	3:54.02	Gert Fredriksson (SWE)	3:55.89
1,000 m Kayak Pairs K2	Sweden	3:34.73	Hungary	3:34.91	Poland	3:37.34
4x500 m Kayak Single Relay K1	Germany*	7:39.43	Hungary	7:44.02	Denmark	7:46.09
1,000 m Canadian Singles C1	János Parti (HUN)	4:33.93	Alexandr Silayev (URS)	4:34.41	Leon Rotman (ROM)	4:35.87
1,000 m Canadian Pairs C2	USSR	4:17.94	Italy	4:20.77	Hungary	4:20.89

CANOEING — WOMEN

EVENT	GOLD		SILVER		BRONZE	
500 m Kayak Singles K1	Antonina Seredina (URS)	2:08.08	Therese Zenz (GER)*	2:08.22	Daniela Walkowiak (POL)	2:10.46
500 m Kayak Pairs K2	USSR	1:54.76	Germany*	1:56.66	Hungary	1:58.22
Single Sculls	Vyacheslav Ivanov (URS)	7:13.96	Achim Hill (GER)*	7:20.21	Teodor Kocerka (POL)	7:21.26
Double Sculls	Czechoslovakia	6:47.50	USSR	6:50.49	Switzerland	6:50.59
Coxless Pairs	USSR	7:02.01	Austria	7:03.17	Finland	7:03.80
Coxed Pairs	Germany*	7:29.14	USSR	7:30.17	USA	7:34.58
Coxless Fours	USA	6:26.26	Italy	6:28.78	USSR	6:29.62
Coxed Fours	Germany*	6:39.12	France	6:41.62	Italy	6:43.72
Coxed Eights	Germany*	5:57.18	Canada	6:01.52	Czechoslovakia	6:04.84

YACHTING

EVENT	GOLD		SILVER		BRONZE	
Finn Class	Paul Elvström (DEN)	8171	Alexandr Chuchelov (URS)	6250	André Neli (BEL)	5934
International Star	USSR	7619	Portugal	6695	USA	6269
Flying Dutchman	Norway	6774	Denmark	5991	Germany*	5882
Dragon	Greece	6733	Argentina	5715	Italy	5704
5.5 m	USA	6900	Denmark	5678	Switzerland	5122

CYCLING

EVENT	GOLD		SILVER		BRONZE	
Individual Road Race (108.75 miles)	Viktor Kapitonov (URS)	4:20:37.0	Livio Trape (ITA)	4:20:37.0	Willy van den Berghen (BEL)	4:20:57.0
100 km Road Team Time Trial	Italy	2:14:33.53	Germany*	2:16:56.31	USSR	2:18:41.67
1,000 m TimeTrial	Sante Gaiardoni (ITA)	1:07.27	Dieter Gieseler (GER)*	1:08.75	Rostislav Vargashkin (URS)	1:08.86
1,000 m Sprint	Sante Gaiardoni (ITA)		Leo Sterckx (BEL)		Valentino Gasparella (ITA)	
2,000 m Tandem	Italy		Germany*		USSR	
4,000 m Team Pursuit	Italy	4:30.90	Germany*	4:35.78	USSR	n/a

EQUESTRIANISM

EVENT	GOLD		SILVER		BRONZE	
Three-Day Event	Lawrence Morgan (AUS)	+ 7.15	Neale Lavis (AUS)	- 16.50	Anton Bühler (SUI)	- 51.21
Three-Day Event (Team)	Australia	-128.18	Switzerland	-386.02	France	-515.71
Grand Prix (Dressage)	Sergey Filatov (URS)	2144.0	Gustav Fischer (SUI)	2087.0	Josef Neckermann (GER)*	2082.0
Grand Prix (Jumping)	Raimondo d'Inzeo (ITA)	-12	Piero d'Inzeo (ITA)	-16	David Broome (GBR)	-23
Grand Prix (Jumping) Team	Germany*	-46.50	USA	-66.00	Italy	-80.50

SHOOTING

EVENT	GOLD		SILVER		BRONZE	
Free Rifle (3 Positions)	Hubert Hammerer (AUT)	1129	Hans Spillmann (SUI)	1127	Vasiliy Borissov (URS)	1127
Small-Bore Rifle (Prone)	Peter Kohnke (GER)*	590	James Hill (USA)	589	Enrico E. Pelliccioni (VEN)	587
Small-Bore Rifle (3-Positions)	Viktor Shamburkin (URS)	1149	Marat Niyasov (URS)	1145	Klaus Zähringer (GER)*	1139
Rapid-Fire Pistol	William McMillan (USA)	587/147	Pentti Linnosvuo (FIN)	587/139	Aleksandr Zabelin (URS)	587/135
Free Pistol (50 m)	Aleksey Gushchin (URS)	560	Makhmud Umarov (URS)	552/26	Yoshihisa Yoshikawa (JPN)	552/20
OlympicTrap Shooting	Ion Dumitrescu (ROM)	192	Galliano Rossini (ITA)	191	Sergey Kalinin (URS)	190

GYMNASTICS — MEN

EVENT	GOLD		SILVER		BRONZE	
Individual Combined Exercises	Boris Shakhlin (URS)	115.95	Takashi Ono (JPN)	115.90	Yuri Titov (URS)	115.60
Team	Japan	575.20	USSR	572.70	Italy	559.05
Parallel Beam	Boris Shakhlin (URS)	19.400	Giovanni Carminucci (ITA)	19.375	Takashi Ono (JPN)	19.350
Floor	Nobuyuki Aihara (JPN)	19.450	Yuri Titow (URS)	19.325	Franco Menichelli (ITA)	19.275
Horse Vault	Boris Shakhlin (URS)	19.350			Vladimir Portnoi (URS)	19.225
	Takashi Ono (JPN)	19.350				
Horizontal Bar	Takashi Ono (JPN)	19.600	Masao Takemoto (JPN)	19.525	Boris Shakhlin (URS)	19.475
					Welik Kapaszow (BUL)	19.475
Rings	Albert Azaryan (URS)	19.725	Boris Shakhlin (URS)	19.500	Takashi Ono (JPN)	19.425
Pommel Horse	Boris Shakhlin (URS)	19.375	Shuji Tsurumi (JPN)	19.150		
	Eugen Ekman (PIN)	19 375				

GYMNASTICS — WOMEN

EVENT	GOLD		SILVER		BRONZE	
Achtkampf. Einzel	Larissa Latynina (URS)	77.031	Sofia Muratova (URS)	76.696	Polina Astakova (URS)	76.164
Team	USSR	382.320	Czechoslovakia	373.323	Romania	372.053
Floor	Larissa Latynina (URS)	19.583	Polina Astakova (URS)	19.532	Tamara Lyukina (URS)	19.449
Horse Vault	Margarita Nikolajeva (URS)	19.316	Sofia Muratova (URS)	19.049	Larissa Latynina (URS)	19.016
Beam	Eva Bosaková (TCH)	19.283	Larissa Latynina (URS)	19.233	Sofia Muratova (URS)	19.232
Asymmetrical Bars	Polina Astakova (URS)	19.616	Larissa Latynina (URS)	19.416	Tamara Lyukina (URS)	19.399

SOCCER

GOLD	SILVER	BRONZE
Yugoslavia	Denmark	Hungary

BASKETBALL

GOLD	SILVER	BRONZE
USA	USSR	Brazil

HOCKEY

GOLD	SILVER	BRONZE
Pakistan	India	Spain

TOKYO 1964

INTRODUCTION

Tokyo 1964

ABOVE: *The rising sun of Japan over the Olympic rings.* Allsport

PREVIOUS PAGE: *Pole vaulter Fred Hansen, of America, training in the Olympic Village.* Allsport

163 EVENTS

93 COUNTRIES

5,140 ATHLETES

	Gold	Silver	Bronze
USA	36	28	28
URS	30	31	35
JPN	16	5	8
GER*	10	21	19
ITA	10	10	7
HUN	10	7	5
POL	7	6	10
AUS	6	2	10
CZE	5	6	3
GBR	4	12	2
BUL	3	5	2
FIN	3		2
NZE	3		2
ROM	2	4	6
NED	2	4	4
TUR	2	3	1
SWE	2	2	4
DEN	2	1	3
YUG	2	1	2
BEL	2		1
FRA	1	8	6
CAN	1	2	1
SUI	1	2	1
BAH	1		
ETH	1		
IND	1		
KOR		2	1
TRI		1	2
TUN		1	1
ARG		1	
CUB		1	
PAK		1	
PHI		1	
IRN			2
BRA			1
GHA			1
IRL			1
KEN			1
MEX			1
NGR			1
URU			1

*Represents a combined German team.

A new satellite network of global communications had been formed since the 1960 games and Tokyo was the first beneficiary of this technological breakthrough. With satellites like Telstar in operation for the first time, the games were broadcast live right into the sitting rooms of the world. It was a new age for the ancient games — one that proved a savior and, at the same time, an occasional curse

Equally significantly, the Tokyo Olympiad was also the first computerized games, with scoring and timekeeping all done electronically.

The decision to award the games to Tokyo represented an act of conciliation towards Japan. Determined to showcase the progress they had made since the end of the war, Japan spent a staggering $3 billion on building new facilities and improving the city's infrastructure.

Despite protests from prisoners who had been held in camps by the Japanese during the war, Emperor Hirohito performed the official opening ceremony. The Olympic flame was brought into the stadium by a young runner who had been born near Hiroshima on the day the atom bomb was dropped there in 1945.

There was no forgiveness for South Africa, however. That nation was no longer welcome because of its apartheid policies and it was to be almost 30 years before its athletes were to reappear on the Olympic arena

The games witnessed one of the biggest upset in its history when America's Billy Mills, a

RIGHT: Tokyo 1964's Commemorative poster. Allsport

part-time Sioux Indian Marine officer, sprinted to victory in the 10,000 meters.

America's Bob Hayes produced what some track experts still believe to be the greatest sprint performance in history. He won the 100 meters and then anchored the US to gold in the 4x100 meters with a final leg so phenomenal it is still talked about today.

Britain also enjoyed one of its most successful games thanks to its women. Mary Rand became the first British woman to strike gold when she took the long jump. Then her team-mate Ann Packer won the 800 meters.

Once again, Oceania dominated the middle-distance events thanks to New Zealand's Peter Snell achieving the 800-1,500 meters double.

Away from the track, the star was Australia's Dawn Fraser, who won her third consecutive 100 meters title and added a relay silver to take her total haul to eight medals, a record for a female swimmer. But she was denied the opportunity of a fourth victory when she was banned by the Australians after an incident at the Imperial Palace.

Joe Frazier, a former worker in a Philadelphia meat locker, won the heavyweight gold medal despite a broken left thumb. He turned professional afterward and went on to enjoy some great clashes with Muhammad Ali.

One of the most successful athletes of the games was the Soviet gymnast Larissa Latynina, winner of two golds, two silvers and two bronzes.

Judo was among the new sports introduced at the behest of the host nation, who believed they

RIGHT: Tokyo 1964's Official Poster. Allsport

were guaranteed every gold medal. But they were shocked when the giant Dutchman Anton Geesink won the open class.

Abebe Bikila retained his Olympic title in the marathon — overcoming the twin handicap of an appendix operation just a few weeks before the games and having to wear shoes. But that led to a sad postscript to the games when Japan's Kokichi Tsuburaya, so distraught at winning "only" a bronze in the marathon, committed suicide because he believed he had let his country down.

ABOVE and RIGHT: *Tokyo 1964's commemorative medal.* Allsport

BELOW RIGHT: *The opening ceremony for Tokyo 1964.* IOC

OPPOSITE PAGE:
TOP: *Yoshinori Sakai, of the host country, ignites the Olympic flame.* IOC

BELOW LEFT: *The Komazawa Olympic Gymnasium is a multi-angular structure that seats 4,000 spectators for wrestling events.* Allsport

BELOW RIGHT: *Tokyo 1964's Olympic torch.* Allsport

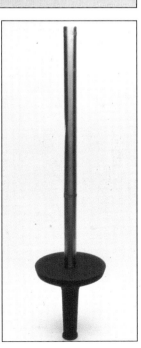

PETER SNELL

Tokyo 1964

Peter Snell was 18 years old before he gave up tennis and took up running but, under the tutelage of the legendary New Zealand coach Arthur Lydiard, he developed quickly. His victories were a triumph for the controversial coaching methods of Lydiard. It was only when, aged 19, he came under his influence that he began to improve and impress nationally, winning the New Zealand titles at 880 yards and the mile in 1959.

Despite a stress fracture that limited his running for two months before the games, the tough program set by coach Lydiard — which included a regular 22-mile hill run — paid dividends in Rome, where he successfully came through four 800 meters races in three days. He was still not considered a threat in the final — yet claimed victory in a time of 1min 46.3sec after an electrifying last 25 meters when he passed the favorite, Roger Moens of Belgium.

Moens approached him afterwards to offer his congratulations. "Who won?" asked Snell. "You did," replied Moens.

Having set world records from 800 meters to the mile, there was more pressure on Snell four years later in Tokyo. He rose to it magnificently as he retained the 800 meters and then added the 1,500 meters gold medal, despite never having raced the distance before he arrived in Tokyo.

It was his strength that crushed the opposition in the 1,500 meters; on the back stretch of the last lap he surged to a 100 meters in 12.7sec to take the lead, and kept that pace before easing off in the final straight to win by 10 yards. Snell's last lap of his only major 1,500 meters race was 52.7sec, with the middle 200 meters in 25 seconds.

He is now a noted exercise physiologist in Dallas, Texas.

Peter Snell of New Zealand won the men's 1,500 m race with a time of 3min 38.1sec.
Allsport

1 9 6 4

DAWN FRASER

Tokyo 1964

The only swimmer to win three consecutive Olympic titles in the same event, the 100 meters freestyle, Australia's Dawn Fraser is generally thought of as the greatest female swimmer of all time.

Her eight Olympic medals (since equaled by Kirtsen Otto) is also a women's record. In all, she set 27 individual world records, with 11 at 100 meters from 64.5sec in the Australian Championships in 1956 to 58.9sec in 1964, a time that was not bettered until eight years later. She broke the minute barrier for the first time in 1962.

In all, she won four gold and four silver medals between 1956 and 1964, and in 1983 was voted Australia's greatest ever Olympian.

Despite her talent, however, she was never far away from controversy. The youngest of eight children from a Sydney suburb, Fraser's clashes with Australian officials eventually ended her career.

At the Rome Olympics she refused to swim in a medley relay and her team-mates stopped talking to her. But her greatest indiscretion came in Tokyo four years later. She led a night time raid to steal a souvenir flag from the Emperor's Palace. She was arrested but charges were dropped and the Emperor gave her a flag as a gift. The Australian Swimming Union was less forgiving, hitting her with a ten-year suspension, later lifted after four years.

She was awarded an MBE in 1967. A film of her life, titled simply *Dawn!* was released in 1979. She became a publican in Sydney's Balmain district and represented that district in the New South Wales parliament from 1988 to 1991.

ANTON GEESINK

Tokyo 1964

Dutchman Anton Geesink provided the Japanese with a massive shock when he became the first Westerner to win a the Judo World Championships in 1961.

By the time the sport of judo was introduced to the Olympic timetable in Tokyo 1964, the giant 6 foot 6 inch Geesink was already a World Champion a second time and shattered the Japanese aura of invincibility by winning the open gold medal.

"I remember everyone in Japan was desperate for one of their players to win and the arena fell silent when I won," Geesink recalled many years later. "Then the crowd rose to applaud me. They appreciated what I had achieved. Even now I cannot visit Japan without someone recognizing me in the street and reminding me of the moment."

He won one more World Championships in 1965 and retired in 1967 after the last of his ten European titles. He went on to write several books on the sport and wrestle professionally in Japan. He remains a noted figure in judo and has served as a member of the International Olympic Committee for many years.

In 1999, he was among several leading IOC members who were alleged to have accepted money for votes from Salt Lake City, who bid successfully to stage the 2002 winter games. It was alleged he had accepted cash to buy a minibus for the Anton Geesink Foundation, a charity trust in his native Holland. Geesink strenuously denied the accusation but after a long investigation he was found guilty — though, unlike some members who were expelled, he escaped with a severe warning.

176

BILLY MILLS

In one of the most shocking upsets in Olympic history, America's Billy Mills came from nowhere to win the 10,000 meters in a games record of 28min 24.4sec. He was immediately surrounding by officials, one of whom asked: "Who are you?"

It was the question on everyone's lips. Humble and calm, Mills, who is half Sioux Indian, explained how he had taken up running to get fit for his boxing and, after losing a couple of fights, decided to stick to the track. He had spent a short time in the Marines before becoming a motor pool officer.

Mills's winning time in Tokyo was a personal best by an incredible 46 seconds. "I'm flabbergasted," he said. "I suppose I was the only person who thought I had a chance."

After the race, reporters asked Australia's Ron Clarke, the favorite who finished third, if he had been worried about Mills. "Worried about him?" Clarke snapped. "I'd never heard of him."

Mills's feat inspired a 1983 movie, *Running Brave*, which he co-wrote with wife Pat and which starred Robby Benson.

"I was running from rejection, from being orphaned," reflects Mills, now living in California.

His mother, who was one quarter Lakota, died when he was seven; his father, three quarters Lakota, died five years later. "The Indians called me mixed blood," says Mills. "They gave me warrior status and a Lakota name, *Makoce Teh'la* (which means "loves his country" or "respects the earth").

In 1965, Mills set a world record in the six-mile run and continued competing for about a year while finishing his stint in the Marines. Although he was not sent to Vietnam, Mills was deeply affected by the many combat deaths of men in his unit. He finally quit running, explaining: "I felt I could not participate in a sport when people were being killed in Vietnam."

After a tour as an official of the Department of the Interior, Mills returned to a career as a successful life insurance salesman and became a motivational speaker. In 1994, he retired from the insurance business so he could devote all his time to speaking to Indian youths and raising money for such charities as Christian Relief Services.

"I've designed my life," he says, "so that I can continue to give."

The American Billy Mills raises his hands in triumph after winning the 10,000 m race. Tunisian and Australian runners placed second and third. Allsport

The Czechoslovakian gymnast Vera Cáslavká captured seven Olympic medals between 1964 and 1968. Allsport

ABOVE: Soviet Galina Prozumenschikova, winner of the gold medal in the 200 m breaststroke, congratulates silver medalist Claudia Ann Kolb of the US Another Soviet, Svetlana Babanina won the bronze. Hulton Deutsch

LEFT: American Don Schollander won gold in the 100 m freestyle. Hulton Deutsch

ABOVE: *America's Henry Carr took gold in the men's 200 m final.* Allsport

ABOVE: *Hans Zdradzila of Czechoslovakia won a gold medal after lifting a total of 445 kg in the middle-weight category. Here he lifts 130 kg.* Allsport

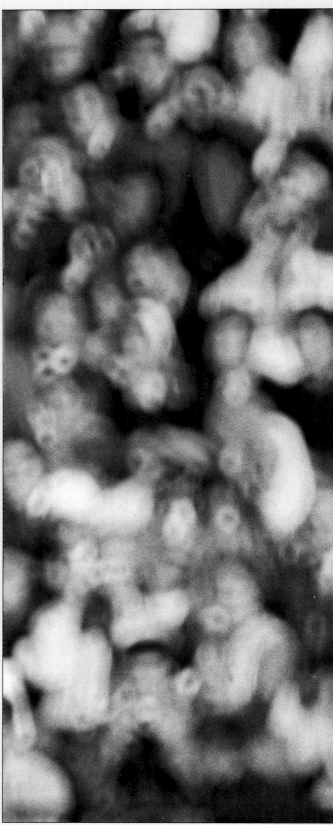

ABOVE: *Pentathlete Mary Rand of Great Britain takes part in the long jump component. She went on to win silver in the pentathlon and gold in the long jump proper.* Hulton Deutsch

ABOVE RIGHT: *America's John Thomas Pennel in the pole vault.* Allsport

Russia's Irina Press and Germany's Karin Balzer battle it out in the women's hurdles. Balzer (right) won the gold, Press placed fourth. Allsport

Larissa Latynina of the Soviet Union took gold in the women's individual floor excercise. Allsport UK

ABOVE: *Bulgarian athletes Nikolai Prodanov and Diana Jorgova exchanged vows in front of the Olympic flame in an Olympic-Shinto ceremony with numerous dignitaries in attendance. The couple honeymooned in Kyoto before returning for the games' closing ceremonies.* Allsport

LEFT: *American long jumper Ralph Boston warms up in the Olympic village.* Hulton Deutsch

TOKYO 1964 OCTOBER 10 -OCTOBER 24

PARTICIPANTS: 5,140

MEN: 4,457

WOMEN: 683

COUNTRIES: 93

SPORTS: 19

EVENTS: 163

FINAL TORCHBEARER: YOSHINORI SAKAI

MEDALS TABLE

PLACE	COUNTRY	GOLD	SILVER	BRONZE
1	USA	36	28	28
2	USSR	30	31	35
3	Japan	16	5	8
4	Germany*	10	21	19
5	Italy	10	10	7

OUTSTANDING ATHLETES

PLACE	NAME (NATIONALITY)	DISCIPLINE	GOLD	SILVER	BRONZE
1	Don Schollander (USA)	Swimming	4		
2	Vera Cáslavská (TCH)	Gymnastics	3	1	
	Yukio Endo (JPN)	Gymnastics	3	1	
	Sharon Stouder (USA)	Swimming	3	1	
3	Stephen Clark (USA)	Swimming	3		

* Represents a combined German team (throughout tables)

ATHLETICS — MEN

EVENT	GOLD		SILVER		BRONZE	
100 m	Robert Hayes (USA)	10.0	Enrique Figuerola (CUB)	10.2	Harry Jerome (CAN)	10.2
200 m	Henry Carr (USA)	20.3	Otis Paul Drayton (USA)	20.5	Edwin Roberts (TRI)	20.6
400 m	Michael Larrabee (USA)	45.1	Wendell Mottley (TRI)	45.2	Andrzej Badenski (POL)	45.6
800 m	Peter Snell (NZL)	1:45.1	William Crothers (CAN)	1:45.6	Wilson Kiprugut (KEN)	1:45.9
1,500 m	Peter Snell (NZL)	3:38.1	Josef Odlozil (TCH)	3:39.6	John Davies (NZI)	3:39.6
5,000 m	Robert Schul (USA)	13:48.8	Harald Norpoth (GER)*	13:49.6	William Dellinger (USA)	13:49.8
10,000 m	William Mills (USA)	28:24.4	Mohamed Gammoudi (TUN)	28:24.8	Ronald Clarke (AUS)	28:25.8
Marathon	Abebe Bikila (ETH)	2:12:11.2	Basil Heatley (GBR)	2:16:19.2	Kokichi Tsuburaya (JPN)	2:16:22.8
110 m Hurdles	Hayes Jones (USA)	13.6	Blaine Lindgren (USA)	13.7	Anatoliy Mikhailov (URS)	13.7
400 m Hurdles	"Rex" Cawley (USA)	49.6	John Cooper (GBR)	50.1	Salvatore Morale (ITA)	50.1
3,000 m Steeplechase	Gaston Roelants (BEL)	8:30.8	Maurice Herriott (GBR)	8:32.4	Ivan Belyayev (URS)	8:33.8
4x100 m	USA	39.0	Poland	39.3	France	39.3
4x400 m	USA	3:00.7	Great Britain	3:01.6	Trinidad	3:01.7
20 km Walk	Kenneth Matthews (GBR)	1:29:34.0	Dieter Lindner (GER)*	31:13.2	Vladimir Golubinichy (URS)	1:31:59.450
50km Walk	Abdon Pamich (ITA)	4:11:12.4	Paul V. Nihill (GBR)	4:11:31.2	Ingvar Pettersson (SWE)	4:14:17.4
High Jump	Valeriy Brumel (URS)	7'1.75"	John Thomas (USA)	2'18"	John Rambo (USA)	7'1"
Pole Vault	Fred Hansen (USA)	16'8.75"	Wolfgang Reinhardt (GER)*	5'05"	Klaus Lehnertz (GER)*	16'4.75"
Long Jump	Lynn Davies (GBR)	26'5.5"	Ralph Boston (USA)	8'03"	Igor Ter-Ovanesyan (URS)	26'2.5"
Triple Jump	Jozef Schmidt (POL)	55'3.25"	Oleg Fedoseyev (URS)	16.58	Viktor Kravchenko (URS)	54'4.25"
Shot	Dallas Long (USA)	66'8.25"	Randy Matson (USA)	20.20	Vilmos Varju (HUN)	63'7.25"
Discus	Al Oerter (USA)	200'1.5"	Ludvik Danek (TCH)	60.52	David Weill (USA)	195'2"
Hammer	Romuald Klim (URS)	228'9.5"	Gyula Zsivótzky (HUN)	69.09	Uwe Beyer (GER)*	223'4.5"
Javelin	Pauli Nevala (FIN)	271'2"	Gergely Kulcsar (HUN)	82.32	Janis Lusis (URS)	264'2"
Decathlon	Willi Holdorf (GER)*	7887	Rein Aun (URS)	7842	Hans-Joachim Walde (GER)*	7809

ATHLETICS — WOMEN

EVENT	GOLD		SILVER		BRONZE	
100 m	Wyomia Tyus (USA)	11.4	Edith McGuire (USA)	11.6	Ewa Klobukowska (POL)**	11.6
200 m	Edith McGuire (USA)	23.0	Irena Kirszenstein (POL)	23.1	Marilyn Black (AUS)	23.1
400 m	Betty Cuthbert (AUS)	52.0	Ann Packer (GBR)	52.2	Judith Amoore (AUS)	53.4
800 m	Ann Packer (GBR)	2:01.1	Maryvonne Dupureur (FRA)	2:01.9	Ann Chamberlain (NZL)	2:02.8
80 m Hurdles	Karin Balzer (GER)*	10.5	Tereza Ciepla (POL)	10.5	Pamela Kilborn (AUS)	10.5
4x100 m	Poland	43.6	USA	43.9	Great Britain	44.0
High Jump	Iolanda Balas (ROM)	6'2.75"	Michele Brown-Mason (AUS)	5'10.75"	Taisia Chenchik (URS)	5'10"
Long Jump	Mary Rand (GBR)	22'2.25"	Irena Kirszenstein (POL)	21'7.75"	Tatyana Schelkanova (URS)	21'0.75"
Shot	Tamara Press (URS)	59'6"	Renate Garisch (GER)*	57'9.25"	Galina Zybina (URS)	57'3"
Discus	Tamara Press (URS)	187'10.5"	Ingrid Lotz (GER)*	187'8"	Lia Manoliu (ROM)	186'10.5"
Javelin	Mihaela Penes (ROM)	187'7"	Marta Rudas (HUN)	191'2"	Yelena Gorchakova (URS)	187'2"
Pentathlon	Irina Press (URS)	5246	Mary Rand (GBR)	5035	Galina Bystrova (URS)	4956

**1967 Barred from competing as a result of a negative sex test

SWIMMING — MEN

EVENT	GOLD		SILVER		BRONZE	
100 m Freestyle	Don Schollander (USA)	53.4	Robert McGregor (GBR)	53.5	Halis-Joachim Klein (GER)*	54.0
400 m Freestyle	Don Schollander (USA)	4:12.2	Frank Wiegand (GER)*	4:14.9	Allan Wood (GBR)	4:15.1
1,500 m Freestyle	Robert Windle (AUS)	17:01.7	John Nelson (USA)	17:03.0	Allan Wood (GBR)	17:07.7
200 m Backstroke	Jed Graef (USA)	2:10.3	Gary Dilley (USA)	2:10.5	Robert Bennett (USA)	2:13.1
200 m Breaststroke	Ian O'Brien (AUS)	2:27.8	Georgy Prokopenko (URS)	2:28.2	Chester Jastremski (USA)	2:29.6
200 m Butterfly	Kevin Berry (AUS)	2:06.6	Carl Robie (USA)	2:07.5	Fred Schmidt (USA)	2:09.3
400 m Medley	Richard Roth (USA)	4:45.4	Roy Saari (USA)	4:47.1	Gerhard Hetz (GER)*	4:51.0
4x100 m Freestyle	USA	3:33.2	Germany*	3:37.2	Australia	3:39.1
4x200 m Freestyle	USA	7:52.1	Germany*	7:59.3	Japan	8:03.8
4x100 m Medley	USA	3:58.4	Germany*	4:01.6	Australia	4:02.3
Springboard Diving	Ken Sitzberger (USA)	159.90	Francis Gorman (USA)	157.63	Larry Andreasen (USA)	143.77
Highboard Diving	Robert Webster (USA)	148.58	Klaus Dibiasi (ITA)	147.54	Thomas Grompf (USA)	146.57
Water Polo	Hungary		Yugoslavia		USSR	

SWIMMING — WOMEN

EVENT	GOLD		SILVER		BRONZE	
100 m Freestyle	Dawn Fraser (AUS)	59.5	Sharon Stouder (USA)	59.9	Kathleen Ellis (USA)	1:00.8
400 m Freestyle	Virginia Duenkel (USA)	4:43.3	Marilyn Ramenofsky (USA)	4:44.6	Terri L. Stickles (USA)	4:47.2
100 m Backstroke	Cathy Ferguson (USA)	1:07.7	Christine Caron (FRA)	1:07.9	Virginia Duenkel (USA)	1:08.0
200 m Breaststroke	Galina Prozumenschikova (URS)	2:46.4	Claudia Kolb (USA)	2:47.6	Svetlana Babanina (URS)	2:48.6
100 m Butterfly	Sharon Stouder (USA)	1:04.7	Ada Kok (HOL)	1:05.6	Kathleen Ellis (USA)	1:06.0
400 m Medley	Donna De Varona (USA)	5:18.7	Sharon Finneran (USA)	5:24.1	Martha Randall (USA)	5:24.2
4x100 m Freestyle	USA	4:03.8	Australia	4:06.9	Netherlands	4:12.0
4x100 m Medley	USA	4:33.9	Netherlands	4:37.0	USSR	4:39.2
Springboard Diving	Ingrid Engel-Krämer (GER)*	145.00	Jeanne Collier (USA)	138.36	Mary Willard (USA)	138.18
Highboard Diving	Lesley Bush (USA)	99.80	Ingrid Engel-Krämer (GER)*	98.45	Galina Alekseyeva (URS)	97.60

WEIGHTLIFTING

EVENT	GOLD		SILVER		BRONZE	
Bantamweight	Aleksey Vakhonin (URS)	357.5	Imre Foldi (HUN)	355.0	Shiro Ichinoseki (JPN)	347.5
Featherweight	Yoshnobu Miyake (JPN)	397.5	Isaac Berger (USA)	382.5	Mieczyslaw Nowak (POL)	377.5
Lightweight	Waldemar Baszanowski (POL)	432.5	Vladimir Kaplunov (URS)	432.5	Marian Zielinski (POL)	420.0
Middleweight	Hans Zdradzila (TCH)	445.0	Viktor Kurentsov (URS)	440.0	Masashi Ouchi (JPN)	437.5
Light-Heavyweight	Rudolf Plukfelder (URS)	475.0	Geza Toth (HUN)	467.5	Gyozo Veres (HUN)	467.5
Middle-Heavyweight	Vladimir Golovanov (URS)	487.5	Louis Martin (GBR)	475.0	Ireneusz Palinski (POL)	467.5
Heavyweight	Leonid Zhabotinsky (URS)	572.5	Yuriy Vlassov (URS)	570.0	Norbert Schemansky (USA)	537.5

WEIGHTLIFTING WEIGHTS

BANTAMWEIGHT	-123.5 lb	FEATHERWEIGHT	-132.25 lb	LIGHTWEIGHT	-148.75 lb
MIDDLEWEIGHT	-165.5 lb	LIGHT-HEAVYWEIGHT	-182 lb	MIDDLE-HEAVYWEIGHT	--198.5 lb
HEAVYWEIGHT	+198.5 lb				

BOXING

EVENT	GOLD	SILVER	BRONZE
Flyweight (-112.5 lb)	Fernando Atzori (ITA)	Artur Olech (POL)	Stanislav Sorokin (URS)
			Robert Carmody (USA)
Bantamweight (-119 lb)	Takao Sakurai (JPN)	Shin-Cho Chung (KOR)	Juan Fabila Mendoza (MEX)
			Washington Rodriguez (URU)
Featherweight (-126 lb)	Stanislav Stepashkin (URS)	Anthony Villanueva (PHI)	Heinz Schulz (GER)*
			Charles Brown (USA)
Lightweight (-132 lb)	Jószef Grudzien (POL)	Vellikton Barannikov (URS)	James McCourt (IRL)
			Ronald Harris (USA)
Light-Welterweight (-140 lb)	Jerzy Kulej (POL)	Yevgeniy Frolov (URS)	Eddie Blay (GHA)
			Habib Galhia (TUN)
Welterweight (-148 lb)	Marian Kasprzyk (POL)	Ritschardas Tamulis (URS)	Pertti Purhonen (FIN)
			Silvano Bertini (ITA)
Light-Middleweight (-157 lb)	Boris Lagutin (URS)	Joseph Gonzales (FRA)	Nojim Maiyegun (NGA)
			Jozef Grzesiak (POL)
Middleweight (-165 lb)	Valeriy Popentschenko (URS)	Emil Schulz (GER)*	Francesco Vallę (ITA)
			Tadeusz Walasek (POL)
Light-Heavyweight (-178.5 lb)	Cosimo Pinto (ITA)	Aleksey Kisselyov (URS)	Alexandar Nikolov (BUL)
			Zbiegniew Pietrzykowski (POL)
Heavyweight (+178.5 lb)	Joe Frazier (USA)	Hans Huber (GER)*	Guiseppe Ros (ITA)
			Vadim Yemelyanov (URS)

GRECO-ROMAN WRESTLING

EVENT	GOLD	SILVER	BRONZE
Flyweight (-114.5 lb)	Tsutomu Hanahara (JPN)	Angel Kerezov (BUL)	Dumitru Pirvulescu (ROM)
Bantamweight (-125.75 lb)	Masamitsu Ichiguchi (JPN)	Vladien Trostiansky (URS)	Ion Cernea (ROM)
Featherweight (-138.75 lb)	Imre Polyák (HUN)	Roman Rurua (URS)	Branislav Martinovic (YUG)
Lightweight (-156.25 lb)	Kazim Ayvaz (TUR)	Valeriu Bularca (ROM)	David Gvantseladze (URS)
Welterweight (-172 lb)	Anatoliy Kolesov (URS)	Cyril Todorov (BUL)	Bertil Nyström (SWE)
Middleweight (-191.75 lb)	Branislav Simic (YUG)	Jiri Kormanik (TCH)	Lothar Metz (GER)*
Light-Heavyweight (-213.75 lb)	Boyan Radev (BUL)	Per Svensson (SWE)	Heinz Kiehl (GER)*
Heavyweight (+213.75 lb)	Istvan Kozma (HUN)	Anatoliy Roschin (URS)	Wilfried Dietrich (GER)*

FREESTYLE WRESTLING

EVENT	GOLD	SILVER	BRONZE
Flyweight (-114.5 lb)	Yoshikatsu Yoshida (JPN)	Chang-Sun Chang (KOR)	Said Aliaakbar Haydari (IRN)
Bantamweight (-125.75 lb)	Yojiro Uetake (JPN)	Hüseyn Akbas (TUR)	Aidyn Ibragimov (URS)
Featherweight (-138.75 lb)	Osamu Watanabe (JPN)	Stantcho Ivanov (BUL)	Nodar Kokaschvili (URS)
Lightweight (-154.25 lb)	Enyu Valtschev (BUL)	Klaus Jürgen Rost (GER)*	Iwao Horiuchi (JPN)
Welterweight (-172 lb)	Ismail Ogan (TUR)	Guliko Sagaradze (URS)	Mohamad-Ali Sanatkaran (IRN)
Middleweight (-191.75 lb)	Prodan Gardschev (BUL)	Hasan Güngör (TUR)	Daniel Brand (USA)
Light-Heavyweight (-213.75 lb)	Alexander Medved (URS)	Ahmet Ayik (TUR)	Said Mustafov (BUL)
Heavyweight (+213.75 lb)	Alexander Ivanitsky (URS)	Liutvi Djiber (BUL)	Hamit Kaplan (TUR)

JUDO

EVENT	GOLD	SILVER	BRONZE
Lightweight (138.75 lb)	Takehide Nakatani (JPN)	Eric Hänni (SUI)	Oleg Stepanov (URS) Aron Bogulubox (URS)
Middleweight (-176.25 lb)	Isao Okano (JPN)	Wolfgang Hofmann (GER)*	James Bergman (USA) Eui-Tae Kim (KOR)
Heavywweight (+205 lb)	Isao Inokuma (JPN)	Al Harold Rogers (USA)	Anzor Kiknadze (URS) Parnaoz Chikviladze (URS)
Open Category	Antonius Geesink (HOL)	Akio Kaminaga (JPN)	Klaus Glahn (GER)* Theodore Boronovskis (AUS)

FENCING

EVENT	GOLD		SILVER		BRONZE	
Individual Foil — Men	Egon Franke (POL)	3	Jean-Claude Magnan (FRA)	2	Daniel Revenu (FRA)	1
Team Foil — Men	USSR		Poland		France	
Individual Épée	Grigoriy Kriss (URS)	2+1	Henry Hoskyns (GBR)	2	Guram Kostova (URS)	1
Team Épée	Hungary		Italy		France	
Individual Sabre	Tibor Pezsa (HUN)	2+1	Claude Arabo (FRA)	2	Umar Mavlikhanov (URS)	1
Team Sabre	USSR		Italy		Poland	
Individual Foil — Women	Ildiko Ujlaki-Rejto (HUN)	2+2	Helga Mees (GER)*	2+1	Antonella Ragno (ITA)	2
Team Foil — Women	Hungary		USSR		Germany*	

MODERN PENTATHLON

EVENT	GOLD		SILVER		BRONZE	
Individual	Ferenc Török (HUN)	5516	Igor Novikov (URS)	5067	Albert Mokeyev (URS)	5039
Team	USSR	14961	USA	14189	Hungary	14173

CANOEING — MEN

EVENT	GOLD		SILVER		BRONZE	
1,000 m Kayak Singles K1	Rolf Peterson (SWE)	3:57.13	Mihaly Hesz (HUN)	3:57.28	Aurel Vernescu (ROM)	4:00.77
1,000 m Kayak Pairs K2	Sweden	3:38.54	Netherlands	3:39.30	Germany*	3:40.69
1,000 m Kayak Fours K4	USSR	3:14.67	Germany*	3:15.39	Romania	3:15.51
1,000 m Canadian Singles C1	Jürgen Eschert (GER)*	4:35.14	Andrei Igorov (ROM)	4:37.89	Yevgeny Penyayev (URS)	4:38.31
1,000 m Canadian Pairs C2	USSR	4:04.64	France	4:06.52	Denmark	4:07.48

CANOEING — WOMEN

EVENT	GOLD		SILVER		BRONZE	
500 m Kayak Singles K1	Ludmila Khvedosyak (URS)	2:12.87	Hilde Lauer (ROM)	2:15.35	Marcia Jones (USA)	2:15.68
500 m Kayak Pairs K2	Germany*	1:56.95	USA	1:59.16	Romania	2:00.25

ROWING

EVENT	GOLD		SILVER		BRONZE	
Single Sculls	Vyacheslav Ivanov (URS)	8:22.51	Achim Hill (GER)*	8:26.24	Gottfried Kottmann (SUI)	8:29.68
Double Sculls	USSR	7:10.66	USA	7:13.16	Czechoslovakia	7:14.23
Coxless Pairs	Canada	7:32.94	Netherlands	7:33.40	Germany*	7:38.63
Coxed Pairs	USA	8:21.23	France	8:23.15	Netherlands	8:23.42
Coxless Fours	Denmark	6:59.30	Great Britain	7:00.47	USA	7:01.37
Coxed Fours	Germany*	7:00.44	Italy	7:02.84	Netherlands	7:06.46
Coxed Eights	USA	6:18.23	Germany*	6:23.29	Czechoslovakia	6:25.11

YACHTING

EVENT	GOLD		SILVER		BRONZE	
Finn Class	Willi Kuhweide (GER)*	7638	Peter Barrett (USA)	6373	Henning Wind (DEN)	6190
International Star	Bahamas	5664	USA	5585	Sweden	5527
Flying Dutchman	New Zealand	6255	Great Britain	5556	USA	5158
Dragon	Denmark	5854	Germany*	5826	USA	5523
5.5 m	Australia	5981	Sweden	5254	USA	5106

CYCLING

EVENT	GOLD		SILVER		BRONZE	
Individual Road Race (121 miles)	Mario Zanin (ITA)	4:39:51.63	Kjell A. Rodian (DEN)	4:39:51.65	Walter Godefroot (BEL)	4:39:51.74
Team Road Race	Netherlands	2:26:31.19	Italy	2:26:55.39	Sweden	2:27:11.52
1,000 m Time-Trial	Patrick Sercu (BEL)	1:09.59	Giovanni Pettenella (ITA)	1:10.09	Pierre Trentin (FRA)	1:10.42.
1,000 m Sprint	Giovanni Pettenella (ITA)		Sergio Bianchetto (ITA)		Daniel Morelon (FRA)	
2,000 m Tandem	Italy		USSR		Germany*	
4,000 m Individual Pursuit	Jiri Daler (TCH)	5:04.75	Giorgio Ursi (ITA)	5:05.96	Preben Isaksson (DEN)	5:01.90
4,000 m Team Pursuit	Germany*	4:35.67	Italy	4:35.74	Netherlands	4:38.99

EQUESTRIANISM

EVENT	GOLD		SILVER		BRONZE	
Three-Day Event	Mauro Checcoli (ITA)	64.40	Carlos Moratorio (ARG)	56.40	Fritz Ligges (GER)*	49.20
Three-Day Event (Team)	Italy	85.80	USA	65.86	Germany	56.73
Grand Prix (Dressage)	Henri Chammartin (SUI)	1504	Harry Boldt (GER)*	1503	Sergey Filatov (URS)	1486
Grand Prix (Dressage) Team	Germany*	2558.0	Switzerland	2526.0	USSR	2311.0
Grand Prix (Jumping)	Pierre Jonqueresh d'Oriola (FRA)	-9	Hermann Schridde (GER)*	-13.75	Peter Robeson (GBR)	-16.00
Grand Prix (Jumping)Team	Germany*	-68.50	France	-77.75	Italy	-88.50

SHOOTING

EVENT	GOLD		SILVER		BRONZE	
Free Rifle (3 Positions)	Gary Anderson (USA)	1153	Shota Kveliashvili (URS)	1144	Martin Gunnarsson (USA)	1136
Small-Bore Rifle (Prone)	Laszló Hammerl (HUN)	597	Lones Wigger (USA)	597	Tommy Pool (USA)	596
Small-Bore Rifle (3 Positions)	Lones Wigger (USA)	1164	Velitchko Khristov (BUL)	1152	Laszló Hammerl (HUN)	1151
Rapid-Fire Pistol	Pentti Linnosvuo (FIN)	592	Ion Tripsa (ROM)	591	Lubomir Nacovsky (TCH)	590
Free Pistol (50 m)	Väino Markkanen (FIN)	560	Franklin Green (USA)	557	Yoshihisa Yoshikawa (JPN)	554
Olympic Trap Shooting	Ennio Mattarelli (ITA)	198	Pavel Senichev (URS)	194/25	William Morris (USA)	194/24

GYMNASTICS — MEN

EVENT	GOLD		SILVER		BRONZE	
Individual Combined Exercises	Yukio Endo (JPN)	115.95	Shuji Tsurumi (JPN)	115.40		
			Viktor Lisitsky (URS)	115.40		
			Boris Shakhlin (URS)	115.40	3-way tie for second place	
Team	Japan	577.95	USSR	575.45	Germany*	565.10
Parallel Bars	Yukio Endo (JPN)	19.675	Shuji Tsurumi (JPN)	19.450	Franco Menichelli (ITA)	19.35
Floor	Franco Menicheiii (ITA)	19.450	Viktor Lisitsky (URS)	19.350		
			Yukio Endo (JPN)	19.350		
Horse Vault	Haruhiro Yamashita (JPN)	19.600	Viktor Lisitsky (URS)	19.325	Hannu Rantakari (FIN)	19.300
Horizontal Bar	Boris Shakhin (URS)	19.625	Yuri Titov (URS)	19.550	Miroslav Cerar (YUG)	19.500
Rings	Takuji Hayata (JPN)	19.475	Franco Menicheilli (ITA)	19.425	Boris Shaklin (URS)	19.400
Pommel Horse	Miroslav Cerar (YUG)	19.525	Shuji Tsurumi (JPN)	19.325	Yuri Tsapenko (URS)	19.200

GYMNASTICS — WOMEN

EVENT	GOLD		SILVER		BRONZE	
Individual Combined Exercises	Vera Cáslavská (TCH)	77.564	Larissa Latynina (URS)	76.998	Polina Astakova (URS)	76.965
Team	USSR	380.890	Czechoslovakia	379.989	Japan	377.889
Floor	Larissa Latynina (URS)	19.599	Polina Astakova(URS)	19.500	Anikó Janosí (HUN)	19.300
Horse Vault	Vera Cáslavská (TCH)	19.483	Larissa Latynina (URS)	19.283		
			Birgit Radochla (GER)*	19.283		
Beam	Vera Cáslavská (TCH)	19.449	Tamara Manina (URS)	19.399	Larissa Latynina (URS)	19.382
Asymmetrical Bars	Polina Astakova (URS)	19.332	Katalin Makray (HUN)	19.216	Larissa Latynina (URS)	19.199

BASKETBALL

GOLD	SILVER	BRONZE
USA	USSR	Brazil

SOCCER

GOLD	SILVER	BRONZE
Hungary	Czechoslovakia	Germany*

HOCKEY

GOLD	SILVER	BRONZE
India	Pakistan	Australia

VOLLEYBALL — MEN

GOLD	SILVER	BRONZE
USSR	Czechoslovakia	Japan

VOLLEYBALL — WOMEN

GOLD	SILVER	BRONZE
Japan	USSR	Poland

INTRODUCTION

Mexico 1968

172
EVENTS

112
COUNTRIES

5,530
ATHLETES

	Gold	Silver	Bronze
USA	45	28	34
URS	29	32	30
JPN	11	7	7
HUN	10	10	12
GDR	9	9	7
FRA	7	3	5
CZE	7	2	4
FRG	5	11	10
AUS	5	7	5
GBR	5	5	3
POL	5	2	11
ROM	4	6	5
ITA	3	4	9
KEN	3	4	2
MEX	3	3	3
YUG	3	3	2
NED	3	3	1
BUL	2	4	3
IRN	2	1	2
SWE	2	1	1
TUR	2		
DEN	1	4	3
CAN	1	3	1
FIN	1	2	1
ETH	1	1	
NOR	1	1	
NZE	1		2
TUN	1		1
PAK	1		
VEN	1		
CUB		4	
AUT		2	2
SUI		1	4
MON		1	3
BRA		1	2
KOR		1	1
UGA		1	1
CAM		1	
JAM		1	
ARG			2
GRE			1
IND			1
TAI			1

This was the games when records were shattered but consciences were pricked. The moral dilemmas began even before the facilities for the XIX Olympiad in Mexico City were even built.

Protests at the cost of hosting the games in a relatively impoverished country led to riots in the streets. Student demonstrations against spending for the games culminated in a confrontation between 10,000 protesters and the Mexican army in which 260 people were killed and another 1,200 were wounded.

The games went ahead, of course, but not before international politics had caused further dissent. African countries, backed by black members of the American team, threatened a boycott if South Africa was admitted and, after long deliberations, the IOC gave in.

The protest that was most memorable, however, involved neither riots nor foreign diplomacy. It amounted to the simple, silent demonstration of US sprinters Tommie Smith and John Carlos.

The pair mounted the podium for the medal ceremonies after the 200 meters dash wearing black gloves and civil rights badges. As the US anthem "The Star-Spangled Banner" was played, they stunned the world by bowing their heads and raising clenched fists in the "black power" salute.

Gold medalist Smith's eyes were cast down during his brief protest. Behind and below him, bronze medalist John Carlos's eyes briefly roved the

RIGHT: The official poster of the 1968 Mexico Summer Olympics. Allsport

stadium. Their arms were ramrod straight but their feet were bare — a reminder, they said, of African-American poverty in the United States. It was a gesture that shook America.

Smith said later that as soon as he raised his fist, he wished it could all be over. He was no natural crusader but he knew the moment offered him a unique opportunity to make his mark for social justice in an America in which equal rights had still not been achieved. "I thought of my parents," he said, "and worried how they would take it and whether they would be hurt."

He added memorably: "It was the fist that scared people. Bowing wouldn't have gotten the response the fist did. It was a silent gesture. I never threw a rock."

The US Olympic Committee disapproved but were unwilling to make martyrs of Smith and Carlos. However, Avery Brundage of the IOC threatened to expel the entire US team if the pair remained unpunished, on the grounds that abuse of the ban on political demonstration would cause the total degeneration of the games.

Two days after their protest, Smith and Carlos were suspended from the US team and given 48 hours to leave the Olympic precincts. It caused a backlash and US runners Lee Evans, Larry James, Ron Freeman and Vince Matthews staged similar protests.

The demonstrations overshadowed what is generally acknowledged to have been the greatest track meet in history. Records galore fell —

Juegos de la XIX Olimpiada – Jeux de la XIXeme Olympiade – Games of the XIXth Olympiad

1968
MEXICO

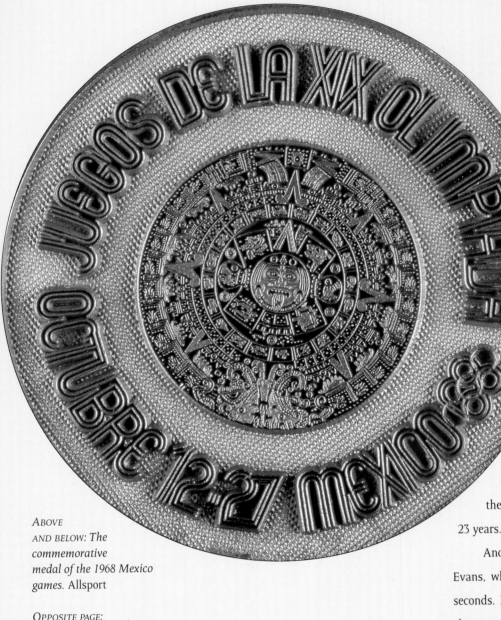

assisted by Mexico City's 7,350-foot (2,240-meter) altitude, which pumped more oxygen into the athlete's muscles.

At the moment that Tommie Smith and John Carlos were being ordered out of the Olympic Village, Bob Beamon, who had opposed their demonstration but was now furious at their suspensions, launched himself into space in the long-jump. His leap of 29 feet 2 inches was almost two feet beyond the previous world mark and stood for 23 years.

Another long-term record was that of Lee Evans, who won the 400 in a world record 43.86 seconds. It took a further 20 years before anyone else managed to crack 44 seconds.

The XIX Olympiad was also notable for the emergence of African distance runners. Kenya's Kip Keino almost failed to make the 1,500 meters because of one of Mexico City's notorious traffic snarl-ups. But he jogged the last mile to the stadium and then raced to a sensational victory over American world record holder Jim Ryun.

Another audience stunner was 16-year-old American Dick Fosbury, who revolutionized high jumping when he invented a new style of clearing the bar which became universally known as the "Fosbury Flop."

ABOVE AND BELOW: The commemorative medal of the 1968 Mexico games. Allsport

OPPOSITE PAGE: TOP RIGHT: The torch used in Mexico. Allsport

BELOW LEFT: Mexican dancers in the Olympic Village. Don Morley

BELOW RIGHT: The opening ceremonies. Allsport

It was African-American athletes, however, for whom the Mexico City games will be remembered. They won seven of the 12 US men's track and field gold medals, setting five world records, while African-American women won three golds and set two world records.

What effect did the protest at Mexico City have on American society? Against a background of disillusionment over Vietnam and civil strife on the streets, the US was facing social and political problems on a massive scale. While some athletes received death threats, many of those in officialdom chose to look the other way. The US Olympic book, for instance, neither mentioned nor printed photographs of the 200 meters awards.

John Carlos comments: "We got letters saying 'You set us back a hundred years,' and others saying 'You freed us.' The verdict is still out."

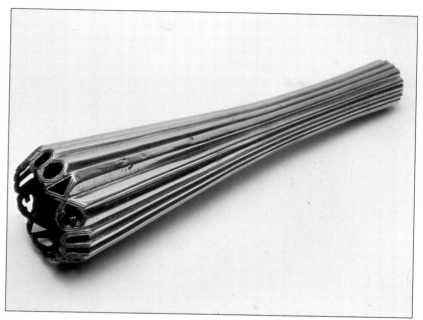

TOMMIE SMITH

American Tommie Smith set a record in the men's 200 m and created a national and international controversy on the medal podium. Hulton Deutsch

American Tommie Smith set a world record of 19.83sec when winning the 200 meters in Mexico City, but his name will be forever linked with the protest he and his team-mate, bronze medalist John Carlos, staged on the medal rostrum.

Mounting the podium barefoot, Smith and Carlos wore civil rights badges. When "The Star-Spangled Banner" was played, they bowed their heads and each one raised one black-gloved hand in the "black power" salute. They later explained that their clenched fists symbolized black strength and unity and their bare feet were a reminder of black poverty in the United States.

Muhammad Ali has called it "the single most courageous act of this century." Arthur Ashe, the former Wimbledon champion, described it as "an inspiration to a generation." However, to Americans of a certain age, it still remains one of the most frightening moments they have ever experienced.

"It was the fist that scared people," Smith says. "White folks would have forgiven the black socks, the silk scarf, the bowed head. But they saw that raised black fist and were afraid.

"It was meant to scare people. Listen, we were young, we had our whole lives in front of us. We knew we giving up everything. Heck, I already had 11 world records, I didn't do it as a claim to fame. It was a message, a sermon of need. It was a cry for help. We didn't say a word, we didn't carry weapons.

"Here I was, the great Tommie Smith, Olympic Champion. When I stepped on the track people saw me as a god. When I stepped off the track I was hungry. I opened the cupboard and saw cockroaches.

"I wanted them to help the real Tommie Smith, instead of helping that caricature who was running. I had to make some kind of stand. Heck, I'm the easiest-going black militant you'll ever find."

The world record of 19.83 Smith set when winning in Mexico City stood for 11 years — but he hopes the legacy of what he did on the podium will endure for many centuries. "I did it because I was afraid to do it," he explains. "Understand? I knew what I was going to do might get me killed. But it had to be done. I felt the necessity for change.

"Oh man, I never felt such a rush of pride. Even hearing 'The Star-Spangled Banner' was pride, though it didn't really represent me. But it was the anthem which represented the country I represented, can you see that?

"They say we demeaned the flag. Hey, no way man. That's my flag, it's what a lot of people who built this country served under the military. Black people died because of that flag."

Two days after their protest, Smith and Carlos were expelled from the US team in Mexico City and ordered home within 48 hours. It served only to rally their team-mates behind them.

Bob Beamon, previously opposed to any type of protest or demonstration, wore black socks to receive his gold medal for his world record in the long jump. Lee Evans, Larry James and Ron Freeman, the gold, silver and bronze medalists respectively in the 400 meters, donned the berets of the militant Black Panthers on the podium.

After Mexico, and graduating from San José State University in 1969, Smith played three seasons of American football with the Cincinnati Benegals and spent a short period running professional track before taking up coaching in Los Angeles.

But there is no doubt what he will always be remembered for. "Who can say how things would have turned out if I'd refused to answer God's call," he reflects. "Sure, I might have been wealthier, but happier? No, I really don't think so."

BOB BEAMON

Has there ever been a single more astonishing athletic performance than that achieved by America's Bob Beamon in Mexico City in 1968 when he leapt 8.90 meters, or 29 feet 2.5 inches?

It was not only the first 29 feet jump, but also the first over 28 feet.

But Beamon nearly did not even make it for the final and it was only thanks to some words of advice from American rival Ralph Boston before his last jump that he managed to get in a qualifying effort.

The night before the final, Beamon did something he had never done before: he had sex. At the moment of orgasm, he wrote in his autobiography, he was suddenly overcome with the feeling that he had ruined his Olympic chances. How wrong he was.

Helped by the maximum permitted wind aid and high altitude of Mexico City, Beamon hit the sand so powerfully with his first jump that he bounced back up and landed outside the pit.

The mark stood as a world record for 23 years until Mike Powell jumped 8.95 meters.

Athletics saved Beamon, who was orphaned before his first birthday and running with a rough New York City street gang by the time he entered his teens.

"Most of my friends from the early years are no longer with us," he attests.

Beamon, who could not read or write, was sent to a high school for troubled teens, where he was encouraged by the school coaches who recognized his long-jump ability. "They didn't give up on me," he says admiringly.

After Mexico City, Beamon earned a degree from Adelphi University and has spent his life helping inner-city children. For 20 years he has lived in Miami and worked for Metro-Dade County's Parks and Recreation Department, organizing track meets as well as art and dance lessons for the local kids.

Bob Beamon, of the US leapt into the history books with a record jump of 29ft 2.5 in. Tony Duffy

KIP KEINO

The emergence of Kenya as a world force in middle and long distance running largely began with Kip Keino in the mid-sixties. His loping stride, toothy smile, and unpredictable tactics made him a huge favorite wherever he raced.

He came to prominence in 1965, becoming the first Kenyan to set a world record when he ran 7min 36.96sec for 3,000 meters and ran the third fastest ever mile in 3min 54.2sec. He won Commonwealth Games titles at three miles and a mile a year later but his greatest triumph came at the 1968 Mexico City Olympics

Stomach cramps ended his 10,000 meters final with two laps to go but four days later he finished second in the 5,000 meters. A traffic jam threatened his arrival for the 1,500 meters but Keino jogged the last mile to the stadium and upset all the odds by front-running his way to a sensational victory over the American world record holder and favorite, Jim Ryun.

Four years later he won further gold in the 3,000 meter steeplechase and a silver in the 1,500 meters.

Keino now lives on Kazi Mingi Farm in Kenya's Western Highlands. When he and his wife Phyllis bought it, the farm was 190 acres of bleak, mountainous scrubland. Twenty-five years of their hard work has turned it green and prosperous. Keino also operates a sporting goods store in nearby Eldoret.

He and Phyllis have been taking in orphans for all 35 years of their married life. They have provided a home for more than 100 children.

Twenty-nine girls and six boys, aged one to 22, now live at Kazi Mingi. They come from all over Kenya and Uganda, representing at least half a dozen tribes.

Keino and Phyllis take in every child sent to them — the malnourished, the malformed, the maltreated. The Keinos treat all the youngsters just as they treat their own five boys and two girls. The children share clothing and quarters.

"They're all my children," he says. "I don't know any different."

The Keinos do not get any steady financial help, though they do receive some donations. The shop in Eldoret is their main source of income.

However, Kazi Mingi is a very self-contained operation. Fruit trees provide bananas, oranges, lemons, apples and tangerines. A large garden produces vegetables. And cow dung and goat droppings are shoveled into the drum of a bio-gas system, which produces energy to light the house.

ABOVE AND RIGHT: Kenya's Kip Keino was a crowd favorite in Mexico. Hulton Deutsch

DICK FOSBURY

Few athletes are remembered for having changed the course of their event, but American Dick Fosbury revolutionized high jumping when he invented the "Fosbury Flop."

It was a new style of clearing the bar that mesmerized spectators at the 1968 Olympics. Until Fosbury came along, most jumpers went over the bar forwards using the straddle technique or sideways with the western roll.

At 16 years old, Fosbury found both techniques too limiting and developed a style which involved running at the bar on a curved approach and turning to jump backwards while arching the back and bringing the lap up high. His perseverance paid off and he won the US Olympic trial with a personal best 2.21 meters.

In Mexico City he won the gold medal clearing 2.24 meters and the hearts and minds of other jumpers who quickly adopted the Flop.

Fosbury never jumped as high again, but the first world record with the Fosbury Flop came in 1973 when Dwight Stones of the US jumped 2.30 meters.

After the Olympics, Fosbury returned to Oregon State University, where he had earlier failed his exams. He was a talk show celebrity, but he was also a student worrying about bills. It was almost a blessing when his celebrity faded and he graduated with an engineering degree in 1972.

He is now an engineer and surveyor in Ketchum, Idaho. Still thin and gangly, Fosbury works out at the Sun Valley Athletic Club. Few of the regulars know his history.

Once a local ski instructor was stunned to learn the identity of the gawky guy in the corner of the gym. "I can't believe I'm looking at an Olympic athlete's body," the man said. "Now I don't feel so bad!"

Dick Fosbury of the US jumped to a gold medal in the high jump with a completely new jumping style, immediately dubbed the "Fosbury Flop."
Hulton Deutsch

207

LEFT: *The basketball stadium, outside (top) and inside (bottom). Tony Duffy*
TOP: *America's Lee Evans captured gold in the 400 m and helped his country to a gold in the 4x400 m relay. Allsport*
ABOVE: *All-American medal winners in the 400 m final. Left to right, Lee Evans (gold), Larry James (silver) and Ron Freeman (bronze). All three wore black berets and gave the Black Power salute during the presentation ceremony. Hulton Deutsch*

MEXICO 1968 OCTOBER 12 - OCTOBER 27

PARTICIPANTS: 5,530

MEN: 4,749

WOMEN: 781

COUNTRIES: 112

SPORTS: 18

EVENTS: 172

FINAL TORCHBEARER: NORMA ENRIQUETA BASILIO DE SOTELO

MEDALS TABLE

PLACE	COUNTRY	GOLD	SILVER	BRONZE
1	USA	45	28	34
2	USSR	29	32	30
3	Japan	11	7	7
4	Hungary	10	10	12
5	GDR*	9	9	7

OUTSTANDING ATHLETES

PLACE	NAME (NATIONALITY)	DISCIPLINE	GOLD	SILVER	BRONZE
1	Vera Caslavska (TCH)	Gymnmstics	4	2	
2	Akinori Nakayama (JPN)	Gymnastics	4	1	1
3	Charles Hickox (USA)	Swimrning	3	1	
4	Sawae Kato (JPN)	Gymnastics	3		1
5	Debbie Meyer (USA)	Swimming	3		

*GDR/FRG indicates two German teams for all Olympic games until 1992.

ATHLETICS — MEN

EVENT	GOLD		SILVER		BRONZE	
100 m	Jim Hines (USA)	9.9	Lennox Miller (JAM)	10.0	Charlie Greene (USA)	10.0
200 m	Tommie Smith (USA)	19.8	Peter Norman (AUS)	20.0	John Carlos (USA)	20.0
400 m	Lee Evans (USA)	43.8	Larry James (USA)	43.9	Ronald Freeman (USA)	44.4
800 m	Ralph Doubell (AUS)	1:44.3	Wilson Kiprugut (KEN)	1:44.5	Thomas Farrell (USA)	1:45.4
1,500 m	Kipchoge Keino (KEN)	3:34.9	Jim Ryun (USA)	3:37.8	Bodo Tümmler(FRG)	3:39.0
5,000 m	Mohamed Gammoudi (TUN)	14:05.0	Kipchoge Keino (KEN)	14:05.2	Naftali Temu (KEN)	14:06
10,000 m	Naftali Temu (KEN)	29:27.4	Mamo Wolde (ETH)	29:28.0	Mohamed Gammoudi (TUN)	29:34.2
Marathon	Mamo Wolde (ETH)	2:20:26.4	Kenji Kimihara (JPN)	2:23:31.0	Michael Ryan (NZL)	2:23:45.0
110 m Hurdles	Willie Davenport (USA)	13.3	Ervin Hall (USA)	13.4	Eddy Ottoz (ITA)	13.4
400 m Hurdles	David Hemery (GBR)	48.12	Gerhard Hennige (FRG)	49.02	John Sherwood (GBR)	49.03
3,000 m Steeplechase	Amos Biwott (KEN)	8:51.0	Benjamm Kogo (KEN)	8:51.6	George Young (USA)	8:51.8
4x100 m	USA	38.2	Cuba	38.3	France	38.4
4x400 m	USA	2:56.1	Kenya	2:59.6	FRG	3:00.5
20 km Walk	Vladimir Golubnichiy (URS)	1:33:58.4	José Pedraza (MEX)	1:34:00.0	Nikolai Smaga (URS)	1:34:03.0
50 km Walk	Christoph Höhne (GDR)	4:20:13.6	Antal Kiss (HUN)	4:30:17.0	Larry Young (USA)	4:31:55.4
High Jump	Dick Fosbury (USA)	7'4.25"	Edward Caruthers (USA)	7'3.5"	Valentin Gavrilov (URS)	7'2.5"
Pole Vault	Robert Seagren (USA)	17'8.5"	Claus Schiprowski (FRG)	17'8.5"	Wolfgang Nordwig (GDR)	17'8"
Long Jump	Bob Beamon (USA)	29'2.5"	Klaus Beer (GDR)	26'10.5"	Ralph Boston (USA)	26'9"
Triple Jump	Viktor Saneyev (URS)	57'0.75"	Nelson Prudencio (BRA)	56'7.75"	Giuseppe Gentile (ITA)	56'5.75"
Shot	Randy Matson (USA)	67'4.5"	George Woods (USA)	66'0"	Eduard Grischin (URS)	65'10.75"
Discus	Al Oerter (USA)	212.5"	Lothar Milde (GDR)	206'11"	Ludvik Danek (TCH)	206'5"
Hammer	Gyula Zsivótzky (HUN)	240'8"	Romuald Klim (URS)	240'5"	Lázár Lovász (HUN)	228'11"
Javelin	Janis Lusis (URS)	295'7"	Jorma Kinneunen (FIN)	290'7"	Gergely Kulcsar (HUN)	285'7.5"
Decathlon	William Toomey (USA)	8193	Hans-Joachim Walde (FRG)	8111	Kurt Bendlin (FRG)	8064

SWIMMING — MEN

EVENT	GOLD		SILVER		BRONZE	
100 m Freestyle	Michael Wenden (AUS)	52.2	Ken Walsh (USA)	52.8	Mark Spitz (USA)	53.0
200 m Freestyle	Michael Wenden (AUS)	1:55.2	Don Schollander (USA)	1:55.8	John Nelson (USA)	1:58.1
400 m Freestyle	Michael Burton (USA)	4:09.0	Ralph Hutton (CAN)	4:11.7	Alain Mosconi (FRA)	4:13.3
1500 m Freestyle	Michael Burton (USA)	16:38.9	John Kinsella (USA)	16:57.3	Gregory Brough (AUS)	17:04.7
100 m Backstroke	Roland Matthes (GDR)	58.7	Charles Hickcox (USA)	1:00.2	Ron Mills (AUS)	1:00.5
200 m Backstroke	Roland Matthes (GDR)	2:09.6	Mitchel Ivey (USA)	2:10.6	Jack Horsley (USA)	2:10.9
100 m Breaststroke	Don McKenzie (USA)	1:07.7	Vladimir Kossinsky (URS)	1:08.0	Nikolai Pankin (URS)	1:08.0
200 m Breaststroke	Felipe Muñoz (MEX)	2:28.7	Vladimir Kossinsky (URS)	2:29.2	Brian Job (USA)	2:29.9
100 m Butterfly	Douglas Russell (USA)	55.9	Mark Spitz (USA)	56.4	Ross Wales (USA)	57.2
200 m Butterfly	Carl Robie (USA)	2:08.7	Martin Woodroffe (GBR)	2:09.0	John Ferris (USA)	2:09.3
200 m Medley	Charles Hickcox (USA)	2:12.0	Gregory Buckingham (USA)	2:13.0	John Ferris (USA)	2:13.3
400 m Medley	Charles Hickcox (USA)	4:48.4	Gary Hall (USA)	4:48.7	Michael Holthaus (FRG)	4:51.4
4x100 m Freestyle Relay	USA	3:31.7	USSR	3:34.2	Australia	3:34.7
4x200 m Freestyle Relay	USA	7:52.3	Australia	7:53.7	USSR	8:01.6
4x100 m Medley Relay	USA	3:54.9	GDR	3:57.5	USSR	4:00.7
Springboard Diving	Bernard Wrightson (USA)	170.15	Klaus Dibiasi (ITA)	159.74	James Henry (USA)	158.09
Highboard Diving	Klaus Dibiasi (ITA)	164.18	Alvaro Gaxiola (MEX)	154.49	Edwin Young (USA)	153.93
Water Polo	Yugoslavia		USSR		Hungary	

SWIMMING — WOMEN

EVENT	GOLD		SILVER		BRONZE	
100 m Freestyle	Jan Henne (USA)	1:00.0	Susan Pedersen (USA)	1:00.3	Linda Gustavson (USA)	1:00.3
200 m Freestyle	Debbie Meyer (USA)	2:10.5	Jan Henne (USA)	2:11.0	Jane Barkman (USA)	2:11.2
400 m Freestyle	Debbie Meyer (USA)	4:31.8	Linda Gustavson (USA)	4:35.5	Karen Moras (AUS)	4:37.0
800 m Freestyle	Debbie Meyer (USA)	9:24.0	Pamela Kruse (USA)	9:35.7	Maria-Teresa Ramirez (MEX)	9:38.5
100 m Backstroke	Kaye Hall (USA)	1:06.2	Elaine Tanner (CAN)	1:06.7	Jane Swagerty (USA)	1:08.1
200 m Backstroke	Lilian Watson (USA)	2:24.8	Elaine Tanner (CAN)	2:27.4	Kaye Hall (USA)	2:28.9
100 m Breaststroke	Djurdjica Bjedov (YUG)	1:15.8	Galina Prozumenschikova (URS)	1:15.9	Sharon Wichman (USA)	1:16.1
200 m Breaststroke	Sharon Wichman (USA)	2:44.4	Djurdjica Bjedov (YUG)	2:46.4	Galina Prozumenschikova (URS)	2:47.0
100 m Butterfly	Lynette McClements (AUS)	1:05.5	Ellie Daniel (USA)	1:05.8	Susan Shields (USA)	1:06.2
200 m Butterfly	Ada Kok (HOL)	2:24.7	Helga Lindner (GDR)	2:24.8	Ellie Daniel (USA)	2:25.9
200 m Medley	Claudia Kolb (USA)	2:24.7	Susan Pedersen (USA)	2:28.8	Jan Helme (USA)	2:31.4
400 m Medley	Claudia Kolb (USA)	5:08.5	Lynn Vidali (USA)	5:22.2	Sabine Steinbach (GDR)	5:25.3
4x100 m Freestyle Relay	USA	4:02.5	FDR	4:05.7	Canada	4:07.2
4x100 m Medley Relay	USA	4:28.3	Australia	4:30.0	FRG	4:36.4
Springboard Diving	Sue Gossick (USA)	150.77	Tamara Pogozheva (URS)	145.30	Keala O'Sullivan (USA)	145.23
Highboard Diving	Milena Duchková (TCH)	109.59	Natalya Lobanova (URS)	105.14	Ann Peterson (USA)	101.11

ATHLETICS — WOMEN

EVENT	GOLD		SILVER		BRONZE	
100 m	WyomiaTyus (USA)	11.0	Barbara Ferrell(USA)	11.1	Irena Szewinska-Kirszenstein (POL)	11.1
200 m	Irena Szewinska-Kirszenstein (POL)	22.5	Raelene Boyle (AUS)	22.7	Jennifer Lamy (AUS)	22.8
400 m	Colerte Besson (FRA)	52.0	Lillian Board (GBR)	52.1	Natalya Pechenkina (URS)	52.2
800 m	Madeline Manning (USA)	2:00.9	Ilona Silai (ROM)	2:02.5	Maria Gommers (HOL)	2:02.6
80 m Hurdles	Maureen Caird (AUS)	10.3	Pam Kilborn (AUS)	10.4	Chi Cheng (TAI)	10.4
4x100 m	USA	42.8	Cuba	43.3	USSR	43.4
High Jump	Miloslava Rezková (TCH)	5'11.5"	Antonina Okorokova (URS)	5'10"	Valentina Kozyr (URS)	5'10.75"
Long Jump	Viorica Viscopoleanu (ROM)	22'4.5"	Sheila Sherwood (GBR)	21'10.75"	Tatyana Talysheva (URS)	21'10"
Shot	Margitta Hehmboldt (GDR)	64'4"	Marita Lange (GDR)	61'7.25"	Nadyezda Chizhova (URS)	63'6"
Discus	Lia Manoliu (ROM)	191'2"	Liesel Westermann (FRG)	189'6"	Jolán Kleiber (HUN)	180'1"
Javelin	Angéla Németh (HUN)	198'0"	Mihaela Penes (ROM)	196'7"	Eva Janko (HUN)	190'5"
Pentathlon	Ingrid Becker (FRG)	5098	Lise Prokop (AUT)	4966	Annamária Tóth (HUN)	4959

BOXING

EVENT	GOLD	SILVER	BRONZE
Light-Flyweight (-105 lb)	Francisco Rodriguez (VEN)	Yong-Ju Jee (KOR)	Harlan Marbley (USA)
			Hubert Skrzypczak (POL)
Flyweight (-112 Ib)	Ricardo Delgado (MEX)	Artur Olech (POL)	Servillo Oliveira (BRA)
			Leo Rwabwogo (UGA)
Bantamweight (-119 Ib)	Valeriy Sokolov (URS)	Eridadi Mukwanga (UGA)	Eiji Morioka (JPN)
			Kyou-Chull Chang (KOR)
Featherweight (-126 Ib)	Antonio Roldan (MEX)	Albert Robinson (USA)	Philipp Waruinge (KEN)
			Ivan Michailov (BUL)
Lightweight (-132 Ib)	Ronald Harris (USA)	Jószef Grudzien (POL)	Calistrat Cutov (ROM)
			Zvonimir Vujin (YUG)
Light-Welterweight (-140lb)	Jerzy Kulej (POL)	Enrique Regueiferos (CUB)	Arto Nilsson (FIN)
			James Wallington (USA)
Welterweight (-148 Ib)	Manfred Wolke (GDR)	Joseph Bessala (CMR)	Vladimir Musalinov (URS)
			Mario Guilloti (ARG)
Light-Middleweight (-157 Ib)	Boris Lagutin (URS)	Rolando Garbey (CUB)	John Baldwin (USA)
			Günther Meier (FRG)
Middleweight (-165 Ib)	Christopher Finnegan (GBR)	Alexey Kisselyov (URS)	Agustin Zaragoza (MEX)
			Alfred Jones (USA)
Light-Heavyweight (-178 Ib)	Dan Poznyak (URS)	Ion Monea (ROM)	Georgy Stankov (BUL)
			Stanislav Gragan (POL)
Heavyweight (+178 Ib)	George Foreman (USA)	Ionas Tschepulis (URS)	Giorgio Bambini (ITA)
			Joaquin Rocha (MEX)

WEIGHTLIFTING

EVENT	GOLD		SILVER		BRONZE	
Bantamweight	Mohammad Nassiri (IRN)	367.5	Imre Földi (HUN)	367.5	Henryk Trebicki (POL)	357.5
Featherweight	Yoshinobu Miyake (JPN)	392.5	Dito Shanidze (URS)	387.5	Yoshiyuki Miyake (JPN)	385.0
Lightweight	Waldemar Baszanowski (POL)	437.5	Parviz Jalayer (IRN)	422.5	Marian Zielinski(POL)	420.0
Middleweight	Viktor Kurentsov (URS)	475.0	Masashi Ouchi (JPN)	455.0	Károly Bakos (HUN)	440.0
Light-Heavyweigh	Boris Selitsky (URS)	485.0	Viktor Belyayev (URS)	485.0	Norbert Ozimek (POL)	472.5
Middle-Heavyweight	Kaarlo Kangasniemi (FIN)	517.5	Jan Talts (URS)	507.5	Marek Golab (POL)	495.0
Heavyweight	Leonid Zhabotinski (URS)	572.5	Serge Reding (BEL)	555.0	Joe Dube (USA)	555.0

WEIGHTLIFTING WEIGHTS

BANTAMWEIGHT	-123.5 lb	FEATHERWEIGHT	-132.25 lb	LIGHTWEIGHT	-148.75 lb
MIDDLEWEIGHT	-165.5 lb	LIGHT-HEAVYWEIGHT	-182 lb	MIDDLE-HEAVYWEIGHT	-198.5 lb
HEAVYWEIGHT	+198.5 lb				

GRECO-ROMAN WRESTLING

EVENT	GOLD	SILVER	BRONZE
Flyweight (-114.5 lb)	Petar Kirov (BUL)	Vladimir Bakulin (URS)	Miroslav Zeman (TCH)
Bantamweight (-125.75 lb)	János Varga (HUN)	Ion Baciu (ROM)	Ivan Kochergin (URS)
Featherweight (-138.75 lb)	Roman Rurua (URS)	Hideo Fujimoto (JPN)	Simeon Popescu (ROM)
Lightweight (-154.75 lb)	Munji Mumemura (JPN)	Stefan Horvat (YUG)	Petros Galaktopoulos (GRE)
Welterweight (-172 lb)	Rudolf Vesper (GDR)	Daniel Robin (FRA)	Károly Bajkó (HUN)
Middleweight (-191.75 lb)	Lothar Metz (GDR)	Valentin Olenik (URS)	Branislav Simic (YUG)
Light-Heavyweight (-213.75 lb)	Boyan Radev (BUL)	Nikolai Yakovenko (URS)	Nicolae Martinescu (ROM)
Heavyweight (+213.75 lb)	István Kozma (HUN)	Anatoli Roschin (URS)	Petr Kment (TCH)

FREESTYLE WRESTLING

EVENT	GOLD	SILVER	BRONZE
Flyweight (-114.5 lb)	Shigeo Nakata (JPN)	Richard Sanders (USA)	Surenjav Sukhbaatar (MGL)
Bantamweight (-125.75 lb)	Yojiro Uetake (JPN)	Donald Behm (USA)	Abutaleb Gorgori (IRN)
Featherweight (-138.75 lb)	Masaaki Kaneko (JPN)	Enyu Todorov (BUL)	Shamseddin Seyed-Abbassi (IRN)
Lighweight (-154.25 lb)	Abdollah M. Ardabili (IRN)	Enyu Valtschev (BUL)	Sereeter Danzandarjaa (MGL)
Welterweight (-172 lb)	Mahmut Atalay (TUR)	Daniel Robin (FRA)	Dagvasuren Purev (MGL)
Middleweight (-191.75 lb)	Boris Gurevitch (URS)	Munkbat Jigjid (MGL)	Prodan Gardschev (BUL)
Light-Heavyweight (-213.75 lb)	Ahmet Ayik (TUR)	Shota Lomidze (URS)	József Csatári (HUN)
Heavyweight (+213.75 lb)	Alexander Medved (URS)	Osman Duraliev (BUL)	Wilfried Dietrich (FRG)

MODERN PENTATHLON

EVENT	GOLD		SILVER		BRONZE	
Individual	Björn Ferm (SWE)	4964	András Balczó (HUN)	4953	Pavel Lednev (URS)	4795
Team	Hungary	14325	USSR	14248	France	13289

FENCING

EVENT	GOLD		SILVER		BRONZE	
Individual Foil — Men	lon Drimba (ROM)	4	Jenö Kamuti (HUN)	3	Daniel Revenu (FRA)	3
Team Foil — Men	France		USSR		Poland	
Individual Épée	Gyözö Kulcsár (HUN)	4+2	Grigory Kriss (URS)	4/10/8	Gianiuigi Saccaro (ITA)	4/10/7
Team Épée	Hungary		USSR		Poland	
Individual Sabre	Jerzy Pawlowski (POL)	4+1	Mark Rakita (URS)	4	Tibor Péisa (HUN)	3
Team Sabre	USSR		Italy		Hungary	
Individual Foil — Women	Elena Novikova (URS)	4	Pilar Roldan (MEX)	3/14	lidiko Ujlaki-Rejtö (HUN)	3/16
Team Foil — Women	USSR		Hungary		Romania	

CANOEING — WOMEN

EVENT	GOLD		SILVER		BRONZE	
500 m Kayak Singles K1	Ludmila Pinayeva (URS)	2:11.09	Renate Breuer (FRG)	2:12.71	Viorica Dumitru (ROM)	2:13.22
500 m Kayak Pairs K2	FRG	1:56.44	Hungary	1:58.60	USSR	1:58.61

CANOEING — MEN

EVENT	GOLD		SILVER		BRONZE	
1,000 m Kayak Single K1	Mihály Hesz (HUN)	4:02.63	Alexander Shaparenko (URS)	4:03.58	Erik Hansen (DEN)	4:04.39
1,000 m Kayak Pairs K2	USSR	3:37.54	Hungary	3:38.44	Austria	3:40.71
1,000 m Kayak Fours K4	Norway	3:14.38	Romania	3:14.81	Hungary	3:15.10
1,000 m Canadian Singles C1	Tibor Tatai (HUN)	4:36.14	Detlef Lewe (FRG)	4:38.31	Vitaly Galkov (URS)	4:40.42
1,000 m Canadian Pairs C2	Romania	4:07.18	Hungary	4:08.77	USSR	4:11.30

ROWING

EVENT	GOLD		SILVER		BRONZE	
Single Sculls	Henri Jan Wienese (HOL)	7:47.80	Jochen Meissner (FRG)	7:52.00	Alberto Demiddi (ARG)	7:57.19
Double Sculls	USSR	6:51.82	Netherlands	6:52.80	USA	6:54.21
Coxless Pairs	GDR	7:26.56	USA	7:26.71	Denmark	7:31.84
Coxed Pairs	Italy	8:04.81	Netherlands	8:06.80	Denmark	8:08.07
Coxless Fours	GDR	6:39.18	Hungary	6:41.64	Italy	6:44.01
Coxed Fours	New Zealand	6:45.62	GDR	6:48.20	Switzerland	6:49.04
Coxed Eights	FRG	6:07.00	Australia	6:07.98	USSR	6:09.11

YACHTING

EVENT	GOLD		SILVER		BRONZE	
Finn Class	Valentin Mankin (URS)	11.7	Hubert Raudaschl (AUT)	53.4	Fabio Albarelli (ITA)	55.1
International Star	USA	14.4	Norway	43.7	Italy	44 7
Flying Dutchman	Great Britain	3.0	FRG	43.7	Brazil	48.4
Dragon	USA	6.0	Denmark	26.4	GDR	32.7
5.5 m	Sweden	8.0	Switzerland	32.0	Great Britain	39.8

CYCLING

EVENT	GOLD		SILVER		BRONZE	
Individual Road Race (122 mi)	Pierfranco Vianelli (ITA)	4:41:25.24	Leif Mortenson (DEN)	4:42:49.71	Gösta Pettersson (SWE)	4:43:15.24
100 km Road Team Time Trial	Netherlands	2:07:49.06	Sweden	2:09:26.60	Italy	2:10:18.74
1,000 m Time Trial	Pierre Trentin (FRA)	1:03.91	Niels-Christian Fredborg (DEN)	1:04.61	Janusz Kierkowski (POL)	1:04.63
1,000 m Sprint	Daniel Morelon (FRA)		Giordano Turrini (ITA)		Pierre Trentin (FRA)	
2,000 m Tandem	France		Netherlands		Belgium	
4,000 m Individual Pursuit	Daniel Rebillard (FRA)	4:41.71	Mogens Frey Jensen (DEN)	4:42.43	Xaver Kurmann (SUI)	4:39.42
4,000 m Team Pursuit	Denmark	4:22.44	FRG*	4:18.94	Italy	4:18.35

*The winning W. German team were demoted to 2nd place owing to an illegal push-start.

EQUESTRIANISM

EVENT	GOLD		SILVER		BRONZE	
Three-Day Event	Jean-Jacques Guyon (FRA)	-38.86	Derek Allhusen (CBR)	-41.61	Michael Page (USA)	-53.31
Three-Day Event (Team)	Great Britain	-175.93	USA	-245.87	Australia	-331.26
Grand Prix (Dressage)	Ivan Kizimov(URS)	1572	Josef Neckermann (FRG)	1546	Reiner Klimke (FRG)	1537
Grand Prix (Dressage)Team	FRG	2699	USSR	2657	Switzerland	2547
Grand Prix (Jumping)	William Steinkraus (USA)	-4	Marion Coakes (GBR)	-8	David Broome (GBR)	-12
Grand Prix (Jumping) Team	Canada	-102.75	France	-110.50	FRG	-117.25

SHOOTING

EVENT	GOLD		SILVER		BRONZE	
Free Rifle (3 Positions)	Gary Anderson (USA)	1157	Vladimir Kornev (URS)	1151	Kurt Müller (SUI)	1148
Small-Bore Rifle (Prone)	Jan Kurka (TCH)	598	László Hammerl (HUN)	598	Ian Ballinger (NZL)	597
Small-Bore Rifle (3 Positions)	Bernd Klingner (FRG)	1157	John Writer (USA)	1156	Vitaly Parkimovich (URS)	1154
Rapid-Fire Pistol	Josef Zapedzki (POL)	593	Marcel Rosca (ROM)	591/147	Renart Suleimanow (URS)	591/146
Free Pistol (50 m)	Grigory Kossykh (URS)	562/30	Heinz Mertel (PRG)	562/26	Harald Vollmar (GDR)	560
Skeet Shooting	Evgeny Petrov (URS)	198/25	Romano Garagnani (ITA)	198/24/25	Konrad Wirnhier (FRG)	198/24/23
Trap Shooting	John Braithwaite (GBR)	198	Thomas Garrigus (USA)	196/25/25	Kurt Czekalla (GDR)	198/25/23

GYMNASTICS — MEN

EVENT	GOLD		SILVER		BRONZE	
Individual Combined Exercises	Sawao Kato (JPN)	115.90	Mikhail Voronin (URS)	115.85	Akinori Nakayama (JPN)	115.65
Team	Japan	575.90	USSR	571.10	GDR	557.15
Parallel Bars	Akinori Nakayama (JPN)	19.475	Mikhail Voronin (URS)	19.425	Viktor Klimenko (URS)	19.225
Floor	Sawao Kato (JPN)	19.475	Akinori Nakayama (JPN)	19.400	Takashi Kato (JPN)	19.275
Horse Vault	Mikhail Voronin (URS)	19.000	Yukio Endo (JPN)	18.950	Sergey Diomidov (URS)	18.925
Horizontal Bar	Mikhail Voronin (URS)	19.550	Eizo Kemmotsu (JPN)	19.375		
	Akinori Nakayama (JPN)	19.550				
Rings	Akinori Nakayama (JPN)	19.450	Mikhail Voronin (URS)	19.325	Sawao Kato (JPN)	19.225
Pommel Horse	Miroslav Cerar (YUG)	19.325	Olli Eino Laiho (FIN)	19.225	Mikhail Voronin (URS)	19.200

GYMNASTICS — WOMEN

EVENT	GOLD		SILVER		BRONZE	
Individual Combined Exercises	Vera Cáslavská (TCH)	78.25	Zinaida Voronina (URS)	76.85	Natalya Kuchinskaya (URS)	76.75
Team	USSR	382.85	Czechoslovakia	382.20	GDR	379.10
Floor	Larissa Petrik (URS)	19.675	Natalya Kuchinshya (URS)	19.650		
	Vera Cáslavská (TCH)	19.675				
Horse Vault	Vera Cáslavská (TCH)	19.775	Erika Zuchold (GDR)	19.625	Zinaida Voronina (URS)	19.500
Beam	Natalya Kuchinskaya (URS)	19.650	Vera Cáslavská (TCH)	19.575	Larissa Petrik (URS)	19.250
Asymmetrical Bars	Vera Cáslavská (TCH)	19.650	Karin Janz (GDR)	19.500	Zinaida Voronina (URS)	19.425

BASKETBALL

GOLD	SILVER	BRONZE
USA	Yugoslavia	USSR

SOCCER

GOLD	SILVER	BRONZE
Hungary	Bulgaria	Japan

HOCKEY

GOLD	SILVER	BRONZE
Pakistan	Australia	India

VOLLEYBALL — MEN

GOLD	SILVER	BRONZE
USSR	Japan	Czechoslovakia

VOLLEYBALL — WOMEN

GOLD	SILVER	BRONZE
USSR	Japan	Poland

RIGHT: Great Britain's Sheila Sherwood, a silver medalist in the long jump. Allsport

MUNICH 1972

INTRODUCTION

Munich 1972

	Gold	Silver	Bronze
URS	50	27	22
USA	33	31	30
GDR	20	23	23
GER	13	11	16
JPN	13	8	8
AUS	8	7	2
POL	7	5	9
HUN	6	13	16
BUL	6	10	5
ITA	5	3	10
SWE	4	6	6
GBR	4	5	9
ROM	3	6	7
FIN	3	1	4
CUB	3	1	4
NED	3	1	1
FRA	2	4	7
CZE	2	4	2
KEN	2	3	4
YUG	2	1	2
NOR	2	1	1
PRK	1	1	3
NZE	1	1	1
UGA	1	1	
DEN	1		
SUI		3	
CAN		2	3
IRN		2	1
BEL		2	
GRE		2	
AUT		1	2
COL		1	2
ARG		1	
KOR		1	
LEB		1	
MEX		1	
MON		1	
PAK		1	
TUN		1	
TUR		1	
BRA			2
ETH			2
GHA			1
IND			1
JAM			1
NIG			1
NGR			1
ESP			1

195 EVENTS

121 COUNTRIES

7,123 ATHLETES

The spirit of the XX Olympiad was joyous and relaxed. The German authorities, recalling the shame of the 1936 Munich games, were determined to erase any hint of militarism. Security police wore casual sporting uniforms and curfews were easily broken. Athletes constantly slipped in and out of the Olympic Village, so it was not an unusual sight when a group of men, dressed casually and carrying sports bags, scaled a fence into the compound at 4:30 in the morning of September 5. Once hidden in a narrow alley, they opened the bags and took out their Kalashnikov assault rifles.

At 4:55am there was a knock on the door of the Israeli team quarters. A wrestling coach opened it, found himself staring into the barrel of a gun and slammed it shut again. With his body pushed against the door in defence, he shouted a warning — silenced when a burst of gunfire through the door killed him. In another room, a weightlifter who tried to hold back the gunmen with just a knife was also shot dead.

The next few hours changed the face of international sports forever as a shocked world witnessed the modern Olympics' great loss of innocence.

The eight guerrillas of the Black September faction of the Palestine Liberation Organization had invaded the Olympic Village to demand the release of about 200 Arabs held on terrorist charges in

Israel. After the first two murders, they took hostage nine other Israeli team members who didn't get out and roped them together on their beds. They said the hostages — wrestlers, weightlifters, a track and field coach, a rifle team coach, and a fencing coach — would all die if their demands were not met.

With the Olympic Village ringed by armor, the German foreign ministry frantically contacted Arab heads of government seeking a mediator, but in vain. The Israeli cabinet also decided not to negotiate with the terrorists. In mid-afternoon, after competition had continued as scheduled, the games were stopped, the IOC unable to say when, or even whether, they would resume.

By nightfall, the German authorities allowed the terrorists to usher their blindfolded hostages into two helicopters and flew them 15 miles to an air base where a Boeing 727 awaited them. But as the terrorists left one of the helicopters, police snipers opened fire. An Arab tossed a grenade into the second helicopter, in which the hostages were still trapped, and it exploded in a fireball.

After the one-hour gunfight, all the Israeli hostages were dead, along with five of the terrorists and a German policeman. Three terrorists were captured.

Athletes attended a memorial service for their fellow Olympians in the main stadium, where IOC president Avery Brundage announced that the games would go on after a 24-hour postponement.

RIGHT: *The Israeli delegation at a memorial service for their murdered peers.* Hulton Getty

There were still dangers — the British team had received death threats from the IRA — and athletes like America's marathon winner Frank Shorter knew that full protection could never be guaranteed. But he summed up the Olympic spirit when he said:

"We went through the stages humans go through in times of brutal stress: from denial to anger, to grief, to resolve. But we could not let this detract from our performance, because that's what they wanted. To surrender in Munich would be to surrender all. We have to say to ourselves, as a society, what we said before the marathon: 'This is as scared as I get — now let's go run.'"

That spirit is nowadays upheld in an entirely modern manner in Munich's old Olympic Park. Created there is the aptly titled "Olympic Spirit," the first of a global chain of multi-media interactive complexes where visitors can "participate" in Olympic events. (Similar centers are planned from Melbourne to London.) In Munich's 1972 Velodrome, a new generation of sports fans can test their skills electronically against athletic giants of the past. They can also learn how even the Munich massacre could not crush the Olympic ideal.

There were plenty of sporting

heroes at Munich. The XXth games saw Australian female swimmer Shane Gould win three gold medals, Soviet gymnast Olga Korbut also won three golds, and American swimmer Mark Spitz won an incredible record seven golds — and seven world records.

As a bizarre footnote to Munich 1972, the US lost the gold medal in basketball to the Soviet Union after they were controversially awarded three tries at the final field goal. In protest, the US team refused their silver medals, which remain in an IOC vault in Switzerland.

RIGHT: Another one of Munich's commemorative pins. Allsport

BELOW RIGHT: The Olympic torch. Allsport

BELOW: Dr. Erwin Lauer Bach of the Bavarian Ministry of Culture, with the Olympic torch handle that allowed cyclists to carry the torch as well. Allsport

225

MARK SPITZ

The star of the 1972 Munich games, Mark Spitz left Germany with a record seven gold medals. The American swimmer had already won two relay golds, a silver, and a bronze at the 1968 games where he had predicted he would be victorious in six events after winning five at the previous year's Pan American Games. But in Munich he reigned supreme.

Spitz's aim was to better the record of four golds at a single games. He launched his attempt with a victory and a world record in the 200 meters butterfly. Then came golds and more world records in the 100 meters and 200 meters freestyle, 100 meters butterfly, and three relays.

All were achieved with a splendid black moustache — a reminder to all those meticulously shorn and shaved adversaries in the pool that Mark Spitz did not have to sacrifice fashion to be the best.

Trouble came when Spitz waved his shoes at the TV cameras and had to convince the International Olympic Committee that he had not been paid to do so. Nevertheless, retiring after the games, Spitz became the first athlete to make a huge post-Olympic splash with corporate America. His endorsement contracts were estimated to be worth $5 million. He appeared on television specials with Bob Hope, Bill Cosby, and Sonny and Cher.

A picture of the moustachioed, rakishly handsome Spitz, posing in just his red-white-and-blue swimsuit and seven gold medals, became the most popular-selling poster of a sports figure. "I'm a commodity, an endorser," Spitz said then.

Today, Spitz lives in Los Angeles with his wife, Suzy (who appeared with him on his third and final *Sports Illustrated* cover the week of their 1973 marriage) and their two sons. He still follows a hectic, eclectic schedule, as he did in Munich, investing in real estate, serving as spokesman for a phone company, and giving motivational speeches. The waterproof Mark Spitz model Swatch watch was the best seller of the company's 1996 Centennial Olympic line.

After failing in a much-publicized attempt to make a comeback and qualify for the 1992 Olympics in the 100 meters butterfly, Spitz stopped swimming for three months. He is now back in the pool, working out with the UCLA masters swim team. "I squeak, rattle, and roll," he says.

But the biggest difference between the mature Spitz and his brash younger self lies in his relaxed enjoyment of the sport. He says: "I have a whole different mission now. I enjoy the camaraderie."

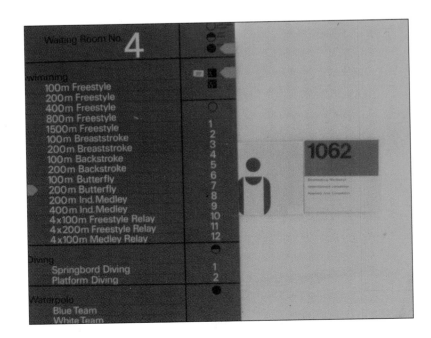

OLGA KORBUT

Superstars in gymnastics are a rare breed but the first, and biggest, was Olga Korbut, a tiny 17-year-old from Grodno in Belarus, who captivated the world at the Munich Olympics. When she performed her daring back flips on the uneven bars and balance beam, TV viewers around the world gasped — and then fell instantly in love with the 4 foot 11 inch, 85 pound dynamo in pigtails.

"I don't believe it!" said ABC's commentator Gordon Maddux when Korbut flung herself into space while performing on the bars. "Give her an 11!"

Korbut's smiling features became a poignant counterpoint to the horrors which unfolded at those games as she won three gold medals and a silver with demonstrations of courage and strength that belied her waif-like features.

Appearing in her first international event, Korbut stole the show from under the nose of the overall champion, Lyudmila Turischeva. Isolated with the Soviet team, Korbut was unaware of the impact she had made until she was inundated with flowers, letters, and telegrams from all over the world. She even had to wear a disguise when she went shopping.

Much has happened to Korbut since 1972. She married folk-rock musician Leonid Bortkevich, and in 1979 they had a son, Richard. But the intervening years have not been full of joy. She is upset that Soviet gymnastics officials did not support her after her

career ended at the Montreal Games in 1976.

Worst of all, says Korbut, the Soviet government failed to alert its citizens about the radiation dangers resulting from the Chernobyl nuclear reactor disaster in 1986. "My family lived in Minsk; we could see the radiation cloud from 180 miles away, but the government never even told us to stay indoors."

Because of the Chernobyl disaster, Korbut has found both a mission in life and a means to exorcise her anger. When friends and relatives became ill, some even dying from what Korbut believes were Chernobyl-related causes, she and Richard underwent cancer tests on a trip to the US.

While their tests were negative, Korbut became convinced during the trip that she needed to get personally involved in aiding Chernobyl victims. Working with the Seattle-based Fred Hutchinson Cancer Research Center, the Olga Korbut Foundation has raised $100,000 for medical supplies, equipment, and training, mainly through speeches and clinics given by Korbut.

Korbut moved to Atlanta in 1991, partly to establish a coaching career there before the 1996 Olympics and partly because of the warm Georgia climate.

"I try not to focus on the annoying things in my past," she says. "It's like the Russian proverb: "If I always watch who steps on my feet, I wouldn't walk."

ULRIKE MEYFARTH

High jumper Ulrike Meyfarth. Tony Duffy

Ulrike Meyfarth leapt into the record books in 1972 when she became the youngest Olympic champion at the age of 16 years 123 days. The German won the high jump title with a new world record of 1.92 meters, the first woman using the Fosbury Flop technique.

Meyfarth's model girl looks made her a favorite of the crowd in Munich and the German tabloids lapped her up. Lean years followed, however, and she failed to qualify for the final in 1976, only to re-emerge as a force in 1981 when she won the World Cup title in Rome and beat Tamara Bycova, her great rival.

She broke the world record in 1982 and again in 1983 before making history again by regaining her Olympic title in Los Angeles in 1984 with a Games record of 2.02 meters. That made hers the longest gap between gold medals.

"The second time was much better because I could appreciate it then," she says. "In Munich everything came too quickly and easily. I thought it was always going to be like that. It was a shock when it wasn't."

Meyfarth retired after the Olympics and now does media work in Germany.

MARY PETERS

On her third attempt at claiming an Olympic title, Britain's Mary Peters won the pentathlon gold medal at Munich with a smile that lit up the entire stadium. At the age of 33, the secretary from Belfast produced two days of fabulous performance to beat the West German favorite, Heide Rosendahl, and set a new world record of 4,801 points.

Peters was fourth in Tokyo, ninth in Mexico City. Munich was her last chance and she took it, dedicating her victory to the city of Belfast, which was then in the midst of the Troubles.

Peters had said before the competition. "The silver medal is useless to me. It has to be the gold or nothing, a gold medal for Belfast. Something good has to happen to our city."

She produced two personal bests on the first day of competition, in the 100 meters hurdles and the high jump. By the end of that first day, when Peters had a 97-point lead in the contest, even the German crowd were rooting for her.

Danger lay ahead, however, because the second day's events included two of Rosendahl's strongest. With just the 200 meters left, Peters knew she had to run a personal best to have a chance of beating her rival. It was an agonizing wait to see if the gap between her 24.08sec and Rosendahl's 22.96 was small enough to win her the gold medal. It was and Rosendahl was the first to congratulate her.

Peters was born in Liverpool but her love affair with Belfast started when her father relocated to the city when she was ten. She made her debut for Northern Ireland in the 1958 Commonwealth Games and for many years was happy to compete internationally without showing much ambition.

"I was always worried that if I was successful, people's attitude towards me would change," she said. "But I won the shot and pentathlon at the 1970 Commonwealth Games and discovered how good it felt to be a winner."

It is an irony that the evil of terrorism should have intruded even on her great moment of triumph. Within 24 hours of her victory, a Palestinian guerrilla attack had resulted in the massacre of 11 Israeli athletes and officials.

"It could so easily have been me," she says. "I had a threat to my life during the Olympics. I was

warned if I went back to Belfast I would be shot and my apartment bombed. But I wanted to go home so I didn't tell anyone about the threat for 20 years."

Not only did Peters ignore the warning, she toured the city in an open truck to show off her gold medal. Peters, who has a track named after her in Belfast, served as President of the British Athletic Federation and concentrates on fund-raising for good causes in Northern Ireland.

Belfast's Mary Peters won a gold in the pentathlon on her third Olympic appearance. Hulton Deutsch

ABOVE: *Heide Rosendahl of West Germany captured gold in the long jump.* Allsport

LEFT: *Valeriy Borsov of the USSR starts in the 100 m sprint; he won gold.* Tony Duffy

ABOVE: *A competitor in the archery competition sets her mark.* Tony Duffy

ABOVE RIGHT: *Runners in the 200 m final start.* Allsport

ABOVE: John Akii-Bua of Uganda gold medalist, in the 400 m hurdles. Allsport

LEFT: Olympic great Jesse Owens appears in Munich. Hulton Deutsch

235

ABOVE: Ludmila Bragina (no.335) of the USSR took gold in this 1,500 m final. Hulton Deutsch

ABOVE RIGHT: Long-distance runner Lasse Viren of Finland. Allsport

ABOVE: *Peter Hodder of the Rhodesian team stands dejected after his team was expelled from the games. Other African nations threatened a boycott the games over Rhodesia's apartheid politics.* Pressens Bild

LEFT: *America's Rod Milburn in the 110 m hurdles.* Tony Duffy

ABOVE: The American team take a victory walk after winning gold in the 4x100 m final. Allsport

ABOVE RIGHT: Germany's Wolfgang Nordwig in the pole vault. Hulton Deutsch

242

ABOVE AND TOP LEFT: The Munich summer games come to a close. Don Morley
LEFT BELOW: Olympic organizers, and the host country, managed to put on a brave and spectacular closing ceremony in spite of the terrorism that had marred the events. In this photo, the scoreboard reads Montreal 1976 — site of the next games. Tony Duffy

MUNICH 1972 AUGUST 26 - SEPTEMBER 11

PARTICIPANTS: 7,123

MEN: 6,065

WOMEN: 1,058

COUNTRIES: 121

SPORTS: 21

EVENTS: 195

FINAL TORCHBEARER: GUNTER ZAHN

MEDALS TABLE

PLACE	COUNTRY	GOLD	SILVER	BRONZE
1	USSR	50	27	22
2	USA	33	31	30
3	GDR	20	23	23
4	West Germany	13	11	16
5	Japan	13	8	8

OUTSTANDING ATHLETES

PLACE	NAME (NATIONALITY)	DISCIPLINE	GOLD	SILVER	BRONZE
1	Mark Spitz (USA)	Swimming	7		
2	Sawao Kato (JPN)	Gymnastics	3	2	
3	Shane Gould (AUS)	Swimming	3	1	1
4	Olga Korbut (URS)	Gymnastics	3	1	
5	Melissa Belote (USA)	Swimming	3		
	Sandra Neilson (USA)	Swimming	3		

RIGHT: Kip Keino of Kenya wins gold. Allsport

ATHLETICS — MEN

EVENT	GOLD		SILVER		BRONZE	
100 m	Valeriy Borsov (URS)	10.14	Robert Taylor (USA)	10.24	Lennox Miller (JAM)	10.33
200 m	Valeriy Borsov (URS)	20.00	Larry Black (USA)	20.19	Pietro Mennea (ITA)	20.30
400 m	Vincent Matthews (USA)	44.66	Wayne Collett (USA)	44.80	Julius Sang (KEN)	44.92
800 m	Dave Wottle (USA)	1:45.9	Yewgeniy Arzhanov (URS)	1:45.9	Mike Boit (KEN)	1:46.0
1,500 m	Pekka Vasala (FIN)	3:36.3	Kipchoge Keino (KEN)	3:36.8	Rodney Dixon (NZL)	3:37.5
5,000 m	Lasse Viren (FIN)	13:26.4	Mohamed Gammoudi (TUN)	13:27.4	Ian Stewart (GBR)	13:27.6
10,000 m	Lasse Viren (FIN)	27:38.4	Emiel Puttemans (BEL)	27:39.6	Miruts Yifter (ETH)	27:41.0
Marathon	Frank Shorter (USA)	2:12:19.8	Karel Lismont (BEL)	2:14:31.8	Mamo Wolde (ETH)	2:15:08.4
110 m Hurdles	Rodney Milburn (USA)	13.24	Guy Drut (FRA)	13.34	Thomas Hill (USA)	13.48
400 m Hurdles	John Akii-Bua (UGA)	47.82	Ralph Mann (USA)	48.51	David Hemery (GBR)	48.52
3,000 m Steeplechase	Kipchoge Keino (KEN)	8:23.6	Benjamin Jipcho (KEN)	8:24.6	Tapio Kantanen (FIN)	8:24.8
4x100 m	USA	38.19	USSR	38.50	FRG	38.79
4x400 m	Kenya	2:59.8	Great Britain	3:00.5	France	3:00.7
20 km Walk	Peter Frenkel (GDR)	1:26:42.4	Vladimir Golubnichiy (URS)	1:26:55.2	Hans Reimann (GDR)	1:27:16.6
50 km Walk	Bernd Kannenberg (FRG)	3:56:11.6	Venjamin Soldatenko (URS)	3:58:24.0	Larry Young (USA)	4:00:46.0
High Jump	Yury Tarmak (URS)	7'3.75"	Stefan Junge (GDR)	7'3"	Dwight Stones (USA)	7'3"
Pole Vault	Wolfgang Nordwig (GDR)	18'0.5"	Robert Seagren (USA)	17'8.5"	Jan Johnson (USA)	17'6.5"
Long Jump	Randy Williams (USA)	27'0"	Hans Baumgartner (FRG)	26'10"	Arme Robinson (USA)	26'4"
Triple Jump	Viktor Saneyev (URS)	56'11"	Jörg Drehmel (GDR)	56'9.25"	Nelson Prudencio (BRA)	55'11.25"
Shot	Wladyslaw Komar (POL)	69'6"	George Woods (USA)	69'5.5"	Hartmut Briesenick (GDR)	69'4.5"
Discus	Ludvik Danek (TCH)	211'3"	Jay Silvester (USA)	208'4"	Rickard Bruch (SWE)	208'0"
Hammer	Anatoliy Bondarchuk (URS)	247'8"	Jochen Sachse (GDR)	245'11"	Vasiliy Khmelevski (URS)	242'10.5"
Javelin	Klaus Wolfermann (FRG)	296'10"	Janis Lusis (URS)	296'9"	William Schmidt (USA)	276'11.5"
Decathlon	Nikolai Avilov (URS)	8454	Leonid Litvinenko (URS)	8035	Ryszard Katus (POL)	7984

ATHLETICS — WOMEN

EVENT	GOLD		SILVER		BRONZE	
100 m	Renate Stecher (GDR)	11.07	Raelene Boyle (AUS)	11.23	Silvia Chivas (CUB)	11.24
200 m	Renate Stecher (GDR)	22.40	Raelene Boyle (AUS)	22.45	Irena Szewinska-Kirszenstein (POL)	22.74
400 m	Monika Zehrt (GDR)	51.08	Rita Wilden (FRG)	51.21	Kathy Hammond (USA)	51.64
800 m	Hildegard Falck (FRG)	1:58.6	Niole Sabaite (URS)	1:58.7	Gunhild Hoffmeister (GDR)	1:59.2
1,500 m	Ludmila Bragina (URS)	4:01.4	Gunhild Hoffmeister (GDR)	4:02.8	Paola Cacchi (ITA)	4:02.9
100 m Hurdles	Annelie Ehrhardt (GDR)	12.59	Valeria Bufanu (ROM)	12.84	Karin Balzer (GDR)	12.90
4x100 m	FRG	42.81	GDR	42.95	Cuba	43.36
4x400 m	GDR	3:23.0	USA	3:25.2	FRG	3:26.5
High Jump	Ulrike Meyfarth (FRG)	6'3.5"	Yordanka Blagoyeva (BUL)	6'2"	Ilona Gusenbauer (AUT)	6'2"
Long Jump	Heide Rosendahl (FRG)	22'3"	Diana Yorgova (BUL)	27'2.5"	Eva Suranova (TCH)	21'10.75"
Shot	Nadyezda Chizhova (URS)	60'0"	Margitta Gummel (GDR)	66'4.75	Ivanka Khristova (BUL)	63'6"
Discus	Faina Melnik (URS)	218'7"	Argentina Menis (ROM)	213'5"	Vassilka Stoyeva (BUL)	211'1"
Javelin	Ruth Fuchs (GDR)	209'7"	Jacqueline Todten (GDR)	205'2"	Kathy Schmidt (USA)	196'8"
Pentathlon	Mary Peters (GBR)	4801	Heide Rosendahl (FRG)	4791	Burglinde Pollak (GDR)	4768

SWIMMING — MEN

EVENT	GOLD		SILVER		BRONZE	
100 Freestyle	Mark Spitz (USA)	51.22	Jerry Heidenreich (USA)	51.65	Vladimir Bure (URS)	51.77
200 m Freestyle	Mark Spitz (USA)	1:52.78	Steven Genter (USA)	1:53.73	Werner Lampe (FRG)	1:53.99
400 m Freestyle	Bradford Cooper (AUS)	4:00.27	Steven Genter (USA)	4:01.94	Tom McBreen (USA)	4:02.64
1,500 m Freestyle	Michael Burton (USA)	15:52.58	Graham Windeatt (AUS)	15:58.48	Douglas Northway (USA)	16:09.25
100 m Backstroke	Roland Matthes (GDR)	56.58	Mike Stamm (USA)	57.70	John Murphy (USA)	58.35
200 m Backstroke	Roland Matthes (USA)	2:02.82	Mike Stamm (USA)	2:04.09	Mitchell Ivey (USA)	2:04.33
100 m Breaststroke	Nobutaka Taguchi (JPN)	1:04.94	Tom Bruce (USA)	1:05.43	John Hencken (USA)	1:05.61
200 m Breaststroke	John Hencken (USA)	2:21.55	David Wilkie (GBR)	2:23.67	NobutakaTaguchi (JPN)	2:23.88
100 m Butterfly	Mark Spitz (USA)	54.27	Bruce Robertson (CAN)	55.56	Jerry Heidenreich (USA)	55.74
200 m Butterfly	Mark Spitz (USA)	2:00.70	Gary Hall (USA)	2:02.86	Robin Backhaus (USA)	2:03.23
200 m Medley	Gunnar Larsson (SWE)	2:07.17	Alexander McKee (USA)	2:08.37	Steven Furniss (USA)	2:08.45
400 m Medley	Gunnar Larsson (SWE)	4:31.981	Alexander McKee (USA)	4:31.983	Andras Hargitay (HUN)	4:32.700
4x100 m Freestyle Relay	USA	3:26.42	USSR	3:29.72	GDR	3:32.42
4x200 m Freestyle Relay	USA	7:35.78	FRG	7:41.69	USSR	7:45.76
4x100 m Medley Relay	USA	3:48.16	GDR	3:52.12	Canada	3:52.26
Springboard Diving	Vladimir Vasin (URS)	594.06	Franco Cagnotto (ITA)	591.63	Craig Lincoln (USA)	577.29
Highboard Diving	Klaus Dibiasi (ITA)	504.12	Richard Rydze (USA)	480.75	Franco Cagnotto (ITA)	475.83
Water Polo	USSR		Hungary		USA	

SWIMMING — WOMEN

EVENT	GOLD		SILVER		BRONZE	
100 m Freestyle	Sandra Neilson (USA)	58.59	Shirley Babashoff (USA)	59.02	Shane Gould (AUS)	59.06
200 m Freestyle	Shane Gould (AUS)	2:03.56	Shirley Babashoff (USA)	2:04.33	Keena Rothhammer (USA)	2:04.92
400 m Freestyle	Shane Gould (AUS)	4:19.04	Novella Calligaris (ITA)	4:22.44	Gudrun Wegner (GDR)	4:23.11
800 m Freestyle	Keena Rothhammer (USA)	8:53.68	Shane Gould (AUS)	8:56.39	Novella Calligaris (ITA)	8:57.46
100 m Backstroke	Melissa Belote (USA)	1:05.78	Andrea Gyarmati (HUN)	1:06.26	Susan Atwood (USA)	1:06.34
200 m Backstroke	Melissa Belote (USA)	2:19.19	Susan Atwood (USA)	2:20.38	Donna Marie Gurr (CAN)	2:23.22
100 m Breaststroke	Catherine Carr (USA)	1:13.58	Galina Stepanova (URS)	1:14.49	Beverley Whitfield (AUS)	1:15.73
200 m Breaststroke	Beverley Whitfield (AUS)	2:41.71	Dana Schoenfield (USA)	2:42.05	Galina Stepanova (URS)	2:42.36
100 m Butterfly	Mayumi Aoki (JPN)	1:03.34	Roswitha Beier (GDR)	1:30.61	Andrea Gyarmati (HUN)	1:03.73
200 m Butterfly	Karen Moe (USA)	2:15.57	Lynn Colella (USA)	2:16.34	Ellie Daniel (USA)	2:16.74
200 m Medley	Shane Gould (AUS)	2:23.07	Kornelia Ender (GDR)	2:23.59	Lynn Vidali (USA)	2:24.06
4x100 m Medley	Gail Neall (AUS)	5:02.97	Leslie Cliff (CAN)	5:03.57	Novella Calligaris (ITA)	5:03.99
4x100 m Freestyle Relay	USA	3:55.19	GDR	3:55.55	FRG	3:57.93
4x100 m Medley Relay	USA	4:20.75	GDR	4:24.91	FRG	4:26.46
Springboard Diving	Maxine King (USA)	450.03	Ulrika Knape (SWE)	434.19	Marina Janicke (GDR)	430.92
Highboard Diving	Ulrika Knape (SWE)	390.00	Milena Duchková (TCH)	370.92	Marina Janicke (GDR)	360.54

BOXING

EVENT	GOLD	SILVER	BRONZE
Light-Flyweight (-105.75) lb)	György Gedo (HUN)	U Gil Kim (PRK)	Enrique Rodriguez (ESP) / Ralph Evans (GBR)
Flyweight (-112.5 lb)	Gheorghi Kostadinov (BUL)	Leo Rwabwogo (UGA)	Douglas Rodriguez (CUB) / Leszek Blazynski (POL)
Bantamweight (-119 lb)	Orlando Marthiez (CUB)	Alfonso Zamora (MEX)	George Turpin (GBR) / Ricardo Carreras (USA)
Featherweight (-126 lb)	Boris Kusnezov (URS)	Philip Waruinge(KEN)	Clemente Rojas (COL) / Andras Botos (HUN)
Lightweight (-132 lb)	Jan Szczepanski (POL)	Laszlo Orban (HUN)	Alfonso Perez (COL) / Samuel Mbugua (KEN)
Light-Welterweight (-140 lb)	Ray Seales (USA)	Anghel Angelov (BUL)	Zvonimir Vujin (YUG) / Issak Daborg (NIG)
Welterweight (-148 lb)	Emilio Correa (CUB)	János Kajdi (HUN)	Dick Tiger Murunga (KEN) / Jesse Valdez (USA)
Light-Middieweight (-157 lb)	Dieter Kottysch (FRG)	Wieslaw Rudkowski (POL)	Alan Minter (GBR) / Peter Tiepold (GDR)
Middieweight (-165 lb)	Vyatcheslav Lemeschev (URS)	Reima Virtanen (FIN)	Marvin Johnson (USA) / Prince Amartey (GHA)
Light-Heavyweight (-178.5 lb)	Mate Parlov (YUG)	Gilberto Carillo (CUB)	Janusz Gortat (POL) / Isaak Ikhouria (NGR)
Heavyweight (+178.5 lb)	Teofilo Stevenson (CUB)	Ion Alexe (ROM)	Peter Hussing (FRG) / Hasse Thomsen (SWE)

WEIGHTLIFTING

EVENT	GOLD		SILVER		BRONZE	
Flyweight	Zymunt Smalcerz (POL)	337.5	Lajos Szuecs (HUN)	330.0	Sandor Holczreiter (HUN)	327.5
Bantamweight)	Imre Földi (HUN)	377.5	Mohammed Nassiri (IRN)	370.0	Gennadi Chetin (URS)	367.5
Featherweight	Norair Nurikyan (BUL)	402.5	Dito Shanidze (URS)	400.0	Janos Benedek (HUN)	390.0
Lightweight	Mukharbi Kirzhinov (URS)	460.0	Mladen Koutchev (BUL)	450.0	Zbigniev Kaczmarek (POL)	437.5
Middleweight	Yordan Bikov (BUL)	485.0	Mohammed Trabulsi (LIB)	472.5	Anselmo Silvino (ITA)	470.0
Light-Heavyweight	Leif Jensen (NOR)	507.5	Norbert Ozimek (POL)	497.5	György Horvath (HUN)	495.0
Middle-Heavyweight	Andon Nikolov (BUL)	525.0	Atanas Chopov (BUL)	517.5	Hans Bettembourg (SWE)	512.5
Heavyweight	Jan Talts (URS)	580.0	Alexander Kraitchev (BUL)	562.5	Stefan Grützner (GDR)	555.0
Super-Heavyweight	Vasiliy Alexeyev (URS)	640.0	Rudolf Mang (FRG)	610.0	Gerd Bonk (GDR)	572.5

WEIGHTLIFTING WEIGHTS

FLYWEIGHT	-114.5 lb	BANTAMWEIGHT	-123.5 lb	FEATHERWEIGHT	-132.25 lb
LIGHTWEIGHT	-148.75 lb	MIDDLEWEIGHT-	-165.5 lb	LIGHT-HEAVYWEIGHT	-182 lb
MIDDLE-HEAVYWEIGHT	-198.5 lb	HEAVYWEIGHT	-242.5 lb	SUPER-HEAVYWEIGHT -	+242.5 lb

FREESTYLE WRESTLING

EVENT	GOLD	SILVER	BRONZE
Light-Flyweight (-105.75 lb)	Roman Dimitriyev (URS)	Ognian Nikolov (BUL)	Ebrahim Javadpour (IRN)
Flyweight (-114.5 lb)	Kiyomi Kato (JPN)	Arsen Alakhverdiev (URS)	Hyong Kim Gwong (PRK)
Bantamweight (-125.75 lb)	Hideaki Yanagida (JPN)	Richard Sanders (USA)	László Klinga (HUN)
Featherweight (-136.5 lb)	Zagalaz Abdulbekov (URS)	Vehbi Akdag (TUR)	Ivan Krastev (BUL)
Lightweight (-149.75 lb)	Dan Gable (USA)	Kikuo Wada (JPN)	Ruslan Ashuralyev (URS)
Welterweight (-163 lb)	Wayne Wells (USA)	Jan Karlsson (SWE)	Adolf Seger (FRG)
Middleweight (-180.75 lb)	Levan Tediashvili(URS)	John Peterson (USA)	Vasile Jorga (ROM)
Light-Heavyweight (-198.25 lb)	Ben Peterson (USA)	Gennadiy Strakhov (URS)	Karoly Bajko (HUN)
Heavyweight (-220.25 lb)	Ivan Yarygin (URS)	Khorloo Baianmunkh (MGL)	Jószef Csatári (HUN)
Super-Heavyweight (+220.25 lb)	Alexander Medved (URS)	Osman Duraliev (BUL)	Chris Taylor (USA)

JUDO

EVENT	GOLD	SILVER	BRONZE
(-138.75 lb)	Takao Kawaguchi (JPN)	Bakhaavaa Buidaa (MGL) *disqualified after positive drug test*	Yong Ik Kim (PRK) / Jean-Jacques Monuier (FRA)
(-154.25 lb)	Toyokazu Nomura (JPN)	Anton Zajkowski (POL)	Anatoliy Novikov (URS) / Dietmar Höttgar (GDR)
(-176.25 lb)	Shinobu Sekine (JPN)	Seung-Lip Oh (KOR)	Brian Jacks (GBR) / Jean-Paul Coché (FRA)
(-205 lb)	Shota Chochoshvili (URS)	David Starbrook (GBR)	Paul Barth (FRG) / Chiaki Ishii (BRA)
(+205 lb)	Wim Ruska (HOL)	Klaus Glahn (FRG)	Givi Onashvili (URS) / Motoki Nishimura (JPN)
Open Class	Wim Ruska (HOL)	Vitaliy Kuznetsov (URS)	Jean-Claude Brondani (FRA) / Angelo Parisi (GBR)

GRECO-ROMAN WRESTLING

EVENT	GOLD	SILVER	BRONZE
Light-Flyweight (-105.75 lb)	Gheorg Berceanu (ROM)	Rahim Ahabadi (IRN)	Stefan Anghelov (BUL)
Flyweight (-114.5 lb)	Petar Kirov (BUL)	Koichiro Hirayama (JPN)	Giuseppe Bognanni (ITA)
Bantamweight (-125.75 lb)	Rustem Kasakov (URS)	Hans-Jürgen Veil (FRG)	Risto Bjorlin (FIN)
Featherweight (-136.5 lb)	Georgi Markov (BUL)	Heinz-Helmut Wehling (GDR)	Kazimierz Lipien (POL)
Lightweight (-149.75 lb)	Shamil Khisamutdinov (URS)	Stoyan Apostolov (BUL)	Gian Matteo Ranzi (ITA)
Welterweight (-163 lb)	Vitezslav Macha (TCH)	Petros Galaktopoulos (GRE)	Jan Karlsson (SWE)
Middleweight (-180.75 lb)	Csaba Hegedus (HUN)	Anatoliy Nazarenko (URS)	Milan Nenadic (YUG)
Light-Heavyweight (-198.25 lb)	Valeriy Rezanzev (URS)	Josip Corak (YUG)	Czeslaw Kwiecinski (POL)
Heavyweight (-220.25 lb)	Nicolae Martinescu (ROM)	Nikolai Yakovenko (URS)	Ferenc Kiss (HUN)
Super-Heavyweight (+220.25 lb)	Anatoliy Roschin (URS)	Alexander Tomov (BUL)	Victor Dolipschi (ROM)

249

FENCING

EVENT	GOLD		SILVER		BRONZE	
Individual Foil — Men	Witold Woyda (POL)	5	Jenö Kamuti (HUN)	4	Christian Noël (FRA)	2
Team Foil — Men	Poland		USSR		France	
Individual Épée	Csaba Fenyresi (HUN)	4	Jacques La Dagaillerie (FRA)	3	Gyözö Kulcsár (HUN)	3
Team Épée	Hungary		Switzerland		USSR	
Individual Sabre	Viktor Sidjak (URS)	4	Peter Maroth (HUN)	3	Vladimir Nazlimov (URS)	3
Team Sabre	Italy		USSR		Hungary	
Individual Foil — Women	Antonella Ragno-Lonzi (ITA)	4	Ildiko Bobis (HUN)	3	Galina Gorokhova (URS)	3
Team Foil — Women	USSR		Hungary		Romania	

MODERN PENTATHLON

EVENT	GOLD		SILVER		BRONZE	
Individual	András Balczó (HUN)	5412	Boris Onischenko (URS)	5335	Pavel Lednev (URS)	5328
Team	USSR	15968	Hungary	15348	Finland	14812

CANOEING — MEN

EVENT	GOLD		SILVER		BRONZE	
1,000 m Kayak Singles K1	Alexander Shaparenko (URS)	3:48.06	Rolf Peterson (SWE)	3:48.35	Geza Csapó (HUN)	3:49.38
1,000 m Kayak Pairs K2	USSR	3:31.23	Hungary	3:32.00	Poland	3:33.83
1,000 Kayak Fours K4	USSR	3:14.02	Romania	3:15.07	Norway	3:15.27
1,000 m Canadian Singles C1	Ivan Patzaichin (ROM)	4:08.94	Tamas Wichmann (HUN)	4:12.42	Detlef Lewe (FRG)	4:13.63
1,000 m Canadian Pairs C2	USSR	3:52.60	Romania	3:52.63	Bulgaria	3:58.10

CANOEING — WOMEN

EVENT	GOLD		SILVER		BRONZE	
500 m Kayak Singles K1	Yulia Ryabchinskaya (URS)	2:03.17	Mieke Jaapies (HOL)	2:04.03	Anna Pfeffer (HUN)	2:05.50
500 m Kayak Pairs K2	USSR	1:53.50	GDR	1:54.30	Romania	1:55.01

ROWING

EVENT	GOLD		SILVER		BRONZE	
Single Sculls	Yuriy Malishev (URS)	7:10.12	Alberto Demiddi (ARG)	7:11.53	Wolfgang Güldenpfennig (GDR)	7:14.45
Double Sculls	USSR	7:01.77	Norway	7:02.58	GDR	7:05.55
Coxless Pairs	GDR	6:53.16	Switzerland	6:57.06	Netherlands	6:58.70
Coxed Pairs	GDR	7:17.25	Czechoslovakia	7:19.57	Romania	7:21.36
Coxless Fours	GDR	6:24.27	New Zealand	6:25.64	FRG	6:28.41
Coxed Fours	FRG	6:31.85	GDR	6:33.30	Czechoslovakia	6:35.64
Coxed Eights	New Zealand	6:08.94	USA	6:11.61	GDR	6:11.67

YACHTING

EVENT	GOLD		SILVER		BRONZE	
Finn Class	Serge Maury (FRA)	58.0	Ilias Hatzipavlis (GRE)	71.0	Viktor Potapov (URS)	74.7
International Star	Australia	28.1	Sweden	44.0	FRG	44.4
Flying Dutchman	Great Britain	22.7	France	40 7	FRG	51.1
International Tempest	USSR	28.1	Great Britain	34.4	USA	47.7
Dragon	Australia	13.7	GDR	41.7	USA	47.7
International Soling	USA	8.7	Sweden	31.7	Canada	47.1

SLALOM RACING

EVENT	GOLD		SILVER		BRONZE	
Kayak Singles	Siegbert Horn (GDR)	268.56	Norbert Sattler (AUT)	270.76	Harald Gimpel (GDR)	277.95
Canadian Singles	Reinhard Eiben (GDR)	315.84	Reinhold Kauder (FRG)	327.89	Jamie McEwan (USA)	335.95
Canadian Pairs	GDR	310.68	FRG	311.90	France	315.10
Kayak Singles (Women)	Angelika Bahmann (GDR)	364.50	Gisela Grothaus (FRG)	398.15	Magdalena Wunderlich (FRG)	400.50

SHOOTING

EVENT	GOLD		SILVER		BRONZE	
Free Rifle (3 Positions)	Lones Wigger (USA)	1155	Boris Melnik (URS)	1155	Lajos Papp (HUN)	1149
Small-Bore Rifle (Prone)	Ho Jun Li (PRK)	599	Viktor Auer (USA)	598	Nicolae Rotaru (ROM)	598
Small-Bore Rifle (3 Positions)	John Writer (USA)	1166	Lanny Bassham (USA)	1157	Werner Lippoldt (GDR)	1153
Rapid-Fire Pistol	Jósef Zapedszki (POL)	595	Ladislav Faita (TCH)	594	Viktor Torshin (URS)	593
Free Pistol (50 m)	Ragnar Shanakar (SWE)	567	Dan Iuga (ROM)	562	Rudolf Dollinger (AUT)	560
Running Game Target	Lakov Zheleziliak (URS)	569	Helmut Bellingrodt (COL)	565	John Kynoch (GBR)	562
Skeet Shooting	Konrad Wirnhier (FRG)	195/25	Evgeny Petrov (URS)	195/24	Michael Buchheim (GDR)	195/23
Trap Shooting	Angelo Scalzone (ITA)	199	Michel Carrega (FRA)	198	Silvano Basagni (ITA)	195

CYCLING

EVENT	GOLD		SILVER		BRONZE	
Individual Road Race (113.25 mi)	Hennie Kuiper (HOL)	4:14:37.0	Kevin Sefton (AUS)	4:15:04.0	Jaime Huelamo (ESP) (Medal withdrawn - disqualified)	
100 km Road Team Trial	USSR	2:11:17.8	Poland	2:11:47.5	(Medal withdrawn HOL disqualified)	
1.000 m Time Trial	Niels Fredborg (DEN)	1:06.44	Danny Clark (AUS)	1:06.87	Jürgen Schütze (GDR)	1:07.02
1.000 m Sprint	Daniel Morelon (FRA)		John Michael Nicholson (AUS)		Omar Phakadze (URS)	
2.000 m Tandem	USSR	GDR	Poland			
4.000 Individual Pursuit	Knut Knudsen (NOR)	4:45.74	Xaver Kurmann (SUI)	4:51.96	Hans Lutz (FRG)	4:50.80
4.000 m Team Pursuit	FRG	4:22.14	GDR	4:25.25	Great Britain	4:23.78

EQUESTRIANISM

EVENT	GOLD		SILVER		BRONZE	
Three-Day Event	Richard Meade (GBR)	57.73	Alessandro Argenton (ITA)	43.33	Jan Jonsson (SWE)	39.67
Three-Day Event Team	Great Britain	95.53	USA	10.81	FRG	18.00
Grand Prix (Dressage)	Liselott Linsenhoff (FRG)	1229	Elena Petruchkova (URS)	1185	Josef Neckermann (FRG)	1177
Grand Prix (Dressage) Team	USSR	5095	FRG	5083	Sweden	4849
Grand Prix (Jumping)	Graziano Mancinelli (ITA)	8/0	Ann Moore (GBR)	8/3	Neal Shapiro (USA)	8/8
Grand Prix (Jumping) Team	FRG	32.00	USA	32.25	Italy	48.00

ARCHERY — MEN

	GOLD		SILVER		BRONZE	
	John William (USA)	2528	Gunnar Jarvil (SWE)	2481	Kyösti Laasonen (FIN)	2467

ARCHERY — WOMEN

	GOLD		SILVER		BRONZE	
	Doreen Wilber (USA)	2424	Irena Szydlowska (POL)	2407	Emma Gapchenko (URS)	2403

GYMNASTICS — MEN

EVENT	GOLD		SILVER		BRONZE	
Individual Combined Exercises	Sawao Kato (JPN)	114.650	Eizo Kenmotsu (JPN)	114.575	Akinori Nakayama (JPN)	114.325
Team	Japan	571.25	USSR	564.05	GDR	559.70
Parallel Bars	Sawao Kato (JPN)	19.475	Shigeru Kasamatsu (JPN)	19.375	Eizo Kenmotsu (JPN)	19.250
Floor	Nikolai Andrianov (URS)	19.175	Akinori Nakayama (JPN)	19.125	Shigeru Kasamatsu (JPN)	19.025
Horse Vault	Klaus Köste (GDR)	18.850	Viktor Klimenko (URS)	18.825	Nikolai Andrianov (URS)	18.800
Horizontal Bar	Mitsuo Tsukahara (JPN)	19.725	Sawao Kato (JPN)	19.525	Shigeru Kasamatsu (JPN)	19.450
Rings	Akinori Nakayama (JPN)	19.350	Mikhail Voronin (URS)	19.275	Mitsuo Tsukahara (JPN)	19.225
Pommel Horse	Viktor Klimenko (URS)	19.125	Sawao Kato (JPN)	19.000	Eizo Kenmotsu (JPN)	18.950

GYMNASTICS — WOMEN

EVENT	GOLD		SILVER		BRONZE	
Individual Combined Exercises	Lyudmila Turischeva (URS)	77.025	Karin Janz (GDR)	76.875	Tamara Lazakovitsch (URS)	76.850
Team	USSR	380.50	GDR	376.55	Hungary	368.25
Floor	Olga Korbut (URS)	19.575	Lyudmila Turischeva (URS)	19.550	Tamara Lazakovitsch (URS)	19.450
Horse Vault	Karin Janz (GDR)	19.525	Erika Zuchold (GDR)	19.275	Lyudmila Turischeva (URS)	19.250
Beam	Olga Korbut (URS)	19.400	Tamara Lazakovitsch (URS)	19.375	Karin Janz (GDR)	18.975
Asymmetrical Bars	Karin Janz (GDR)	19.675	Olga Korbut (URS)	19.450		
			Erika Zuchold (GDR)	19.450		

BASKETBALL

GOLD	SILVER	BRONZE
USSR	USA	Cuba

SOCCER

GOLD	SILVER	BRONZE
Poland	Hungary	*USSR
		*GDR

*GDR and USSR declared joint bronze medallists as result was still a draw at end of extra time.

HOCKEY

GOLD	SILVER	BRONZE
West Germany	Pakistan	India

VOLLEYBALL — MEN

GOLD	SILVER	BRONZE
Japan	GDR	USSR

VOLLEYBALL — WOMEN

GOLD	SILVER	BRONZE
USSR	Japan	North Korea

MONTREAL 1976

INTRODUCTION

198
EVENTS

92
COUNTRIES

6,028
ATHLETES

Montreal 1976

	Gold	Silver	Bronze
URS	49	41	35
GDR	40	25	25
USA	34	35	25
FRG	10	12	17
JPN	9	6	10
POL	7	6	13
BUL	6	9	7
CUB	6	4	3
ROM	4	9	14
HUN	4	5	13
FIN	4	2	
SWE	4	1	
GBR	3	5	5
ITA	2	7	4
FRA	2	3	4
YUG	2	3	3
CZE	2	2	4
NZE	2	1	1
COR	1	1	4
SUI	1	1	2
JAM	1	1	
NOR	1	1	
PRK	1	1	
DEN	1		2
MEX	1		1
TRI	1		
CAN		5	6
BEL		3	3
NED		2	3
POR		2	
ESP		2	
AUS		1	4
IRN		1	1
MON		1	
VEN		1	
BRA			2
AUT			1
BER			1
PAK			1
PUR			1
THA			1

The Montreal Olympic Games were born of a political compromise and had the ironic counter-effect of financially crippling a city and scaring off Olympic bidders for years.

The picturesque city of Montreal, on the St. Lawrence River, was awarded the games because the International Olympic Committee couldn't decide between bids from the two Cold War superpowers vying for Los Angeles and Moscow as venues for 1976. But on the second round of voting, Los Angeles threw its support behind "neutral" Canada... and Montreal got the Olympics and a billion-dollar tax bill the Canadians are, to a degree, still paying off.

So ambitious was Montreal in trying to produce a breathtaking series of stadiums and arenas that it proved impossible to complete work on the facilities in time. The opening ceremony, in Canada's dual tongues of French and English, took place in improvised conditions. Bad planning, under-budgeting, industrial disputes and an especially harsh winter had not helped.

But what finally threatened to turn the games into a disaster area was the collapse of the the economy in the aftermath of the 1973 oil crisis. The original construction estimate of $310 million grew to $1.2 billion but even so, the Olympic Stadium was not completed in time for the start of the games. An added burden was the cost of a 16,000-strong security force, to guard against any recurrence of 1972's Munich terrorism, at a cost of at least $100 million.

In the event, there was no terrorism... but there was plenty of politics. Twenty-four of the 116 registered teams boycotted the games — some announcing their decision just 48 hours before the start. Mainly African nations, they were protesting against the inclusion in the Olympics of New Zealand, whose rugby team had recently toured apartheid South Africa. Thus only about 6,000 athletes took part in Montreal's spectacular, more than a thousand fewer than at Munich.

Yet athletically the games were amazing. The shining stars included three examples of small nations' athletes defeating the world powers. Fourteen-year-old Nadia Comaneci (Romania) will be forever famous for recording the first perfect "10" on the bars. Alberto "The Horse" Juantorena (Cuba) won the 400 and 800 meters, the only man other than American Paul Pilgrim in 1906 to achieve such a feat in the same games. And Lasse Viren (Finland) amazingly repeated his Munich double in the 5,000 and 10,000 meters four years earlier, the first person ever to have achieved such a feat in two Olympiads. Amazingly, Viren competed in the marathon later in the Montreal games, finishing a respectable fifth.

Another hero of the games was American: track gold medalist Bruce Jenner. With his stylishly long hair and boyish good looks, Jenner became an all-American pin-up and "cover boy" after winning the decathlon.

A commemorative medal from the 1976 Montreal Summer Olympics. Allsport

Jenner's effort, along with that of fellow American gold medalist Edwin Moses who set a world record in the 400 meters hurdles, helped the US forget its failure to win the 100 meters and 110 meters hurdles for the first time since 1928.

Other notables were the East German women, who took nine gold medals in the 14 track and field events. East Germany (with 11 golds), along with the US (13), also dominated the swimming competitions. Britain's David Wilkie broke the pattern briefly in the 200 meters breaststroke.

But the athlete who became most famous as a result of the Montreal Olympics was boxer Sugar Ray Leonard whose triumph in the light-welterweight class led to fame and fortune as a professional.

Despite the passage of time, a series of plaques recognizing all the gold medalists remain pristine and shining around a fountain outside the Olympic Stadium, which is just four miles from downtown Montreal.

The final cost to the city of the 1976 Games has never been satisfactorily added up — because it's still growing and some of the debts remain unpaid. For instance, the stadium's original retractable roof, which had never worked effectively, finally gave up the ghost in 1991. A new retractable roof was installed at a cost of $25 million (CAN) but partly collapsed under the weight of a winter's snow. Proposals have recently been mooted to demolish the jinxed stadium — but the cost of that would be at least $3 million!

All the problems, however, can never detract from the enduring image of Montreal... Nadia Comaneci flawlessly bending her tiny 4 foot 11 inch form to win three gold medals, a silver and a bronze.

MAIN: *The torch used to light the Olympic flame in Montreal.* Allsport

LEFT: *Dancers at the opening ceremony.* Don Morley

NADIA COMANECI

OPPOSITE PAGE AND BELOW:
The diminutive Romanian gymnast, Nadia Comaneci, became Montreal's darling with her flawless performances and grace.
Allsport/Hulton Deutsch

The 14-year-old Romanian Nadia Comaneci lacked Olga Korbut's charisma but she became the first gymnast to score a perfect ten with her performances on the uneven bars and balance beam in Montreal. She ended the competition with seven perfect scores, three gold medals, and the overall title.

Celebrity status was as hard for her as it had been for Korbut. When asked what her greatest wish was, the startled Comaneci replied: "I want to go home."

Though her father, Gheorghe, an auto mechanic, and her mother, Stefania, divorced a year later, she struggled on to another triumph in Moscow in 1980. Then at 19, reaching the end of her competitive career, she quit.

Shortly afterwards, it was said she had an affair with Nicu Ceausescu — son of the Romanian dictator — though she denies it.

She eventually took a government coaching post and, prohibited from traveling to the West because she was considered too valuable to let slip away, languished in frustrated obscurity until 1989.

That year she chose her own way out. ("I used to say I'd rather die in a free country than live in a Communist one," she says.) She walked six hours in darkness to cross the Hungarian border, where Romanian emigré Constantin Panait, a Florida roofer who engineered her defection, was waiting. Panait took her via Vienna to the United States.

For a time, exposure to the West worked a garish transformation on Comaneci's lithe, gamin beauty. Traveling with Panait across the US and living out of motel rooms, she began turning up in public overweight, in heavy makeup and stiletto heels.

It was widely assumed that she and Panait, who was married with four children, were lovers — though she now claims that was not true. Instead, she says, she was a virtual hostage to Panait, who pocketed her fees from performances and TV interviews and threatened her with deportation if she exposed him.

She eventually manufactured her escape and in 1996 wed her longtime beau, the US gold medalist Bart Conner. The couple now run a gymnastics school in their adopted hometown of Norman, Oklahoma.

ALBERTO JUANTORENA

The giant Cuban with the shock of fuzzy hair and nine-foot stride — which earned him the nickname "El Caballo" ("The Horse") — won a unique double in 1976 when he took the 400 meters and 800 meters titles.

In the 800 meters he set a new world record of 1min 43.50sec and it was thought that he would take the event into unchartered territory but he only improved that time once.

Missing from the two-lap event because of the African boycott was Mike Boit of Kenya, and when the two raced in 1977 in two epic duels, Juantorena won them both.

Juantorena believed he would run only the 400, but he was goaded into some 800 meters training by his coach under the guise of trying to develop additional stamina. When he was finally told he was to run both races, Juantorena refused.

"I said, no way," Juantorena recalls. "My coach was running behind me for two weeks, trying to convince me to do it."

Juantorena's concern was that because the 800 came first he would be left too drained to compete in the 400. "I was really afraid," he says. Accordingly, Juantorena carefully eased through the final parts of his qualifying heats. When he looked back at the field seven times during his 400 semi-final, "everybody criticized me," he says.

Come the final, his 400 meters win in 44.26sec was the fastest time ever run at sea level.

He went to Moscow to defend both titles but had to withdraw from the 800 meters with injury after finishing fourth in the 400 meters.

His last major appearance was at the 1983 World Championships where he had to be stretchered from the stadium after tripping over the track curb.

He will be in Sydney as President of the Cuban Athletics Federation and member of the International Amateur Athletic Federation.

LEFT: Alberto Jauntorena of Cuba captured two gold medals in track events at Montreal. Tony Duffy

LASSE VIREN

Winner of the 5,000 meters and 10,000 meters in the Munich Olympics in 1972, Finland's Lasse Viren repeated the double four years later in Montreal — a feat not even the legendary Paavo Nurmi had achieved. In 1976, he was placed fifth in the Olympic marathon only a day after the 5,000 meters final.

Viren had an uncanny knack of being able to peak at the right time, although he went into the 1972 games as a virtual unknown. He had finished seventh and 17th in the 5,000 meters and 10,000 meters at the 1971 European Championships in Helsinki.

But he did set a two mile world record of 8min 14.00sec prior to the games in Munich. In the 5,000 meters final in Munich he won in 13min 26.42sec after a fast last 2,000 meters. However, he saved his most devastating form for the longer distances. On lap 12 of the 10,000 meters he stumbled and fell, but recovered himself, getting up to win in a new world record of 27min 38.35sec.

Viren was constantly linked with rumors of blood doping and in between Olympic Games failed to impress, although he set a world record for 5,000 meters late in 1972 of 13min 16.4sec. In the 1980 games in Moscow he was fifth in the 10,000 meters and dropped out of the marathon after 25 kilometers.

In 1994, Viren sold his four gold medals for $200,000 apiece. He insisted that his decision to sell was not based on any financial hardship. "What does it matter if they are with me or somewhere else?" he asked.

Viren now serves as a respected member of the Finnish parliament.

BRUCE JENNER

The golden boy of American track and field in the seventies, Bruce Jenner went to the 1976 Olympics with a sure sense of his own destiny. It was to be his last competition before retirement and he was confident of victory.

Tenth in the 1972 games, he won 12 out of 13 decathlons between 1974 and 1976. The Olympics was due to have been a battle between Jenner and the defending champion Mykola Avilov of the Soviet Union but the American was in sparkling form, scoring five personal bests on the opening day.

There was no catching him and he went on to win the gold medal with a world record 8,618 points.

He proved to be just as good at cashing in on his athletic achievements, becoming a millionaire with his own sports promotion company and forging a lucrative career in films, TV, sponsorship and advertising. He even appeared in the TV series, "C.H.i.P.S."

He had it all: a house in Malibu that he shared with his wife, Chrystie, and a portfolio of endorsements for such all-American products as Wheaties.

But a decade later, Jenner felt like a has-been. In 1980 he had met Linda Thompson, the late Elvis Presley's former live-in lover, and wound up in a messy divorce from Chrystie, his first wife.

The marriage to Linda lasted barely five years, a failure she blamed on Jenner's frequent travels as a sports commentator. He then married Kris Kardashian, who he met on a blind date in 1990. They wed five months later.

The couple now live in a five-bedroom, French-style country chateau in Los Angeles with their daughter Kendall Nicole, named after Nicole Simpson, O.J. Simpson's murdered wife who was a close family friend.

Jenner now owns a family conglomerate comprising infomercials ("SuperFit" with Bruce and Kris Jenner), exercise products (like stair-climbing machines), and an aircraft sales company (Jenner is a keen flier).

RIGHT: American Bruce Jenner found success off the track after his 1976 decathlon gold. Tony Duffy

ABOVE: *New Zealander John Walker ran to gold in the 1,500 m event.* Tony Duffy

ABOVE LEFT: Kornelia Ender became the first East German woman to win gold in the water. Hulton Deutsch

ABOVE RIGHT: Miklos Nemeth of Hungary won gold in the javelin and set a world record. Allsport

Soviet athlete Victor Saneyev jumped 56'8.75" in the triple jump to win gold. Tony Duffy

ABOVE: *Vasiliy Alexyev of the Soviet Union won gold in the super-heavyweight, weightlifing division.* Allsport

LEFT: *Lasse Viren of Finland (foreground) winner of the 5,000 m event.* Tony Duffy

MONTREAL 1976 JULY 17 - AUGUST 1

PARTICIPANTS: 6,028

MEN: 4,781

WOMEN: 1,247

COUNTRIES: 92

SPORTS: 21

EVENTS: 198

FINAL TORCHBEARERS

SANDRA HENDERSON & STEPHANE PREFONTAINE

MEDALS TABLE

PLACE	COUNTRY	GOLD	SILVER	BRONZE
1	USSR	49	41	35
2	GDR	40	25	25
3	USA	34	35	25
4	FRG	10	12	17
5	Japan	9	6	10

OUTSTANDING ATHLETES

PLACE	NAME (NATIONALITY)	DISCIPLINE	GOLD	SILVER	BRONZE
1	Nikolai Andrinov(URS)	Gymnastics	4	2	1
2	Kornelia Ender (GDR)	Swimming	4	1	
3	John Naber (USA)	Swimming	4	1	
	Nadia Comaneci (ROM)	Gymnastics	3	1	1
	Nelli Kim (URS)	Gymnastics	3	1	

ATHLETICS — MEN

EVENT	GOLD		SILVER		BRONZE	
100 m	Hasely Crawford (TRI)	10.06	Donald Quarrie (JAM)	10.08	Valeriy Borsov (URS)	10.14
200 m	Donald Quarrie (JAM)	20.23	Millard Hampton (USA)	20.29	Dwayne Evans (USA)	20.43
400 m	Alberto Juantorena (CUB)	44.26	Fred Newhouse (USA)	44.40	Herman Fnazier (USA)	44.95
800 m	Alberto Juantorena (CUB)	1:43.5	Ivo van Damme (BEL)	1:43.9	Richard Wohlhuter (USA)	1:44.1
1, 500 m	John Walker (NZL)	3:39.2	Ivo van Damme (BEL)	3:39.3	Paul-Heinz Wellmann (FRG)	3:39.3
5, 000 m	Lasse Viren (FIN)	13:24.8	Dick Quax (NZL)	13:25.2	Klaus-P. Hildenbrand (FRG)	13:25.4
10, 000 m	Lasse Viren (FIN)	27:44.4	Carlos Lopez (POR)	27:45.2	Brendan Foster (GBR)	27:54.9
Marathon	Waldermar Cierpinski (GDR)	2:09:55.0	Frank Shorter (USA)	2:10:45.8	Karel Lismont (BEL)	2:11:12.6
110 m Hurdles	Guy Drut (FRA)	13.30	Alejandro Casanas (CUB)	13.33	Willie Davenport (USA)	13.38
400 m Hurdles	Edwin Moses (USA)	47.64	Michad Shine (USA)	48.69	Yevgeniy Gavrilenko (URS)	49.45
3,000 m Steeplechase	Anders Gärderud (SWE)	8:08.0	Bronislaw Malinowski (POL)	8:09.1	Frank Baumgartl (GDR)	8:10.4
4x100 m	USA	38.33	GDR	38.66	USSR	38.78
4x400 m	USA	2:58.65	Poland	3:01.43	FRG	3:01.98
20 km Walk	Daniel Bautista (MEX)	1:24:40.6	Hans-Peter Reimann (GDR)	1:25:13.8	Peter Frenkel (GDR)	1:25:29.4
High Jump	Jacek Wszola (POL)	7'4.5"	Gregory Joy (CAN)	7'3.25"	Dwight Stones (USA)	7'3"
Pole Vault	Tadeusz Slusarski (POL)	18'0.5"	Antti Kalliomäki (FIN)	18'0'5"	David Roberts (USA)	18'0.5"
Long Jump	Arnie Robinson (USA)	27'4.25"	Randy Williams (USA)	26'7.25"	Frank Wartenberg (GDR)	26'3.75"
Triple Jump	Viktor Saneyev (URS)	56'8.75"	James Butts (USA)	56'8.5"	Joao de Oliveira (BRA)	55'5.5"
Shot	Udo Beyer (GDR)	69'0.75"	Yevgeniy Mironov (URS)	69'0"	Alexander Baryshnikov (URS)	68'10.75"
Discus	Mac Wilkins (USA)	221'5"	Wolfgang Schmidt (GDR)	217'3"	John Powell (USA)	215'7"
Hammer	Yuriy Sedykh (URS)	254'4"	Alexey Spiridonov (URS)	249'7"	Anatoliy Bondarchuk (URS)	247'8"
Javelin	Miklos Nemeth (HUN)	310'4"	Hannu Siitonen (FIN)	288'5"	Gheorghe Megelea (ROM)	285'11"
Decathlon	Bruce Jenner (USA)	8618	Guido Kratschmer (FRG)	8411	Nikolai Avilov (URS)	8369

ATHLETICS — WOMEN

EVENT	GOLD		SILVER		BRONZE	
100 m	Annegret Richter (FRG)	11.08	Renate Stecher (GDR)	11.13	Inge Helten (FRG)	11.17
200 m	Bärbel Eckert (GDR)	22.37	Annegret Richter (FRG)	22.39	Renate Stecher (GDR)	22.47
400 m	Irena Szewinska (POL)	49.29	Christina Brehmer (GDR)	50.51	Ellen Streidt (GDR)	50.55
800 m	Tatyana Kazankina URS)	1:54.9	Nikolina Shtereva (BUL)	1:55.4	Elfie Zinn (GDR)	1:55.6
1, 500 m	Tatyana Kazankina (URS)	4:05.5	Gunhild Hoffmeister (GDR)	4:06.0	Ulrike Klapezynski (GDR)	4:06.1
100 m Hurdles	Johanna Schaller (GDR)	12.77	Tatyana Anisimova (URS)	12.78	Natalya Lebedeva (URS)	12.80
4x100 m	GDR	42.55	FRG	42.59	USSR	43.09
4x400 m	GDR	3:19.2	USA	3:22.8	USSR	3:24.2
High Jump	Rosemarie Ackermann (GDR)	6'4"	Sara Simeoni (ITA)	6'3.25"	Yordanka Blagoyeva (BUL)	6'3.25"
Long Jump	Angela Voight (GDR)	22'0.75"	Kathy McMillan (USA)	21'10.25"	Lidia Alfeyeva (USR)	21'8"
Shot	Ivanka Khristova (BUL)	69'5.25"	Nadyezda Chizhova (URS)	68'9.25"	Helena Fibingerova (TCH)	67'9.75"
Discus	Evelin Schlaak (GDR)	226'4"	Maria Vergova (BUL)	220'9"	Gabriele Hinzmann (GDR)	219'3"
Javelin	Ruth Fuchs (GDR)	209'7"	Marion Becker (FRG)	212'3"	Kathy Schmidt (USA)	209'10"
Pentathlon	Siegrun Siegl (GDR)	4745	Christine Laser (GDR)	4745	Burglinde Polak (GDR)	4740

SWIMMING — WOMEN

EVENT	GOLD		SILVER		BRONZE	
100 m Freestyle	Kornelia Ender (GDR)	55.65	Petra Priemer (GDR)	56.49	Enith Brigitha (HOL)	56.65
200 m Freestyle	Kornelia Ender (GDR)	1:59.26	Shirley Babashoff (USA)	2:01.22	Enith Brigitha (HOL)	2:01.40
400 m Freestyle	Petra Thümer (GDR)	4:09.89	Shirley Babashoff (USA)	4:10.46	Shannon Smith (CAN)	4:14.60
800 m Freestyle	Petra Thümer (GDR)	8:37.14	Shirley Babashoff (USA)	8:37.59	Wendy Weinberg (USA)	8:42.60
100 m Backstroke	Ulrike Richter (GDR)	1:01.83	Birgit Treiber (GDR)	1:03.41	Nancy Garapick (CAN)	1:03.71
200 m Backstroke	Ulrike Richter (GDR)	2:13.43	Birgit Treiber (GDR)	2:14.97	Nancy Garapick (CAN)	2:15.60
100 m Breaststroke	Hannelore Anke (GDR)	1:11.16	Lubov Rusanova (URS)	1:13.04	Marina Koscheveya (URS)	1:13.30
200 m Breaststroke	Marina Koscheveya (URS)	2:33.35	Marina Yurchenia (URS)	2:36.08	Lubow Rusanova (URS)	2:36.22
100 m Butterfly	Kornelia Ender (GDR)	1:00.13	Andrea Pollack (GDR)	1:00.98	Wendy Boglioli (USA)	1:01.17
200 m Butterfly	Andrea Pollack (GDR)	2:11.41	Ulrike Tauber (GDR)	2:12.50	Rosemarie Gabriel (GDR)	2:12.86
400 m Medley	Ulrike Tauber (GDR)	4:42.77	Cheryl Gibson (CAN)	4:48.10	Becky Smith (CAN)	4:50.48
4x100 m Freestyle	USA	3:44.82	GDR	3:45.50	Canada	3:48.81
4x100 m Medley	GDR	4:07.95	USA	4:14.55	Canada	4:15.22
Springboard Diving	Jennifer Chandler (USA)	506.19	Christa Kohler (GDR)	469.41	Cynthia McIngvale (USA)	466.83
Highboard Diving	Elena Vaytsekhovskaya (URS)	406.59	Ulrika Knape (SWE)	402.60	Deborah Wilson (USA)	401.07

SWIMMING — MEN

EVENT	GOLD		SILVER		BRONZE	
100 m Freestyle	Jim Montgomery (USA)	49.99	Jack Babashoff (USA)	50.81	Peter Nocke (FRG)	51.31
200 m Freestyle	Bruce Furniss (USA)	1:50.29	John Naber (USA)	1:50.50	Jim Montgomery (USA)	1:50.58
400 m Freestyle	Brian Goodell (USA)	3:51.93	Tim Shaw (USA)	3:52.54	Vladimir Raskatov (URS)	3:55.76
1, 500 m Freestyle	Brian Goodell (USA)	15:02.40	Bobby Hackett (USA)	15:03.91	Stephen Holland (AUS)	15:04.66
100 m Backstroke	John Naber (USA)	55.49	Peter Rocca (USA)	56.34	Roland Matthes (GDR)	57.22
200 m Backstroke	John Naber (USA)	1:59.19	Peter Rocca (USA)	2:00.55	Dan Harrigan (USA)	2:01.35
100 m Breaststroke	John Hencken (USA)	1:03.11	David Wilkie (GBR)	1:03.43	Arvidas Iuozaytis (URS)	1:04.23
200 m Breaststroke	David Wilkie (GBR)	2:15.11	John Hencken (USA)	2:17.26	Richard Colella (USA)	2:19.20
100 m Butterfly	Matt Vogel (USA)	54.35	Joe Bottom (USA)	54.50	Gary Hall (USA)	54.65
200 m Butterfly	Mike Bruner (USA)	1:59.23	Steven Gregg (USA)	1:59.54	Bill Forrester (USA)	1:59.96
400 m Medley	Rod Strachan (USA)	4:23.68	Alexander McKee (USA)	4:24.62	Andrei Smirnov (URS)	4:26.90
4x200 m Freestyle	USA	7:23.22	USSR	7:27.97	Great Britain	7:32.11
4x100 m Medley	USA	3:42.22	Canada	3:45.94	FRG	3:47.29
Springboard Diving	Phil Boggs (USA)	619.05	Franco Cagnotto (ITA)	570.48	Alexander Kosenkov (URS)	567.24
Highboard Diving	Klaus Dibiasi (ITA)	600.51	Greg Louganis (USA)	576.99	Vladimir Aleynik (URS)	548.61
Water Polo	Hungary		Italy		Netherlands	

FREESTYLE WRESTLING

EVENT	GOLD	SILVER	BRONZE
Light-Flyweight (-105.75 lb)	Khassan Issayev (BUL)	Roman Dmitriev (URS)	Akira Kudo (JPN)
Flyweight (-114.5 lb)	Yuji Takada (JPN)	Alexander Ivanov (URS)	Hae Sup Jeon (KOR)
Bantamweight (-125.75 lb)	Vladimir Umin (URS)	Hans-Dieter Bruchert (GDR)	Masao Arai (JPN)
Featherweight (-136.5 lb)	Jung Mo Yang (KOR)	Zeveg Oidov (MGL)	Gene Davis (USA)
Lightweight (-149.75 lb)	Pavel Pinigin (URS)	Lloyd Keaser (USA)	Yasaburo Sugawara (JPN)
Welterweight (-163 lb)	Jiichiro Date (JPN)	Mansour Barzegar (IRN)	Stanley Dziedzic (USA)
Middleweight (-180.75 lb)	John Peterson (USA)	Viktor Novoshilev (URS)	Adolf Seger (FRG)
Light-Heavyweight (-198.25 lb)	Levan Tediashvili (URS)	Benjamin Peterson (USA)	Stelica Morcov (ROM)
Heavyweight (-220.25 lb)	Ivan Yarygin (URS)	Russell Hellickson (USA)	Dimo Kostov (BUL)
Super-Heavyweight (+ 220.25 lb)	Soslan Andyev (URS)	Jószef Balla (HUN)	Ladislav Simon (ROM)

WEIGHTLIFTING

EVENT	GOLD		SILVER		BRONZE	
Flyweight	Alexander Voronin (URS)	242.5	György Koszegi (HUN)	237.5	Mohammed Nassiri (IRN)	235
Bantamweight	Norair Nurikyan (BUL)	262.5	Grzegorz Cziura (POL)	252.5	Kenichi Ando (JPN)	250.0
Featherweight	Nikolai Kolesnikov (URS)	285.0	Georgi Todorov (BUL)	280.0	Kazumasa Hirai (JPN)	275.0
Lightweight	Pjotr Korol (URS)	305.0	Daniel Senet (FRA)	300.0	Kazimierz Czarnicki (POL)	295.0
Middleweight	Yordan Mitkov (BUL)	335.0	Vartan Militosyan (URS)	330.0	Peter Wenzel (GDR)	327.5
Light-Heavyweight	Valery Shariy (URS)	365.0	Trendachil Stoichev (BUL)	360.0	Peter Baczako (HUN)	345.0
Middle-Heavyweight	David Rigert (URS)	382.5	Lee James (USA)	362.5	Atanas Chopov (BUL)	360.0
Heavyweight	Yury Zaitsev (URS)	385.0	Krastio Semerdiev (BUL)	385.0	Tadeusz Rutkowski (POL)	377.5
Super-Heavyweight	Vasiliy Alexeyev (URS)	440.0	Gerd Bonk (GDR)	405.0	Helmut Losch (GDR)	387.5

WEIGHTLIFTING WEIGHTS

BANTAMWEIGHT	-123.5 lb	FEATHERWEIGHT'S	-132.25 lb	LIGHTWEIGHT	-148.75 lb
MIDDLEWEIGHT	-165.5 lb	LIGHT-HEAVYWEIGHT	-182 lb	MIDDLE-HEAVYWEIGHT	-198.5 lb
HEAVYWEIGHT	+198.5 lb	SUPER-HEAVYWEIGHT	+247.3 lb		

BOXING

EVENT	GOLD	SILVER	BRONZE
Light-Flyweigsht (-105.75 lb)	Jorge Hernandez (CUB)	Byong Uk Li (PRK)	Payao Pooltarat (THA)
			Orlando Maldonado (PUR)
Flyweight (-112.5 lb)	Leo Randolph (USA)	Ramon Duvalon (CUB)	David Torosyan (URS)
			Leszek Blazynski (POL)
Bantamweight (-119 lb)	Yong Jo Gu (PRK)	Charles Mooney (USA)	Parrick Cowdell (GBR)
			Chulsoon Hwang (KOR)
Featherweight (-126 lb)	Angel Herrera (CUB)	Richard Nowakowski (GDR)	Leszek Kosedowski (POL)
			Juan Paredes (MEX)
Lightweight (-132 lb)	Howard Davis (USA)	Simion Cutov (ROM)	Vasiliy Solomin (URS)
			Ace Rusevski (YUG)
Light-Welterweight (-140 lb)	Sugar Ray Leonard (USA)	Andres Aldama (CUB)	Wladimir Kolev (BUL)
			Kacimierz Szcerba (POL)
Welterweight (-148 lb)	Jochen Bachfeld (GDR)	Pedro Gamarro (VEN)	Reinhard Skricek (FRC)
			Victor Zilberman (ROM)
Light-Middleweight (-157 lb)	Jerzy Rybicki (POL)	Tadija Kacar (YUG)	Viktor Savechenko (URS)
			Rolando Garbey (CUB)
Middleweight (-165 lb)	Michael Spinks (USA)	Rufat Riskiev (URS)	Alec Nastac (ROM)
			Luis Martinez (CUB)
Light-Heavyweight (-178.5 lb)	Leon Spinks (USA)	Sixto Soria (CUB)	Costica Danifoiu (ROM)
			Janusz Gortat (POL)
Heavyweight (+178.5 lb)	Teofilo Stevenson (CUB)	Mircea Simon (ROM)	Johnny Tate (USA)
			Clarence Hill (BER)

GRECO-ROMAN WRESTLING

EVENT	GOLD	SILVER	BRONZE
Light-Flyweight (-105.75 lb)	Alexey Shumakov (URS)	Gheorge Berceanu (ROM)	Stefan Anghelov (BUL)
Flyweight (-114.5 lb)	Vitaly Konstantinov (URS)	Nicu Ginga (ROM)	Koichiro Hirayama (JPN)
Bantamweight (-125.75 lb)	Pertti Ukkola (FIN)	Ivan Frgic (YUG)	Farhat Mustafin (URS)
Featherweight (-136.5 lb)	Kazimierz Lipien (POL)	Nelson Davidian (URS)	Laszlo Reczi (HUN)
Lightweight (-149.75 lb)	Suren Nalbandyan (URS)	Stefan Rusu (ROM)	Heinz-Helmut Wehling (GDR)
Welterweight (-163 lb)	Anatoliy Bykov (URS)	Vitezslav Macha (TCH)	Karl-Heinz Helbing (FRG)
Middleweight (-180.75 lb)	Momir Petkovic (YUG)	Vladimir Cheboksarov (URS)	Ivan Kolev (BUL)
Light-Heavyweight (-198.25 lb)	Valeriy Rezanzev (URS)	Stoyan Nikolov (BUL)	Czeslaw Kwiecinski (POL)
Heavyweight (-220.25 lb)	Nikolai Bolboshin (URS)	Kamen Goranov (BUL)	Andrzej Skrzylewski (POL)
Super-Heavyweight (+220.25 lb)	Alexander Kolchinski (URS)	Alexander Tomov (BUL)	Roman Codreanu (ROM)

FENCING

EVENT	GOLD		SILVER		BRONZE	
Individual Foil — Men	Fabio dal Zotto (ITA)	4	Alexander Romankov (URS)	4	Bernard Talvard (FRA)	3
Team Foil — Men	FRG		Italy		France	
Individual Épée	Alexander Pusch (FRG)	3/2	Jürgen Hehn (FRG)	3/1	Gyözö Kulcsár (HUN)	3/0
Team Épée	Sweden		FRG		Switzerland	
Individual Sabre	Viktor Krovopouskov (URS)	5	Vladimir Nazlimov (URS)	4	Viktor Sidjak (URS)	3
Team Sabre	USSR		Italy		Romania	
Individual Foil — Women	Ildiko Schwarczenberger (HUN)	4/1	Maria Consolata Collino (ITA)	4/0	Elena Belova (URS)	3
Team Foil — Women	USSR		France		Hungary	

JUDO

EVENT	GOLD	SILVER	BRONZE
Lightweight (-138.75 lb)	Hector Rodriguez (CUB)	Eun-Kyung Chang (KOR)	Jozsef Tuncsik (HUN)
			Felice Mariani (ITA)
Welterweight (-154.25 lb)	Vladimir Nevzorov (URS)	Koji Kuramoto (JPN)	Patrick Vial (FRA)
			Marian Talaj (POL)
Middleweight (-176.25 lb)	Isamu Sonoda (JPN)	Valeriy Dvoinikov (URS)	Slavko Obadov (YUG)
			Yung-Chul Park (KOR)
Light-Heavyweight (-205	Kazuhiro Ninomiya (JPN)	Ramaz Harshiladze (URS)	David Starbrook (GBR)
			Jörg Röthlisberger (SUI)
Heavyweight (+205 lb)	Sergey Novikov (URS)	Günther Neureuther (FRG)	Allen Coage (USA)
			Sumio Endo (JPN)
Open Class	Haruki Uemura (JPN)	Keith Remfry (GBR)	Jeaki Cho (KOR)
			Shota Chochoshvili (URS)

MODERN PENTATHLON

EVENT	GOLD		SILVER		BRONZE	
Individual	Janusz Pyciak-Peciak (POL)	5520	Pavel Lednev (URS)	5485	Jan Bartu (TCH)	5466
Team	Great Britain	15559	Czechoslovakia	15451	Hungary	15395

CANOEING — MEN

EVENT	GOLD		SILVER		BRONZE	
500 m Kayak Singles K1	Vasile Diba (ROM)	1:46.11	Zoltan Sztanity (HUN)	1:46.95	Rüdiger Helm (GDR)	1:48.30
1,000 m Kayak Singles K1	Rüdiger Hebn (GDR)	3:48.20	Geza Csapó (HUN)	3:48.34	Vasile Diba (ROM)	3:49.65
500 m Kayak Pairs K2	GDR	1:35.87	USSR	1:36.81	Romania	1:37.43
1,000 m Kayak Pairs K2	USSR	3:29.01	GDR	3:29.33	Hungary	3:30.36
1,000 m Kayak Fours K4	USSR	3:08.69	Spain	3:08.95	GDR	3:10.76
500 m Canadian Singles C1	Alexander Rogov (URS)	1:59.23	John Wood (CAN)	1:59.58	Matja Ljubek (YUG)	1:59.60
1,000 m Canadian Singles C1	Matja Ljubek (YUG)	4:09.51	Vasiliy Urchenko (URS)	4:12.57	Tamás Wichmann (HUN)	4:14.11
500 m Canadian Pairs C2	USSR	1:45.81	Poland	1:47.77	Hungary	1:48.35
1,000 m Canadian Pairs C2	USSR	3:52.76	Romania	3:54.28	Hungary	3:55.66

CANOEING — WOMEN

EVENT	GOLD		SILVER		BRONZE	
500 m Kayak Singles K1	Carola Zirzow (GDR)	2:01.05	Tatyana Korshunova (URS)	2:03.07	Klara Rajnai (HUN)	2:05.01
500 m Kayak Pairs K2	USSR	1:51.15	Hungary	1:51.69	GDR	1:51.81

ROWING — MEN

EVENT	GOLD		SILVER		BRONZE	
Single Sculls	Pertti Karppinen (FIN)	7:29.03	Peter-Michael Kolbe (FRG)	7:31.67	Joachim Dreifke (GDR)	7:38.03
Doubles Sculls	Norway	7:13.20	Great Britain	7:15.25	GDR	7:17.45
Coxless Pairs	GDR	7:23.31	USA	7:26.73	FRG	7:30.03
Coxed Pairs	GDR	7:58.99	USSR	8:01.82	Czechoslovakia	8:03.28
Coxless Quadruple Sculls	GDR	6:18.65	USSR	6:19.89	Czechoslovakia	6:21.77
Coxless Fours	GDR	6:37.42	Norway	6:41.22	USSR	6:42.52
Coxed Fours	USSR	6:40.22	GDR	6:42.70	FRG	6:46.96
Coxed Eights	GDR	5:58.29	Great Britain	6:00.82	New Zealand	6:03.51

ROWING — WOMEN

EVENT	GOLD		SILVER		BRONZE	
Single Sculls	Christina Scheiblich (GDR)	4:05.56	Joan Lind (USA)	4:06.21	Elena Antonova (URS)	4:10.24
Double Sculls	Bulgaria	3:44.36	GDR	3:47.86	USSR	3:49.93
Coxless Pairs	Bulgaria	4:01.22	GDR	4:01.61	FRG	4:02.35
Coxed Quadruple Skulls	GDR	3:29.99	USSR	3:32.49	Romania	3:32.76
Coxed Fours	GDR	3:45.08	Bulgaria	3:48.24	USSR	3:49.38
Coxed Eights	GDR	3:33.32	USSR	3:36.17	USA	3:38.68

YACHTING

EVENT	GOLD		SILVER		BRONZE	
Finn Class	Jochen Schürmann (GDR)	35.4	Andrey Balashov (URS)	39.7	John Bertrand (AUS)	46.4
International Tempest	Sweden	14.0	USSR	30.4	USA	32.7
Flying Dutchman	FRG	34.7	Great Britain	51.7	Brazil	52.1
International Tornado	Great Britain	18.0	USA	36.0	FRG	37.7
International 470	FRG	42.4	Spain	49.7	Australia	57.0
International Sailing	Denmark	46.7	USA	47.4	GDR	47.4

CYCLING

EVENT	GOLD		SILVER		BRONZE	
Individual Road Race (108.25 mi)	Bernt Johansson (SWE)	4:46:52	Giuseppe Martinelli (ITA)	4:47:23	Mieczyl Nowich (POL)	4:47:23
100 km Road Team Trial	USSR	2:08:53	Poland	2:09:13	Denmark	2:12:20
1,000 m Time Trial	Klaus-Jürgen Grünke (GDR)	1:05.927	Michel Vaarten (BEL)	1:07.516	Niels Fredborg (DEN)	1:07.617
1,000 Sprint	Anton Tkac (TCH)		Daniel Morelon (FRA)		Hans-Jürgen Geschke (GDR)	
4,000 m Individual Pursuit	Gregor Bratn (FRG)	4:47.61	Herman Ponsteen (HOL)	4:49.72	Thomas Huschke (GDR)	4:52.71
4,000 m Team Pursuit	FRG	4:21.06	USSR	4:27.15	Great Britain	4:22.41

EQUESTRIANISM

EVENT	GOLD		SILVER		BRONZE	
Three-Day Event	Edmund Coffin (USA)	114.99	John Plumb (USA)	125.85	Karl Schultz (FRG)	129.45
Three-Day Event (Team)	USA	441.00	FRG	584.60	Australia	599.54
Grand Prix (Dressage)	Christine Stückelberger (SUI)	1486	Harry Boldt (FRG)	1435	Reiner Klimke (FRG)	1395
Grand Prix (Dressage) Team	FRG	5155	Switzerland	4684	USA	4670
Grand Prix (Jumping)	Alwin Schockemöhle (FRG)	0	Michel Vaillancourt (CAN)	12/4	Francois Mathy (BEL)	12/8
Grand Prix (Jumping) Team	France	40	FRG	44	Belgium	63

SHOOTING

EVENT	GOLD		SILVER		BRONZE	
Small-Bow Rifle (Prone)	Karlheinz Smieszek (FRG)	599	Ulrich Lind (FRG)	597	Gennadiy Lushchikov(URS)	595
Small Bore Rifle (3 Positions)	Lanny Bassham (USA)	1162	Margaret Murdock (USA)	1162	Werner Seibold (FRG)	1160
Rapid-Fire Pistol	Norbert Klaar (GDR)	597	Jurgen Wiefel (GDR)	596	Roberto Ferraris (ITA)	595
Free Pistol (50 m)	Uwe Potteck (GDR)	573	Harald Vollmar (GDR)	567	Rudolf Dollinger (AUT)	562
Running GameTarget	Alexander Gasov (URS)	579	Alexander Kedyarov (URS)	576	Jerzy Greszkiewicz (POL)	571
Skeet Shooting	Josef Panacek (TCH)	198	Eric Swinkels (HOL)	198	Wieslaw Gawlikowski (POL)	196
Trap Shooting	Donald Haldeman (USA)	190	Armando Silva Marques (POR)	189	Ubaldesco Baldi (ITA)	189

ARCHERY — WOMEN

GOLD		SILVER		BRONZE	
Luann Ryan (USA)	2499	Valentina Kovpan (URS)	2460	Zebiniso Rustamova (URS)	2407

ARCHERY — MEN

GOLD		SILVER		BRONZE	
Darrell Pace (USA)	2571	Hiroshi Michinaga (JPN)	2502	Giancarlo Ferrari (ITA)	2495

GYMNASTICS — MEN

EVENT	GOLD		SILVER		BRONZE	
Individual Combined Excercises	Nikolai Andrianov (URS)	116.650	Sawao Kato (JPN)	115.650	MitsuoTsukahara (JPN)	115.575
Team	Japan	576.85	USSR	576.45	GDR	564.65
Parallel Bars	Sawao Kato (JPN)	19.675	Nikolai Andrianov (URS)	19.500	Mirsuo Tsukahara (JPN)	19.475
Floor	Nikolai Andrianov (URS)	19.450	Vladimir Marchenko (URS)	19.425	Peter Korman (USA)	19.300
Horse Vault	Nikolai Andrianov (URS)	19.450	MitsuoTsukahara (JPN)	19.375	Hiroshi Kajiyama (JPN)	19.275
Horizontal Bars	MitsuoTsukahara (JPN)	19.675	Eizo Kenmotsu (JPN)	19.500	Henri Boerio (FRA)	19.475
					Eberhard Gienger (FRG)	19.475
Rings	Nikolai Andrianov (URS)	19.650	Alexander Ditiatin (URS)	19.550	Dan Grecu (ROM)	19.500
Pommel Horse	Zoltan Magyar (HUN)	19.700	Eizo Kenmotsu (JPN)	19.575	Nikolai Andrianov (URS)	19.525

GYMNASTICS — WOMEN

EVENT	GOLD		SILVER		BRONZE	
Individual Combined Excercises	Nadia Comaneci (ROM)	79.275	Nelli Kim (URS)	78.675	Lyudmila Turischeva (URS)	78.625
Team	USSR	390.35	Romania	387.15	GDR	385.10
Floor	Nelli Kim (URS)	19.850	Lyudmila Turischeva (URS)	19.825	Nadia Comaneci (ROM)	19.750
Horse Vault	Nelli Kim (URS)	19.800	Carola Dombeck (GDR)	19.650		
			Lyudmila Turischeva (URS)	19.650		
Beam	Nadia Comaneci (ROM)	19.950	Olga Korbut (URS)	19.725	Teodora Ungureanu (ROM)	19.700
Asymmetrical Bars	Nadia Comaneci (ROM)	20.000	Teodora Ungureanu (ROM)	19.800	Marta Egervari (HUN)	19.775
Gruppen-Gymnastik	Sweden	74.20	USSR	73.00	Poland	74.00

BASKETBALL — MEN

GOLD	SILVER	BRONZE
USA	Yugoslavia	USSR

BASKETBALL — WOMEN

GOLD	SILVER	BRONZE
USSR	USA	Bulgaria

SOCCER

GOLD	SILVER	BRONZE
GDR	Poland	USSR

HANDBALL — MEN

GOLD	SILVER	BRONZE
USSR	Romania	Poland

HANDBALL — WOMEN

GOLD	SILVER	BRONZE
USSR	GDR	Hungary

HOCKEY

GOLD	SILVER	BRONZE
New Zealand	Australia	Pakistan

VOLLEYBALL — MEN

GOLD	SILVER	BRONZE
Poland	USSR	Cuba

VOLLEYBALL — WOMEN

GOLD	SILVER	BRONZE
Japan	USSR	South Korea

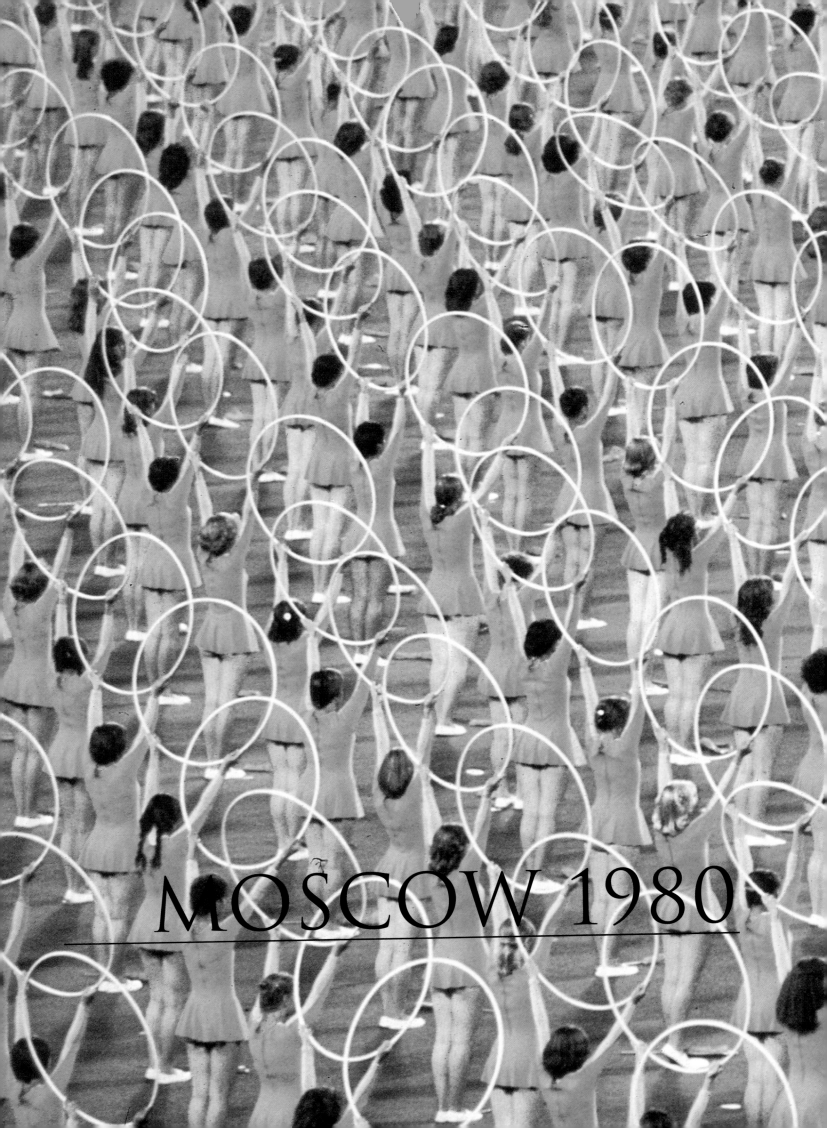

MOSCOW 1980

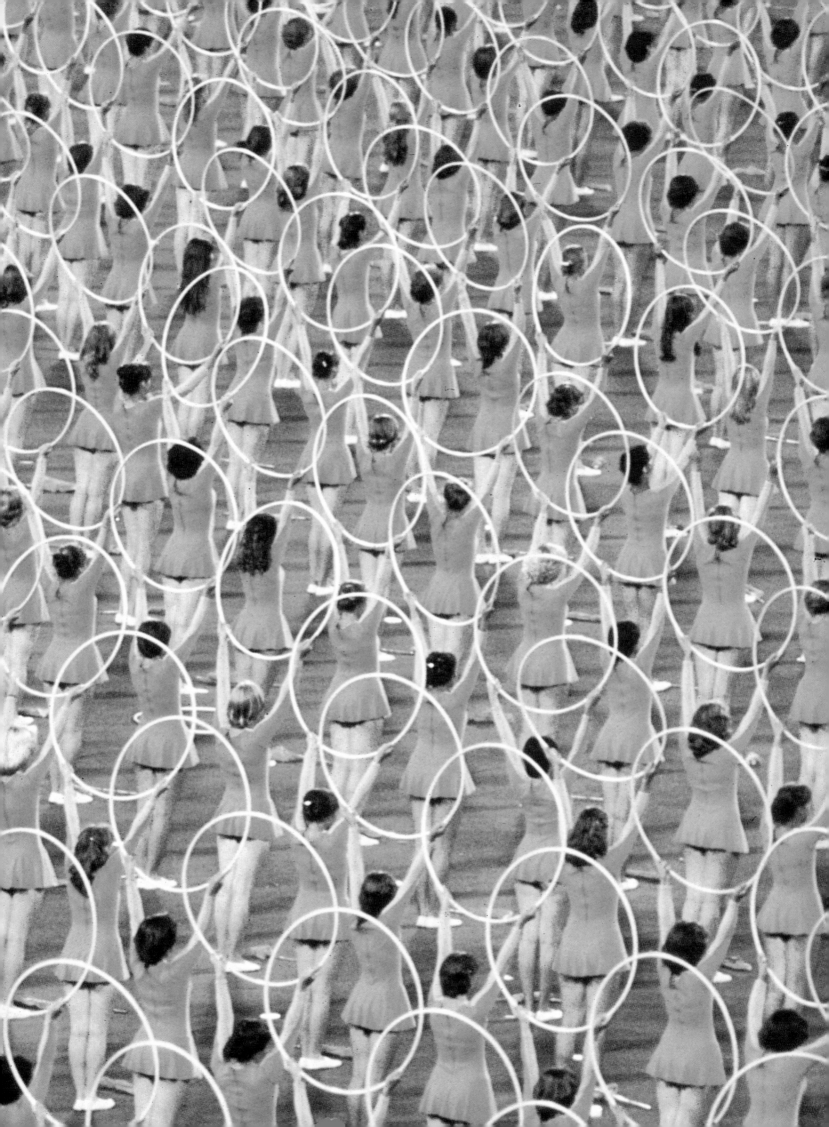

INTRODUCTION

Moscow 1980

ABOVE: *A close-up of the games' commemorative pin.* Allsport

PREVIOUS PAGES: *Colorfully costumed dancers help open the 1980 Moscow summer games.* Allsport-France

204
EVENTS

80
COUNTRIES

5,217
ATHLETES

	Gold	Silver	Bronze
URS	80	69	46
GDR	47	37	42
BUL	8	16	17
CUB	8	7	5
ITA	8	3	4
HUN	7	10	15
ROM	6	6	13
FRA	6	5	3
GBR	5	7	9
POL	3	14	15
SWE	3	3	6
FIN	3	1	4
CZE	2	3	9
YUG	2	3	4
AUS	2	2	5
DEN	2	1	2
BRA	2	-	2
ETH	2		2
SUI	2		
ESP	1	3	2
AUT	1	2	1
GRE	1		2
BEL	1		
IND	1		
ZIM	1		
PRK		3	2
MON		2	2
TAN		2	
MEX		1	3
NED		1	2
IRL		1	1
UGA		1	
VEN		1	
JAM			3
GUY			1
LEB			1

The cold war blew a big draught through the 1980 Olympics. Angered by the Soviet Union's invasion of Afghanistan the previous year, US President Jimmy Carter directed a boycott of the Moscow games.

No fewer than 61 nations refused to go to Moscow, including the United States, West Germany and Japan. Only 81 — including, ironically, Afghanistan — attended. The US, however, continued to trade with the Soviet Union.

Britain's athletes, including future Tory politician Sebastian Coe, bravely stood up to Prime Minister Margaret Thatcher and refused to heed her calls not to go. However, those who worked in the civil service were refused permission to attend.

But Britain, like many other nations, decided to stage their own protests, such as marching under the Olympic flag or having the Olympic hymn played at medals ceremonies instead of their own national anthems.

The games ran with clockwork efficiency. President Leonid Brezhnev had conscripted almost the entire city to attend events and support the Olympics. Running in parallel with the games were many human rights protests. But when the press tried to report them, they usually found their telephone line went dead for several hours, causing them to miss their deadline.

The absence of so many nations failed to take the gloss off one of the most anticipated clashes in

RIGHT: A full-view of the official commemorative pin of the 1980 Moscow Summer Olympics. Allsport

Olympic history: Coe versus Steve Ovett in the 800 and 1,500 meters.

The British pair had been trading world records on the European circuit while carefully avoiding meeting each other. There was no hiding place in the magnificent 103,000-capacity Lenin Stadium and the races lived up to the hype, even though they each won the 'wrong' event. Ovett was the favourite for the 1,500 meters but took the 800 meters and Coe won the 1,500 meters.

Scotland's Allan Wells became the first Briton to win the Olympic 100 meters for 56 years but had to live with jibes he wouldn't have triumphed if the Americans had been there. To complete an exceptional games for Britain, Daley Thompson won the decathlon.

Ethiopia's Miruts Yifter repeated Lasse Viren's 5,000 and 10,000 meters double while East Germany's Waldemar Cierpinski became only the second man to successfully defend his marathon title.

Unusually, the star of the gymnastics hall was not a woman but a man, in the shape of Aleksandr Dityatin. He won a record eight medals and his maximum 10.00 in the horse vault was the first ever awarded to a male gymnast in the Olympics.

Amid suspicions that something was not quite right, East Germany's female swimmers won an incredible 26 of the available 35 medals. Many competitors commented on their masculine

RIGHT PHOTO: Dancers at the opening ceremony. Allsport

appearance and deep voices. It was only 15 years later that it was confirmed they had all been on state-sponsored doping programmes.

Cuba, naturally, were enthusiastic supporters of the games and provided one of the highlights when the giant heavyweight boxer Teofilo Stevenson became the first man to win the same event in three games.

Despite the boycott, the standard in all events was very high. Yet, when the curtain came down on these games, there remained a real fear that perhaps this was the end. Coming after the terrorist atrocity in Munich and the financial disaster of Montreal, Moscow appeared to many observers to be the final nail in the coffin.

Two views of the official commemorative medal from the Moscow summer games.
Allsport

MAIN PHOTO: The torch used to light the Olympic flame in Moscow.

BELOW: An acrobatic display at the opening ceremony. Allsport

SEBASTIAN COE

BELOW: Steve Ovett of Great Britain seen after his 800 m victory. Tony Duffy

BELOW RIGHT AND OPPOSITE PAGE: Rival, Sebastian Coe (no. 254), also of Great Britain, captured gold in the 1,500 m event instead. Tony Duffy

The 800 and 1,500 meters finals at the 1980 Olympics in Moscow were probably the most eagerly awaited track races of all time.

Britain's two middle-distance heroes — Seb Coe, the world record holder at 800 meters, and Steve Ovett, world record holder for the mile — were going to meet at last. This was crunch time.

First up was the 800 meters, the one Coe was expected to win. But in a rough, untidy race, it was Ovett who kept his nerve to win in 1min 45.40sec. Coe, a bag of nerves, spent the race at the back of the field, leaving it too late to make his move.

Coe reacted badly to the defeat and looked a picture of misery as he received his silver medal.

Six days later Coe was rejuvenated, Ovett jaded as they met in the final of the 1,500 meters. Running the perfect race this time, Coe's famous double kick around the final bend was too much for Ovett, who had to settle for bronze behind Jurgen Straub, the East German who had done so much to make it a fast race.

With one gold medal apiece, each won in the other's favorite event, Coe and Ovett never raced again in their prime, due to market forces and injury. By the time they did meet again, at the Los Angeles Olympics four years later, Ovett had succumbed to a virus and the local pollution. Brazil's Joaquim Cruz and British rival Steve Cram had emerged at 800

meters and 1,500 meters respectively and Coe was back to his best after 12 months spent combating a blood disorder.

The result? Coe won another 800 meters silver medal behind Cruz, while Ovett struggled home last and Coe became the first man to retain his Olympic 1,500 meters title in an Olympic record 3min 32.53sec, ahead of Cram — both of them celebrating while Ovett was taken to hospital having stepped off the track with 300 meters to go.

Shortly after Coe controversially failed to make Britain's 1988 Olympic team, he was chosen by the Conservative Party to stand for parliament and in 1993 was elected as the MP for Falmouth. Coe was touted as a future health secretary, even a future prime minister. But he lost his seat in the Labour landslide of 1997. He is now the private secretary to William Hague, the new leader of the Conservatives, and combines that role with helping find sponsors for Britain's elite televised meetings.

Coe still runs five miles five days per week and in 1995 ran the London Marathon in under three hours.

Ovett has spent much of his time since retirement was forced upon him by a knee injury, renovating Kinmout House, a Scottish stately home built for the Marquess of Queensberry.

TEOFILO STEVENSON

Teofilo Stevenson won the Olympic heavyweight gold medal a record three times between 1972 and 1980 and was regarded as the best prospect since Muhammad Ali but the giant Cuban steadfastly held out against the offers that came his way to turn professional. At one stage he was offered $2 million and even a shot at Ali's world title but he remained unmoved.

"I don't believe in professionalism, only revolution," Stevenson said. "I tell these men from America, the promoters, that money means nothing to me. What is eight million dollars against eight million Cubans who love me?"

Opinion is divided on whether Stevenson would have cut the mustard as a professional. As an amateur, however, he had no equal — winning 309 out of 321 bouts and amassing 72 international gold medals.

Stevenson does not seem to have suffered unduly by not turning pro. He dwells among his countrymen like a towering Cuban peacock, occupying high positions within the government's sports programs and gaining sufficient attention from the island's women to have attracted four wives, a testimony to his eclectic taste. His first wife was a dance instructor, his second an industrial engineer, his third a doctor, and his present wife is a criminal attorney.

Stevenson always fought from an upright position, and he maintains that posture today. When people talk to him, his eyes look downward, but his head remains high. His firm jaw seems to be locked at a right-angle to his straight-spined back.

Although they never fought, Stevenson and Ali have struck up a great friendship. He was Ali's guest in the United States during 1995 and Ali has visited him in Havana.

WALDEMAR CIERPINSKI

Only two men have won two Olympic marathon titles. Abebe Bikila won in 1960 and 1964, Waldemar Cierpinski in 1976 and 1980.

Cierpinski was an unknown force when he lined up against the defending champion Frank Shorter in Montreal. But when the American surged just after half-way he was shocked to find the East German on his shoulder.

Cierpinski eventually pulled away to win in 2 hrs 9min 55sec, an Olympic record and personal best by two-and-a-half minutes. His win was a shock even to the East Germans.

Between Olympics, Cierpinski looked anything but a champion and was ranked only third in his own country in 1979. But he got it right when it mattered most in Moscow in 1980 and won in 2 hrs 11min 3sec. He aimed for a third win in Los Angeles in 1984 but that was ruled out by the Eastern Bloc's boycott.

Shorter, the man he beat in 1976, now says he has evidence that Cierpinski participated in East Germany's long-suspected performance-enhancement drugs program and is lobbying to have him disqualified by the International Olympic Committee.

Life has been good since that day in Montreal for Cierpinski. Even now, despite the doping revelations, he is still considered a national legend. When the Berlin Wall came down in 1989, he cashed in on his fame and respect by opening a chain of sporting goods stores bearing his name throughout what was once East Germany.

There is no doubt that Cierpinski was one of the greatest successes of the fabled East German system. As a child growing up outside Halle, he displayed an early talent for running, racing the bus to school and often winning. He saw sports as a way out of what he feared would be a dull life as a worker on a collective farm.

Like other successful athletes in East Germany, he was approached to become an informer for the secret police, the Stasi. In 1973, he signed on with the spy organization, which was interested in getting information on athletes who might try to defect.

Under the code name "Willi," Cierpinski won high marks from the Stasi for his cooperation, although a look at his Stasi file, which is available to the public, shows that he gave next to no information

MIRUTS YIFTER

A man of mystery with a blistering sprint finish, Ethiopia's Miruts Yifter earned the affectionate nickname "Yifter the Shifter" after his golden double at the Moscow Olympics in 1980. He won the 5,000 meters and 10,000 meters, both with electrifying bursts of speed over the final 300 meters.

The little man from Ethiopia, who had six children but has always been unsure about his own birth date, had tried for eight years to win a gold medal at 5,000 meters.

In 1972, his bronze medal in the 10,000 meters in Munich was marred by his disqualification from the 5,000 meters for failing to to turn up on time for his heat. He claimed a political conspiracy against him within the Ethiopian team, although subsequent explanations have suggested that he was misdirected at the at the check-in gate or that he spent too long in the toilet before the start.

that was overtly incriminating. Cierpinski says: "I never ratted."

During his running career, Cierpinski was a true believer in the system. He belonged to the Communist Party, quoted Marx, and gave speeches at the annual ruling party congresses. He was also one of East Germany's best loved sports figures. Twice, he was voted East German athlete of the year.

After his win in Moscow, a jubilant sports announcer urged his listeners to take action. "Fathers, have courage! Name your sons Waldemar." Many did.

When asked whether he took steroids, Cierpinski bristles. "These accusations are absurd," he says. "I'm confronted every other day with something like this. It's aggravating."

Yifter was then robbed of the chance of redemption in 1976 by the African boycott of the Montreal games over New Zealand's rugby tour of South Africa. And, in 1984, Yifter's chances of emulating Mamo Wolde and the great Abebe Bikila by winning the marathon were ruined when the Soviet Bloc pulled out of the Los Angeles games and the Ethiopians, then under Marxist rule, supported the boycott.

A generation of Ethiopian boys grew up wanting to be like Yifter. His name still evokes incredible respect in Addis Ababa, where there is a street named after him.

Yet the man himself fled his homeland in 1997 — using the opportunity of an invitation to appear as guest of honor at a North American Ethiopian Sports Festival in Los Angeles. He is now in Canada seeking political asylum. He fears he will never again see his family or his homeland where he is worshipped.

Yifter is a member of the Amhara ethnic group, who once held sway in Ethiopia and now make up roughly 30 per cent of the country's population. He claims there is widespread fear among the Amharas because the new government in Ethiopia is led by a president from the formerly secessionist province of Tigre. Yifter says he is being victimized because of his name.

"Throughout my life I was running for the people of Ethiopia and for my beloved flag," he says. "The reason I have left my country is that people who were educated, people who had every kind of talent, have been removed by the government because of their ethnic background. They have been fired. I have seen them on the street with their kids begging. So I don't get peace of mind. The Government is unfair."

Yifter, who had lost his job as a coach with the Ethiopian national team, claims he was beaten up by security forces there. When he arrived in Canada, his shins were horrifically scarred — the result, he claims, of a recent beating. "I reported the incident but I was ignored," he says.

He was given a hero's welcome in Toronto. The Ethiopian community set him up with an apartment, furniture and a lawyer to represent his case before the Canadian Refugee Board.

Of his flight to freedom, he says: "I didn't indicate anything to my family," he says. "I didn't want emotions to become involved. There is a saying in Ethiopia that if a man wants to do something he must keep things in his heart.

"When I left Ethiopia I was deeply depressed and full of sorrow. It is totally sad. I have no words to explain."

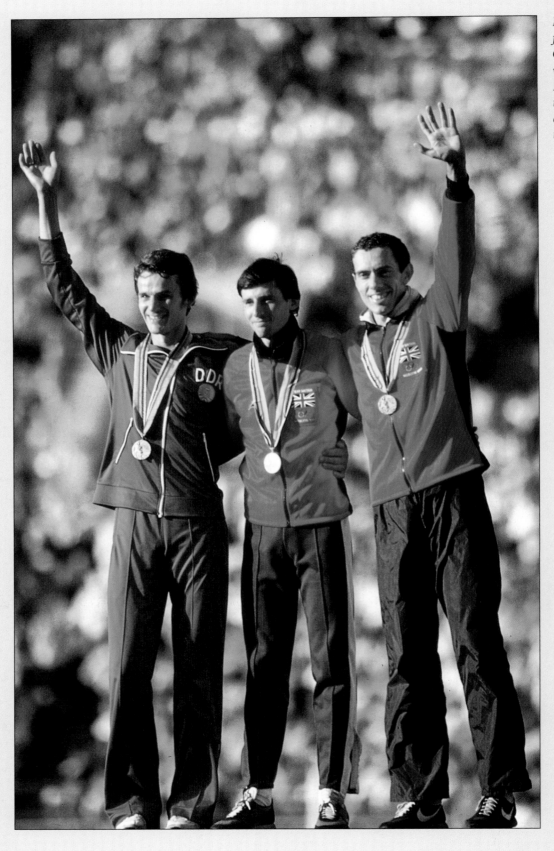

*Medalists in the 1,500 m
final were (l to r) West
Germany's Juürgen Straub
with the silver, Great
Britain's Sebastian Coe with
the gold and Steve Ovett,
also of Great Britain, with
the bronze. Tony Duffy*

TOP LEFT: *Daley Thompson,*
of Great Britain, jubilant
after winning gold in the
decathlon. Allsport

ABOVE: *Duncan Goodhew,*
of Great Britain, a winner in
the 100 m breaststroke,
comes up for air. Tony
Duffy

LEFT: *Another view*
of Moscow's opening
ceremony. Allsport

MOSCOW 1980 JULY 19 - AUGUST 3

PARTICIPANTS: 5,217
MEN: 4,043
WOMEN: 1,124
COUNTRIES: 80
SPORTS: 21
EVENTS: 204

FINAL TORCHBEARER: SERGEY BELOV

MEDALS TABLE

PLACE	COUNTRY	GOLD	SILVER	BRONZE
1	USSR	80	69	46
2	GDR	47	37	42
3	Bulgaria	8	16	17
4	Cuba	8	7	5
5	Italy	8	3	4

OUTSTANDING ATHLETES

PLACE	NAME (NATIONALITY)	DISCIPLINE	GOLD	SILVER	BRONZE
1	Alexander Ditiatin (URS)	Gymnastics	3	4	1
2	Caren Metschuk (GDR)	Swimming	3	1	
3	Barbara Krause (GDR)	Swimming	3		
	Rica Reinisch (GDR)	Swimming	3		
	Vladimir Salnikov (URS)	Swimming	3		
	Vladimir Parfenovich (URS)	Canoeing	3		

ATHLETICS — WOMEN

EVENT	GOLD		SILVER		BRONZE	
100 m	Ludmila Kondratyeva (URS)	11.06	Marlies Göhr (GDR)	11.07	Ingrid Auerswald (GDR)	11.14
200 m	Bärbel Wöckel (GDR)	22.03	Natalya Bochina (URS)	22.19	Merlene Ottey (JAM)	22.20
400 m	Marita Koch (GDR)	48.88	Jarmila Kratochvilova (TCH)	49.46	Christina Lathan (GDR)	49.66
800 m	Nadyezda Olizarenko (URS)	1:53.2	Olga Mineyeva (URS)	1:54.9	Tatyana Providokhina (URS)	1:55.5
1,500 m	Tatyana Kasankina (URS)	3:56.6	Christiane Wartenberg (GDR)	3:57.8	Nadyezda Olizarenko (URS)	3:59.6
100 m Hurdles	Vera Komisova (URS)	12.56	Johanna Klier (GDR)	12.63	Lucyna Langer (POL)	12.65
4x100 m	GDR	41.60	USSR	42.10	Great Britain	42.43
4x400 m	USSR	3:20.2	GDR	3:20.4	Great Britain	3:27.5
High Jump	Sara Simeoni (ITA)	6'5.5"	Urszula Kielan (POL)	6'4.5"	Jutta Kirst (GDR)	6'4.5"
Long Jump	Tatyana Kolpakova (URS)	23'2"	Brigitte Wujak (GDR)	23'1.25"	Tatyana Skachko (URS)	23'0"
Shot	Ilona Slupianek (GDR)	73'6.25"	Svetlana Krachevskaya (URS)	70'3.25"	Margitta Pufe (GDR)	69'6.75"
Discus	Evelin Jahl (GDR)	229'6"	Maria Petkova-Vergova (BUL)	222'9"	Tatyana Lesovaya (URS)	221'1"
Javelin	Maria Caridad-Colon (CUB)	224'5"	Saida Gunba (URS)	222'2"	Ute Hommola (GDR)	218'4"
Pentathlon	Nadyezda Tkachenko (URS)	5083	Olga Rukavishnikova (URS)	4937	Olga Kuragina (URS)	4875

ATHLETICS — MEN

EVENT	GOLD		SILVER		BRONZE	
100 m	Allan Wells (GBR)	10.25	Silvio Leonard (CUB)	10.25	Petar Petrov (BUL)	10.39
200 m	Pietro Mennea (ITA)	20.19	Allan Wells (GBR)	20.21	Donald Quarrie (JAM)	20.29
400 m	Viktor Markin (URS)	44.60	Richard Mitchell (AUS)	44.84	Frank Schaffer (GDR)	44.87
800 m	Steve Ovett (GBR)	1:45.4	Sebastian Coe (GBR)	1:45.9	Nikolai Kirov (URS)	1:46.0
1,500 m	Sebastian Coe (GBR)	3:38.4	Jürgen Straub (GDR)	3:38.8	Steve Ovett (GBR)	3:39.0
5,000 m	Miruts Yifter (ETH)	13:21.0	Suleiman Nyambui (TAN)	13:21.6	Kaarlo Maaninka (PIN)	13:22.0
10,000 m	Miruts Yifter (ETH)	27:42.7	Kaarlo Maaninka (FIN)	27:44.3	Mohammed Kedir (ETH)	27:44.7
Marathon	Waldemar Cierpinski (GDR)	2:11:03	Gerard Nijboer (HOL)	2:11:20	Sat Dzhumanazarov (URS)	2:11:35
110 m Hurdles	Thomas Munkelt (GDR)	13.39	Alejandro Casanas (CUB)	13.40	Alexander Puchkov (URS)	13.44
400 m Hurdles	Volker Beck (GDR)	48.70	Vasiliy Arkhipenko (URS)	48.86	Gary Oakes (GBR)	49.11
3000 m Steeplechase	Bronislaw Malinowski (POL)	8:09.7	Filbert Bayi (TAN)	8:12.5	Eshetu Tura (ETH)	8:13.6
4x100 m	USSR	38.26	Poland	38.33	France	38.53
4x400 m	USSR	3:01.1	GDR	3:01.3	Italy	3:04.3
20 km Walk	Maurizio Damilano (ITA)	1:23:35.5	Pyotr Pochenchuk (URS)	1:24:45.4	Roland Wieser (GDR)	1:25:58.2
50 km Walk	Hartwig Gander (GDR)	3:49:24	Jorge Llopart (ESP)	3:51:25	Yevgeniy Ivchenko (URS)	3:56:32
High Jump	Gerd Wessig (GDR)	7'8.75"	Jacek Wszola (POL)	7'7"	Jörg Freimuth (GDR)	7'7"
Pole Vault	Wladislaw Kozakiewicz (POL)	18'11.5"	Konstantin Volkov (URS)	18'6.5"		
			Tadeusz Slusarski (POL)	18'6.5"		
Long Jump	Lutz Dombrowki (GDR)	28'0.25"	Frank Paschek (GDR)	26'11.25"	Valeri Podluzhniy (URS)	26'10"
Triple Jump	Jaak Uudmae (URS)	56'11"	Viktor Saneyev (URS)	56'6.75"	Joao de Oliveira (BRA)	56'6"
Shot	Vladimir Kiselyev (URS)	70'0.5"	Alexander Baryshnikov (URS)	69'2"	Udo Beyer (GDR)	69'1.25"
Discus	Viktor Rashchupkin (URS)	218'7"	Imrich Bugar (TCH)	217'9"	Luis Delis (CUB)	217'7"
Hammer	Yuriy Sedykh (URS)	268'4"	Sergey Litvinov (URS)	264'6"	Yuriy Tamm (URS)	259'0"
Javelin	Dainis Kula (URS)	299'2"	Alexander Makarov (URS)	294'1"	Wolfgang Hanisch (GDR)	284'6"
Decathlon	Daley Thompson (GBR)	8495	Yuriy Kutsenko (URS)	8331	Sergey Zhelanov (URS)	8135

SWIMMING — MEN

EVENT	GOLD		SILVER		BRONZE	
100 m Freestyle	Jörg Woithe (GDR)	50.40	Per Alvar Holmertz (SWE)	50.91	Per Johansson (SWE)	51.29
200 m Freestyle	Sergey Kopliakov (URS)	1:49.81	Andrej Krylov (URS)	1:50.76	Graeme Brewer (AUS)	1:51.60
400 m Freestyle	Vladimir Salnikov (URS)	3:51.31	Andrej Krylov (URS)	3:53.24	Ivar Stukolkin (URS)	3:53.95
1,500 m Freestyle	Vladimir Salnikov (URS)	14:58.27	Alexander Chaev (URS)	15:14.30	Max Metzker (AUS)	15:14.49
100 m Backstroke	Bengt Baron (SWE)	56.63	Viktor Kusnetsov (URS)	56.99	Vladimir Dolgov (URS)	57.63
200 m Backstroke	Sandor Wladar (HUN)	2:01.93	Zoltan Verraszto (HUN)	2:02.40	Mark Kerry (AUS)	2:03.14
100 m Breaststroke	Duncan Goodhew (GBR)	1:03.34	Arsen Miskarov (URS)	1:03.82	Peter Evans (AUS)	1:03.96
200 m Breaststroke	Robertas Schulpa (URS)	2:15.85	Alban Vermes (HUN)	2:16.93	Arsen Miskarov (URS)	2:17.28
100 m Butterfly	Paer Arvidsson (SWE)	54.92	Roger Pyttel (GDR)	54.94	David Lopez (ESP)	55.13
200 m Butterfly	Sergey Fesenko (URS)	1:59.76	Philip Hubble (GBR)	2:01.20	Roger Pyttel (GDR)	2:01.39
400 m Medley	Alexander Sidorenko (URS)	4:22:89	Sergey Fesenko (URS)	4:23.43	Zoltan Verraszto (HUN)	4:24.24
4x200 m Freestyle	USSR	7:23.50	GDR	7:28.60	Brazil	7:29.30
4x100 m Medley	Australia	3:45.70	USSR	3:45.92	Great Britain	3:47.71
Springboard Diving	Alexander Portnov (URS)	905.025	Carlos Giron (MEX)	892.140	Franco Cagnotto (ITA)	871.500
Highboard Diving	Falk Hoffmann (GDR)	835.650	Vladimir Heynik (URS)	819.705	David Ambartsumyan (URS)	817.440
Water Polo	USSR		Yugoslavia		Hungary	

SWIMMING — WOMEN

EVENT	GOLD		SILVER		BRONZE	
100 m Freestyle	Barbara Krause (GDR)	54.79	Caren Metschuk (GDR)	55.16	Ines Diers (GDR)	55.65
200 m Freestyle	Barbara Krause (GDR)	1:58.33	Ines Diers (GDR)	1:59.64	Carmela Schmitt (GDR)	2:01.44
400 m Freestyle	Ines Diers (GDR)	4:08.76	Petra Schneider (GDR)	4:09.16	Carmela Schmitt (GDR)	4:10.86
800 m Freestyle	Michelle Ford (AUS)	8:28.90	Ines Diers (GDR)	8:32.55	Heike Dähne (GDR)	8:33.48
100 m Backstroke	Rica Reinisch (GDR)	1:00.86	Ina Kleber (GDR)	1:02.07	Petra Riedel (GDR)	1:02.64
200 m Backstroke	Rica Reinisch (GDR)	2:11.77	Cornelia Polit (GDR)	2:13.75	Birgit Treiber (GDR)	2:14.14
100 m Breaststroke	Ute Geweniger (GDR)	1:10.22	Elvira Vasilkova (URS)	1:10.41	Susanne Schultz-Nielsson (DEN)	1:11.16
200 m Breaststroke	Lina Kachushite (URS)	2:29.54	Svetlana Varganova (URS)	2:29.61	Yulia Bogdanova (URS)	2:32.39
100 m Butterfly	Caren Metschuk (GDR)	1:00.42	Andrea Pollack (GDR)	1:00.90	Christiane Knacke (GDR)	1:01.44
200 m Butterfly	Ines Geissler (GDR)	2:10.44	Sybille Schönrock (GDR)	2:10.45	Michelle Ford (AUS)	2:11.66
400 m Medley	Petra Schneider (GDR)	4:36.29	Sharon Davies (GBR)	4:46.83	Agnieszka Czopek (POL)	4:48.17
4x100 m Freestyle	GDR	3:42.71	Sweden	3:48.93	Netherlands	3:49.51
4x100 Medley	GDR	4:06.67	Great Britain	4:12.24	USSR	4:13.61
Springboard Diving	Irina Kalinina (URS)	725.910	Martina Proeber (GDR)	698.895	Karin Guthke (GDR)	685.245
Highboard Diving	Maruna Jäschke (GDR)	595.250	Servard Emirzyan (URS)	576.466	Liana Tsotadze (URS)	575.925

BOXING

EVENT	GOLD	SILVER	BRONZE
Light-Flyweight (-105.75 lb)	Shamil Sabirov (URS)	Hipolito Ramos (CUB)	Ismail Mustafov (BUL) / Byong Uk Li (PRK)
Flyweight (-112.25 lb)	Petar Lessov (BUL)	Viktor Miroshnichenko (URS)	Janos Varadi (HUN) / Hugh Russell (IRL)
Bantamweight (-119 lb)	Juan Bautista Hernandez (CUB)	Bernardo José Pinango (VEN)	Michael Anthony (GUY) / Dimitru Cipere (ROM)
Featherweight (-126 lb)	Rudi Fink (GDR)	Adolfo Horta (CUB)	Krzysztof Kosedowski (POL) / Viktor Rybakov (URS)
Lightweight (-132 lb)	Angel Herrera (CUB)	Viktor Demianenko (URS)	Richard Nowakowski (GDR) / Kazimierz Adach (POL)
Light-Welterweight (-140 lb)	Patrizio Oliva (ITA)	Serik Konakbayev (URS)	Anthony Willis (GBR) / José Aguilar (CUB)
Welterweight (-148 lb)	Andres Aldania (CUB)	John Mugabi (UGA)	Karl-Heinz Krüger (GDR) / Kazimierz Szczerba (POL)
Light-Middleweight (-157 lb)	Armando Martinez (CUB)	Alexander Koshkin (URS)	Detlef Kästner (GDR) / Jan Franck (TCH)
Middleweight (-165 lb)	José Gomez (CUB)	Viktor Savchenko (URS)	Valentin Silaghi (ROM) / Jerzy Rybicki (POL)
Light-Heavyweight (-178.5 lb)	Slobodan Kacar (YUG)	Pawel Skrzecz (POL)	Herbert Bauch (GDR) / Ricardo Rojas (CUB)
Heavyweight (+178.5 lb)	Teofilo Stevenson (CUB)	Pjotr Zayev (URS)	Istvan Levai (HUN) / Jürgen Fanghänel (GDR)

FENCING

EVENT	GOLD		SILVER		BRONZE	
Individual Foil — Men	Vladimir Smirnov (URS)	4	Pascal Jolyot (FRA)	4	Alexander Romankov (URS)	5
Team Foil — Men	France		USSR		Poland	
Individual Épée	Johan Harmenberg (SWE)	4	Ernõ Kolczonay (HUN)	3	Philippe Riboud (FRA)	3
Team Épée	France		Poland		USSR	
Individual Sabre	Viktor Krovopouskov (URS)	4	Mikhail Burtsev (URS)	4	Imre Gedovari (HUN)	3
Team Sabre	USSR		Italy		Hungary	
Individual Foil — Women	Pascale Trinquet (FRA)	4	Magda Maros (HUN)	3	Barbara Wysoczanska (POL)	
Team Foil — Women	France		USSR		Hungary	

FREESTYLE WRESTLING

EVENT	GOLD	SILVER	BRONZE
Light-Flyweight (-105.75 lb)	Claudio Pollio (ITA)	Se Hong Jang (PRK)	Sergey Kornilayev (URS)
Flyweight (-114.5 lb)	Anatoliy Beloglazov (URS)	Wladyslaw Stecyk (POL)	Nermedin Selimov (BUL)
Bantamweight (-119 lb)	Sergey Beloglazov (URS)	Ho Pyong Li (PRK)	Dugarsuren Quinbold (MGL)
Featherweight (-136.5 lb)	Magomedgasan Abushev (URS)	Mikho Dukov (BUL)	Georges Hadjionnides (GRE)
Lightweight (-149.75 lb)	Saipulla Absaidov (URS)	Ivan Yankov (BUL)	Saban Sejdi (YUG)
Welterweight (-163 lb)	Valentin Raitschev (BUL)	Jamtsying Davaajav (MGL)	Dan Karabin (TCH)
Middleweight (-180.75 lb)	Ismail Abilov (BUL)	Mahomet Aratsilov (URS)	István Kovacs (HUN)
Light-Heavyweight (-198.25 lb)	Sanasar Oganesyan (URS)	Uwe Neupert (GDR)	Alexander Cichon (POL)
Heavyweight (-220.5 lb)	Ilya Mate (URS)	Slavtcho Tchervenkov (BUL)	Julius Strnisko (TCH)
Super-Heavyweight (+220.5 lb)	Soslan Andiev (URS)	Jószef Balla (HUN)	Adam Sandurski (POL)

GRECO-ROMAN WRESTLING

EVENT	GOLD	SILVER	BRONZE
Light-Flyweight (-105.75 lb)	Zaksylik Ushkempirov (URS)	Constantin Alexandru (ROM)	Ferenc Seres (HUN)
Flyweight (-114.5 lb)	Vakhtang Blagidze (URS)	Lajos Racz (HUN)	Mladen Mladenov (BUL)
Bantamweight (-125.75 lb)	Shamil Serikov (URS)	Jozef Lipien (POL)	Benni Ljungbeck (SWE)
Featherweight (-136.5 lb)	Stilianos Migiakis (GRE)	István Tóth (HUN)	Boris Kramorenko (URS)
Lightweight (-149.74 lb)	Stefan Rusu (ROM)	Andrzej Supron (POL)	Lars-Erik Skjöld (SWE)
Welterweight (-163 lb)	Ferenc Kocsis (HUN)	Anatoliy Bykov (URS)	Mikko Huhtala (FIN)
Middleweight (-180.75 lb)	Gennadiy Korban (URS)	Jan Polgowicz (POL)	Pavel Pavlov (BUL)
Light-Heavyweight (-198.25 lb)	Norbert Nottny (HUN)	Igor Kanygin (URS)	Petre Disu (ROM)
Heavyweight (-220.5 lb)	Gheorghi Raikov (BUL)	Roman Bierla (POL)	Vasile Andrei (ROM)
Super-Heavyweight (+220.5 lb)	Alexander Kolchinski (URS)	Alexander Tomov (BUL)	Hassan Bchara (LIB)

WEIGHTLIFTING

EVENT	GOLD		SILVER		BRONZE	
Flyweight	Kanybek Osmonaliev (URS)	540 lb	Ho Bong Chol (PRK)	540 lb	Han Gyong Si (PRK)	540 lb
Bantamweight	Daniel Nunez (CUB)	606.25 lb	Yurik Sarkisian (URS)	595 lb	Tadeusz Dembonczyk (POL)	584 lb
Featherweight	Viktor Mazin (URS)	639.25 lb	Stefan Dimitrov (BUL)	633.25 lb	Marek Seweryn (POL)	622.25 lb
Lightweight	Yanko Rusev (BUL)	755 lb	Joachim Kunz (GDR)	738 lb	Mintcho Pachov (BUL)	716 lb
Middleweight	Asen Zlatev (BUL)	793.5 lb	Alexander Pervy (URS)	788 lb	Nedeltcho Kolev (BUL)	760 lb
Light-Heavyweight	Yurik Vardanjan (URS)	881.75 lb	Blagoi Blagoyev (BUL)	821 lb	Dusan Poliacik (TCH)	810 lb
Middle-Heavyweight	Peter Baczako (HUN)	832 lb	Rumen Alexandrov (BUL)	826.5 lb	Frank Mantek (GDR)	815 lb
First Heavyweight	Ota Zaremba (CSR)	870.75 lb	Igor Nikitin (URS)	865.5 lb	Alberto Blanco (CUB)	848 lbs
Second Heavyweight	Leonid Taranenko (URS)	931.25 lb	Valentin Christov (BUL)	492.75 lb	György Szalai (HUN)	859.6 lb
Super-Heavyweight	Sultan Rakhmanov (URS)	970 lb	Jürgen Heuser (GDR)	903.75 lb	Tadeusz Rutkowski (POL)	898.25 lb

WEIGHTLIFTING WEIGHTS

FLYWEIGHT	-114.5 lb	BANTAMWEIGHT	-123.25 lb	FEATHERWEIGHT	-132.25 lb
LIGHTWEIGHT	-148.75 lb	MIDDLEWEIGHT	-165.5 lb	LIGHT-HEAVYWEIGHT	-182 lb
MIDDLE-HEAVYWEIGHT	-198.5 lb	FIRST-HEAVYWEIGHT	-220.5 lb	SECOND-HEAVYWEIGHT	-242.5 lb
SUPER-HEAVYWEIGHT	+242.5 lb				

MODERN PENTATHLON

EVENT	GOLD		SILVER		BRONZE	
Individual	Anatoliy Starostin (URS)	5568	Tamás Szombathelyi (HUN)	5502	Pavel Lednev (URS)	5282
Team	USSR	16126	Hungary	15912	Sweden	15845

JUDO

EVENT	GOLD	SILVER	BRONZE
Super-Lightweight (-132.5 lb)	Thierry Rey (FRA)	José Rodrigez (CUB)	Tibor Kincses (HUN) / Aramby Emizh (URS)
Welterweight (-143.25 lb)	Nikolai Solodukhin (URS)	Tsendying Damdin (MGL)	Ilian Nedkov (BUL) / Janusz Pawlowski (POL)
Lightweight (-156.5 lb)	Enzio Gamba (ITA)	Neil Adams (GBR)	Karl Heniz Lehmann (GDR) / Ravdan Davaadalai (MGL)
Light-Middleweight (-171.75 lb)	Shota Khabaleri (URS)	Juan Ferrer (CUB)	Bernard Tchoullouyan (FRA) / Harald Heinke (GDR)
Middleweight (-189.5 lb)	Jorg Rothlisberger (SUI)	Isaac Azcuy (CUB)	Dedev Ultsch (GDR) / Alexander Yatskevich (URS)
Light-Heavyweight (-209.25 lb)	Robert van de Walle (BEL)	Tengiz Khubuluri (URS)	Dietmar Lorenz (GDR) / Henk Numann (HOL)
Heavyweight (+209.25 lb)	Angelo Parisi (FRA)	Dimitar Zaprianov (BUL)	Vladimir Kocman (TCH) / Radomir Kovacevic (YUG)
Open Class	Dietmar Lorenz (GDR)	Angelo Parisi (FRA)	Andras Ozsvar (HUN) / Arthur Mapp (GBR)

ROWING — WOMEN

EVENT	GOLD		SILVER		BRONZE	
Single Sculls	Sanda Toma (ROM)	3:40:69	Antonina Makhina (URS)	3:41.65	Marena Schröter (GDR)	3:43.54
Double Sculls	USSR	3:16.27	GDR	3:17.63	Romania	3:18.91
Coxless Pairs	GDR	3:30.49	Poland	3:30.95	Bulgaria	3:32.39
Coxless Quadruple Sculls	GDR	3:15.32	USSR	3:15.73	Bulgaria	3:16.10
Coxed Fours	GDR	3:16.27	Bulgaria	3:20.75	USSR	3:20.92
Coxed Eights	GDR	3:03.32	USSR	3:04.29	Romania	3:05.63

ROWING — MEN

EVENT	GOLD		SILVER		BRONZE	
Single Sculls	Pertti Karppinen (FIN)	7:09.61	Vasiliy Yakusha (URS)	7:11.66	Peter Kersten (GDR)	7:14.88
Doubles Sculls	GDR	6:24.33	Yugoslavia	6:26.34	Czechoslovakia	6:29.07
Coxless Pairs	GDR	6:48.01	USSR	6:50.50	Great Britain	6:51.47
Coxed Pairs	GDR	7:02.54	USSR	7:03.35	Yugoslavia	7:04.92
Coxless Quadruple Sculls	GDR	5:49.81	USSR	5:51.47	Bulgaria	5:52.38
Coxless Fours	GDR	6:08.17	USSR	6:11.81	Great Britain	6:16.58
CoxedFours	GDR	6:14.51	USSR	6:19.05	Poland	6:22.52
Coxed Eights	GDR	5:49.05	Great Britain	5:51.92	USSR	5:52.66

CANOEING — WOMEN

EVENT	GOLD		SILVER		BRONZE	
500 m Kayak Singles K1	Birgit Fischer (GDR)	1:57.96	Vanya Ghecheva (BUL)	1:59.48	Antonina Melnikova (URS)	1:59.66
500 m Kayak Pairs K2	GDR	1:43.88	USSR	1:46.91	Hungary	1:47.95

CANOEING — MEN

EVENT	GOLD		SILVER		BRONZE	
500 m Kayak Singles K1	Vladimir Parfenovich (URS)	1:43.43	John Sumegi (AUS)	1:44.12	Vasile Diba (ROM)	1:44.90
1,000 m Kayak Singles K1	Rüdiger Helm (GDR)	3:48.77	Alain Lebas (FRA)	3:50.20	Ion Birladeanu (ROM)	3:50.49
500 m Kayak Pairs K2	USSR	1:32.38	Spain	1:33.65	GDR	1:34.00
1,000 m Kayak Pairs K2	USSR	3:26.72	Hungary	3:28.49	Spain	3:28.66
1,000 m Kayak Fours K4	GDR	3:13.76	Romania	3:15.35	Bulgaria	3:15.46
500 m Canadian Singles C1	Sergey Postrekhin (URS)	1:53.37	Lubomir Lubenov (BUL)	1:53.49	Olaf Heukrodt (GDR)	1:54.38
1,000 m Canadian Singles C1	Lubomir Lubenov (BUL)	4:12.38	Sergey Postrekhin (URS)	4:13.53	Eckhard Leue (GDR)	4:15.02
500 m Canadian Pairs C2	Hungary	1:43.39	Romania	1:44.12	Bulgaria	1:44.83
1,000 m Canadian Pairs C2	Romania	3:47.65	GDR	3:49.93	USSR	3:51.28

YACHTING

EVENT	GOLD		SILVER		BRONZE	
Finn-Class	Esko Rechardt (FIN)	36.7	Wolgang Mayrhofer (AUT)	46.7	Andrei Balaschov (URS)	47.4
International Star	USSR	24.7	Austria	31.7	Italy	36.1
Flying Dutchman	Spain	19.0	Ireland	30.0	Hungary	45.7
International Tornado	Brazil	21.4	Denmark	30.4	Sweden	33.7
International 470	Brazil	36.4	GDR	38.7	Finland	39.7
International Soling	Denmark	23.0	USSR	30.4	Greece	31.4

CYCLING

EVENT	GOLD		SILVER		BRONZE	
Individual Road Race (117.5 m)	Sergey Sukoruchenkov (URS)	4:48:28	Czeslaw Lang (POL)	4:51:26	Yuriy Barinov (URS)	4:51:26
100 km Road Team Time Trial	USSR	2:01:21.7	GDR	2:02:53.2	Czechoslovakia	2:02:53.9
1,000 m Time Trial	Lothar Thoms (GDR)	1:02.955	Alexander Pantilov (URS)	1:04.845	David Weller (JAM)	1:05.241
1,000 m Sprint	Lutz Hesslich (GDR)		Yave Cahard (FRA)		Sergey Kopylov (URS)	
4,000 m Individual Pursuit	Robert Dill-Bundi (SUI)	4:35.66	Alain Bondue (FRA)	4:42.96	Hans-Henrik Oersted (DEN)	4:36.54
4,000 m Team Pursuit	USSR	4:15.70	GDR	4:19.67	Czechoslovakia	n/a

EQUESTRIANISM

EVENT	GOLD		SILVER		BRONZE	
Three-Day Event	Federico Roman (ITA)	-108.60	Alexander Blinov (URS)	-120.80	Yuriy Salnikov (URS)	-151.60
Three-Day Event Team	USSR	-457.00	Italy	-656.20	Mexico	-1172.85
Grand Prix (Dressage)	Elisabeth Theurer(AUT)	1370	Yuriy Kovshov (URS)	1300	Viktor Ugrjumov (URS)	1234
Grand Prix (Dressage) Team	USSR	4383.0	Bulgaria	3580.0	Romania	3346.0
Grand Prix (Jumping)	Jan Kowalczyk (POL)	-8	Nikolai Korolkov (URS)	-9 50	Joaquin Perez de las Heras (MEX)	-12
Grand Prix (Jumping) Team	USSR	-16.00	Poland	-32.00	Mexico	-39.25

SHOOTING

EVENT	GOLD		SILVER		BRONZE	
Small-Bore Rifle (Prone)	Karoly Varga (HUN)	599	Hellfried Heilfort (GDR)	599	Petar Zapianov (BUL)	598
Small-Bore Rifle (3 Positions)	Viktor Vlassow (URS)	1173	Bernd Hartstein (GDR)	1166	Sven Johansson (SWE)	1165
Rapid-Fire Pistol	Corneliu Ion (ROM)	596	Jürgen Wiefel (GDR)	596	Gerhard Petrisch (AUT)	596
Free Pistol (50 m)	Alexander Melentyev (URS)	581	Harald Vollmar (GDR)	568	Lubcho Diakov (BUL)	565
Running Game Target	Igor Sokolow (URS)	589	Thomas Pfeffer (GDR)	589	Alexander Gasov (URS)	587
Skeet Shooting	Hans Kjeld Rasmussen (DEN)	196	Lars-Göran Carlsson (SWE)	196	Roberto Castrillo (CUB)	196
Trap Shooting	Luciano Giovanetti (ITA)	198	Rustam Yambulatov (URS)	196	Jörg Damme (GDR)	196

ARCHERY — WOMEN

	GOLD		SILVER		BRONZE	
	Keto Losaberidse (URS)	2491	Natalya Butuzova (URS)	2477	Paivi Merilouto (FIN)	2449

ARCHERY — MEN

	GOLD		SILVER		BRONZE	
	Tomi Poikalainen (FIN)	2455	Boris Isachenko (URS)	2452	Alexander Gazov (URS)	2449

GYMNASTICS — MEN

EVENT	GOLD		SILVER		BRONZE	
Individual Combined Exercises	Alexander Ditiatin (URS)	118.650	Nikolai Andrianov (URS)	118.225	Stoyan Deltschev (BUL)	118.000
Team	USSR	589.60	GDR	581.15	Hungary	575.00
Parallel Bars	Alexander Tkatschov (URS)	19.775	Alexander Ditiatin (URS)	19.750	Roland Brückner (GDR)	19.650
Floor	Roland Brückner (GDR)	19.750	Nikolai Andrianov (URS)	19.725	Alexander Ditiatin (URS)	19.700
Horse Vault	Nikolai Andrianow (URS)	19.825	Alexander Ditiatin (URS)	19.800	Roland Brückner (GDR)	19.775
Horizontal Bar	Stojan Deltschev (BUL)	19.825	Alexander Ditiatin (URS)	19.750	Nikolai Andrianov (URS)	19.675
Rings	Alexander Ditiatin (URS)	19.875	Alexander Tkachov (URS)	19.725	Jiri Tabák (TCH)	19.600
Pommel Horse	Zoltan Magyar (HUN)	19.925	Alexander Ditiatin (URS)	19.800	Michael Nikolay (GDR)	19.775

GYMNASTICS — WOMEN

EVENT	GOLD		SILVER		BRONZE	
Individual Combined Exercises	Yelena Davydova (URS)	79.150	Nadia Comaneci (ROM)	79.075		
			Maxi Gnauck (GDR)	79.075		
Team	USSR	394.90	Romania	393.50	GDR	392.55
Floor	Nadia Comaneci (ROM)	19.875			Maxi Gnauck (GDR)	19.825
	Nelli Kim (URS)	19.875			Natalya Shaposhnikova (URS)	19.825
Horse Vault	Natalya Shaposhnikova (URS)	19.725	Steffi Kräker (GDR)	19.675	Melita Ruhn (ROM)	19.650
Beam	Nadia Comaneci (ROM)	19.800	Yelena Davydova (URS)	19.750	Natalya Shaposhnikova (URS)	19.725
Asymmetrical Bars	Maxi Gnauck (GDR)	19.875	Emilia Eberle (ROM)	19.850	Maria Filatova (URS)	19.775
					Steffi Kräker (GDR)	19.775
					Melita Ruhn (ROM)	19.775

BASKETBALL — MEN

	GOLD		SILVER		BRONZE	
	Yugoslavia		Italy		USSR	

BASKETBALL — WOMEN

GOLD	SILVER	BRONZE
USSR	Bulgaria	Yugoslavia

SOCCER

GOLD	SILVER	BRONZE
Czechoslovakia	GDR	USSR

HANDBALL — MEN

GOLD	SILVER	BRONZE
GDR	USSR	Romania

HANDBALL — WOMEN

GOLD	SILVER	BRONZE
USSR	Yugoslavia	GDR

HOCKEY— MEN

GOLD	SILVER	BRONZE
India	Spain	USSR

HOCKEY— WOMEN

GOLD	SILVER	BRONZE
Zimbabwe	Czechoslovakia	USSR

VOLLEYBALL — MEN

GOLD	SILVER	BRONZE
USSR	Bulgaria	Romania

VOLLEYBALL — WOMEN

GOLD	SILVER	BRONZE
USSR	GDR	Bulgaria

LOS ANGELES 1984

INTRODUCTION

ABOVE: *The official commorative pin for the Los Angeles Olympics.* Allsport

PREVIOUS PAGE: *Gold medal winning diver, Greg Louganis of the USA.* Tony Duffy

221
EVENTS

140
COUNTRIES

6,797
ATHLETES

Los Angeles 1984

	Gold	Silver	Bronze
USA	83	61	30
ROM	20	16	17
FRG	17	19	23
CHN	15	8	9
ITA	14	6	12
CAN	10	18	16
JPN	10	8	14
NZE	8	1	2
YUG	7	4	7
KOR	6	6	7
GBR	5	10	22
FRA	5	7	16
NED	5	2	6
AUS	4	8	12
FIN	4	2	6
SWE	2	11	6
MEX	2	3	1
MOR	2		
BRA	1	5	2
ESP	1	2	2
BEL	1	1	2
AUT	1	1	1
KEN	1		2
POR	1		2
PAK	1		
SUI		4	4
DEN		3	3
JAM		1	2
NOR		1	2
GRE		1	1
NGR		1	1
PUR		1	1
COL		1	
EGY		1	
IRL		1	
IVC		1	
PER		1	
SYR		1	
THA		1	
TUR			3
VEN			3
ALG			2
CAM			1
DOM			1
ICE			1
TAI		1	
ZAM		1	

The Soviet Union retaliated for the mass boycott of the 1980 Moscow Olympics by staying away from the 1984 games in Los Angeles. The Russians managed to keep most of their Eastern Bloc satelites away, too, the most notable exception being Romania.

The decision to miss the games was announced on the same day that the Olympic flame arrived on American soil, with the Soviets claiming that they would not be traveling because they did not believe the US could guarantee their team's safety.

However, this was not the disaster it had been four years earlier, as a combination of great performances and unbounded patriotism helped turn the Los Angeles Olympics into what many deemed to be the most successful event in the history of the games.

One of the largest TV audiences in history, approximately 2,500 million, tuned in for the games. Television rights alone amounted to $287 million and private sponsorship helped swell the profit to an amazing $230 million. It showed the International Olympic Committee how to make millions on its own and convinced the world that maybe the games was worth saving.

Organisers pulled out all the stops to produce a stunning spectacle. The Memorial Coliseum, site for the 1932 games, was fully refurbished and had a capacity of 92,607.

The final runner on the torch relay was Gina Hemphill, a great granddaughter of the great Jesse Owens. She handed over the torch to Rafer

RIGHT: Two commemorative pins. Allsport

Johnson, the 1960 Olympic decathlon champion, who lit the flame on top of the stadium peristyle by means of a 96-step hydraulic slip-stair.

There then followed a three-hour Hollywood-style extravaganza opening ceremony which set the tone for the rest of the games.

Attendances were remarkable and, by the end of the games, had topped 5.7 million. The biggest attendance was for the final of the football where a crowd of 101,799 gathered at the Pasadena Bowl to watch France beat Brazil.

The games also produced some of the greatest athletic prowess in history, topped by the four gold-medal performance of Carl Lewis. Matching the Owens feat of 48 years earlier, Lewis won the 100 and 200 meters, the long jump and anchored the 4x100 meters relay to victory.

Seb Coe and Daley Thompson, two of Britain's great champions from Moscow, returned to retain their titles in the 1,500 meters and decathlon respectively. It represented quite a turnaround in fortunes for Coe, who at the start of the year had been so stricken with illness he had been reduced to training with young teenagers at his club in London.

301

The most controversial moment of the games came in the women's 3,000 meters where the American favourite Mary Decker was tripped by Zola Budd, an 18-year-old South African circumventing the ban on her country's athletes by competing under the British flag.

Los Angeles produced an American gymnast to take on all the Olgas and Nadias who had previously held sway. She was Mary Lou Retton, who became the first US woman to win the all-around gymnastics gold.

The absence of the Eastern Bloc allowed the host nation to claim the lion's share of the medals. They won 83 golds compared to Romania, the next best with 20.

Unfortunately, it was not all glory, glory. A record 12 competitors were disqualified after testing positive for performance-enhancing drugs, including Finland's 10,000 meters silver medalist Martti Vainio. Several years later it also emerged that many other positive tests had been quietly covered up.

ABOVE:
A commemorative medal.
Allsport

BELLOW:
Another commemorative Pin from the Los Angeles games. Allsport

RIGHT: *Rafer Johnson lighting the Olympic flame.*
Steve Powell

BELOW: *The Olympic Torch.* Allsport

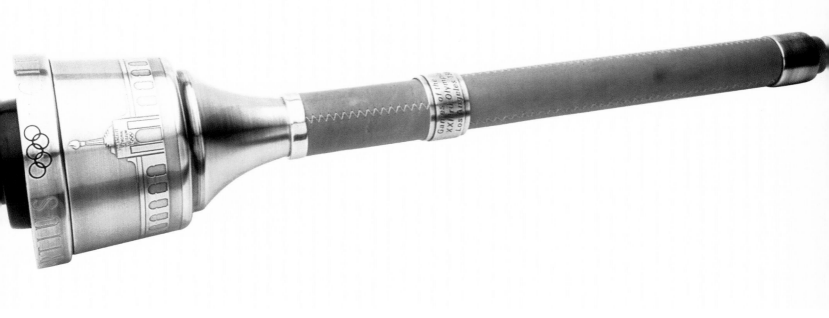

CARL LEWIS

ABOVE: The greatest athlete in history — Carl Lewis of the USA. Tony Duffy

BELOW: Already celebrating gold for his participation as the anchor leg in the USA 100 m relay team. Steve Powell

FAR RIGHT: Carl Lewis on the run-up before leaping to take first place in the Long jump. David Cannon

Carl Lewis is arguably the greatest athlete in history. At his peak, accelerating into apparent overdrive at 60 meters, there was no finer sight in athletics than Lewis winning a 100 meters. Tall and long legged, Lewis epitomized grace and style at speed.

In a career stretching back to 1981, he won nine Olympic golds, eight World Championship golds, set two world records, ran the greatest number of sub-10 second 100 meters and consistently long jumped beyond 28 feet.

In front of his own crowd at the 1984 Los Angeles games he emulated the achievement of the great Jesse Owens' — winning four gold medals in the 100 and 200 meters, the long jump, and the 4x100 meters relay.

In 1988, he retained his 100 meters and long jump titles and four years later again won the long jump crown and anchored the US 4x100 meters team to victory. He bowed out in Atlanta in 1996 when, at the age of 35, he won a record fourth consecutive long jump gold.

It tied him in gold medals with Paavo Nurmi, the legendary Finnish distance runner, who won gold nine times between 1920 and 1928.

It also put him in the rarefied company of American discus thrower Al Oerter, the first track and field performer to win four consecutive golds in one event.

But, medals notwithstanding, he has never really been the sport's golden boy. At the Los Angeles games, Lewis was booed for passing on his final four jumps to conserve his energy and for not challenging Bob Beamon's then world record of 8.90 meters.

He showed up late for press conferences, complained about ill-paid amateur athletes not being allowed to be capitalists too, flaunted flamboyant clothing and hairstyles, and gave the impression of being full of himself.

Instant fame, he says now, was "a tough adjustment for someone 21 years old. I did good things and bad things, but I learned through all of it."

Lewis grew up in an athletic family. His mother was a top hurdler and his sister, Carol, was the nation's best high school long jumper and a future world champion. Though small for his age, his talent was evident even before he reached his teens.

He won a long jump competition at age 12 that was attended by Owens, who pointed the puny Lewis out to other children. "I was starry eyed and crazy," Lewis remembered. "For someone like Jesse Owens to pick me out and make me an example was amazing."

By his senior year of high school in Willingboro, New Jersey, Lewis was ranked fifth in the world in the long jump. He was recruited by Houston coach Tom Tellez, who remained his mentor till the end of his career, as a long jumper.

He was still 18 when he placed second in the long jump at the US trials and qualified for the 1980 Olympics, but could not go to Moscow because of the American boycott. Lewis won his first national title in the 100 meters in 1981. He went on to win six more national titles in the 100, as well as two World Championships.

Lewis, a vegetarian since 1989, was meticulous in maintaining his body, sculpting it into a finely muscled shape carrying only three percent body fat.

Remarkably, Lewis' impact has been even greater off the track than on it. He helped professionalize the sport, and by extension the Olympics, with his demands and huge racing contracts. He remains one of Nike's top spokesmen. He also pushed for the sport's leaders in the United States to modernize their marketing methods to promote track on a par with American football and basketball.

"He was concerned about where track and field should go. He always had a lot more vision down the line of where the sport should be," Tellez said. "The older generation didn't understand Carl."

Lewis said simply: "I was a big liberal in a conservative sport."

Perhaps he was just too good and too fast. Fans were awed by his talent instead of inspired by his achievements.

JOAN BENOIT

Joan Benoit of the USA wins the women's marathon. Tony Duffy

Joan Benoit's victory in the inaugural women's marathon at the 1984 games in Los Angeles ranks among the best performances of all time.

The American's win in 2hr 24min 52sec was the result of the most audacious tactics which left her out in front, on her own, after just three miles. Despite the presence in the field of world champion Grete Waitz, Benoit made her break, opened a huge lead and hung onto it all the way to the finish inside the LA Coliseum. The fact that she made the start line at all was astonishing. Only 17 days before the compulsory US trial race she was forced to undergo arthroscopic surgery on her right knee but she recovered sufficiently to win the trial in 2hr 31min 4sec.

Like many top class road runners, she took up running in her teens as a means of keeping fit for another sport. In her case, it was skiing, but that was soon abandoned when her love of running took over.

She ran her first marathon in Bermuda in 1979, to satisfy her curiosity about the distance, and finished second in 2hr 50min 54sec. She went on to set two world bests at the marathon and was the first woman to run inside 2hr 25min when she won the 1983 Boston Marathon. She married Scott Samuelson in 1984 and now spends much of her time with her husband and their two children at their home in Maine, but still races several times a year.

DALEY THOMPSON

Recently voted Britain's greatest ever sportsman, Daley Thompson never failed to capture the public's imagination during the years he reigned supreme in the decathlon. A showman by nature, Thompson's antics often masked his fierce determination to be the best.

Between 1978 and 1986 he was unbeatable. He held Olympic, World, European, and Commonwealth titles. At Montreal in 1976, when he was 18, Thompson observed Bruce Jenner's triumph from the shade of 18th place and had an outlandish notion. Even before his 1980 victory in Moscow, he confided it to the 1948 and 1952 Olympic champion Bob Mathias. "I got a postcard from Russia," Mathias recalls. "All it said was 'I'm going for three'."

After victories at the 1982 European and Commonwealth Games and winning the first ever World Championship title in 1983, Thompson met the world record holder, Jurgen Hingsen, head on at the Los Angeles Olympics in 1984. Thompson won and equaled the German's world record. In LA, Thompson was a wonderful character. If you asked how he was, he probably replied: "A little short of fantastic." During his career, Thompson often heard the description "world's greatest athlete" — in fact, he has been called the greatest of all time — but has never seriously proclaimed the title. "It's merely a tag," he says.

He does, however, feel kinship with Jim Thorpe, the 1912 Olympic decathlon champion. "We're all his descendants — Mathias, Rafer Johnson, Jenner, me.

We've all shared something. It's passed down from one to the next." His full name is Francis Morgan Thompson. "Daley" is a corruption of "Ayodele," an African endearment bestowed by his Nigerian father and mispronounced by his Scottish mother. It means "joy enters the house." He always expected to be famous. "Since forever, I always thought I was going to be the best in the world at something. My school friends used to laugh at me, but I kept searching for the thing that would express who I am. As soon as I found the decathlon, I knew it was me."

"In any walk of life, there'll always be a bloke more talented in this or that, who's smarter in some way, or richer, or faster, or just better suited. But can the thing that he was given be lined up against everything you've got?"

At 6 foot and half an inch and 195 pounds, he was much too thick and chunky for track, though not nearly brawny or flexible enough for the field, Thompson was ideally constructed for none of the ten events. "Would have I changed anything at all? Sure, I would. I'd have liked Paul Newman's eyes," he jokes.

There were more European and Commonwealth titles after Los Angeles but the run came to an end at the 1987 World Championships in Rome and a year later, Thompson could only finish fourth at the Seoul Olympics. Today, happily married with a family, he finds an outlet for his talent as the fitness coach for the English Premiership soccer club Wimbledon and turning out for their reserve side as a center back.

MARY LOU RETTON

Both Olga Korbut and Nadia Comaneci commanded an army of fans in the United States, a country desperate to produce its own gymnastics star. Its wish was granted when the Soviet Bloc boycotted the Los Angeles Olympics in 1984.

As a bubbly 16-year-old, Mary Lou Retton thrilled fans with stunning flips and a perfect 10 vault, performed not once but twice with equal precision. She remains the only American to win the Olympic All Around title and was the first US woman to earn a gold medal in gymnastics.

Born in the coal mining town of Fairmont, West Virginia, Retton was one of five children. Her father fixed transportation cables for the miners, and money was always scarce.

But her parents stressed a strong work ethic to Mary. "We were taught that you can't wait around your whole life for people to give you things," Retton recalls. "You have to make them happen. And you make them happen through hard work."

She left home at 14 to train with a top coach in Houston, having begun gymnastics at age seven.

After retiring in 1986, Retton married former University of Texas quarterback Shannon Kelley and has two children. She now writes a daily newspaper column and works as a TV commentator. Her newest project is hosting a TV show for young children, *Mary Lou's Flip Flop Shop*.

The outstanding gymnast, Mary-Lou Retton, captured the hearts of America. Steve Powell

307

TOP: *The Japanese gymnast Koji Gushiken.* Steve Powell

ABOVE: *The three outstanding British middle distance runners — Steve Ovett, Steve Cram and Sebastian Coe in the 1,500 m final. Coe won gold, and Cram silver.* Steve Powell

ABOVE: *Greg Louganis of the USA won gold in both the springboard diving and the highboard diving events.* Alvin Chung

ABOVE LEFT: *Edwin Moses — USA 400 m hurdles champion and long-standing record holder.* David Cannon

ABOVE RIGHT: *Marti Vainio and Alberto Cova in the 10,000 m final. The Italian Cova was the winner in a time of 27min 47.54sec.* Steve Powell

LOS ANGELES JULY 28 - AUGUST 12

PARTICIPANTS: 6,797

MEN: 5,230

WOMEN: 1,567

COUNTRIES: 40

SPORTS: 21

EVENTS: 221

FINAL TORCHBEARER: RAFER JOHNSON

MEDALS TABLE

PLACE	COUNTRY	GOLD	SILVER	BRONZE
1	USA	83	61	30
2	Romania	20	16	17
3	FRG	17	19	23
4	China	15	8	9
5	Italy	14	6	12

OUTSTANDING ATHLETES

PLACE	NAME (NATIONALITY)	DISCIPLINE	GOLD	SILVER	BRONZE
1	Jecaterina Szabó (ROM)	Gymnastics	4	1	
2	Carl Lewis (USA)	Athletics	4		
3	Li Ning (CHN)	Gymnastics	3	2	1
4	Valerie Brisco-Hooks (USA)	Athletics	3		
	Richard Carey (USA)	Swimming	3		
	Ian Ferguson (NZL)	Canoeing	3		

ATHLETICS — MEN

EVENT	GOLD		SILVER		BRONZE	
100 m	Carl Lewis (USA)	9.99	Sam Graddy (USA)	10.19	Ben Johnson (CAN)	10.22
200 m	Carl Lewis (USA)	19.80	Kirk Baptiste (USA)	19.96	Thomas Jefferson (USA)	20.26
400 m	Alonzo Babers (USA)	44.27	Gabriel Tiacoh (CIV)	44.54	Antonio McKay (USA)	44.71
800 m	Joaquim Cruz (BRA)	1:43.00	Sebastian Coe (GBR)	1:43.64	Earl Jones (USA)	1:43.83
1,500 m	Sebastian Coe (GBR)	3:32.53	Steve Cram (GBR)	3:33.40	José Abascal (ESP)	3:34.30
5,000 m	Said Aouita (MAR)	13:05.59	Markus Ryffel (SUI)	13:07.54	Antoaio Leitao (POR)	13:09.20
10,000 m	Alberto Cova (ITA)	27:47.54	Michael McLeod (GBR)*	28:06.22	Mike Musyoki (KEN)	28:06.46
Marathon	Carlos Lopes (POR)	2:09:21	John Treacy (IRL)	2:09:56	Charles Spedding (GBR)	2:09:58
110 m Hurdles	Roger Kingdom (USA)	13.20	Greg Foster (USA)	13.23	Arto Bryggare (FIN)	13.40
400 m Hurdies	Edwin Moses (USA)	47.75	Danny Harris (USA)	48.13	Harald Schmid (FRG)	48.19
3,000 m Steeplechase	Julius Korir (KEN)	8:11.80	Joseph Mahmoud (FRA)	8:13.31	Brian Diemer (USA)	8:14.06
4x100 m	USA	37.83	Jamaica	38.62	Canada	38.70
4x400 m	USA	2:57.91	Great Britain	2:59.13	Nigeria	2:59.32
20 km Walk	Ernesto Canto (MEX)	1:23:13	Raul Gonzalez (MEX)	1:23:20	Maurizio Damilano (ITA)	1:23:26
50 km Walk	Raul Gonzalez (MEX)	3:37:26	Bo Gustafsson (SWE)	3:53:19	Sandro Bellucci (ITA)	3:53:45
Long Jump	Carl Lewis (USA)	28'0.25	Gary Honey (AUS)	27'0.5	Giovanni Evangelisti (ITA)	27'0.5"
High Jump	Dietmar Mögenburg (FRG)	7'81.5"	Patrik Sjöberg (SWE)	7'7.75"	Jianhua Zhu (CHN)	7'7"
Pole Vault	Pierre Quinon (FRA)	18'0.25"	Mike Tully (USA)	18'6.5"	Earl Bell (USA)	18'4.5"
Triple Jump	Al Joyner (USA)	56'7.5"	Mike Conley (USA)	56'4.5"	Keith Connor (GBR)	55'4.5"
Shot	Alessandro Andrei (ITA)	69'9"	Michael Carter (USA)	69'2.5"	Dave Laut (USA)	68'9.75"
Discus	Rolf Danneberg (FRG)	218'6"	Mac Wilkins (USA)	217'6"	John Powell (USA)	214'9"
Hammer	Juha Tiainen (FIN)	256'2"	Karl-Hans Riehm (FRG)	255'10"	Klaus Ploghaus (FRG)	251'7"
Javelin	Aro Härkönen (FIN)	284'8"	David Ottley (GBR)	281'3"	Kenth Eldebrink (SWE)	274'8"
Decathlon	Daley Thompson (GBR)	8798	Jürgen Hingsen (FRG)	8673	Siegfried Wentz (FRG)	8412

*Martti Väiniö (FIN) disqualified from 2nd position after failing a drugs test

ATHLETICS — WOMEN

EVENT	GOLD		SILVER		BRONZE	
100m	Evelyn Ashford (USA)	10.97	Alice Brown (USA)	11.13	Merlene Ottey (JAM)	11.16
200 m	Valerie Brisco-Hooks (USA)	21.81	Florence Griffth (USA)	22.04	Merlene Ottey (JAM)	22.09
400 m	Valerie Brisco-Hooks (USA)	48.83	Chandra Cheeseborough (USA)	49.05	Kathryn Cook (GBR)	49.42
800 m	Doina Melinte (ROM)	1:57.60	Kim Gallagher (USA)	1:58.63	Fita Lovin (ROM)	1:58.83
1,500 m	Gabriella Dorio (ITA)	4:03.25	Doina Melinte (ROM)	4:03.76	Maricica Puica (ROM)	4:04.15
3,000 m	Maricica Puica (ROM)	8:35.96	Wendy Sly (GBR)	8:39.47	Lynn Williams (CAN)	8:42.14
Marathon	Joan Benoit (USA)	2:24:52	Grete Waitz (NOR)	2:26:18	Rosa Mota (POR)	2:26:57
100 m Hurdles	Benita Fitzgerald-Brown (USA)	12.84	Shirley Strong (GBR)	12.88	Kim Turner (USA)	13.06
					Michele Chardonnet (FRA)	13.06
400 m Hurdles	Nawal El Moutawakel (MAR)	54.61	Judi Brown (USA)	55.20	Cristina Cojocaru (ROM)	55.41
4x100 m	USA	41.65	Canada	42.77	Great Britain	43.11
4x400m	USA	3:18.29	Canada	3:21.21	FRG	3:22.98
High Jump	Ulrike Meyfarth (FRG)	6' 7 25"	Sara Simeoni (ITA)	6'6.75"	Joni Huntley (USA)	6'5.5"
Long Jump	Anis Stanciu-Cusmir (ROM)	22'10"	Vali Ionescu (ROM)	22'4.25"	Susan Hearnshaw (GBR)	22'3.75"
Shot	Claudia Losch (FRG)	67'2.25"	Mihaela Loghin (ROM)	67'2"	Gael Martin (AUS)	62'11.5"
Discus	Ria Stalman (HOL)	214'5"	Leslie Deniz (USA)	212'9"	Florenta Craciunescu (ROM)	208'9"
Javelin	Tessa Sanderson (GBR)	228'2"	Tiina Lillak (FIN)	226'4"	Fatima Whitbread (GBR)	220'5"
Heptathlon	Glynis Nunn (AUS)	6390	Jackie Joyner (USA)	6385	Sabine Everts (FRG)	6363

BOXING

EVENT	GOLD	SILVER	BRONZE
Light-Flyweight (-105.75 lb)	Paul Gonzales (USA)	Salvatore Todisco (ITA)	Keith Mwila (ZAM) José Marcelino Bolivar (VEN)
Flyweight (-112.5 lb)	Steven McCrory (USA)	Redzep Redzepovski (YUG)	Eyup Can (TUR) Ibrahim Bilali (KEN)
Bantamweight (-119 lb)	Maurizio Stecca (ITA)	Hector Lopez (MEX)	Dale Walters (CAN) Pedro Nolasco (DOM)
Featherweight (-126 lb)	Meldrick Taylor (USA)	Peter Konyegwachie (NGR)	Omar Catari Peraza (VEN) Turgut Aykac (TUR)
Lightweight (-132 lb)	Pernell Whitaker (USA)	Luis Ortiz (PUR)	Martin Ndongo Ebanga (CMR) Chi-Sung Cun (KOR)
Light-Welterweight (-140 lb)	Jerry Page (USA)	Dhawee Umponmaha (THA)	Mirko Puzovic (YUG) Mircea Fulger (ROM)
Welterweight (-148 lb)	Mark Breland (USA)	Young-Su An (KOR)	Joni Nyman (FIN) Luciano Bruno (ITA)
Light-Middlewright (-157 lb)	Frank Tate (USA)	Shawn O'Sullivan (CAN)	Manfred Zielonka (FRG) Christophe Tiozzo (FRA)
Middleweight (-165 lb)	Joon-Sup Ship (KOR)	Virgil Hill (USA)	Mohammed Zaoui (ALG) Aristides Gonzales (PUR)
Light-Heavyweight (-178.5 lb)	Anton Josipovi´c (YUG)	Kevin Barry (NZL)	Mustapha Moussa (ALG) Evander Holyfield (USA)
Heavyweight (-200.5 lb)	Henry Tillman (USA)	Willie Dewit (CAN)	Angelo Musone (ITA) Arnold Vanderlijde (HOL)
Super-Heavyweight (+200.5 lb)	Tyrell Biggs (USA)	Francesco Damiani (ITA)	Robert Wells (GBR) Azis Salihu (YUG)

JUDO

EVENT	GOLD	SILVER	BRONZE
Super-Lighrweight (-132.5 lb)	Shinji Hosokawa (JPN)	Jae-Jup Kim (KOR)	Edward Liddle (USA) Neil Eckersley (GBR)
Welterweight (-143.25 lb)	Yoshiyuki Matsuoka (JPN)	Jung-Oh Hwang (KOR)	Josef Reiter (AUT) Marc Alexandre (FRA)
Lightweight (-156.5 lb)	Ahn-Beyong Keun (KOR)	Ezio Gamba (ITA)	Luis Onmura (BRA) Kerrith Brown (GBR)
Light-Middleweight (-171.75 lb)	Frank Wieneke (FRG)	Neil Adams (GBR)	Mircea Fratica (ROM) Michel Nowak (FRA)
Middleweight (-189.5 lb)	Peter Seisenbacher (AUT)	Robert Berland (USA)	Walter Carmona (BRA) Seiki Nose (JPN)
Light-Heavyweight (-209.25 lb)	Hyoung Zoo Ha (KOR)	Douglas Vieira (BRA)	Günther Neureuther (FRG) Bjarni Fridriksson (ISL)
Heavyweight (+209.25 lb)	Hitoshi Saito (JPN)	Angelo Parisi (FRA)	Mark Berger (CAN) Yong-Chul Cho (KOR)
Open Class	Yasuhiro Yamashita (JPN)	Mohamed Rashwan (EGY)	Arthur Schnabel (FRG) Mihai Cioc (ROM)

SYNCHRONIZED SWIMMING

	GOLD		SILVER		BRONZE	
Solo	Tracie Ruiz (USA)	198.467	Carolyn Waldo (CAN)	195.300	Miwako Motoyoshi (JPN)	187.050
Duet	USA	99.00	Canada	98.20	Japan	97.00

SWIMMING — WOMEN

EVENT	GOLD		SILVER		BRONZE	
100 m Freestyle	Carrie Steinseifer (USA)	55.92			Annemarie Verstappen (HOL)	56.08
	Nancy Hogshead (USA)	55.92				
200 m Freestyle	Mary Wayte (USA)	1:59.23	Cynthia Woodhead (USA)	1:59.50	Annemarie Verstappen (HOL)	1:59.69
400 m Freestyle	Tiffany Cohen (USA)	4:07.10	Sarah Hardcastle (GBR)	4:10.27	June Croft (GBR)	4:11.49
800 m Freestyle	Tiffany Cohen (USA)	8:24.95	Michelle Richardson (USA)	8:30.73	Sarah Hardcastle (GBR)	8:32.60
100 m Backstroke	Theresa Andrews (USA)	1:02.55	Betsy Mitchell (USA)	1:02.63	Jolanda de Rover (HOL)	1:02.91
200 m Backstroke	Jolanda de Rover (HOL)	2:12.38	Amy White (USA)	2:13.04	Aneta Patrascoiu (ROM)	2:13.29
100 m Breaststroke	Petra Van Staveren (HOL)	1:09.88	Anne Ottenbrite (CAN)	1:10.69	Catherine Poirot (FRA)	1:10.70
200 m Breaststroke	Anne Ottenbrite (CAN)	2:30.38	Susan Rapp (USA)	2:31.15	Ingrid Lempereur (BEL)	2:31.40
100 m Butterfly	Mary T. Meagher (USA)	59.26	Jenna Johnson (USA)	1:00.19	Karin Seick (FRG)	1:00.36
200 m Butterfly	Mary T. Meagher (USA)	2:06.90	Karen Philipps (AUS)	2:10.56	Ina Beyermann (FRG)	2:11.91
200 m Medley	Tracy Caulkins (USA)	2:12.64	Nancy Hogshead (USA)	2:15.17	Michele Pearson (AUS)	2:15.92
400 m Medley	Tracy Caulkins (USA)	4:39.24	Suzanne Landells (AUS)	4:48.30	Petra Zindler (FRG)	4:48.57
4x400 m Freestyle Relay	USA	3:43.43	Netherlands	3:44.40	FRG	3:45.56
4x100 m Medley Relay	USA	4:08.34	FRG	4:11.97	Canada	4:12.98
Springboard Diving	Silvie Bernier (CAN)	530.70	Kelly McCormick (USA)	527.46	Christina Seufert (USA)	517.62
Highboard Diving	Jihong Zhou (CHN)	378.81	Michele Mitchell (USA)	367.35	Wendy Wyland (USA)	365.52

SWIMMING — MEN

EVENT	GOLD		SILVER		BRONZE	
100 m Freestyle	Ambrose Gaines (USA)	49.80	Mark Stockwell (AUS)	50.24	Per Johansson (SWE)	50.31
200 m Freestyle	Michael Gross (FRG)	1:47.44	Michael Heath (USA)	1:49.10	Thomas Fahrner (FRG)	1:49.69
400 m Freestyle	George Dicarlo (USA)	3:51.23	John Mykkanen (USA)	3:51.49	Justin Lemberg (AUS)	3:51.79
1.500 m Freestyle	Michael O'Brien (USA)	15:05.20	George Dicarlo (USA)	15:10.59	Stefan Pfeiffer (FRG)	15:12.11
100 m Backstroke	Richard Carey (USA)	55.79	David Wilson (USA)	56.35	Mike West (CAN)	56.49
200 m Backstroke	Richard Carey (USA)	2:00.23	Frederic Delcourt (FRA)	2:01.75	Cameron Henning (CAN)	2:02.37
100 m Breaststroke	Steve Lundquist (USA)	1:01.65	Victor Davis (CAN)	1:01.99	Peter Evans (AUS)	1:02.97
200 m Breaststroke	Victor Davis (CAN)	2:13.34	Glenn Beringen (AUS)	2:15.79	Etienne Dagon (SUI)	2:17.41
100 m Butterfly	Michael Gross (FRG)	53.08	Pablo Morales (USA)	53.23	Glenn Buchanan (AUS)	53.85
200 Butterfly	Jon Sieben (AUS)	1:57.04	Michael Gross (FRG)	1:57.40	Rafael Vidal Castro (VEN)	1:57.51
200 m Medley	Alex Baumann (CAN)	2:01.42	Pedro Morales (USA)	2:03.05	Neil Cochran (GBR)	2:04.38
400 m Medley	Alex Baumann (CAN)	4:17.41	Ricardo Prado (BRA)	4:18.45	Robert Woodhouse (AUS)	4:20.50
4x100 Freestyle Relay	USA	3:19.03	Australia	3:19.68	Sweden	3:22.69
4x200 Freestyle Relay	USA	7:16.59	FRG	7:16.73	Great Britain	7:24.78
4x100 m Medley Relay	USA	3:39.30	Canada	3:43.23	Australia	3:43.25
Springboard Diving	Greg Louganis (USA)	754.41	Tan Liangde (CHN)	662.31	Ronald Merriott (USA)	661.32
Highboard Diving	Greg Louganis (USA)	710.91	Bruce Kimball (USA)	643.50	Li Kongzhen (CHN)	638.28
Water Polo	Yugoslavia		USA		FRG	

WEIGHTLIFTING

EVENT	GOLD		SILVER		BRONZE	
Flyweight	Guoqiang Zeng (CHN)	518 lb	Peishun Zhou (CHN)	518 lb	Kazushito Manabe (JPN)	512.5 lb
Bantamweight	Shude Wu (CHN)	589.5 lb	Runming Lai (CHN)	584 lb	Masahiro Kotaka (JPN)	556.5 lb
Featherweight	Weiqiang Chen (CHN)	622.75 lb	Gelu Radu (ROM)	617.25 lb	Wen-YeeTsai (KOR)	600.75 lb
Lightweight	Jingyuan Yao (CHN)	705.25 lb	Andrei Socaci (ROM)	688.75 lb	Jouni Gronman (FIN)	688.75 lb
Middleweight	Karl-Heinz Radschinsky (FRG)	749.5 lb	Jacques Demers (FRA)	738.5 lb	Dragomir Cioroslan (ROM)	733 lb
Light-Heavyweight	Petre Becheru (ROM)	782.5 lb	Robert Kabbas (AUS)	755 lb	Ryoji Isaoka (JPN)	749.5 lb
Middle-Heavyweight	Nicu Vlad (ROM)	865.25 lb	Petre Dumitru (ROM)	793.5 lb	David Mercer (GBR)	771 lb
First Heavyweight	Rolf Milser (FRG)	848.75 lb	Vasile Gropa (ROM)	843.25 lb	Pekka Niemi (FIN)	810 lb
Second Heavyweight	Norberto Oberburger (ITA)	859.75 lb	Stefan Tasnadi (ROM)	837.75 lb	Guy Carlton (USA)	832 lb
Super-Heavyweight	Dean Lukin (AUS)	909.25 lb	Mario Martinez (USA)	903.75 lb	Manfred Nerlinger (FRG)	876.25 lb

WEIGHTLIFTING WEIGHTS

FLYWEIGHT	-114.5 lb	BANTAMWEIGHT	-123.5 lb	FEATHERWEIGHT	-132.25 lb
LIGHTWEIGHT	-148.75 lb	MIDDLEWEIGHT-	-165.5 lb	LIGHT-HEAVYWEIGHT	-182 lb
MIDDLE-HEAVYWEIGHT	-198.5 lb	FIRST-HEAVYWEIGHT	-220.5 lb	SECOND-HEAVYWEIGHT -	-242 lb
SUPER-HEAVYWEIGHT	+242 lb				

GRECO-ROMAN WRESTLING

EVENT	GOLD	SILVER	BRONZE
Light-Flyweight (-105.75 lb)	Vincenzo Maenza (ITA)	Markus Scherer (FRG)	Ikuzo Saito (JPN)
Flyweight (-114.5 lb)	Atsuji Miyahara (JPN)	Daniel Aceves (MEX)	Dae-Du Bang (KOR)
Bantamweight (-125.75 lb)	Pasquale Passarelli (FRG)	Masaki Eto (JPN)	Haralambos Holidis (GRE)
Featherweight (-136.5 lb)	Weon-Kee Kim (KOR)	Kentolle Johansson (SWE)	Hugo Dietsche (SUI)
Lightweight (-149.75 lb)	Vlado Lisjak (YUG)	Tapio Sipila (FIN)	James Martinez (USA)
Welterweight (-163 lb)	Jonko Salomäki (FIN)	Roger Tallroth (SWE)	Stefan Rusu (ROM)
Middleweight (-180.75 lb)	Ion Draica (ROM)	Dimitrios Thanopoulos (GRE)	Soren Claeson (SWE)
Light-Heavyweight (-198.25 lb)	Steven Fraser (USA)	Ilie Matei (ROM)	Frank Andersson (SWE)
Heavyweight (-220.5 lb)	Vasile Andrei (ROM)	Greg Glbson (USA)	Jozef Tertelje (YUG)
Super-Heavyweight (+220.5 lb)	Jeffrey Blatnick (USA)	Refik Memisevic (YUG)	Victor Dolipschi (ROM)

FREESTYLE WRESTLING

EVENT	GOLD	SILVER	BRONZE
Light-Flyweight (-105.75 lb)	Robert Weaver (USA)	Takashi Irie (JPN)	Son-Gab Do (KOR)
Flyweight (-114.5 lb)	Saban Trstena (YUG)	Jong-Kiu Kim (KOR)	Yuji Takada (JPN)
Bantamweight (-125.75 lb)	Hideaki Tomiyama (JPN)	Barry Davis (USA)	Eui-Kon Kim (KOR)
Featherweight (-136.5 lb)	Randy Lewis (USA)	Kosei Akaishi (JPN)	Jung-Keun Lee (KOR)
Lightweight (-149.75 lb)	In-Tak You (KOR)	Andrew Rein (USA)	Jukka Rauhala (FIN)
Welterweight (-163 lb)	David Shultz (USA)	Martin Knosp (FRG)	Saban Sejdi (YUG)
Middleweight (-180.75 lb)	Mark Shultz (USA)	Hideyuki Nagashima (JPN)	Chris Rinke (CAN)
Light-Heavyweight (-198.25 lb)	Ed Banach (USA)	Akira Ota (JPN)	Noel Loban (GBR)
Heavyweight (-220.5 lb)	Lou Banach (USA)	Joseph Atiyeh (SYR)	Vasile Pascasu (ROM)
Super-Heavyweight (+220.5 lb)	Bruce Baumgartner (USA)	Bob Molle (CAN)	Ayhan Taskin (TUR)

MODERN PENTATHLON

EVENT	GOLD		SILVER		BRONZE	
Individual	Daniele Masala (ITA)	5,469	Svante Rasmusson (SWE)	5,456	Carlo Massullo (ITA)	5,406
Team	Italy	16,060	USA	15,568	France	15,565

FENCING

EVENT	GOLD	SILVER	BRONZE
Individual Foil — Men	Mauro Numa (ITA)	Matthias Behr (FRG)	Stefano Cerioni (ITA)
Team Foil — Men	Italy	FRG	France
Individual Épée	Philippe Boisse (FRA)	Björne Vaggo (SWE)	Philippe Riboud (FRA)
Team Épée	FRG	France	Italy
Individual Sabre	Jean-François Lamour (FRA)	Marco Marin (ITA)	Peter Westbrook (USA)
Team Sabre	Italy	France	Romania
Individual Foil — Women	Ju Jie Luan (CHN)	Cornelia Hanisch (FRG)	Dorina Vaccaroni (ITA)
Team Foil — Women	FRG	Romania	France

YACHTING

EVENT	GOLD		SILVER		BRONZE	
Finn Class	Russel Coutes (NZL)	34.7	John Bertrand (USA)	37.0	Terry Neilson (CAN)	37.7
International Star	USA	29.7	FRG	41.4	Italy	43.5
Flying Dutchman	USA	19.7	Canada	22.7	Great Britain	48.7
International Tornado	New Zealand	14.7	USA	37.0	Australia	50.4
International 470	Spain	33.7	USA	43.0	France	49.9
International Sailing	USA	33.7	Brazil	43.4	Canada	49.7
Windglider Class	Stephan van den Berg (HOL)	27.7	Randall Steele (USA)	46.0	Bruce Kendall (NZL)	46.4

CANOEING — WOMEN

EVENT	GOLD		SILVER		BRONZE	
500 m Kayak Singles K1	Agneta Andersson (SWE)	1:58.72	Barbara Schüttpelz (FRG)	1:59.93	Annemiek Derckx (HOL)	2:00.11
500 m Kayak Pairs K2	Sweden	1:45.25	Canada	1:47.13	FRG	1:47.32
500 m Kayak Fours K4	Romania	1:38.34	Sweden	1:38.87	Canada	1:39.40

CANOEING — MEN

EVENT	GOLD		SILVER		BRONZE	
500 m Kayak Singles K1	Ian Ferguson (NZL)	1:47.84	Lars-Erik Moberg (SWE)	1:48.18	Bernard Bregeon (FRA)	1:48.41
1,000 m Kayak Singles K1	Alan Thompson (NZL)	3:45.73	Milan Janic (YUG)	3:46.88	Greg Barton (USA)	3:47.38
500 m Kayak Pairs K2	New Zealand	1:34.21	Sweden	1:35.26	Canada	1:35.41
1,000 m Kayak Pairs K2	Canada	3:24.22	France	3:25.97	Australia	3:26.80
1,000 m Kayak Fours K4	New Zealand	3:02.28	Sweden	3:02.81	France	3:03.94
500 m Canadian Single C1	Larry Cain (CAN)	1:57.01	Henning Jakobsen (DEN)	1:58.45	Costica Olaru (ROM)	1:59.86
1,000 m Canadian Singles C1	Ulrich Eicke (FRG)	4:06.32	Larry Cain (CAN)	4:08.67	Henning Jakobsen (DEN)	4:09.50
500 m Canadian Pairs C2	Yugoslavia	1:43.67	Romania	1:45.68	Spain	1:47.71
1,000 m Canadian Pairs C2	Romania	3:40.60	Yugoslavia	3:41.56	France	3:48.01

ROWING — MEN

EVENT	GOLD		SILVER		BRONZE	
Single Sculls	Pertti Karppinen (FIN)	7:00.24	Peter Michael Kolbe (FRG)	7:02.19	Robert Mills (CAN)	7:10.38
Doubles Sculls	USA	6:36.87	Belgium	6:38.19	Yugoslavia	6:39.59
Coxless Pairs	Romania	6:45.39	Spain	6:48.47	Norway	6:51.81
Coxed Pairs	Italy	7:05.99	Romania	7:11.21	USA	7:12.81
Coxless Quadruple Sculls	FRG	5:57.55	Australia	5:57.98	Canada	5:59.07
Coxless Fours	New Zealand	6:03.48	USA	6:06.10	Denmark	6:07.72
Coxed Fours	Great Britain	6:18.64	USA	6:20.28	New Zealand	6:23.68
Coxed Eights	Canada	5:41.32	USA	5:41.74	Australia	5:42.40

ROWING — WOMEN

EVENT	GOLD		SILVER		BRONZE	
Single Sculls	Valeria Racila (ROM)	3:40.68	Charlotte Geer (USA)	3:43.89	Ann Haesebrouck (BEL)	3:45.72
Double Sculls	Romania	3:26.77	Netherlands	3:29.13	Canada	3:29.82
Coxless Pairs	Romania	3:32.60	Canada	3:36.06	FRG	3:40.50
Coxed Quadruple Sculls	Romania	3:14.11	USA	3:15.57	Denmark	3:16.02
Coxed Fours	Romania	3:19.38	Canada	3:21.55	Australia	3:23.29
Coxed Eights	USA	2:59.80	Romania	3:00.87	Netherlands	3:02.92

SHOOTING

EVENT	GOLD		SILVER		BRONZE	
Small-Bore Rifle (Prone)	Edward Etzel (USA)	599	Michel Bury (FRA)	596	Michael Sullivan (GBR)	596
Small-Bore Rifle (3 Positions)	Malcolm Cooper (GBR)	1173	Daniel Nipkow (SUI)	1163	Alister Allan (GBR)	1162
Rapid Fire Pistol	Takeo Kamachi (JPN)	595	Corneliu Ion (ROM)	593	Rauno Bies (FIN)	591
Free Pistol (50 m)	Xu Haifeng (CHN)	566	Ragnar Skanaker (SWE)	565	Yifu Wang (CHN)	564
Running Game Target	Yuwei Li (CHN)	587	Helmut Bellingrodt (COL)	584	Shiping Huang (CHN)	581
Skeet Shooting	Matthew Dryke (USA)	198	Ole Riber Rasmussen (DEN)	196/25	Luca Scribani-Rossi (ITA)	196/24
Trap Shooting	Luciano Giovanetti (ITA)	192	Francisco Boza (PER)	192	Daniel Carlisle (USA)	192
Air Rifle	Philippe Heberle (FRA)	589	Andreas Kronthaler (AUT)	581	Barry Dagger (GBR)	587
Women Sport Pistol	Linda Thom (CAN)	585	Ruby Fox (USA)	585	Patricia Dench (AUS)	583
Women Standard Rifle	Xiaoxuan Wu (CHN)	581	Ulrike Holmer (FRG)	578	Wanda Jewell (USA)	578
Women Air Rifle	Pat Spurgin (USA)	393	Edith Gufler (ITA)	391	Xiaoxuan Wu (CHN)	389

ARCHERY — MEN

EVENT	GOLD		SILVER		BRONZE	
	Darrell Pace (USA)	2,616	Richard McKinney (USA)	2,564	Hiroshi Yamamoto (JPN))	2,563

ARCHERY — WOMEN

EVENT	GOLD		SILVER		BRONZE	
	Hyang-Soon Seo (KOR)	2,568	Lingjuan Li (CHN)	2,559	Jin-Ho Kim (KOR)	2,555

CYCLING — MEN

EVENT	GOLD		SILVER		BRONZE	
Road Race (118.25 mi)	Alexi Grewal (USA)	4:59.57	Steve Bauer (CAN)	4:59.7	Dag Otto Lauritzen (NOR)	5:00.18
100 km Road Team Time Trial	Italy	1:58.28	Switzerland	2:02.38	USA	2:02.46
1,000 m Time Trial	Fredy Schmidtke (FRG)	1:06.10	Curtis Harnett (CAN)	1:06.44	Fabrice Colas (FRA)	1:06.65
1,000 m Sprint	Mark Gorski (USA)		Nelson Vails (USA)		Tsutomu Sakamoto (JPN)	
4,000 m Individual Pursuit	Steve Hegg (USA)	4:39.35	Rolf Gölz (FRG)	4:43.82	Leonand Nitz (USA)	4:44.03
4,000 m Team Pursuit	Australia	4:25.99	USA	4:29.85	FRG	4:25.60
Individual Points Race	Roger Ilegems (BEL)		Uwe Messerschmidt (FRG)		José Manuel Youshimatz (MEX)	

CYCLING — WOMEN

EVENT	GOLD		SILVER	BRONZE
Women Road Race (49.25 mi)	Connie Carpenter-Phinney (USA)	2:11.14	Rebecca Twigg (USA)	Sandra Schumacher (FRG)

EQUESTRIANISM

EVENT	GOLD		SILVER		BRONZE	
Three-Day Event	Mark Todd (NZL)	51.60	Karen Stives (USA)	54.20	Virginia Holgate (GBR)	56.80
Three-Day Event Team	USA	186.180	Great Britain	189.20	FRG	234
Grand Prix (Dressage)	Reiner Klimke (FRG)	1,504	Anne Grethe Jensen (DEN)	1,442	Otto Hofer (SUI)	1,364
Grand Prix (Dressage) Team	FRG	4,955	Switzerland	4,673	Sweden	4,630
Grand Prix (Jumping)	Joe Fargis (USA)		Conrad Homfeld (USA)	-4	Heidi Robbiani (SUI)	-8
Grand Prix (Jumping) Team	USA	12.00	Great Britain	36.75	FRG	39.25

GYMNASTICS — MEN

EVENT	GOLD		SILVER		BRONZE	
Individual Combined Exercises	Koji Gushiken (JPN)	118.700	Peter Vidmar (USA)	118.675	Li Ning (CHN)	118.575
Team	USA	591.40	China	590.80	Japan	586.70
Parallel Bars	Bart Conner (USA)	19.950	Nobuyuki Kajitani (JPN)	19.925	Mitchell Gaylord (USA)	19.850
Floor	Li Ning (CHN)	19.925	Yun Lou (CHN)	19.775	Koji Sotomura (JPN)	19.700
					Philippe Vatuone (FRA)	19.700
Horse Vault	Yun Lou (CHN)	19.950	Li Ning (CHN)	19.825		
			Mitchell Gaylord (USA)	19.825		
			Koji Gushiken (JPN)	19.825		
			Shinji Morisue (JPN)	19.825		
Horizontal Bar	Shinji Morisue (JPN)	20.000	Tong Fei (CHN)	19.955	Koji Gushiken (JPN)	19.950
Rings	Koji Gushiken (JPN)	19.850	Mitchell Gaylord (USA)	19.825		
	Li Ning (CHN)	19.850				
Pommel Horse	Li Ning (CHN)	19.950			Timothy Daggett (USA)	19.825
	Peter Vidmar (USA)	19.950				

GYMNASTICS — WOMEN

EVENT	GOLD		SILVER		BRONZE	
Individual Combined Exercises	Mary Lou Retton (USA)	79.175	Ecaterina Szabó (ROM)	79.125	Simona Pauca (ROM)	78.675
Team	Romania	392.20	USA	391.20	China	388.60
Floor	Ecaterina Szabó (ROM)	19.975	Julianne McNamara (USA)	19.950	Mary Lou Retton (USA)	19.775
Horse Vault	EcaterinaSzabó (ROM)	19.875	Mary Lou Retton (USA)	19.850	Lavinia Agache (ROM)	19.750
Beam	Simona Pauca (ROM)	19.800			Kathy Johnson (USA)	19.650
	Ecaterina Szabó (ROM)	19.800				
Asymmetrical Bars	Yanhong Ma (CHN)	19.950			Mary Lou Retton (USA)	19.800
	Julianne Mc Namara (USA)	19.950				
Modern Rhythmic	Lori Fung (CAN)	57.950	Doina Staiculescu (ROM)	57.900	Regina Weber (FRG)	57.700

BASKETBALL — MEN

GOLD	SILVER	BRONZE
USA	Spain	Yugoslavia

BASKETBALL — WOMEN

GOLD	SILVER	BRONZE
USA	South Korea	China

SOCCER

GOLD	SILVER	BRONZE
France	Brazil	Yugoslavia

HANDBALL — MEN

GOLD	SILVER	BRONZE
Yugoslavia	FRG	Romania

TENNIS — MEN

	GOLD	SILVER	BRONZE
Individual	Miloslav Mecir (TCH)	Tim Mayotte (USA)	Stefan Edberg (SWE)
			Brad Gilbert (USA)
Doubles	Ken Flach/Robert Seguso (USA)	Emilio Sanchez/Sergio Casal (ESP)	Stefan Edberg/Anders Jarryd (SWE)
			Miroslav Mecir/Milan Srejber (TCH)

TENNIS — WOMEN

	GOLD	SILVER	BRONZE
Individual	Steffi Graf (FRG)	Gabriela Sabatini (ARG)	Zina Garrison (USA)
			Manuela Maleeva (BUL)
Doubles	Pam Shriver/Zina Garrison (USA)	Jana Novotna/Helena Sukova (TCH)	Steffi Graf/Claudia Kohde-Kilsch (FRG)
			Elizabeth Smylie/Wendy Turnball (AUS)

HANDBALL — WOMEN

GOLD	SILVER	BRONZE
Yugoslavia	South Korea	China

HOCKEY — MEN

GOLD	SILVER	BRONZE
Pakistan	FRG	Great Britain

HOCKEY — WOMEN

GOLD	SILVER	BRONZE
Netherlands	FRG	USA

VOLLEYBALL — MEN

GOLD	SILVER	BRONZE
USA	Brazil	Italy

VOLLEYBALL — WOMEN

GOLD	SILVER	BRONZE
China	USA	Japan

SEOUL 1988

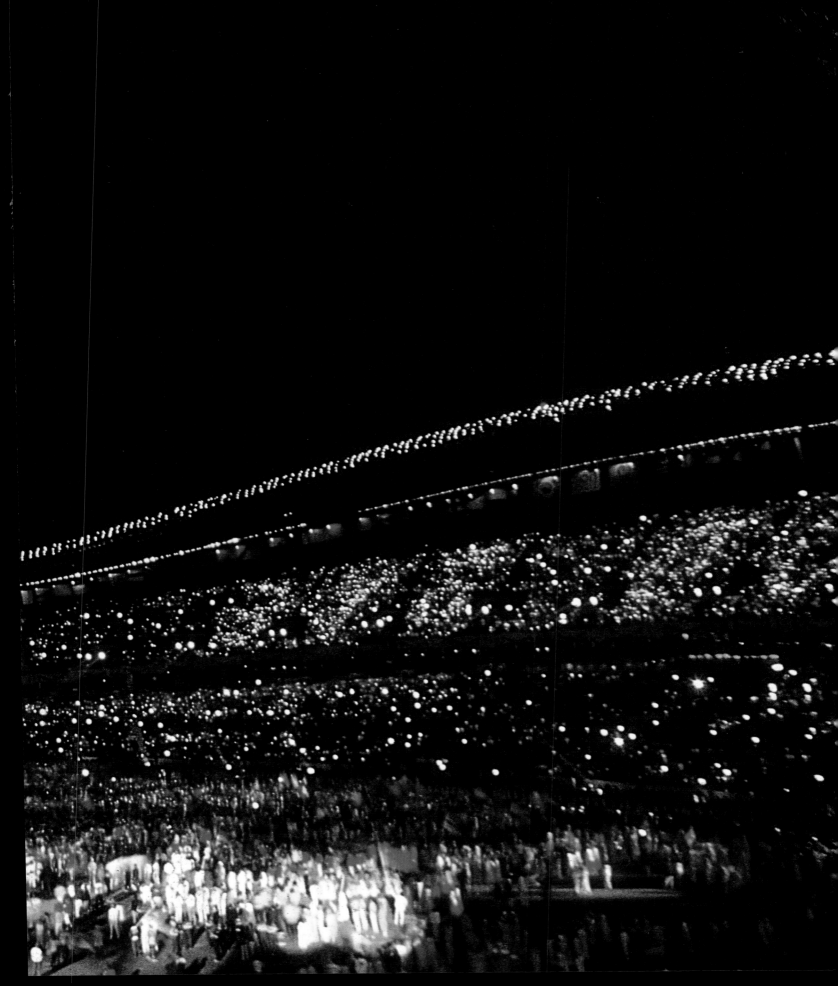

INTRODUCTION

Seoul 1988

ABOVE: Close-up of the commemorative pin.
Allsport

PREVIOUS PAGE: One of the spectacular highlights of the closing ceremony of Seoul 1988.
Allsport

237
EVENTS

159
COUNTRIES

8,465
ATHLETES

	Gold	Silver	Bronze
URS	55	31	46
GER	37	35	30
USA	36	31	27
KOR	12	11	10
FRG	11	14	15
HUN	11	6	6
BUL	10	12	13
ROM	7	11	6
FRA	6	4	6
ITA	6	4	4
CHN	5	11	12
GBR	5	10	9
KEN	5	2	2
JPN	4	3	7
AUS	3	6	5
YUG	3	4	5
CZE	3	3	2
NZE	3	2	8
CAN	3	2	5
POL	2	5	9
NOR	2	3	
NED	2	2	5
DEN	2	1	1
BRA	1	2	3
FIN	1	1	2
ESP	1	1	2
TUR	1	1	
MOR	1		2
AUT	1		
POR	1		
SUR	1		
SWE		4	7
SUI		2	2
JAM		2	
ARG		1	1
CHN		1	
CRC		1	
INA		1	
IRN		1	
NLA		1	
PER		1	
SEN		1	
VIR		1	
BEL			2
MEX			2
COL			1
DJI			1
GRE			1
MON			1
PAK			1
PHI			1
THA			1

The choice to host the 1988 Olympiad of South Korea, a country technically at war with neighboring North Korea, seemed like asking for trouble. Yet in the end, the large-scale boycotts that had dogged Moscow and Los Angeles did not occur. All the leading Olympic nations turned up in Seoul, with the notable exceptions of Cuba and Ethiopia. Nicaragua and, of course, North Korea also stayed away. The Olympic Committee could afford to congratulate themselves.

It had been touch and go. With the Demilitarized Zone separating North and South Korea just 35 miles away, Seoul seemed the very recipe for superpower confrontation.

North Korea had demanded that it co-host the games, and two fatal bombings were linked by Seoul to the North's early efforts to sabotage the planned event. A thaw in East-West relations meant that all such attempts failed and Seoul completed its ambitious plans to construct a whole new Olympia, a lead which cities around the world have since taken. Thus, for the first time in 12 years, the Americans and Soviets were able to compete against one another.

The games in Seoul showed that, thanks to diplomacy and compromise, the Olympics had evolved into a new era, largely free of the politics which had dogged it off the field for most of its first 92 years. Seoul was praised as an international melting pot and as a theater of sporting excellence.

RIGHT: A commemorative pin from Seoul 1988. Allsport

But in the end, the damage done to the XXIVth Olympiad came from an unexpected quarter...

Canadian sprinter Ben Johnson had won the 100 meters race, beating his US arch rival Carl Lewis in a world record of 9.79 seconds. The 26-year-old national hero immediately handed his medal to his mother Gloria. "I won the gold for her," he said touchingly.

Three days later, there was a knock on the door of Johnson's room at two o'clock in the morning. He answered it to his grim-faced coach who told him he was to be stripped of his record because he had tested positive for the anabolic steroid stanozolol. Humiliatingly, Johnson had to ask his mother for the return of his precious gold, which he placed in the hand of a weeping Canadian team official.

From that moment, rumor and scandal swept Seoul. Many athletes felt under a cloud of suspicion. As Johnson flew home in disgrace, the entire 64-strong Canadian track and field team volunteered themselves for mass dope testing — though the games officials declined their offer.

Suddenly the games were marred, not just by Johnson's guilt but by other examples of cheating, bad manners, and temper tantrums. Two other gold medalists, Bulgarian weightlifters Mitko Grablev and Angel Guenchev, and several other minor athletes were disqualified by the IOC for using banned substances.

RIGHT: Part of the opening ceremony for the Seoul 1988 Olympics. Jean-Marc Loubat

ABOVE: Seoul commemorative medal. Allsport

RIGHT: One of the coveted gold medals. Allsport USA

OPPOSITE PAGE and OVERLEAF: Scenes from the opening ceremony Seoul 1988. Jean-Marc Loubat/Gray Mortimore

OPPOSITE PAGE RIGHT: The Seoul Olympic torch. Allsport

Yet the games produced many valid feats, not least in the Iron Curtain countries' storming return to the Olympics after their Los Angeles boycott. The Soviet Union took 132 medals (55 of them golds) and East Germany 102 medals (37 golds), knocking the US into third slot with 94 medals (36 golds).

East German swimmer Kristin Otto gained six golds, the most ever won by a female in Olympic history, and coming close to equaling Mark Spitz's 1972 record. Of the US swimmers, Matt Biondi won five golds, a silver, and a bronze. Team-mate Janet Evans won three golds.

America's Greg Louganis is as much remembered for his misjudgment in the run-ups. In a reverse two-and-a-half somersault in the pike position, he banged his head on the springboard and required stitches to close the cut, yet finished his Olympic career with two more gold medals. He had already won springboard and platform golds in Los Angeles in 1984 and repeated the double in Seoul.

The addition of tennis as a medal sport for the first time since 1924 brought fresh glamor to the 1988 games — particularly in the form of West Germany's Steffi Graf, and Czechoslovakia's Miloslav Mecir won the men's singles.

It was also the games that saw the glamorous Florence Griffith Joyner win golds in the 100 meters, 200 meters, and 4x200 meters relay, and a silver in the 4x400 meters relay. Flo Jo, as she became known, set a world record of 21.34 seconds over 200 meters. She also ran the fastest ever Olympic time over 100 meters — but this was discounted as a record because it was judged to be wind assisted.

Yet even at the moment of Flo Jo's triumph, the shadow of drugs muted the euphoria. The string of amazing performances with which she rewrote the record books inevitably led to suspicions that she had used performance enhancing aids. Despite all the triumphs of Seoul, the legacy was sadly one of shame.

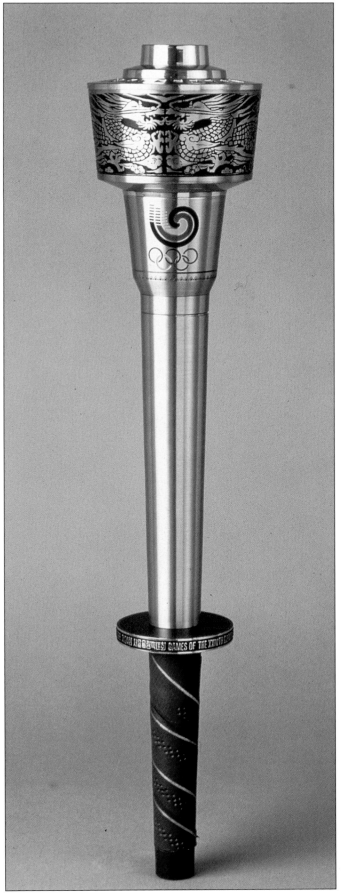

FLORENCE GRIFFITH JOYNER

Seoul 1988

The world could only look on in astonishment in 1988 as America's Florence Griffith Joyner, a good but not outstanding sprinter previously, rewrote the record books with a series of amazing performances.

The phenomenal achievements of Griffith Joyner — wife of the 1984 Olympic triple jump gold medalist Al Joyner and the sister-in-law of Jackie Joyner Kersee, the world record holder in the heptathlon and the 1984 and 1988 Olympic champion — inevitably led to suspicions that she had used banned performance enhancing drugs.

She always denied the allegations but her sudden death in 1998, at the age of 38, from a heart attack convinced many that she was using anabolic steroids and human growth hormone. Her death came in the week which marked the tenth anniversary of her amazing performances in Seoul.

Griffith Joyner was born in the Los Angeles suburb of Watts, the seventh of eleven children. She first displayed her athletic prowess as a five-year-old in the Mojave desert where she became speedy enough to catch a rabbit.

She earned silver medals in the 200 meters at the 1984 Olympics and 1987 World Championships but had done nothing to suggest, at the age of 27, that she was about to become the greatest female athlete in history.

Dressed in a selection of multi-colored, one legged leotards and wearing her equally colorful fingernails dangerously long, Griffith Joyner began her sensational summer of 1988 by winning her 100 meters quarter final at the US trials in 10.49sec, slashing more than two tenths of a second off Evelyn Ashford's four-year-old world record. She followed it with a US record of 21.77sec for the 200 meters.

Flo Jo, as she became known, repeated the form at the Seoul Olympics, winning the 100 meters in 10.54sec and setting two world records at 200 meters in 21.34sec. A silver medal in the 4x400 meters relay, in which she ran a 48.07 sec leg, made her the athlete of the games.

At this point she promptly retired because, she claimed, she wanted take advantage of the lucrative commercial opportunities which had opened up for her. A number of claims that she intended to return to the track were largely ignored.

Her decision to hang up her spikes, however, followed the worldwide clampdown on doping in the wake of the scandal surrounding Ben Johnson. Griffith Joyner's team-mate Carl Lewis regularly cast doubts over her massive improvement but she never took legal action against him.

After Seoul, she had a daughter Mary in 1990 and concentrated on a career in public speaking and acting. She marketed her own collection of athletic wear and a line in nail varnish and was chosen in 1996 by Bill Clinton to replace Arnold Schwarzenegger as chair of the President's Council on Physical Fitness and Sports.

After her death, Clinton said: "Flo Jo earned the right to be called the world's fastest woman. We were dazzled by her speed, humbled by her talent, and captivated by her style."

ABOVE: *American great Florence Griffith-Joyner comes first in the 100 m.* Steve Powell

RIGHT: *Her haul of Seoul Olympic medals.* Tony Duffy

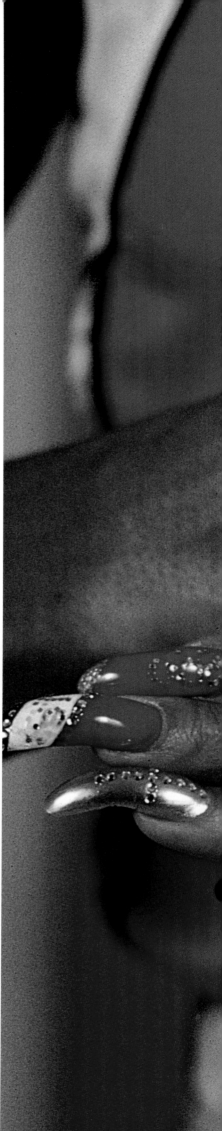

KRISTIN OTTO

A tall and powerful swimmer, East Germany's Kristin Otto dominated the 1988 Olympics in Seoul, winning six gold medals, the most ever won by a female in Olympic history.

The Seoul games came before the East was opened up and the 22-year-old Otto won golds in all the events she entered. She demonstrated unique versatility by winning 100 meters titles at three strokes: freestyle, backstroke, and butterfly as well as golds at the 50 meters freestyle and 4x100 meters freestyle and medley relays.

Otto started swimming at the age of six and, as was customary for top East German hopes, started sports school at 11. Her first national title was at 100 meters backstroke in 1982.

Before Seoul, she had won three gold medals at the 1982 World Championships, four at the 1986 World Championships and five at the 1987 European Championships. She missed the Los Angeles games in 1984 because of her country's boycott.

After her multiple medal efforts in Seoul, Otto had a quiet time at the 1989 European Championships, restricting herself to just two events — and two gold medals — before retiring.

But her record remains tarnished by the revelation in East German documents uncovered in 1994 that she had been among a group of swimmers fed a steady diet of banned performance enhancing drugs, most notably testosterone, throughout her career.

She has always denied knowingly taken any banned drug and now coaches in Hannover and commentates on swimming for German television.

The East German swimmer Kristin Otto proudly holds her six gold medals — the most any woman has won at an Olympic event. They were for the 100 m freestyle, backstroke and butterfly, the 50 m freestyle, and the 4 x 100 m freestyle and medley. Allsport

STEFFI GRAF

Quite simply, one of the greatest tennis players of all time, on top of everything else, Germany's Steffi Graf has a superb record at the Olympic Games.

For a ten-year period starting in 1987, Graf was ranked either number one or number two in the world list and was only the fifth player in history, man or woman, to win tennis' Grand Slam — that is to win Wimbledon and the Australian, French, and US Open tournaments in the same year.

Graf did it in 1988, the year when she completed what was called the "Golden Slam" by winning the Olympic title at the sport's reintroduction to the games in Seoul. She previously won the title when tennis was a demonstration sport in Los Angeles.

She has won 21 Grand Slam titles in all, including six Wimbledons. But for Graf, who was an outstanding 800 meters runner as a girl, the Olympics remain something special.

"It's great being at the games with all the great athletes from other sports," she said. "It's not like a Grand Slam. You walk into the dining room and you might see Carl Lewis, Michael Jordan, or Linford Christie. You suddenly find yourself nudging your friends and saying, 'Look who's over there.' You're a fan again."

"To look at the Olympic record books and find my name alongside people like Jesse Owens, it blows your mind. It helps remind you why you came into sport in the first place."

During the last few years, Graf has played through numerous health and injury problems and in 1995 won the US Open while her father, Peter, was in prison in Germany awaiting trial on tax evasion charges. He subsequently served two and half years. She announced her retirement from competitive tennis after Wimbledon in 1999.

It was hardly a surprise when Steffi Graff won the ladies tennis gold medal on its reintroduction as an Olympic sport at the Seoul Olympics. Pascal Rondeau

GREG LOUGANIS

Greg Louganis of the USA is, perhaps, the greatest diver the world has ever seen. Tony Duffy

Hailed as the greatest diver ever, America's Greg Louganis was a problem child whose life and career took a sensational turn in 1988.

Given up for adoption by his 15-year-old parents, he suffered at school because he was dyslexic, he started smoking at nine years old, and, as he entered his teens, he was virtually an alcoholic. But he discovered diving and at 16 qualified for the 1976 Olympic Games in Montreal, where he finished sixth in the springboard event and won a silver medal in the platform.

Absent from Moscow because of the US boycott, Louganis won springboard and platform gold medals in Los Angeles in 1984, the former by a record margin of 94 points. He repeated the double four years later in Seoul where he qualified for the springboard final despite misjudging a reverse two and a half somersault in the pike position and cracking his head on the board on his way down.

Louganis revealed in 1995 that he had been diagnosed as HIV positive six months before the games and had been terrified that blood spilled in the pool may have infected other divers. His coach, who knew about Louganis' condition, and his doctor, who did not, later took AIDS tests which proved negative.

After the games, he found the courage to leave his abusive lover and then fell into a deep depression after nursing his dying father.

Alone and quite possibly moving from HIV to AIDS, Louganis took on the theatrical role of an AIDS sufferer in a New York play. That experience, particularly seeing how many of his new colleagues lived more easily with their sexual orientation than he ever had, gave Louganis the strength to refashion his life and come out at the 1994 Gay Games. He has since taken an active role in gay issues.

The man who rules the Olympics with a rod of iron — J. A. Samaranch the International Olympic Committee President. Allsport

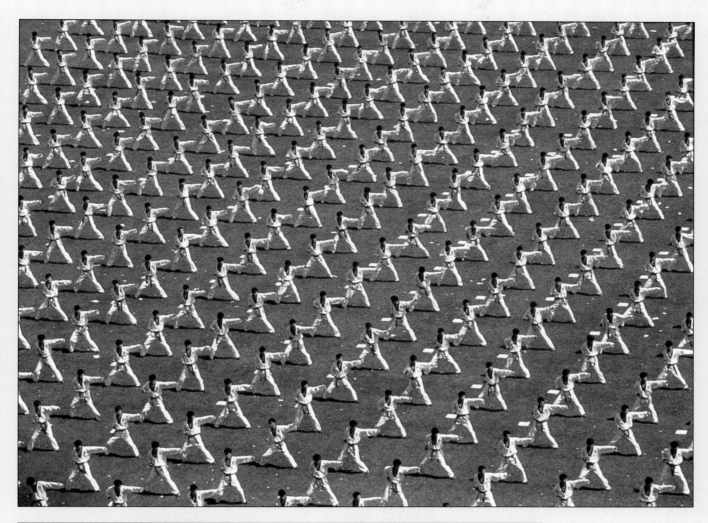

ABOVE: *Another scene from the opening ceremony for Seoul 1988.* Gerard Vandystadt

LEFT: *The Olympic torch, brought by relay runners all the way from Greece, enters the stadium to resounding applause.* Bob Martin

TOP: *The 4x 100 m USA ladies' team win gold.* Mike Powell

ABOVE: *Florence Griffith Joyner praying for help while waiting her leg of the 4x 400 m Relay.* Tony Duffy

RIGHT: *On the podium for the 100 m medals presentation: first, Ben Johnson, second, Carl Lewis, third, Linford Christie. Johnson was later stripped of his medal after failing a drugs test.* Gray Mortimore

Adrian Moorhouse celebrating his win in the 100 m breaststroke final. Simon Bruty

ABOVE: *Soviet athlete Gintautas Umaras takes first in the 4,000 m individual pursuit cycling event.* Mike Powell

BOTTOM: *The men's 400 m hurdles.* Gerard Vandystadt

OVERLEAF: *A pole vaulter hopes to clear the bar.* Allsport

341

ABOVE: *A Bulgarian pole vaulter prepares to make his jump.* Mike Powell

ABOVE RIGHT: *Marathon runners round a bend.* Simon Bruty

Soviet players celebrate their basketball victory with coach Alexandre Gomelski. Joe Patronite

A Korean competitor stages a personal sit-in during the Seoul games. Allsport

ABOVE: Canada's Ben Johnson took the 100 m sprint in a record 9.79 seconds but was stripped of his medal after failing a drugs test.
Simon Bruty

ABOVE RIGHT: Morocco's Brahim Boutaib on his way to a gold medal in the 10,000 m run. Tony Duffy

SEOUL 1988 SEPTEMBER 17 - OCTOBER 2

PARTICIPANTS: 8,465

MEN: 6,279

WOMEN: 2,186

COUNTRIES: 159

SPORTS: 23

EVENTS: 237

FINAL TORCHBEARERS: SON KEE-CHUNG, LIM CHUN-AE, CHUNG SUN-MAN, KIM WON-TAK, SOHN MI-CHUNG

MEDALS TABLE

PLACE	COUNTRY	GOLD	SILVER	BRONZE
1	USSR	55	31	46
2	GDR	37	35	30
3	USA	36	31	27
4	South Korea	12	11	10
5	FRG	11	14	15

OUTSTANDING ATHLETES

PLACE	NAME (NATIONALITY)	DISCIPLINE	GOLD	SILVER	BRONZE
1	Kristin Otto (GDR)	Swimming	6		
2	Matt Biondi (USA)	Swimming	5		1
3	Vladimir Artemov (URS)	Gymnastics	4	1	
4	Daniela Silivas (ROM)	Gymnastics	3	2	1
5	Florence Griffith-Joyner (USA)	Athletics	3	1	

ATHLETICS — MEN

EVENT	GOLD		SILVER		BRONZE	
100 m*	Carl Lewis (USA)	9.92*	Linford Christie (GBR)	9.97	Calvin Smith (USA)	9.99
200 m	Joe DeLoach (USA)	19.75	Carl Lewis (USA)	19.79	Robson da Silva (BRA)	20.04
400 m	Steven Lewis (USA)	43.87	Butch Reynolds (USA)	43.93	Danny Everett (USA)	44 09
800m	Paul Ereng (KEN)	1:43.45	Joaquim Cruz (BRA)	1:43.90	Said Aouita (MAR)	1:44.06
1,500 m	Peter Rono (KEN)	3:35.96	Peter Elliott (GBR)	3:36.15	Jens-Peter Herold (GDR)	3:36.21
5,000 m	John Ngugi (KEN)	13:11.70	Dieter Baumann (FRG)	13:15.52	Hansjörg Kunze (GDR)	13:15.73
10,000 m	Brahim Boutaib (MAR)	27:21.44	Salvatore Antibo (ITA)	27:23.55	Kipkemboy Kimeli (KEN)	27:25.16
Marathon	Gelindo Bordin (ITA)	2:10:32	Douglas Wakihuriu (KEN)	2:10:47	Ahmed Saleh (DIJ)	2:10:59
110 m Hurdles	Roger Kingdom (USA)	12.98	Colin Jackson (GBR)	13.28	Anthony Campbell (USA)	13.38
400 m Hurdles	Andre Philipps (USA)	47.19	Amadou Dia Ba (SEN)	47.23	Edwin Moses (USA)	47.56
3,000 m Steeplechase	Julius Kariuki (KEN)	8:05.51	Peter Koech (KEN)	8:06.79	Mark Rowland (GBR)	8:07.96
4x100 m	USSR	38.19	Great Britain	38.28	France	38.40
4x400 m	USA	2:56.16	Jamaica	3:00.30	FRG	3:00.56
20 km Walk	Jozef Pribilinec (TCH)	1:19.57	Ronald Weigel (GDR)	1:20.00	Maurizio Damilano (lTA)	1:20:14
50 km Walk	Vyacheslav Ivanenko (URS)	3:38:29	Ronald Weigel (GDR)	3:38:56	Hartwig Gauder (GDR)	3:39:45
High Jump	Gennadi Avdeyenko (URS)	7'9.75"	Hollis Conway (USA)	7'8"	Rudolf Povarnitsin (URS)	7'8.75"
					Patrick Sjöberg (SWE)	7'8.75"
Pole Vault	Sergei Bubka (URS)	19'4"	Rodion Gataullin (URS)	19'2"	Grigori Yegorov (URS)	19'0.25"
Long Jump	Carl Lewis (USA)	28'7.5"	Mike Powell (USA)	27'10.25"	Larry Myricks (USA)	27'1.75"
Triple Jump	Khristo Markov (BUL)	57'9.5"	Igor Lapshin (URS)	57'5.75"	Alexander Kovalenko (URS)	57'2"
Shot	Ulf Timmermann (GDR)	73'8.75"	Randy Barnes (USA)	73'5.5"	Werner Günthör (SUI)	72'1"
Discus	Jurgen Schult (GDR)	225'9"	Romas Ubartas (URS)	221'5"	Rolf Danneberg(FRG)	221'1"
Hammer	Sergeiy Litvinov (URS)	278'2"	Yuriy Sedych (URS)	274'10"	Yuriy Tamm (URS)	266'3"
Javelin	Tapio Korjus (FIN)	276'6"	Jan Zelezny (TCH)	276'0"	Seppo Räty (FIN)	273'2"
Decathlon	Christian Schenk (GDR)	8488	Torsten Voss (GDR)	8399	Dave Steen (CAN)	8328

*Race Winner Ben Johnson (Can: 9.79) was disqualified for failing a drugs test

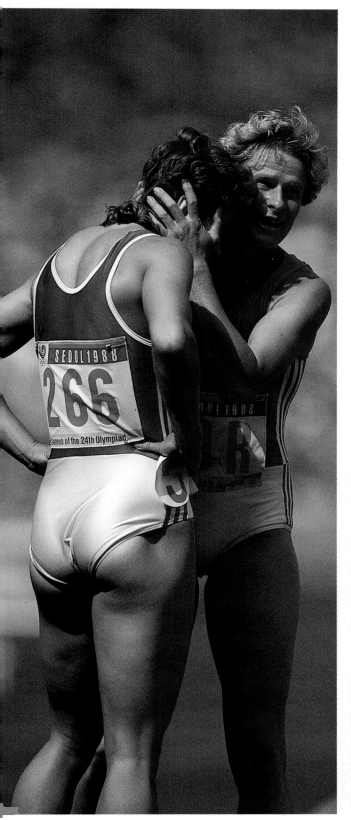

LEFT: *American gymnast, Ken Suter goes through his routine.* Pascal Rondeau

ABOVE LEFT: *Ingrid Lange comforts her teammate after they took silver in the 4 x 100 m relay.* Bob Martin

ABOVE RIGHT: *Julius Kariuki of Kenya leading Peter Koech in the 3,000 m steeplechase final.* Tony Duffy

SWIMMING — MEN

EVENT	GOLD		SILVER		BRONZE	
50 m Freestyle	Matt Biondi (USA)	22.14	Thomas Jager (USA)	22.36	Gennadi Prigoda (URS)	22.71
100 m Freestyle	Matt Biondi (USA)	48.63	Christopher Jacobs (USA)	49.08	Stephan Caron (FRA)	49.62
200 m Freestyle	Duncan Armstrong (AUS)	1:47.25	Anders Holmertz (SWE)	1:47.89	Matt Biondi (USA)	1:47.99
400 m Freestyle	Uwe Dassler (GDR)	3:46.95	Duncan Armstrong (AUS)	3:47.15	Artur Wojdat (POL)	3:47.34
1,500 m Freestyle	Vladimir Salnikov (URS)	15:00.40	Stefan Pfeiffer (FRG)	15:02.69	Uwe Dassler (GDR)	15:06.15
100 m Backstroke	Daichi Suzuki (JPN)	55.05	David Berkhoff (USA)	55.18	Igor Polianski (URS)	55.20
200 m Backstroke	Igor Polianski (URS)	1:59.37	Frank Baltrusch (GDR)	1:59.60	Paul Kingsman (NZL)	2:00.48
100 m Breaststroke	Adrian Moorhouse (GBR)	1:02.04	Károly Guttler (HUN)	1:02.05	Dimitri Volkov (URS)	1:02.20
200 m Breaststroke	Jozef Szábó (HUN)	2:13.52	Nick Gillingham (GBR)	2:14.12	Sergio Lopez (ESP)	2:15.21
100 m Butterfly	Anthony Nesty (SUR)	53.00	Matt Biondi (USA)	53.01	Andy Jameson (GBR)	53.30
200 m Butterfly	Michael Gross (FRG)	1:56.94	Benny Nielsen (DEN)	1:58.24	Anthony Mosse (NZL)	1:58.28
200 m Medley	Tamas Darnyi (HUN)	2:00.17	Patrick Kuhl (GDR)	2:01.61	Vadim Yaroshchuk (URS)	2:02.40
400 m Medley	Tamas Darnyi (HUN)	4:14.75	David Wharton (USA)	4:17.36	Stefano Battistelli (ITA)	4:18.01
4x100 m Freestyle	USA	3:16.53	USSR	3:18.33	GDR	3:19.82
4x200 m Freestyle	USA	7:12.51	GDR	7:13.68	FRG	7:14.35
4x100 m Medley	USA	3:36.93	Canada	3:39.28	USSR	3:39.96
Springboard Diving	Greg Louganis (USA)	730.80	Liangde Tan (CHN)	704.88	Deliang Li (CHN)	665.28
Highboard Diving	Greg Louganis (USA)	638.61	Ni Xiong (CHN)	637.47	Jesus Mena (MEX)	594.93
Water Polo	Yugoslavia		USA		USSR	

SYNCHRONIZED SWIMMING

	GOLD		SILVER		BRONZE	
Solo	Carolyn Waldo (CAN)	200.150	Tracie Ruiz-Conforto (USA)	197.633	Mikako Kotani (JPN)	191.850
Duet	Canada	197.717	USA	197.284	Japan	190.959

BOXING

EVENT	GOLD	SILVER	BRONZE
Light-Flyweight (-105.75 lb)	Ivailo Christov (BUL)	Michael Carbajal (USA)	Robert Isaszegi (HUN) Leopoldo Serantes (PHI)
Flyweight (-112.5 lb)	Kim Kwang Sun (KOR)	Andreas Tews (GDR)	Mario Gonzalez (MEX) Timofei Skriabin (URS)
Bantamweight (-119 lb)	Kennedy McKinney (USA)	Alexander Christov (BUL)	Phajol Moolsan (THA) Jorge Julio Rocha (COL)
Featherweight (-126 lb)	Giovanni Parisi (ITA)	Daniel Dumitrescu (ROM)	Abdelhak Achik (MAR) Lee Jae Hiuk (KOR)
Lightweight (- 132 lb)	Andreas Zülow (GDR)	George Cramne (SWE)	Nerguy Enchbat (MGL) Romallis Ellis (USA)
Light-Welterweight (-140 lb)	Vyacheslav Yanovski (URS)	Graham Cheney (AUS)	Reiner Gies (FRG) Lans Myberg (SWE)
Welterweight (-148 lb)	Robert Wangila (KEN)	Laurent Boudouani (FRA)	Jan Dydak (POL) Kenneth Gould (USA)
Light-Middleweight (- 157 lb)	Park Si Hun (KOR)	Roy Jones (USA)	Richard Woodhall (GBR) Raymond Downey (CAN)
Middleweight (-165 lb)	Henry Maske (GDR)	Egerton Marcus (CAN)	Chris Sande (KEN) Hussain Syed (PAK)
Light-Heavyweight (-178.5 lb)	Andrew Maynard (USA)	Nuramgomed Shanavasov (URS)	Henryk Petrich (POL) Damir Skaro (YUG)
Heavyweight (-200.5 lb)	Ray Mercer (USA)	Baik Hyun Man (KOR)	Andrzej Golota (POL) Arnold Vanderlijde (HOL)
Super-Heavyweight (+200.5 lb)	Lennox Lewis (CAN)	Riddick Bowe (USA)	Alexander Miroshnichenko (URS) Janusz Zarenkiewicz (POL)

ATHLETICS — WOMEN

EVENT	GOLD		SILVER		BRONZE	
100 m	Florence Griffith-Joyner (USA)	10.54	Evelyn Ashford (USA)	10.83	Heike Drechsler (GDR)	10.85
200 m	Florence Griffith-Joyner (USA)	21.34	Grace Jackson (JAM)	21.72	Heike Drechsler (GDR)	21.95
400 m	Olga Brizgina (URS)	48.65	Petra Müller (GDR)	49.45	Olga Nasarova (URS)	49.90
800 m	Sigrun Wodars (GDR)	1:56.10	Christine Wachtel (GDR)	1:56.64	Kim Gallagher (USA)	1:56.91
1,500 m	Paula Ivan (ROM)	3:53.96	Lelute Baikauskaite (URS)	4:00.24	Tatyana Samolenko (URS)	4:00.30
3,000 m	Tatyana Samolenko (URS)	8:26.53	Paula Ivan (ROM)	8:27.15	Yvonne Murray (GBR)	8:29.02
10,000 m	Olga Bondarenko (URS)	31:05.21	Elizabeth McColgan (GBR)	31:08.44	Yelena Yupiveva (URS)	31:19.82
Marathon	Rosa Mota (POR)	2:25:40	Lisa Martin (AUS)	2:25:53	Katrin Dörre (GDR)	2:26:21
100 m Hurdles	Yordanka Donkova (BUL)	12.38	Gloria Siebert (GDR)	12.61	Claudia Zaczkewicz (FRG)	12.75
400 m Hurdles	Debra Flintoff-King (AUS)	53.17	Tatyana Ledovskaya (URS)	53.18	Ellen Fiedler (GDR)	53.63
4x100 m	USA	41.98	GDR	42.09	USSR	42.75
4x400 m	USSR	3:15.18	USA	3:15.51	GDR	3:18.29
High Jump	Louise Ritter (USA)	6'8"	Stefka Kostadinova (BUL)	6'7"	Tamara Bykova (URS)	6'6.25"
Long Jump	Jackie Joyner-Kersee (USA)	24'3.5"	Heike Drechsler (GDR)	23'8.25"	Galina Chistyakova (URS)	23'4"
Shot	Natalia Lisovskaya (URS)	72'11.75"	Kathrin Neimke (GDR)	69'1.5"	Meisu Li (CHN)	69'1.25"
Discus	Martina Hellmann (GDR)	237'2"	Diana Gansky (GDR)	235'10"	Szvetanka Christova (BUL)	228'10"
Javelin	Petra Felke (GDR)	245'0"	Fatima Whitbread (GBR)	230'8"	Beate Koch (GDR)	220'9"
Heptathlon	Jackie Joyner-Kersee (USA)	7291	Sabine John (GDR)	6897	Anke Behiner (GDR)	6858

ABOVE: *Daley Thompson of Great Britain competing in the pole vault portion of the decathlon.* Gerard Vandystadt

ABOVE LEFT: *Colin Jackson leads Roger Kingdom in the 110 m hurdles.* Gray Mortimore

TOP LEFT: *West Germany's Christian Schenk won the decathlon.* Steve Powell

357

SWIMMING — WOMEN

EVENT	GOLD		SILVER		BRONZE	
50 m Freestyle	Kristin Otto (GDR)	25.49	Wenyi Yang (CHN)	25.64	Katrin Meissner (GDR)	25.71
					Jill Sterkel (USA)	25.71
100 m Freestyle	Kristin Otto (GDR)	54.93	Yong Zhuang (CHN)	55.47	Cathérine Plewinski (FRA)	55.49
200 m Freestyle	Heike Friedrich (GDR)	1:57.65	Sivia Poll (CRC)	1:58.67	Manuela Stellmach (GDR)	1:59.01
400 m Freestyle	Janet Evans (USA)	4:03.85	Heike Friedrich (GDR)	4:05.94	Anke Möhring (GDR)	4:06.62
800 m Freestyle	Janet Evans (USA)	8:20.20	Astrid Strauss (GDR)	8:22.09	Julie McDonald (AUS)	8:22.93
100 m Backstroke	Kristin Otto (GDR)	1:00.89	Krisztina Egerszegy (HUN)	1:01.56	Cornelia Sirch (GDR)	1:01.57
200 m Backstroke	Krisztna Egerszegy (HUN)	2:09.29	Kathrin Zimmermann (GDR)	2:10.61	Cornelia Sirch (GDR)	2:11.45
100 m Breaststroke	Tania Dangalakova (BUL)	1:07.95	Antonella Frenkeva (BUL)	1:08.74	Silke Horner (GDR)	1:08.83
200 m Breaststroke	Silke Horner (GDR)	2:26.71	Xiaomin Huang (CHN)	2:27.49	Antoaneta Frenkeva (BUL)	2:28.34
100 m Butterfly	Kriston Otto (GDR)	59.00	Birte Weigang (GDR)	59.45	Hong Quian (CHN)	59.52
200 m Butterfy	Kathleen Nord (GDR)	2:09.51	Birte Weigang (GDR)	2:09.91	Mary T. Meagher (USA)	2:10.80
200 m Medley	Daniela Hunger (GDR)	2:12.59	Elena Dendeberova (URS)	2:13.31	Noemi lidiko Lung (ROM)	2:14.85
400 m Medley	Janet Evans (USA)	4:37.76	Noemi Lung (ROM)	4:39.46	Daniela Hunger (GDR)	4:39.76
4x100 m Freestyle	GDR	3:40.63	Netherlands	3:43.39	USA	3:44.25
4x100 m Medley	GDR	4:03.74	USA	4:07.90	Canada	4:10.49
Springboard Diving	Min Gao (CHN)	580.23	Qing Li (CHN)	534.33	Kelly McCormick (USA)	533.19
Highboard Diving	Yanmei Xu (CHN)	445.20	Michele Mitchell (USA)	436.95	Wendy Lian Williams (USA)	400.44

JUDO

EVENT	GOLD	SILVER	BRONZE
Super-Lighrweight (-132.5 Ib)	Kim Jae Yup (KOR)	Kevin Asano (USA)	Shinji Hosokawa (JPN)
			Amiran Totikashvili (URS)
Half-Lightweight (-143.25 Ib)	Lee Kyung Keun (KOR)	Janusz Pawlowski (POL)	Bruno Carabetta (FRA)
			Yosuke Yamamoto (JPN)
Lightweight (-156.5 Ib)	Marc Alexandre (FRA)	Sven Loll (GDR)	Michael Swain (USA)
			Georgiy Tenadze (URS)
Light-Middleweight (-171.75 Ib)	Waldemar Legien (POL)	Frank Wieneke (FRG)	Torsten Bréchôt (GDR)
			Bashir Varayev (URS)
Middleweight (-189.5 Ib)	Peter Seisenbacher (AUT)	Vladimir Chestakov (URS)	Ben Spijkers (HOL)
			Akinobu Osako (JPN)
Light-Heavyweight (-209.25 Ib)	Aurelio Miguel (BRA)	Marc Meiling (FRG)	Robert van de Walle (BEL)
			Dennis Stewart (GBR)
Heavyweight (+ 209.5 Ib)	Hitoshi Saito (JPN)	Henry Stöhr (GDR)	Cho Young Chul (KOR)
			Grigory Verichev (URS)

FENCING

EVENT	GOLD	SILVER	BRONZE
Individual Foil — Men	Stefano Cerioni (ITA)	Udo Wagner (GDR)	Alexander Romankov (URS)
Team Foil — Men	USSR	FRG	Hungary
Individual Épée	Jean-François Lamour (FRA)	Janusz Olech (POL)	Giovanni Scalzo (ITA)
Team Épée	Hungary	USSR	Italy
Individual Sabre	Arnd Schmitt (FRG)	Philippe Riboud (FRA)	Andrei Shuvalov (URS)
Team Sabre	France	FRG	USSR
Individual Foil — Women	Anja Fichtel (FRG)	Sabine Bau (FRG)	Zita Funkenhauser (FRG)
Team Foil - Women	FRG	Italy	Hungary

WEIGHTLIFTING

EVENT	GOLD		SILVER		BRONZE	
Flyweight	Sevdalin Marinov (BUL)	595 lb	Byung-Kwan Chun (KOR)	573 lb	Zhuoquiang He (CHN)	567.5 lbs
Bantamweight	Oken Mirzoian (URS)	644 lb	Yiangqiang He (CHN)	633.75 lb	Shoubin Liu (CHN)	589.25 lbs
Featherweight	Nahim Süleymanoglu (TUR)	755 lb	Stefan Topourov (BUL)	688.75 lb	Huanming Ye (CHN)	633.75 lbs
Lightweight	Joachim Kunz (GDR)	749.5 lb	Israil Militosian (URS)	744 lb	Jinhe Li (CHN)	716.5 lbs
Middleweight	Borislav Gidikov (BUL)	826 lb	Ingo Steinhöfel (GDR)	793 lb	Alexander Varbanov (BUL)	788 lbs
Light-Heavyweight	Israil Arsamakov (URS)	832 lb	Istvan Messzi (HUN)	815.5 lb	Lee Hyung Kun (KOR)	810 lbs
Middle-Heavyweight	Anatoli Khrapaty (URS)	412 lb	Nail Muchamediarov(URS)	881.75 lb	Slawomir Zawada (POL)	881.75 lbs
First Heavyweight 100 kg	Pavel Kuznetzov (URS)	936.75 lb	Nicu Vlad (ROM)	887.25 lb	Peter Immesberger (FRG)	870.75 lbs
Second Heavyweight	Juri Zacharevich (URS)	1,003 lb	Jozse Jacso (HUN)	942.5 lb	Ronny Weller (GDR)	936.75 lbs
Super-Heavyweight	Alexander Kurlovich (URS)	1,019 lb	Manfred Nerlinger (FRG)	947.75 lb	Marun Zawieja (FRG)	914.75 lbs

WEIGHTLIFTING WEIGHTS

FLYWEIGHT	-114.5 lb	BANTAMWEIGHT	-123.5 lb	FEATHERWEIGHT	-132.25 lb
LIGHTWEIGHT	-148.75 lb	MIDDLEWEIGHT-	165.5 lb	LIGHT-HEAVYWEIGHT -	-182 lb
MIDDLE-HEAVYWEIGHT	-182.5 lb	FIRST-HEAVYWEIGHT	-220.5 lb	SECOND-HEAVYWEIGHT --	-242.5 lb
SUPER-HEAVYWEIGHT	+242.5.5 lb				

GRECO-ROMAN WRESTLING

EVENT	GOLD	SILVER	BRONZE
Light-Flyweight (-105.75 lb)	Vincenzo Maenza (ITA)	Andrzej Chlab (POL)	Bratan Tzenov (BUL)
Flyweight (-114.5 lb)	Jon Rönningen (NOR)	Atsuji Miyahara (JPN)	Lee Jae Suk (KOR)
Bantamweight (-125.75 lb)	Andras Sike (HUN)	Stoyan Balov (BUL)	Haralambos Holidis (GRE)
Featherweight (-136.5 lb)	Kamandar Madzhidov (URS)	Yivko Vangyelov (BUL)	An Dae Hyun (KOR)
Lightweight (-149.75 lb)	Levon Zhulfalakian (URS)	Kim Sung Moon (KOR)	Tapio Sipilä (FIN)
Welterweight (-163.75 lb)	Kim Young Nam (KOR)	Daulet Turlykanow (URS)	Jozef Tracz (POL)
Middleweight (-180.75 lb)	Mikhail Mamiashvili (URS)	Tibor Komaronyi (HUN)	Kim Sang Kyu (KOR)
Light-Heavyweight (-198.25 lb)	Atanas Komchev (BUL)	Harri Koskela (FIN)	Vladimir Popov (URS)
Heavyweight (-220.5 lb)	Andrzej Wronski (POL)	Gerhard Himmel (FRG)	Dennis Koslowski (USA)
Super-Heavyweight (+220.5 lb)	Aleksander Karelin (URS)	Rangel Guerovski (BUL)	Tonzas Johansson (SWE)

Anke Behiner, Sabine John and Innes Schulz in the heptathlon 800 m. Gray Mortimore

Jackie Joyner-Kersee of the USA winning the heptathlon gold. Bob Martin

PAGE 365: *The Olympic flame and flag* Allsport

FREESTYLE WRESTLING

EVENT	GOLD	SILVER	BRONZE
Light-Flyweight (-105.75 lb)	Takashi Kobayashi (JPN)	Ivan Tzonov (BUL)	Sergey Karamchakov (URS)
Flyweight (-114.5 lb)	Mitsuru Sato (JPN)	Saban Trstena (YUG)	Vladimir Togusov (URS)
Bantam (-125.75 lb)	Sergey Beloglassov (URS)	Askari Mohammadian (IRN)	Noh Kyung Sun (KOR)
Featherweight (-114.5 lb)	John Smith (USA)	Stephan Sarkissian (URS)	Simeon Schterev (BUL)
Lightweight (-149.75 lb)	Arsen Fadzayev (URS)	Park Jang Soon (KOR)	Nate Carr (USA)
Welterweight (-163 lb)	Kenneth Monday (USA)	Adlan Vanayev (URS)	Rakhmad Sofiadi (BUL)
Middleweight (-180.75 lb)	Han Myung Woo (KOR)	Necmi Gencalp (TUR)	Josef Lohyna (TCH)
Light-Heavyweight (-198.25 lb)	Macharbek Hadanchev (URS)	Akira Ota (JPN)	Kim Tae Woo (KOR)
Heavyweight (-220.5 lb)	Vasile Puscasu (ROM)	Leri Kabelow (URS)	William Scherer (USA)
Super-Heavyweight (+220.5 lb)	David Gobedishvili (URS)	Bruce Baumgartner (USA)	Andreas Schröder (GDR)

MODERN PENTATHLON

EVENT	GOLD		SILVER		BRONZE	
Individual	Janós Marntinek (HUN)	5404	Carlo Massullo (ITA)	5379	Vachtang Yagorashvili (URS)	5367
Team	Hungary	15886	Italy	15571	Great Britain	15276

ROWING — WOMEN

EVENT	GOLD		SILVER		BRONZE	
Single Sculls	Jutra Behrendt (GDR)	7:47.19	Anne Marden (USA)	7:50.28	Magdalena Georgieva (BUL)	7:53.65
Double Sculls	GDR	7:00.48	Romania	7:04.36	Bulgaria	7:06.03
Coxless Pairs	Romania	7:28.13	Bulgaria	7:31.95	New Zealand	7:35.68
Coxed Quadruple Sculls	GDR	6:21.06	USSR	6:23.47	Romania	6:23.81
Coxed Fours	GDR	6:56.00	China	6:58.78	Romania	7:01.13
Coxed Eights	GDR	6:15.17	Romania	6:17.44	China	6:21.83

CANOEING — MEN

EVENT	GOLD		SILVER		BRONZE	
500 m Kayak Singles K1	Zsolt Gyulay (HUN)	1:44.82	Andreas Stähle (GDR)	1:46.38	Paul MacDonald (NZL)	1:46.46
1,000 m Kayak Singles K1	Greg Barton (USA)	3:55.27	Grant Davies (AUS)	3:55.28	André Wohllebe (GDR)	3:55.55
500 m Kayak Pairs K2	New Zealand	1:33.98	USSR	1:34.15	Hungary	1:34.32
1,000 m Kayak Pairs K2	USA	3:32.42	New Zealand	3:32 71	Australia	3:33.76
1,000 m Kayak Fours K4	Hungary	3:00.20	USSR	3:01.40	GDR	3:02.37
500 m Canadian Singles C1	Olaf Heukrodt (GDR)	1:56.42	Mikhail Slivinski (URS)	1:57.26	Martin Marinov (BUL)	1:57.27
1,000 m Canadian Singles C1	Ivan Klementiev (URS)	4:12.78	Jörg Schmidt (GDR)	4:15.83	Nikolai Bukalov (URS)	4:18.94
500 m Canadian Pairs C2	USSR	1:41 77	Poland	1:43.61	France	1:43.81
1,000 m Canadian Pairs C2	USSR	3:48.36	GDR	3:51.44	Poland	3:54.33

CANOEING — WOMEN

EVENT	GOLD		SILVER		BRONZE	
500 m Kayak Singles K1	Vania Guechava (BUL)	1:55.19	Birgit Schmidt (GDR)	1:55.31	Izabela Dylewska (POL)	1:57.38
500 m Kayak Pairs K2	GDR	1:43.46	Bulgaria	1:44.06	Netherlands	1:46.00
500 m Kayak Fours K4	GDR	1:40.78	Hungary	1:41.88	Bulgaria	1:42.63

YACHTING

EVENT	GOLD		SILVER		BRONZE	
Finn Class	José Luis Doreste (ESP)	38.1	Peter Holmberg (ISV)	40.4	John Cutler (NZL)	45.0
International Star	Great Britain	45.7	USA	48.0	Brazil	50.0
Flying Dutchman	Denmark	31.4	Norway	37.4	Canada	48.4
International Tornado	France	16.0	New Zealand	35.4	Brazil	40.1
470 Women	USA	26.7	Sweden	40.0	USSR	45.4
470 Men	France	34.7	USSR	46.0	USA	51.0
International Soling	GDR	11.7	USA	14.0	Denmark	52.7
Surfing	Bruce Kendall (NZL)	35.4	Jan Boersma (AHO)	42.7	Michael Gebhardt (USA)	48.0

ROWING — MEN

EVENT	GOLD		SILVER		BRONZE	
Single Sculls	Thomas Lange (GDR)	6:49.86	Peter-Michael Kolbe (FRG)	6:54.77	Eric Verdonk (NZL)	6:58.66
Double Sculls	Netherlands	6:21.13	Switzerland	6:22.59	USSR	6:22.87
Coxless Pairs	Great Britain	6:36.84	Romania	6:38.06	Yugoslavia	6:41.01
Coxed Pairs	Italy	6:58.79	GDR	7:00.63	Great Britain	7:01.95
Coxless Quadruple Sculls	Italy	5:53.37	Norway	5:55.08	GDR	5:56.13
Coxless Fours	GDR	6:03.11	USA	6:05.33	FRG	6:06.22
Coxed Fours	GDR	6:10.74	Romania	6:13.58	New Zealand	6:15.78
Coxed Eights	FRG	5:46.05	USSR	5:48.01	USA	5:48.26

CYCLING — MEN

EVENT	GOLD		SILVER		BRONZE	
Road Race (122.25 mi)	Olaf Ludwig (GDR)	4:32:22	Bernd Gröne (FRG)	4:32:25	Christian Henn (FRG)	4:32:46
100 km Road TeamTime Trial	GDR	1:57:47.7	Poland	1:57:54.2	Sweden	1:59:47.3
Sprint	Lutz Hesslich (GDR)		Nikolai Kovche (URS)		Gary Neiwand (AUS)	
1,000 m Time Trial	Alexander Kirichenko (URS)	1:04.499	Martin Vinnicombe(AUS)	1:04.784	Robert Lechner(FRG)	1:05.114
4,000 m Individual Pursuit	Gintautus Umaras (URS)	4:32.00	Dean Woods (AUS)	4:35.00	Bernd Dittert (GDR)	4:34.17
4,000 m Team Pursuit	USSR	4:13.31	GDR	4:14.09	Australia	4:16.02
Individual Points Race	Dan Frost (DEN)	38	Leo Peelen (HOL)	26	Marat Ganeyev (URS)	46/1

CYCLING — WOMEN

EVENT	GOLD		SILVER		BRONZE	
Road Race (51 mi)	Monique Knol (HOL)	2:00:52	Jutta Niehaus (FRG)		Laima Zilporite (URS)	
Sprint	Erika Salumiá (URS)		Christa Luding-Rothenburg (GDR)		Connie Paraskevin-Young (USA)	

SHOOTING — MEN

EVENT	GOLD		SILVER		BRONZE	
Small-Bore Rifle (Prone)	Miroslav Varga (TCH)	703.9	Young Chul Cha (KOR)	702.8	Attila Zahonyi (HUN)	701.9
Small-Bore Rifle (3 Positions)	Malcolm Cooper (GBR)	1279.3	Alister Allan (GBR)	1275.6	Kirill Ivanov (URS)	1275.0
Rapid-Fire Pistol	Afanasi Kuzmin (URS)	698	Ralf Schumann (GDR)	696	Zoltan Kovacs (HUN)	693
Free Pistol (50 m)	Sorin Babii (ROM)	660	Ragnar Skanaker (SWE)	657	Igor Bassinski (URS)	657
Running Game Target	Tor Heiestad (NOR)	689	Shiping Huang (CHN)	687	Gennadi Avramenko (URS)	686
Air Pistol	Taniou Kiriakov (BUL)	687.9	Erich Buljung (USA)	687.9	Haifeng Xu (CHN)	684.5
Skeet Shooting	Axel Wegner (GDR)	222	Alfonso de Iruarrizaga (CHI)	221	Jorge Guardiola (ESP)	220
Trap Shooting	Dimitri Monakov (URS)	222.8	Miloslaw Bednarik (TCH)	694.2	Trans Peeters (FRG)	694.0
Air Rifle	Goran Maksimovic (YUG)	695.6	Nicolas Berthelot (FRA)	694.2	Johann Riederer (FRG)	694.0

SHOOTING — WOMEN

EVENT	GOLD		SILVER		BRONZE	
Sports Pistol	Nino Salukvadze (URS)	690	Tomoko Hasegawa (JPN)	686	Jasna Sekaric (YUG)	686
Small-Bore Rifle (3 Positions)	Silvia Sperber (FRG)	685.6	Vessela Lecheva (BUL)	683.2	Valentina Cherkassova (URS)	681.4
Air Rifle	Irina Chilova (URS)	498.5	Silvia Sperber (FRG)	497.5	Anna Malukina (URS)	495.8
Air Pistol	Jasna Sekaric YUG)	489.5	Nino Salukvadze (URS)	487.9	Marina Dobrancheva (URS)	485.2

ARCHERY — MEN

EVENT	GOLD		SILVER		BRONZE	
Individual	Jay Barrs (USA)	338	Park Sung Soo (KOR)	336	Vladimir Echeyev (URS)	335
Team	South Korea	986	USA	972	Great Britain	968

Gelindo Bordin of Italy (579) wins the marathon. Mike Powell

Weightlifter Tsai Wen Yee of Taiwan. Gerard Vandystadt

ARCHERY — WOMEN

EVENT	GOLD		SILVER		BRONZE	
Individual	Kim Soo Nyung (KOR)	344	Wang Hee Kyung (KOR)	332	Yun Young Sook (KOR)	327
Team	South Korea	982	Indonesia	952	USA	952

EQUESTRIANISM

EVENT	GOLD		SILVER		BRONZE	
Three-Day Event	Mark Todd (NZL)	42.60	Ian Stark (GBR)	52.80	Virginia Leng (GBR)	62.00
Three-Day Event Team	FRG	225.95	Great Britain	256.80	New Zealand	271.20
Grand Prix (Dressage)	Nicole Uphoff (FRG)	1521	Margitt Otto-Crepin (FRA)	1462	Christine Stückelberger (SUI)	1417
Gralid Prix (Dressage) Team	FRG	4302	Switzerland	4164	Canada	3969
Grand Prix (Jumping)	Pierre Durand (FRA)	1.25	Greg Best (USA)	4.00	Karsten Huck (FRG)	4.00
Grand Prix (Jumping) Team	FRG	17.25	USA	20.50	France	27.50

GYMNASTICS — MEN

EVENT	GOLD		SILVER		BRONZE	
Individual Combined Exercises	Vladinur Artemov (URS)	119 125	Valeri Lyukin (URS)	119.025	Dimitri Biloserchev (URS)	118.975
Team	USSR	593.35	GDR	588.45	Japan	585.60
Parallel Bars	Vladimir Artemov (URS)	19.925	Valeri Lyukill (URS)	19.900	Sven Tippelt (GDR)	19.750
Floor	Sergei Kharkov (URS)	19.925	Vladimir Artemov (URS)	19.900	Yun Lou (CHN)	19.850
Horse Vault	Yun Lou (CHN)	19.875	Sylvio Kroll (GDR)	19.862	Park Jong Hoon (KOR)	19.775
Horizontal Bar	Vladimir Artemov (URS)	19.900			Holger Behrendt (Gl)R)	19.800
	Valeri Lukin (URS)	19.900			Marius Gherman (ROM)	19.800
Rings	Holger Behrendt (GDR)	19.925			Sven Tippelt (GDR)	19.875
	Dimitri Biloserchev (URS)	19.925				
Pommel Horse	Lubomir Guraskolv (BUL)	19.950				
	Zsolt Borkai (HUN)	19.950				
	Dimitri Biloserchev (URS)	19.950				

GYMNASTICS — WOMEN

EVENT	GOLD		SILVER		BRONZE	
Individual Combined Exercises	Elena Shushunova (URS)	79 662	Daniela Silivas (ROM)	79.637	Svetlana Boginskaya (URS)	79 400
Team	USSR	395.475	Romania	394.125	GDR	390.875
Floor	Daniela Silivas (ROM)	19.937	Svetlana Boginskaya (URS)	19.887	Diana Doudeva (BUL)	19.850
Horse Vault	Svetlana Boginskaya (URS)	19.905	Gabriela Potorac (ROM)	19.830	Daniela Silivas (ROM)	19.818
Beam	Daniela Silivas (ROM)	19.924	Elena Shushunova (URS)	19.875	Gabriela Potorac (ROM)	19.837
					Phoebe Mills (USA)	19.837
Asymmetrical Bars	Daniela Silivas (ROM)	20.000	Dagmar Kersten (GDR)	19.987	Elena Shusanova (URS)	19.962
Modern Rhythmic	Marina Lobach (URS)	60 000	Adriana Dunavska (BUL)	59.950	Alexandra Timoshenko (URS)	59.875

TENNIS — MEN

	GOLD	SILVER	BRONZE
Individual	Miloslav Mecir (TCH)	Tim Mayotte (USA)	Stefan Edberg (SWE)
			Brad Gilbert (USA)
Doubles	Ken Flach / Robert Seguso (USA)	Emilio Sanchez / Sergio Casal (ESP)	Steftan Edberg / AndersJarryd (SWE)
			Miroslav Mecir / Milan Srejber (TCH)

TENNIS — WOMEN

	GOLD	SILVER	BRONZE
Individual	Steffi Graf (FRG)	Gabriela Sabatini (ARG)	Zina Garrison (USA)
			Manuela Maleeva (BUL)
Doubles	Pam Shriver / Zina Garrison (USA)	Jana Novotna / Helena Sukova (TCH)	Steffi Graf / Claudia Kohde-Kilsch (FRG)
			Elizabeth Smylie / Wendy Turnball (AUS)

TABLE TENNIS — MEN

	GOLD	SILVER	BRONZE
Singles	Yoo Nam Kyu (KOR)	Kim Ki Taik (KOR)	Erik Lindh (SWE)
Doubles	China	Yugoslavia	South Korea

ABOVE LEFT: *An emotional Canadian women's track team. Gray Mortimore*

LEFT: *American Florence Griffith Joyner won the 100 m gold. Mike Powell*

ABOVE: *America's Carl Lewis in the 100 m heats. Mike Powell*

TABLE TENNIS — WOMEN

	GOLD	SILVER	BRONZE
Individual	Jing Chen (CHN)	Huifeng Li (CHN)	Zhimin Jiao(CHN)
Doubles	South Korea	China	Yugoslavia

BASKETBALL — MEN

GOLD	SILVER	BRONZE
USSR	Yugoslavia	USA

BASKETBALL — WOMEN

GOLD	SILVER	BRONZE
USA	Yugoslavia	USSR

SOCCER

GOLD	SILVER	BRONZE
USSR	Brazil	FRG

England and Germany playing hockey in the summer games. Simon Bruty

HANDBALL — MEN

GOLD	SILVER	BRONZE
USSR	South Korea	Yugoslavia

HANDBALL — WOMEN

GOLD	SILVER	BRONZE
South Korea	Norvay	USSR

HOCKEY — MEN

GOLD	SILVER	BRONZE
Great Britain	FRG	Netherlands

Above: Yugoslavian basketball ace Dino Rajda at play. Joe Patronite

Above right: Great Britain versus Australia. Great Britain eventually won gold in hockey. David Cannon

HOCKEY — WOMEN

GOLD	SILVER	BRONZE
Australia	South Korea	Netherlands

VOLLEYBALL — MEN

GOLD	SILVER	BRONZE
USA	USSR	Argentina

VOLLEYBALL — WOMEN

GOLD	SILVER	BRONZE
USSR	Peru	China

The torch arrives.

FAR LEFT: Gymnast Lou Yun of China. Pascal Rondea

ABOVE AND LEFT: Marathon competitors. Pascal Rondeau

PREVIOUS PAGE: The 4x100 m relay final. Tony Duffy

ABOVE: *Valeri Lukin of the Soviet Union placed second in the all round men's individual gymnastics competition.* Mike Powell

LEFT: *Steve Lewis of the United States won the 400 m gold.* Steve Powell

RIGHT: *West German, Thomas Duerst qualifies for the 4,000 m individual pursuit.* Mike Powell

OVERLEAF: *An aerial view of the women's 82 km road race.* Billy Stickland

ABOVE: *Jackie Joyner-Kersee, showing the athleticism that put her first in the women's heptathlon.* Tony Duffy

OPPOSITE PAGE TOP: *The closing ceremony at Seoul 1988.* David Cannon
BOTTOM: *A gold medal from Seoul 1988.* Allsport

BARCELONA 1992

INTRODUCTION

Barcelona 1992

PREVIOUS PAGE AND ABOVE: *A diver leaps from the board, with Barcelona's spectacular skyline as her backdrop at the 1992 Olympic summer games.* Bob Martin

BOTTOM RIGHT: *South African president Nelson Mandela accompanied his nation's team to Barcelona.* David Leah

257
EVENTS

169
COUNTRIES

9,364
ATHLETES

	Gold	Silver	Bronze
EUN	45	38	29
USA	37	34	37
GER	33	21	28
CHN	16	22	16
CUB	14	6	11
ESP	13	7	2
KOR	12	5	12
HUN	11	12	7
FRA	8	5	16
AUS	7	9	11
ITA	6	5	8
CAN	6	5	7
GBR	5	3	12
ROM	4	6	8
CZE	4	2	1
PKR	4		5
JPN	3	8	11
BUL	3	7	6
POL	3	6	10
NED	2	6	7
KEN	2	4	2
NOR	2	4	1
TUR	2	2	2
INA	2	2	1
BRA	2	1	
GRE	2		
SWE	1	7	4
NZL	1	4	5
FIN	1	2	2
DEN	1	1	4
MOR	1	1	1
IRL	1	1	
ETH	1		2
ALG	1		1
EST	1		1
LTU	1		1
SUI	1		
JAM		3	1
NIG		3	1
LAT		2	1
SAF		2	
AUT		2	
NAM		2	
BEL		1	2
CRO		1	2
IRN		1	2
IOP		1	2
ISR		1	1
MEX		1	
PER		1	
TPE		1	
MON			2
SLO			2
ARG			1
BAH			1
COL			1
GHA			1
MAL			1
PAK			1
PHI			1
PUR			1
QAT			1
SUR			1
THA			1

What a welcome! These were the games when the International Olympic Committee, which four years ago had seen the end of the US-Soviet boycotts, now saw the reemergence of other national teams on the sporting stage. With the Berlin Wall gone, German athletes competed as one team for the first time since 1952. And with the fall of apartheid, South Africa's international banishment was ended.

What made the Barcelona Olympics so astonishingly successful, however, was the sheer enthusiasm of the hosts. About $8 billion was spent on the Olympics in the year Spanish IOC president Juan Antonio Samaranch brought the games to his homeland of Catalonia. The Catalans had always defended their independence of language and spirit from the rest of Spain. The arrival of the games, however, had an unexpected bonus in unifying them with the rest of their countrymen.

The benefits were clear to see — in that the triumphal staging of the Olympics coincided with

the triumph of Spanish athletes, who won
13 gold medals in Barcelona. Before
then, Spain had won only four
gold medals in the history of the
Summer Olympics.

The incentive was not
only patriotism. The Spanish
poured money into the games like
concrete into the foundations of the
many new and refurbished stadia. The
government granted $160 million, almost
matched by a consortium of major corporations, so
that hundreds of Spanish athletes could devote
themselves to intensive training. There was a $1
million trust for each gold medal winner.
And there was even $1 million to pamper and
train a horse named Fino Barcelona '92 which
was competing in the equestrian events. (It finished 19th!)

No wonder Spanish athletes like Fermin
Cacho suddenly showed the
rest of the world a clean pair
of heels — in his case, storming past the leaders in the straight
to steal the 1,500 meters.

It was the year that money talked. For the
games now welcomed pros, including the multi-
million-dollar stars of the NBA. The American
basketball "dream team," featuring Michael
Jordan and Magic Johnson, swept the field and
won gold by an average of 40 points a game.

America's Carl Lewis won his third consecutive long jump gold. Gail Devers, who almost lost her feet to a blood disorder, won the women's 100 meters. And Jackie Joyner-Kersee was unbeatable in the heptahtlon.

But the medals were well spread across the international spectrum. A "Unified Team" represented the old Soviet Union, among whose members Vitali Scherbo was Barcelona's star, winning six gymnastics gold medals.

Krisztina Egerszegi, who became the youngest swimmer ever to take an Olympic gold medal in 1988, retained her 200 meters backstroke title in Barcelona with the second fastest time in history and an Olympic record. The "Hungarian Mouse" added the 100 meters backstroke and the 400 meters medley titles.

At the other end of the age scale, Britain's Linford Christie decided on one last bid for Olympic glory at the age of 32 — and became the oldest man in history to win the 100 meters title.

And a former shepherdess from Ethiopia named Derartu Tulu outpaced South African Lana Meyer to win the 10,000 meters. When she ran a lap of honor alongside her white rival, the true spirit of the Olympic games was again clear to see.

Barcelona

LINFORD CHRISTIE

He will not thank anyone for reminding him but Britain's golden sprinter Linford Christie outpaced Father Time to win his Olympic 100 meters gold medal in Barcelona. "I'm the best — I am a remarkable athlete," Christie said simply.

The skinny Jamaican-born kid, who came to England when he was seven and started running a year later, never lacked confidence. "I thought I had all the talent in the world but I didn't train that much. I just messed around."

When he started, he had to borrow spikes from his school gym and he did not have a track suit — he ran in his jeans.

Overshadowed at first by the Americans and Ben Johnson, Christie outlasted them all and was still competing at a high level well into his late thirties. He claimed he was "living proof" that it was possible with the right training and the right attitude to transform yourself into a world-beater.

Yet in his early days, while Christie's ability on the track was never in doubt, the problem was getting him onto one. Instead of training, he preferred partying or hanging around the West London Stadium that would eventually be renamed in his honor, playing dominoes.

In 1984, the then 24-year-old failed to make Great Britain's team for the Los Angeles Olympics, even in the sprint relay. In his autobiography, entitled *To be Honest With You*, Christie admitted: "I reckoned I had all the talent in the world. Guys who were training couldn't beat me. So why did I need to bother? Training was so tedious."

Christie took stock of his career and within two years of that rejection, he had been crowned European Champion indoors, at 200 meters, and out at 100 meters. His time for the 100 meters had come tumbling down from 10.42sec to 10.04sec.

In the next decade, Christie established himself as Britain's greatest ever sprinter and its most successful athlete in history. By the time he retired from competition after leading the men's team to a second European Cup title in Munich in 1997, he had won a record 23 major championship medals of which 10 were gold.

But, for Christie, his career was often a stormy ride with officialdom, fellow athletes and, most notably, the media. Christie announced his retirement, or threatened to quit, several times in the ensuing years but as each championships came he would be there winning medals.

The first global success came at the 1988 Olympics when he was promoted to the silver medal behind American rival Carl Lewis after the "winner," Canadian Ben Johnson, fell foul of the drug testers. Johnson's positive test also brought a belated bronze for the Briton from the World Championships in 1987 where he had originally finished fourth.

Christie successfully defended his European title in 1990 and also won his first Commonwealth crown. But when he finished just out of the medals at the 1991 World Championships it seemed that elusive global gold was going to be beyond him.

Retirement beckoned again, only to be forestalled by a van-load of mail from his fans who successfully pleaded with him to reconsider. "Best decision I ever made," Christie was to say 12 months later.

At 32, he decided to have one last-gasp crack at Olympic glory and blazed down the Barcelona track to become the oldest man in history to win the 100 meters title.

Christie could justifiably claim to be the world's fastest man in 1992. And a year later he came within just 0.01 of a second of grabbing the actual world record from Lewis. The consolation, though, was that the time was clocked in the World Championships final in Stuttgart. History was made again as he became the first man to hold all four major titles.

However, a new generation of sprinters were quickly catching up and in 1995 — hampered by a hamstring injury and a long dispute with British officials — he was sixth as his world title went to Canada's Donovan Bailey.

Twelve months later, after a "will-he won't-he go to Atlanta?" saga that became tedious, he was eventually dethroned as Olympic champion in sensational fashion.

Christie incurred two false starts in the Centennial Stadium, leaving cynics to suggest he could not bear to be beaten on the track. He did cross the finish line, though, long after Bailey had claimed the gold.

It was not the greatest of ways to bow out of major championships, but it somehow seemed to sum up his career. Controversial to the end.

Christie is now coaching and guiding some of Britain's most promising athletes via the management company, Nuff Respect, which he originally set up with hurdler Colin Jackson. The name was taken from the street argot of young blacks. And Christie's record on the track has demanded respect ever since.

Linford Christie of Great Britain. Tony Duffy

JACKIE JOYNER-KERSEE

Jackie Joyner-Kersee could have been a star at basketball, made a decent living, and left it at that. But she wanted to be a pioneer, too... Because she knew the toughest steps in her journey were the ones that carried her up and out of East St. Louis, Illinois, the place she called home and which government statistics call America's worst ghetto.

But it did not take long for her to set her sights on the horizon, and not much longer after that to begin practicing to reach it.

As a little girl, Jackie was running and jumping off the three-foot-high porch of her grandmother's house, where she was raised, into sand she carried off from a nearby park in little bags. "I jumped until my mother came home from work," Joyner-Kersee said.

Even though she came from one of the most downtrodden areas of the country, her dream was to become an Olympic athlete, "but never did I dream I would win all those medals," she said.

Joyner-Kersee won Illinois prep titles in track and basketball, and become a star in both sports at the University of California. But it was track that gave real context to her sheer grace and power, that made her stand out.

She won six Olympic medals, including three golds (the heptathlon in 1988 and 1992 and the long jump in 1988), four world titles, four Goodwill Games victories, 14 national championships, the world record in the heptathlon, and the American record in the long jump.

Yet her most memorable Olympic performance was a bronze medal. In the Atlanta Olympics in 1996, she was laid low by nagging leg injuries and drained by her running battle with asthma and forced to pull out of the heptathlon. Joyner-Kersee returned to the track a few days later to compete in the long jump and slipped to sixth place before her final jump.

Where she found the energy for the last one, let alone a strong enough effort to secure a bronze medal, was one of the most impressive displays of willpower in recent memory.

Joyner-Kersee now has a sports marketing business to tend to and a charitable foundation that raised nearly $7 million to build a community center to replace the one where she played as a child.

LEFT: American track star Jackie Joyner-Kersee carries the flag after winning the gold in Barcelona's heptathlon. Tony Duffy

OVERLEAF: Men's 3,000 m steeplechase. Mike Powell

DERARTU TULU

Derartu Tulu completed a previously unthinkable four-year graduation from shepherdess in a remote Ethiopian highland farming settlement to Olympic 10,000 meters champion in Barcelona.

She ran away from Elana Meyer to win the Barcelona gold and then ran with the white South African on a lap of honor which represented the games's most powerful rainbow symbol.

She was rewarded with gifts of jewelry and gold. The new government, stepping out of the infamous shadow of the Mengistu regime and spotting an Olympian public relations asset in its push for international recognition, provided her with 5,000 pounds and 500 acres of prime land just outside Addis, while promoting her to the rank of major in the prison service.

She had been plucked from the thin air of her home province of Arsi in 1988. "I was just being a shepherd, running here and there," she recalled, "but never aiming to be a runner."

That raw youngster from a family of 10, who was still blinking nervously into the flashlights after her Barcelona win, bears no resemblance to the poised, mature twenty-something who has developed quite a taste for sophisticated fashion trappings on her European travels.

Yet Tulu has not forgotten her roots. She is called the mother of the athletes for the dutiful way she encourages and coaxes the children she describes as "the brothers and sisters who will follow me."

"She has charm but real toughness too," said Haile Gebrselassie, Ethiopia's great male runner.

When you think that Tulu comes from a community where most girls are married at the age of 11 or 12, you know she has had to work hard to get where she is.

KRISZTINA EGERSZEGI

Hungary's Krisztina Egerszegi took the 1988 Olympic 200 meters backstroke in Seoul when aged just 14 years and 40 days to become the youngest swimmer ever to take Olympic gold. Known as "Eger" (Hungarian for mouse), she achieved her fantastic feat despite being the lightest in the field by 40 pounds.

Egerszegi took the event into new territory at the 1991 World Championships when she improved the world record by almost two seconds to 2min 6.62sec. She was rewarded with a ten-minute standing ovation.

Known for her effortless style, Egerszegi retained her title in Barcelona with the second fastest time in history and an Olympic record. She added the 100 meters backstroke and the 400 meters medley titles. Then in Atlanta in 1996 she blistered the field in the 200 meters backstroke and became the first swimmer in history to win five Olympic gold medals.

Mark Spitz won seven gold medals in Munich in 1972, but three of those came in relays. Egerszegi didn't get that kind of help. Indeed she said that she passed up a chance to swim the 100 meters backstroke in Atlanta to be on a relay team with her Hungarian team-mates.

It also meant she became the only swimmer besides Australia's Dawn Fraser in 1956-64, to win the same event in three different Olympics.

"I like all the gold medals, but the last one is the best," said Egerszegi.

Even when she just ten, Roland Matthes had commented on her perfect technique and had predicted that she would leave the rest of the world behind in the backstroke. Before her eighteenth birthday the schoolgirl had fulfilled his prophecy.

Now retired, Egerszegi owns a restaurant, "The Mousehole," in Budapest.

OPPOSITE PAGE: The Olympic Flame Barcelona 1992. Gary Newkirk

TOP: Barcelona General Palace Montjuic. Bernard Asset

ABOVE: Carl Lewis crossed the finish line in the 4x100 m semi-final. Gerard Vandystadt

TOP: *America's Gail Devers falls down during the womens 100 m hurdles.* Allsport

ABOVE: *The American women's relay team celebrate their 4 x 100 m gold.* Gerard Vandystadt

OPPOSITE PAGE: *Carl Lewis of the United States wins the gold in the long jump.* Mike Powell

OPPOSITE PAGE: Ellen Van Langen of Holland wins the 800 m final. Gray Mortimore

ABOVE: America's Gail Devers in the 100 m hurdles. Mike Powell

ABOVE LEFT: *American Jo Jennings dejected in the high jump.* Gerard Vandystadt

ABOVE RIGHT: *Mike Conley of the USA placed first in the triple jump.* Gray Mortimore

BARCELONA 1992

JULY 25 – AUGUST 8

PARTICIPANTS: 9,364 / MEN: 6,657 WOMEN: 2,707
COUNTRIES: 169 SPORTS: 24 EVENTS: 257

FINAL TORCHBEARER: ANTONIO REBOLLO

MEDALS TABLE

PLACE	COUNTRY	GOLD	SILVER	BRONZE
1	Unified Team	45	38	29
2	USA	37	34	37
3	Germany	33	21	28
4	China	16	22	16
5	Cuba	14	6	11

OUTSTANDING ATHLETES

PLACE	NAME (NATIONALITY)	DISCIPLINE	GOLD	SILVER	BRONZE
1	Vital Sherbo (EUN)	Gymnastics	6		
2	Yevgeniy Sadoviy (EUN)	Swimming	3		
3	Krisztina Egerszegy (HUN)	Swimming	3		
4	Alexander Popov (EUN)	Swimming	2	2	
5	Tatyana Goutsou (EUN)	Gymnastics	2	1	1

ATHLETICS — MEN

EVENT	GOLD		SILVER		BRONZE	
100 m	Linford Christie (GBR)	9.96	Frank Fredericks (NAM)	10.02	Dennis Mitchell (USA)	10.04
200 m	Mike Marsh (USA)	20.01	Frank Fredericks (NAM)	20.13	Michael Bates (USA)	20.38
400 m	Quincy Watts (USA)	43.50	Steve Lewis (USA)	44.21	Samson Kitur (KEN)	44.24
800 m	William Tanui (KEN)	1:43.66	Nixon Kiprotich (KEN)	1:43.70	Johnny Gray (USA)	1:43.97
1,500 m	Fermin Ruiz (ESP)	3:40.12	Rachid El Basir (ESP)	3:40.62	Mohamed Sulaiman (QAT)	3:40.69
5,000 m	Dieter Baumann (GER)	13:12.52	Paul Bitok (KEN)	13:12.71	Fita Bayisa (ETH)	13:13.03
10,000 m	Khalid Skah (MAR)	27:46.70	Richard Chelimo (KEN)	27:47.72	Addis Abebe (ETH)	28:00.07
Marathon	Young-Cho Hwang (KOR)	2:13:23	Koichi Morishita (JPN)	2:13:45	Stephan Freigang (GER)	2:14:00
110 m Hurdles	Mark McKoy (CAN)	13.12	Tony Dees (USA)	13.24	Jack Pierce (USA)	13.26
400 m Hurdles	Kevin Young (USA)	46.78	Winthrop Graham (JAM)	47.66	Kriss Akabusi (GBR)	47.82
3,000 m Steeplechase	Mathew Birir (KEN)	8:08.84	Patrick Sang (KEN)	8:09.55	William Mutwol (KEN)	8:10.74
4x100 m	USA	37.40	Nigeria	37.98	Cuba	38.00
4x400 m	USA	2:55.74	Cuba	2:59.51	Great Britain	2:59.73
20 km Walk	Daniel Montero Plaza (ESP)	1:21:45	Guillaume Leblanc (CAN)	1:22:25	Giovanni De Benedictis (ITA)	1:23:11
50 km Walk	Andrey Perlov (EUN)	3:50.13	Carlos Carbajal (MEX)	3:52:09	Ronald Weigel (GER)	3:53:45
High Jump	Javier Sotomayor (CUB)	7'8"	Patrick Sjöberg (SWE)	7'8"	Artur Partyka (POL)	7'8"
					Timothy Forsyth (AUS)	7'8"
					Hollis Conway (GBR)	7'8"
Pole Vault	Maxim Tarrassov (EUN)	19'0.25"	Igor Trandellkow (EUN)	19'0.25"	Javier Garcia (ESP)	18'10"
Long Jump	Carl Lewis (USA)	28'5.25"	Mike Powell (USA)	28'4"	Joe Greene (USA)	27'4.25"
Triple Jump	Michael Conley (USA)	59'7.25"	Charles Simpkins (USA)	57'8.75"	Frank Rutherford (BAH)	56'11.25"
Shot	Michael Stulce (USA)	71'2"	James Doehring (USA)	68'9"	Vyacheslav Lycho (EUN)	68'8.25"
Discus	Romas Ubartas (LIT)	213'7"	Jurgen Schult (GER)	213'0"	Roberto Moya (CUB)	210'4"
Javelin	Jan Zelezny (TCH)	294'2"	Seppo Räty (FIN)	284'1.5"	Steve Backley (GBR)	273'6.5"
Hammer	Andrey Abdulvalyev (EUN)	270'9.5"	Igor Astapkovich (EUN)	268'10.5"	Igor Nikulin (EUN)	266'11.75"
Decathlon	Robert Zillelik (TCH)	8611	Antonio Penalver (ESP)	8412	David Johnson USA)	8309

ABOVE: *Mike Powell of America a silver medallist in the long jump*. Mike Powell.
OPPOSITE PAGE: *Runners in the 100 m heat*. Gerard Vandystadt

414

SWIMMING — MEN

EVENT	GOLD		SILVER		BRONZE	
50 m Freestyle	Alexander Popov (EUN)	21.91	Matt Biondi (USA)	22.09	Tom Jager (USA)	22.30
100 m Freestyle	Alexander Popov (EUN)	49.02	Gustavo Borges (BRA)	49.43	Stephan Caron (FRA)	49.50
200 m Freestyle	Yevgeniy Sadovyi (EUN)	1:46.70	Anders Holmertz (SWE)	1:46.86	Antti Kasvio (FIN)	1:47.63
400 m Freestyle	Yevgeniy Sadovyi (EUN)	3:45.00	Kieren Perkins (AUS)	3:45.16	Anders Hohlmertz (SWE)	3:46.77
1,500 m Freestyle	Kieren Perkins (AUS)	14:43.48	Glen Housman (AUS)	14:55.29	Jörg Hoffman (GER)	15:02.29
100 m Backstroke	Mark Tewksbury (CAN)	53.98	Jeff Rouse (USA)	54.04	David Berkhoff (USA)	54.78
200 m Backstroke	Martin Lopez-Zubero (ESP)	1:58.47	Vladimir Selkov (EUN)	1:58.87	Stefano Battistelli (ITA)	1:59.40
100 m Breaststroke	Nelson Diebel (USA)	1:01.50	Norbert Rosza (HUN)	1:01.68	Philip Rogers (AUS)	1:01.76
200 m Breaststroke	Mike Barrowman (USA)	2:10.16	Norbert Rozsa (HUN)	2:11.23	Nick Gillingham (GBR)	2:11.29
100 m Butterfly	Pablo Morales (USA)	53.32	Rafal Szukala (POL)	53.35	Anthony Nesty (SUR)	53.41
200 m Butterfly	Melvin Stewart (USA)	1:56.26	Danyon Loader (NZL)	1:57.93	Frank Esposito (FRA)	1:58.51
200 m Medley	Tamas Darnyi (HUN)	2:00.76	Gregory Burgess (USA)	2:00.97	Attila Czene (HUN)	2:01.00
400 m Medley	Tamas Darnyi (HUN)	4:14.23	Eric Namesnik (USA)	4:15.57	Luca Sacchi (ITA)	4:16.34
4x100 m Freestyle	USA	3:16.74	Unified Team	3:17.56	Germany	3:17.90
4x200 m Freestyle	Unified Team	7:11.95	Sweden	7:15.51	USA	7:16.23
4x100 m Medley	USA	3:36.93	Unified Team	3:38.56	Canada	3:39.66
Springboard Diving	Mark Lenzi (USA)	676.53	Lingde Tan (CHN)	645.57	Dmitri Sautin (EUN)	627.78
Highboard Diving	Shuwei Sun (CHN)	677.31	Scott Donie (USA)	633.63	Ni Xiong (CHN)	600.15
Water Polo	Italy		Spain		Unified Team	

SYNCHRONIZED SWIMMING

	GOLD		SILVER		BRONZE	
Solo	Kristen Babb-Sprague (USA)	191.848	Sylvie Frechette (CAN)	191.717	Fumiko Okuno (JPN)	187.056
Duet	USA	192.175	Canada	189.394	Japan	186.868

BOXING

EVENT	GOLD	SILVER	BRONZE
Light-Flyweight (-105.75 lb)	Rogelio Marcelo Garcia (CUB)	Daniel Bojinov (BUL)	Jan Quast (GER)
			Roel Velasco (PHI)
Flyweight (-112.5 lb)	Chol Su Choi (PRK)	Raul Gonzales (CUB)	Istvan Kovacs (HUN)
			Timothy Austin (USA)
Bantamweight (-119 lb)	Joel Casamayor (CUB)	Wayne McCullough (IRL)	Mohamed Achik (MAR)
			Gxvalag Sik Li (PRK)
Featherweight (-126 lb)	Andreas Tews (GER)	Faustino Reyes (ESP)	Hocine Soltani (ALG)
			Ramazi Paliani (EUN)
Lightweight (- 132 lb)	Oscar de la Hoya (USA)	Marco Rudolph (GER)	Sung Sik Hong (KOR)
			Namjil Bayarsaikhan (MGL)
Light-Welterweight (-140 lb)	Hector Vinent (CUB)	Mark Leduc (CAN)	Jyri Kjäll (FIN)
			Leonard Doroftei (ROM)
Welterweight (-148 lb)	Michael Carruth (IRL)	Juan Hernandez (CUB)	Anibal Acevedo Santiago (PUR)
			Arkom Chenglai (THA)
Light-Middleweight (-157 lb)	Juan Lemus Garcia (CUB)	Orhan Delibas (HOL)	Robin Reid (GBR)
			Gyorgy Mizsei (HUN)
Middleweight (-165 lb)	Ariel Hernandez (CUB)	Chris Byrd (USA)	Chris Johnson (CAN)
			Seung Bae Lee (KOR)
Light-Heavyweight (-178.5 lb)	Torsten May (GER)	Rostislav Saulischni (EUN)	Zoltan Beres (HUN)
			Wojciech Bartnik (POL)
Heavyweight (-200.5 lb)	Felix Savon (CUB)	David Izonretei (NGR)	Arnold Vanderlijde (HOL)
			David Tua (NZL)
Super-Heavyweight (+200.5 lb)	Roberto Balado Mendez (CUB)	Richard Igbineghu (NGR)	Brian Nielsen (DEN)
			Swilen Aldinow Rusinov (BUL)

TOP: *Tamas Darnyo of Hungary captured gold in the 400 m medley.* Simon Bruty

ABOVE: *Sharon Davies of Great Britain in the pool.* Bob Martin

LEFT: *Canadian silver medalist, Sylvie Frechette, in the solo synchronized swimming category.* David Leah

ATHLETICS — WOMEN

EVENT	GOLD		SILVER		BRONZE	
100 m	Gail Devers (USA)	10.82	Juliet Cuthbert (JAM)	10.83	Irina Privalova (EUN)	10.84
200 m	Gwen Torrence (USA)	21.81	Juliet Cuthbert (JAM)	22.02	Merlene Ottey (JAM)	22.09
400 m	Marie-Jose Perec (FRA)	48.83	Olga Brysgina (EUN)	49.05	Ximena Gaviria (COL)	49.64
800 m	Ellen Van Langen (HOL)	1:55.54	Lilia Nurutdinova (EUN)	1:55.99	Ana Quirot (CUB)	1:56.80
1,500 m	Hassiba Boulmerka (ALG)	3:55.30	Ludmilla Rogacheva (EUN)	3:56.91	Yunxia Qu (CHN)	3:57.08
3,000 m	Yelena Romanova (EUN)	8:46.04	Tatyana Dorovskich (EUN)	8:46.85	Angela Chalmers (CAN)	8:47.22
10,000 m	Derartu Tulu (ETH)	31:06.02	Elena Meyer (RSA)	31:11.75	Lynn Jennings (USA)	31:19.89
Marathon	Valentina Yegorova (EUN)	2:32:41	Yuko Arimori (JPN)	2:32:49	Lorraine Moller (NZL)	2:33:59
100 m Hurdles	Paraskevi Patoulidou (GRE)	12.64	Lavonna Martin (USA)	12.69	Jordanka Donkova (BUL)	12.70
400 m Hurdles	Sally Gunnell (GBR)	53.23	Sandra Farmer-Patrick (USA)	53.69	Janeene Vickers (USA)	54.31
4x100 m	USA	42.11	Unified Team	42.16	Nigeria	42.81
4x400 m	Unified Team	3:20.20	USA	3:20.92	Great Britain	3:24.23
10 km Walk	Yueling Chen (CHN)	44:32	Yelena Nikolayeva (EUN)	44:33	Chunxiu Li (CHN)	44:41
High Jump	Heike Henkel (GER)	6'7.25"	Galina Astafei (ROM)	6'6.5"	Joanet Quintero (CUB)	6'5.5"
Long Jump	HeikeDrechler (GER)	23'5"	Inessa Kravets (EUN)	23'4.25"	Jackie Joyner-Kersee (USA)	23'2.25"
Shot	Svetlana Kriveleova (EUN)	69'1"	Zhihong Huang (CHN)	67'1.75"	Kathrin Neimke (GER)	64'10.5"
Discus	Maritza Marten (CUB)	229'10"	Zvetanka Christova (BUL)	222'4.5"	Daniela Costian (AUS)	217'3.75"
Javelin	Silke Renke (GER)	224'2.5"	Natalya Shikolenko (EUN)	223'11.25"	Karen Forkel (GER)	219'4"
Heptathlon	Jackie Joyner-Kersee (USA)	7044	Irina Belova (EUN)	6845	Sabine Braun (GER)	6649

SWIMMING — WOMEN

EVENT	GOLD		SILVER		BRONZE	
50 m Freestyle	Wenyi Yang (CHN)	24.79	Yong Zhuang (CHN)	25.08	Angel Martino (USA)	25.23
100 m Freestyle	Yong Zhuang (CHN)	54.64	Jenny Thompson (USA)	54.84	Franziska von Almsick (GER)	54.94
200 m Freestyle	Nicole Haislett (USA)	1:57.90	Franziska von Almsick (GER)	1:58.00	Kerstin Kielgass (GER)	1:59.67
400 m Freestyle	Dagmar Hase (GER)	4:07.18	Janet Evans (USA)	4:07.37	Hayley Lewis (AUS)	4:11.22
800 m Freestyle	Janet Evans (USA)	8:25.52	Hayley Lewis (AUS)	8:30.34	Jana Hanke (GER)	8:30.99
100 m Backstroke	Krisztina Egerszegi (HUN)	1:00.68	Tunde Szabo (HUN)	1:01.14	Lea Loveless (USA)	1:01.43
200 m Backstroke	Krisztina Egerszegi (HUN)	2:07.06	Dagmar Hase (GER)	2:09.46	Nicole Stevenson (AUS)	2:10.20
100 m Breaststroke	Yelena Rudkovskaya (EUN)	1:08.00	Anita Nall (USA)	1:08.17	Samantha Riley (AUS)	1:09.25
200 m Breaststroke	Kyoko Iwasaki (JPN)	2:26.65	Li Lin (CHN)	2:26.85	Anita Nall (USA)	2:26.88
100 m Butterfly	Hong Qian (CHN)	58.62	Christine Ahmann-Leighton (USA)	58.74	Cathérine Plewinski (FRA)	59.01
200 m Butterfly	Summer Sanders (USA)	2:08.67	Xiaohong Walig (CHN)	2:09.01	Susan O'Neill (AUS)	2:09.03
200 m Medley	Li Lin (CHN)	2:11.65	Summer Sanders (USA)	2:11.91	Daniela Hunger (GER)	2:13.92
400 m Medley	Krisztina Egerszegy (HUN)	4:36.54	Li Lin (CHN)	4:36.73	Summer Sanders (USA)	4:37.58
4x100 m Freestyle	USA	3:39.46	China	3:40.12	Germany	3:41.60
4x100 Medley	USA	4:02.54	Germany	4:05.19	Unified Team	4:06.44
Springboard Diving	Min Gao (CHN)	572.40	Irina Laschko (EUN)	514.14	Brita Baldus (GER)	503.07
Highboard Diving	Mingxia Fu (CHN)	461.43	Yelena Miroschina (EUN)	411.63	Mary Ellen Clark (USA)	401.91

JUDO — MEN

EVENT	GOLD	SILVER	BRONZE
(-132.5 lb)	Nazim Gusseinov (EUN)	Hyun Yoon (KOR)	Tadanor Koshino (JPN)
			Richard Trautmann (GER)
(-143.25 lb)	Rogerio Sampaio Cardoso (BRA)	Jozsef Csak (HUN)	Udo Quellmalz (GER)
			Israel Hernandez-Planas (CUB)
(-156.5 lb)	Toshihiko Koga (JPN)	Bertalan Haitos (HUN)	Hoon Chung (KOR)
			Shay Oren Smadga (ISR)
(-171.75 lb)	Hidehiko Yoshida (JPN)	Jason Morris (USA)	Bertrand Damasian (FRA)
			Byung-Joo Kim (KOR)
(-189.5 lb)	Waldemar Legian (POL)	Pascal Tayot (FRA)	Hirotaka Okada (JPN)
			Nicolas Gill (CAN)
(-209.25 lb)	Antal Kovacs (HUN)	Raymond Stevens (GBR)	Theo Meijer (HOL)
			Dimitri Sergeyev (EUN)
(+209.25 lb)	David Shashaleshvili (EUN)	Naoya Ogawa (JPN)	David Douillet (FRA)
			Imre Csosz (HUN)

JUDO — WOMEN

EVENT	GOLD	SILVER	BRONZE
(-105.75 lb)	Cecile Nowak (FRA)	Ryoko Tamura (JPN)	Hulya Senyurt (TUR)
			Amarilis Savon Carmenaty (CUB)
(-114.5 lb)	Almudena Munoz (ESP)	Noriko Mizogushi (JPN)	Zhongyun Li (CHN)
			Susan Rendle (GBR)
(-123.5 lb)	Miriam Blasco (ESP)	Nicola Fairbrother (GBR)	Chiyori Tateno (JPN)
			Driulis Gonzales Morales (CUB)
(-134.5 lb)	Cathérine Fleury (FRA)	Yael Arad (ISR)	Di Zhang (CHN)
			Yelena Petrova (EUN)
(-145.5 lb)	Odalis Reve Jimenez (CUB)	Emanuela Pierantozzi (ITA)	Heidi Rakels (BEL)
			Kate Howey (GBR)
(-158.75 lb)	Mi-Jung Kim (KOR)	Yoko Tanabe (JPN)	Laetitia Meignan (FRA)
			Irene de Kok (HOL)
(+158.75 lb)	Xiaoyan Zhuang (CHN)	Estela Rodriquez Villanueva (CUB)	Natalia Lupino (FRA)
			Yoko Sakaue (JPN)

ABOVE: *Draped in the Union Flag, Sally Gunnell of Great Britain, celebrates her win in the 400 m hurdles.* Mike Hewitt

ABOVE: Fireworks explode over Barcelona's opening ceremony celebrations. Mike Powell

FENCING

EVENT	GOLD	SILVER	BRONZE
Individual Foil — Men	Philippe Omnes (FRA)	Sergey Golubitski (EUN)	Elvis Gregory (CUB)
Team Foil — Men	Germany	Cuba	Poland
Individual Sabre	Benco Szabo (HUN)	Marco Marin (ITA)	Jean-François Lamour (FRA)
Team Sabre	EUN	Hungary	France
Individual Épée	Eric Srecki (FRA)	Pavel Kolobkov (EUN)	Jean-Michel Henry (FRA)
Team Épée	Germany	Hungary	Unified Team
Individual Team — Women	Giovanna Trillini (ITA)	Huifeng Wang (CHN)	Tatyana Sadovskaya (EUN)
Team Foil — Women	Italy	Germany	Romania

WEIGHTLIFTING

EVENT	GOLD	SILVER	BRONZE
Flyweight	Ivan Ivanov (BUL)	Qisheng Lin (CHN)	Traian Joachim Ciharean (ROM)
Bantamweight	Byung-Kwan Chun (KOR)	Shoubin Liu (CHN)	Jianming Luo (CHN)
Featherweight	Naim Suleymanoglu (TUR)	Nikolai Peshalov (BUL)	Yinggiang He (CHN)
Lightweight	Israel Militosiyan (EUN)	Yoto Yotov (BUL)	Andreas Behm GER)
Middleweight	Fedor Kassapu (EUN)	Pablo Rodriguez (CUB)	Myong Nam Kim (PRK)
Light-Heavyweight	Pyrros Dimas (GRE)	Krzysztof Siemion (POL)	Ibragim Samadov (EUN)
Middle-Heavyweight	Kakhi Kakhiasvili (EUN)	Sergey Syrtsov (EUN	Sergiusz Wolczanieki (POL)
100 kg	Viktor Tregubov (EUN)	Timur Taimassov (EUN)	Waldemar Malak (POL)
First Heavyweight	Ronny Weller (GER)	Artur Akoev (EUN)	Stefan Botev (BUL)
Second Super-Heavy weight	Alexander Kurlovich (EUN)	Leonid Taranenko (EUN)	Manfred Nerlinger (GER)

WEIGHTLIFTING WEIGHTS

FLYWEIGHT	-114.5 lb	BANTAMWEIGHT	-123.25 lb	FEATHERWEIGHT	-132.25 lb
LIGHTWEIGHT	-148.75 lb	MIDDLEWEIGHT	-165.5 lb	LIGHT-HEAVYWEIGHT	-182 lb
MIDDLE-HEAVYWEIGHT	-198.5 lb	FIRST-HEAVYWEIGHT	-220.5 lb	SECOND-HEAVYWEIGHT	- 242.5 lb
SUPER-HEAVYWEIGHT	+242.5 lb				

GRECO-ROMAN WRESTLING

EVENT	GOLD	SILVER	BRONZE
Light-Flyweight (-105.75 lb)	Oleg Kucherenko (EUN)	Vincenzo Maenza (ITA)	Wilber Sanchez (CUB)
Flyweight (-114.5 lb)	Jon Rönningen (NOR)	Alfred Ter-Mkrychan (EUN)	Kyung Kap Min (KOR)
Bantamweight (-125.75 lb)	Han Bong An (KOR)	Rifat Yildiz (GER)	Zetian Shang (CHN)
Featherweight (-136.5 lb)	Akif Pirim (TUR)	Sergey Martynov (EUN)	Juan Maren (CUB)
Lightweight (-149.75 lb)	Attila Repka (HUN)	Islan Duguchiyev (EUN)	Rodney Smith (USA)
Welterweight (-163 lb)	Minazakhan Iskandarian (EUN)	Jozef Tracz (POL)	Torbjörn Kornbakk (SWE)
Middleweight (-180.75 lb)	Peter Farkas (HUN)	Pjotr Stepien (POL)	Daulet Turhlyhanov (EUN)
Light-Heavyweight (-198.25 lb)	Maik Bullmann GER)	Hakki Basar (TUR)	Gogui Koguashvili (EUN)
Heavyweight (-220.5 lb)	Hector Milian (CUB)	Dennis Koslowski (USA)	Sergey Demiashkiievich (EUN)
Super-Heavyweight (+220.5 lb)	Alexander Karelin (EUN)	Tomas Johansson (SWE)	Ion Grigoras (ROM)

MODERN PENTATHLON

EVENT	GOLD		SILVER		BRONZE	
Individual	Arkadlusz Skrzypaszek (POL)	5559	Attila Mizser (HUN)	5446	Eduard Zanovka (EUN)	5361
Team	Poland	16018	Unified Team	15924	Italy	15760

ROWING — WOMEN

EVENT	GOLD		SILVER		BRONZE	
Single Sculls	Elisabeta Lipa (ROM)	7:25.54	Annelies Bredael (BEL)	7:26.64	Silken Laumann (CAN)	7:28.85
Double Sculls	Germany	6:49.00	Romania	6:51.47	China	6:55.16
Coxless Pairs	Canada	7:06.22	Germany	7:07.96	USA	7:08.11
Coxless Quadruple Sculls	Germany	6:20.18	Romania	6:24.34	Unified Team	6:25.07
Coxless Fours	Canada	6:30.85	USA	6:31.86	Germany	6:32.34
Coxed Eights	Canada	6:02.62	Romania	6:06.26	Germany	6:07.80

FREESTYLE WRESTLING

EVENT	GOLD	SILVER	BRONZE
Light-Flyweight (-105.75 lb)	Il Kim (PRK)	Jong-Shin Kim (KOR)	Vugar Orudyev (EUN)
Flyweight (-114.5 lb)	Hak-Son Li (PRK)	Harry Lee Jones (USA)	Valentin Jordanov (BUL)
Bantamweight (-125.75 lb)	Alejandro Puerto (CUB)	Sergey Smal (EUN)	Yong-Sik Kim (PRK)
Featherweight (-136.5 lb)	John Smith (USA)	Asgari Mohammedian (IRN)	Lazaro Reinoso (CUB)
Lightweight (-149.75 lb)	Arsen Fadzayev (EUN)	Valentin Getsov (BUL)	Kosei Akaishi (JPN)
Welterweight (-163 lb)	Jang-Soon Park (KOR)	Kenneth Monday (USA)	Amir Khadem (IRN)
Middleweight (-180.75 lb)	Kevin Jackson (USA)	Elemadi Jabrailov (EUN)	Rasul Khadem (IRN)
Light-Heavyweight (-198.25 lb)	Maharbeg Chadartsev (EUN)	Kenan Simsek (TUR)	Christopher Campbell (USA)
Heavyweight (-220.5 lb)	Leri Chabelov (EUN)	Heiko Balz (GER)	Ali Kayali (TUR)
Super-Heavyweight (+220.5 lb)	Bruce Baumgartner (USA)	Jeffrey Thue (CAN)	David Gobedyishuili (EUN)

ROWING — MEN

EVENT	GOLD		SILVER		BRONZE	
Single Sculls	Thomas Lange (GER)	6:51.40	Vaclav Chalupa (TCH)	6:52.93	Kajetan Broniewski (POL)	6:56.82
Doubles Sculls	Australia	6:17.32	Austria	6:18.42	Netherlands	6:22.82
Coxless Pairs	Great Britain	6:27.72	Germany	6:32.68	Slovenia	6:33.43
Coxed Pairs	Geat Britain	6:49.83	Italy	6:50.98	Romania	6:51.58
Coxless Quadruple Sculls	Germany	5:45.17	Norway	5:47.09	Italy	5:47.33
Coxless Fours	Australia	5:55.04	USA	5:56.68	Slovenia	5:58.24
Coxed Fours	Romania	5:59.37	Germany	6:00.34	Poland	6:03.27
Coxed Eights	Canada	5:29.53	Romania	5:29.67	Germany	5:31.00

CANOE SLALOM — MEN

EVENT	GOLD		SILVER		BRONZE	
Kayak 1	Pierpaolo Ferrazzi (ITA)	106.89	Sylvain Curinier (FRA)	107.06	Jochen Lettmann (GER)	108.52
Canadian 1	Lukas Pollert (TCH)	113.69	Gareth Marriott (GBR)	116.48	Jacky Avril (FRA)	117.18
Canadian 2	USA	122.41	Czech Republic	124.25	France	124.38

CANOE SLALOM — WOMEN

EVENT	GOLD		SILVER		BRONZE	
Kayak 1	Elisabeth Micheler (GER)	126.41	Danielle Woodward (AUS)	128.27	Dana Chladek (USA)	131.75

CANOEING — WOMEN

EVENT	GOLD		SILVER		BRONZE	
500 m Kayak Singles K1	Birgit Schmidt (GER)	1:51.60	Rita Koban (HUN)	1:51.96	Izabella Dylewska (POL)	1:52.36
500 m Kayak Pairs K2	Germany	1:40.29	Sweden	1:40.41	Hungary	1:40.81
500 m Kayak Fours K4	Hungary	1:38.22	Germany	1:38.47	Sweden	1:39.79

CANOEING — MEN

EVENT	GOLD		SILVER		BRONZE	
500 m Kayak Singles K1	Mikko Kolehmainen (FIN)	1:40.34	Zsolt Gyulay (HUN)	1:40.64	Knut Holman (NOR)	1:40.71
1,000 m Canadian Singles C1	Clint Robinson (AUS)	3:37.26	Knut Holman (NOR)	3:37.50	Greg Barton (USA)	3:37 93
500 m Kayak Pairs K2	Germany	1:28.27	Poland	1:29.84	Italy	1:30.00
1,000 m Kayak Pairs K2	Germany	3:16.10	Sweden	3:17.70	Poland	3:18.86
1,000 m Kayak Fours K4	Germany	2:54.18	Hungary	2:54.82	Australia	2:56.97
500 m Canadian Singles C1	Nikolai Buchalov (BUL)	1:51.15	Michail Slivinski (EUN)	1:51.40	Olaf Heukrodt (GER)	1:53.00
1,000 m Canadian Singles C1	Nikolai Buchalov (BUL)	4:05.92	Ivan Klementyev (LET)	4:06.60	Gyorgy Zala (HUN)	4:07.35
500 m Canadian Pairs C2	Unified Team	1:41.54	Germany	1:41.68	Bulgaria	1:41.94
1,000 m Canadian Pairs C2	Germany	3:37.42	Denmark	3:39.26	France	3:54.51

YACHTING

EVENT	GOLD		SILVER		BRONZE	
Finn Class	José van der Ploeg (ESP)	33.4	Brian Ledbetter (USA)	54.7	Craig Monk (NZL)	64.7
International Star	USA	31.4	New Zealand	58.4	Canada	62.7
Flying Dutchman	Spain	29.7	USA	32.7	Denmark	37.7
International Tornado	France	40.4	USA	42.0	Australia	44.4
470 Men	Spain	50.0	USA	66.7	Estonia	68.7
470 Women	Spain	30.7	New Zealand	39.7	USA	42.4
International Soling	Denmark	34.0	USA	24.4	Great Britain	48.0
Lechner A-390 Men	Franck David (FRA)	70.7	Mike Gebhardt (USA)	71.1	Lars Kleppich (AUS)	98.7
Lechner A-390 Women	Barbara Kendall (NZL)	47.8	Xiaodong Zhang (CHN)	65.8	Dorien de Vries (HOL)	68.7
Europa Class	Linda Andersen (NOR)	48.7	Natalia Perena (ESP)	57.4	Julia Trotman (USA)	62.7

427

OPPOSITE PAGE: America's John Smith took gold in the featherweight freestyle wrestling final. Mike Powell

ABOVE: A torchbearer enters the stadium during the opening ceremony. Chris Cole

SHOOTING — MEN

EVENT	GOLD		SILVER		BRONZE	
Small-Bore Rifle (Prone)	Eun-Chul Lee (KOR)	702.5	Harald Stenvaag (NOR)	701.4	Steven Pletikosic (IOP)	701.1
Small-Bore Rifle (3 Positions)	Grachia Petikian (EUN)	1267.4	Robert Foth (USA)	1266.6	Ryohei Koba (JPN)	1265.9
Rapid-Fire Pistol	Ralf Schumann (GER)	885	Afanassis Kusmin (LET)	882	Vladimir Vochmianin (EUN)	882
Free Pistol (50 m)	Konstantin Lukashik (EUN)	658.0	Yifu Wang (CHN)	657.0	Ragnar Skanakar (SWE)	657.0
Running Game Target	Michael Jakosits (GER)	673	Anatoliy Asrabayev (EUN)	672	Lubos Racansky (TCH)	670
Air Pistol	Yifu Wang (CHN)	6848	Sergei Plianov (EUN)	684.1	Sorin Babii (ROM)	684.1
Skeet Shooting	Shan Zhang (CHN)	223	Juan Jorge Giha Yahur (PER)	222	Bruno Rossetti (ITA)	222
Trap Shooting	Petr Hrdlicka (TCH)	219	Kazumi Watanabe (JPN)	9	Marco Venturini (ITA)	218
Air Rifle	Yuriy Fedkin (EUN)	695.3	Franck Badiou (FRA)	691.9	Johann Riederer (GER)	691.7

SHOOTING — WOMEN

EVENT	GOLD		SILVER		BRONZE	
Sports Pistol (3 positions)	Marina Logvienko (EUN)	684	Duihong Li (CHN)	680	Dorzhsuren Munkbajar (MGL)	679
Small Bore Rifle	Launi Meili (USA)	684.3	Nonka Matova (BUL)	682.7	Malgorzata Ksiazkiewicz (POL)	681.5
Air Rifle	Yeo Kab-Soon (KOR)	498.2	Vesela Lecheva (BUL)	495.3	Aranka Binder (IOP)	495.1
Air Pistol	Marina Logvinenko (EUN)	486.4	Jasna Sekaric (IOP)	486.4	Maria Grusdeva (BUL)	481.6

EQUESTRIANISM

EVENT	GOLD		SILVER		BRONZE	
Three-Day Event	Matthew Ryan (AUS)	70.0	Herbert Blöcker (GER)	81.3	Blyth Tait (NZL)	87.6
Three-Day Event Team	Australia	288.6	New Zealand	290.8	Germany	300.3
Grand Prix (Dressage)	Nicole Uphoff (GER)	1768	Isabelle Werth (GER)	1762	Klaus Balkenhol (GER)	1694
Gralid Prix (Dressage) Team	Germany	5224	Netherlands	4742	USA	4643
Grand Prix (Jumping)	Ludger Beerbaum (GER)	0.00	Piet Raymakers (HOL)	0.25	Norman Joio (USA)	.75
Grand Prix (Jumping)	Netherlands	12	Austria	16.75	France	24.75

OVERLEAF: *The Olympic flame, as the sun sets on the final day of Barcelona's summer games.* Shaun Botterill

ARCHERY — MEN

EVENT	GOLD		SILVER		BRONZE	
Individual	Sebastien Flut (FRA)	542	Jae-Hun Chung (KOR)	542	Simon Terry (GBR)	528
Team	Spain		Finland		Great Britain	

ARCHERY — WOMEN

EVENT	GOLD		SILVER		BRONZE	
Individual	Cho Youn-Jeong (KOR)	552	Kim Nyung Soo (KOR)	543	Natalia Valeyeva (EUN)	526
Team	South Korea	966	China	917	Unified Team	948

CYCLING — WOMEN

EVENT	GOLD		SILVER		BRONZE	
Road Race	Kathryn Watt (AUS)	2:04.42	Jeannie Longo-Ciprelli (FRA)	2:05.02	Monique Knol (HOL)	2:05.03
Sprint	Erika Salumäe (EST)		Annett Neumann (GER)		Ingrid Haringa (HOL)	
3,000 m Individual Pursuit	Petra Rossner (GER)	3:41.753	Kathryn Watt (AUS)	3:43.438	Rebecca Twigg (USA)	3:52.429

CYCLING — MEN

EVENT	GOLD		SILVER		BRONZE	
Road Race	Fabio Casartelli (ITA)	4:35:21	Hendrick Dekker (HOL)	4:35:22	Dainis Ozols (LET)	4:35:24
100 km Road Team Time Trial	Germany	2:01:39	Italy	2:02:39	France	2:05:25
Sprint	Jens Fiedler (GER)		Gary Neiwand (AUS)		Curtis Harnett (CAN)	
1,000 m Time Trial	Jose Moreno Perinan (ESP)	1:03.342	Shane Kelly (AUS)	1:04.288	Erin Hartwell (USA)	1:04.753
4,000 m Individual Pursuit	Christopher Boardman (GBR)		Jens Lehmann (GER)		Gary Anderson (NZL)	
4,000 m Team Pursuit	Germany	4:08.791	Australia	4:10.218	Denmark	4:15.860
Individual Points Race	Giovanni Lombardi (ITA)		Leon van Bon (HOL)		Cedric Mathy (BEL)	

GYMNASTICS — MEN

EVENT	GOLD		SILVER		BRONZE	
Individual Combined Exercises	Vitali Sherbo (EUN)	59.025	Grigoriy Misyutin (EUN)	58.925	Valeri Belenki (EUN)	58 625
Individual Team	Unified Team	585.450	China	580.375	Japan	578.250
Parallel Bars	Vitali Sherbo (EUN)	9.900	Linyao Guo (CHN)	9.800	Igor Korobchinski (EUN)	9.800
	Li Jing (CHN)	9.812			Masayuki Matsunaga (JPN)	9.800
Floor	Xiaosahung Li (CHN)	9.925	Grigoriy Misyutin (EUN)	9.787	Yukio Ikatani (JPN)	9.787
Horse Vault	Vitali Sherbo (EUN)	9.856	Grigoriy Misyutin (EUN)	9.781	Ok Ryul Yoo (KOR)	9.762
Horizontal Bar	Trent Dimas (USA)	9.875	Grigoriy Misyutin (EUN)	9.837	Andreas Wecker (GER)	9.837
Rings	Vitali Sherbo (EUN)	9.937	Li Jing (CHN)	9.875	Andreas Wecker (GER)	9.862
					Xiaoshuang Li (CHN)	9.862
Pommel Horse	Vitali Sherbo (EUN)	9.925	Gil-Su Pae (PRK)	9.925	Andreas Wecker (GER)	9.887

GYMNASTICS — WOMEN

EVENT	GOLD		SILVER		BRONZE	
Individual Combined Exercises	Tatjana Gutsu (EUN)	39.737	Shannon Miller (USA)	39.725	Lavinia Milosovici (ROM)	39.687
Team	Unified Team	395.666	Romania	395.079	USA	394.704
Floor	Lavinia Milosovici (ROM)	10.000	Henrietta Onodi (HUN)	9.950	Cristina Bontas (ROM)	9.912
					Tatyana Gutsu (EUN)	9.912
					Shannon Miller (USA)	9.912
Horse Vault	Henrietta Onodi (HUN)	9.925	Lavinia Milosovici (ROM)	9.925	Tatyanka Lyssenko (EUN)	9.912
Beam	Tatyana Lyssenko (EUN)	9.975	Lu Li (CHN)	9.912	Shannon Miller (USA)	9.9612
Asymmetrical Bars	Lu Li (CHN)	10.00	Tatyana Gutsu (EUN)	9.975	Shannon Miller (USA)	9.9612
Modern Rhythmic	Alexandra Timoshenko (EUN)	59.037	Carolina Pascual (ESP)	58.100	Oksana Skaldina (EUN)	57.912

TENNIS — MEN

	GOLD	SILVER	BRONZE
Singles	Marc Rosset (SUI)	Jordi Arrese (ESP)	Goran Ivanisevic (CRO)
			Andrey Cherkassov (EUN)
Doubles	Boris Becker / Michael Stich (GER)	Wayne Ferreira / Piet Norval (RSA)	Goran vanisevic / Goran Prpic (ROM)
			Javier Frana / Christian Miniussi (ARG)

TENNIS — WOMEN

	GOLD	SILVER	BRONZE
Singles	Jennifer Capriati (USA)	Steff Graf (GER)	Mary Jo Fernandez (USA)
			Arantxa Sanchez-Vicario (ESP)
Doubles	Gigi Fernandez / MaryJo Fernandez (USA)	Conchita Martinez / Arantxa Sanchez-Vicario (ESP)	Leila Meshki/Natalia Zvereva (EUN)
			Rachel McQuillan/Nicole Proris (AUS)

TABLE TENNIS — MEN

	GOLD	SILVER	BRONZE
Singles	Jan-Ove Waldner (SWE)	Jean-Philippe Gatien (FRA)	Wenge Ma (CHN)
			Kim Taek-Soo (KOR)
Doubles	China	Germany	Korea

HANDBALL — WOMEN

	GOLD	SILVER	BRONZE
	South Korea	Norway	Unified Team

HOCKEY — MEN

	GOLD	SILVER	BRONZE
	Germany	Australia	Pakistan

TABLE TENNIS — WOMEN

	GOLD	SILVER	BRONZE
Singles	Yaping Deng (CHN)	Hong Qiao (CHN)	Jung Hwa Hyun (KOR)
			Ben Hui Li (PRK)
Doubles	Cuba	China	South Korea

Olympic opening and closing ceremonies have become more and more flamboyant: festive occasions in which colour, design and movement are used to conjure up a spectacle that can be enjoyed by the whole world watching on television. These photographs show glimpses of Barcelona's opening (above) and closing ceremonies. Chris Cole, Simon Bruty

BASKETBALL — MEN

GOLD	SILVER	BRONZE
USA	Croatia	Lithuania

BASKETBALL — WOMEN

GOLD	SILVER	BRONZE
Unified Team	China	USA

SOCCER

GOLD	SILVER	BRONZE
Spain	Poland	Ghana

HANDBALL — MEN

GOLD	SILVER	BRONZE
Unified Team	Sweden	France

HOCKEY — WOMEN

GOLD	SILVER	BRONZE
Spain	Germany	Great Britain

VOLLEYBALL — MEN

	GOLD	SILVER	BRONZE
	Brazil	Netherlands	USA

VOLLEYBALL — WOMEN

	GOLD	SILVER	BRONZE
	Cuba	Unified Team	USA

BADMINTON — MEN

	GOLD	SILVER	BRONZE
Singles	Alan Budi Kusuma (INA)	Ardy Wiranata (INA)	Thomas Stuer-Lauridsen (DEN)
			Hermawan Susanto (INA)
Doubles	South Korea	Indonesia	China
			Malaysia

BADMINTON — WOMEN

	GOLD	SILVER	BRONZE
Singles	Susi Susanti (INA)	Soo Hyun Bang (KOR)	Hua Huang (CHN)
			Jiuhong Tang (CHN)
Doubles	South Korea	China	China

BASEBALL

	GOLD	SILVER	BRONZE
	Cuba	Chinese Taipai	Japan

Scenes from Barcelona's spectacular opening ceremony. Shaun Botterill, Simon Bruty

Atlanta 1996

ABOVE: *Atlanta native, boxer Evander Holyfield.*
Ross Kinnaird

PREVIOUS PAGE: *The opening ceremony of the 1996 Olympic Games in Atlanta, Georgia.*
Billy Stickland

271 EVENTS

197 COUNTRIES

10,310 ATHLETES

	Gold	Silver	Bronze
USA	44	32	25
RUS	26	21	16
GER	20	18	27
CHN	16	22	12
FRA	15	7	15
ITA	13	10	12
AUS	9	9	23
CUB	9	8	8
UKR	9	2	12
KOR	7	15	5
POL	7	5	5
HUN	7	4	10
ESP	5	6	6
ROM	4	7	9
NED	4	5	10
GRE	4	4	
CZE	4	3	4
SUI	4	3	
DEN	4	1	1
TUR	4	1	1
CAN	3	11	8
BUL	3	7	5
JPN	3	6	5
KAZ	3	4	4
BRA	3	3	9
NZL	3	2	1
RSA	3	1	1
IRL	3		1
SWE	2	4	2
NOR	2	2	3
BEL	2	2	2
NGR	2	1	3
PRK	2	1	2
ALG	2		1
ETH	2		1
GBR	1	8	6
BLR	1	6	8
KEN	1	4	3
JAM	1	3	2
FIN	1	2	1
INA	1	1	2
YUG	1	1	2
IRI	1	1	1
SVK	1	1	1
ARM	1	1	
CRO	1	1	
POR	1		1
THA	1		1
BDI	1		
CRC	1		
ECU	1		
HKG	1		
SYR	1		
ARG		2	1
NAM		2	
SLO		2	
AUT		1	2
MAS		1	1
MDA		1	1
UZB		1	1
AZE		1	
BAH		1	
TPE		1	
LAT		1	
PHI		1	
TGA		1	
ZAM		1	
GEO			2
MAR			2
TRI			2
IND			1
ISR			1
LTU			1
MEX			1
MGL			1
MOZ			1
PUR			1
TUN			1
UGA			1

This was supposed to be more than a mere international sports competition. This wasn't just the Olympic Games; it wasn't even just the Centennial Games. It was the Atlanta games. It was the city which was center stage.

Before the games, city officials were already talking of "international" Atlanta, the "capital of the twentieth century," the "hi-tech metropolis of the future."

Andrew Young, the celebrated former mayor who was instrumental in attracting the games to Atlanta, was quoted as saying: "We want to be for the world what London was in the 17th and 18th centuries."

The reality turned out to be something different. When Juan Antonio Samaranch, the president of the International Olympic Committee, spoke at the closing ceremonies of the games, he opened his remarks with "Well done, Atlanta," rather than the traditional lauding of the city for staging the "best games ever."

In truth, the organisation of the Atlanta games left a lot to be desired. Things did not run smoothly. Worse, the chief image that most television viewers took away from Atlanta — sports aside — was of small-town commercialism.

The games had other troubles... the bombing at the crowded Centennial Olympic Park chief among them. Flying shrapnel killed Alice Hawthorne, a 44-year-old mother from Albany, and the blast injured more than 100 other people. Turkish journalist Melih Uzunyol, 40, died of a

RIGHT: *American boxer Evander Holyfield carries the Olympic flame. Holyfield was an Olympic medalist in the 1984 Los Angeles games.* Ross Kinnaird

heart attack while hurrying to cover the explosion. More than anything, that bombing underscored the fragility of the Olympic notions of peace and understanding through sport. Yet the crowds seemed determined not to give in to violence or fear. Three days after the blast, people returned to the reopened park, pausing for a touching tribute to the victims.

Even the competitions themselves seemed to counter the violence with uplifting images and outstanding athletic accomplishments.

There was Ethiopian Fatuma Roba, who appeared almost tireless as she ran, beaming, into Olympic Stadium to capture gold in the women's marathon. There was Josiah Thugwane who became the first black South African to strike gold in the men's event and, there was Marie-José Perec, the elegant Frenchwoman who equalled Michael Johnson's feat by winning the women's 200 and 400 meters events.

Of course, the Americans, led by Johnson, won the most medals at the Atlanta Games. But even Johnson had to share some of his glitter with 35-year-old Carl Lewis, who showed the grit of a true champion, refusing against the odds to yield ground to younger athletes.

He was on the verge of elimination in the preliminary round of the long jump. But he pulled off a qualifying leap on his last attempt, and went on to win the event and his ninth gold medal at his fourth Olympic games.

Britain's Steve Redgrave, another Olympic veteran, struck gold for the fourth consecutive time in the rowing.

At the other end of the age spectrum, the biggest stars were the US gymnasts who captured the country's hearts by winning the all-round team title amid unprecedented scenes. Kerri Strugg became the hero of the hour when, her leg strapped heavily after an earlier injury, appeared on the mat to take the final vault and ensure victory. All the members of the team became teenage millionairesses overnight.

Then there was Michelle Smith in the swimming pool. The Irishwoman came from seemingly nowhere to claim three gold medals amid allegations she was using performance-enhancing drugs. Even President Bill Clinton found himself having to defend her.

In 1999 she was banned for two years after being caught trying to manipulate a drugs sample. By then, her Olympic dream, rather like Atlanta's, appeared to be a rather tarnished one.

ABOVE AND LOWER INSET:
A close-up of Atlanta's commemorative medal.
Allsport

RIGHT: America's Amy Van Dyken displays her four Atlanta gold medals in swimming. Ross Kinnaird

OPPOSITE PAGE
LEFT: The torch used in the Atlanta games. Allsport

RIGHT: Downtown Atlanta, site of the women's marathon. Gary M. Prior

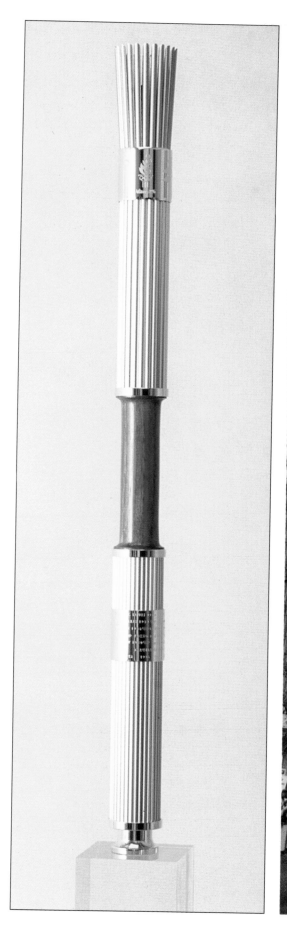

a 🔥 1996

MICHAEL JOHNSON

Michael Johnson of the United States did something in Atlanta no other man had ever achieved in an Olympics: win both the 400 and 200 meters gold medals. Only four others even made the finals in both — a combination of speed and power that have defied a century of Olympians, recalling the 400-800 double by Cuba's Alberto Juantorena in 1976.

Having won the 400 meters, Johnson completed the double in some style when he won the 200 meters in 19.32sec. That took 0.34 of a second off the already startling world record he owned. His winning margin of 0.36sec was the largest in a men's Olympic 200 final since Jesse Owens beat Mack Robinson in 1936, by 20.7 to 21.1. Cut that 19.32 in half and it produced back-to-back 100 meters times of 9.66sec. (Earlier in the games, Canada's Donovan Bailey set the world 100 record at a comparatively crawling 9.84.)

The whole long campaign toward his final was "pressure," Johnson said — he had already done the 200/400 double at the 1995 World Championships and then requested that the Olympic schedule be changed to accommodate the double in Atlanta. Johnson had in the past tried to argue against the all-or-nothing nature of the Olympic track competition.

He failed in Barcelona, advancing no farther than the 200 meters semi-finals because of a suspected case of food poisoning. The smallest of troubles can derail the grandest of plans. It can be the twinge of a muscle or the luck of the lean. In Johnson's case, it was a plate of sausages and meats, Spanish style. That cost him both his Olympic moment and the ability to trust any food more exotic than the Big Mac.

"I don't need the Olympic Games to validate Michael Johnson," he said immediately after that. His next act, in privacy, was to cry in his father's arms.

Johnson is the most meticulous of men, so narrow of focus that he even broke up with a girlfriend in order to simplify his life during training.

At the other extreme, he is the severest of competitors, one who enters an almost frightening trance before the race. "The Danger Zone," he calls it.

Johnson grew up in Dallas as no one's prodigy. Nor did he impress the masses in high school, wearing black-frame glasses and a necktie. He even carried a briefcase to school. He resists these tales of a "nerd" gone straight.

"It was the style in those days to look nice," he protested. He will tell you that he now is very hip, liking fast cars almost as much as fast times.

The highest earning athlete in history, who can command up to $100,000 an appearance, he hopes to repeat his double in Sydney in 2000.

America's Michael Johnson set a world record in the 200 meter sprint. Mike Powell

PREVIOUS PAGE: Italy's Enrico Vecchi makes the throw during the Cuba-Italy matchup. Cuba eventually won gold. Rick Stewart

MICHELLE DE BRUIN

Michelle De Bruin's Olympic triumphs were over-shadowed from the word go by poolside rumors that performance-enhancing drugs were behind her rapid improvement.

De Bruin — then known as Michelle Smith — torpedoed her way through the waters of the Georgia Tech Aquatic center in Atlanta to win three gold medals. In just five days that shocked the swimming world the 28-year-old emerged from obscurity to seal a date with President Bill Clinton, who hugged her and advised her to ignore all the critics.

Hardly had she stopped the clock on the opening night of competition at the Centennial Olympics to win the first of her three golds, with parents Brian and Pat proudly watching, than the whispers began.

She was snubbed by her swimming rivals and the greatest moment in Ireland's Olympic — indeed sporting — history was undermined by the rumors which eventually led to a four-year ban in 1998 after she was found guilty of manipulating a sample in an attempt to mask the fact she had taken anabolic steroids. When the rumors began during the Atlanta Olympics, the Irish called it a witch-hunt, with Pat Hickey, president of the country's Olympic Council, criticizing the Americans for their "Uncle Sam" attitude.

De Bruin did return to a heroine's welcome, with a red carpet awaiting her at the steps of the aircraft at Dublin Airport, where she was greeted by then-President Mary Robinson. But those whispers turned into a tidal wave of suspicion and innuendo which De Bruin's constant denials did nothing to quell.

The millions of pounds in endorsements that should have followed her phenomenal performances in Atlanta (when she also won a bronze) and again at the 1997 European Championships in Seville never arrived. The charming De Bruin, with her long golden hair and infectious smile, was a natural for television, but those appearances were few and far between.

The presence of Dutch husband Erik De Bruin, a former discus thrower whose own past was clouded by a positive drugs test and a four-year ban, ensured her achievements would always be cloaked in suspicion. They had met in the athletes' village in Barcelona four years earlier when De Bruin was there purely to make up the numbers. How could a woman whose country had no Olympic size pool expect to challenge the world's best? But after Erik De Bruin took over her coaching in 1993, the improvements began.

Nevertheless, she still went into the Atlanta Olympics unheralded and thought unlikely to figure in the medal count. De Bruin's husband put her subsequent dramatic turnaround down to his training methods and her iron will and commitment to a regime that could see her swimming several hours a day.

The training certainly broadened her shoulders. But since stunning her rivals in Atlanta, those shoulders have been used to bear the brunt of the constant claims about the "secret" of her success.

452

SVETLANA MASTERKOVA

Svetlana Masterkova's ascent towards the top of her sport was staggering. In 1993, a good but not exceptional two-lap performer going stale from over-racing, she decided to take a break and start a family with her husband, Asiate Saitov, a Russian professional cyclist based in Spain.

In Atlanta, the mother of 17-month-old Anastasia, Masterkova, returned after two seasons out to win Olympic gold at 800 meters and 1,500 meters.

Masterkova was not the first athlete to be physically revitalized by the hormonal stimulus and improved vascular activity which stems from the body's change in pregnancy. The psychological benefits are many, too. At 28, she came across on the track like a mom enjoying a break at night school.

After she won the 800 meters final in Atlanta, a Russian fan cried, "Do it again, Svetlana," and she obliged by sprinting maniacally up both straights for the fastest lap of honor in history.

The Russian team coaches did not want her to run the 800 meters in Atlanta, preferring her to concentrate on the 1,500 meters but she ignored them, and her two-lap victory, forged from the front with subtle pace variations, proved a masterpiece of control and poise. Though she had run only one 1,500 meters before Atlanta, she toyed with the field to complete the double.

She was born and raised in the small Siberian town of Achinsk, about as near to Tokyo as it is to Moscow, some five hours away by plane. Masterkova lost her first race at school, but was so jealous when the winner received a puppet that she vowed to carry on until she won one too.

It was not much fun, though. She recalls: "I would get up at six o'clock but it was so bad I needed a hot shower and hot tea before I went out and a lot of clothes whenever I ran. My nose would get frozen too."

At 18, she went to Moscow; at 23 she ran the year's fastest 800 meters, and at 25 she won a world indoor silver medal. But with the old Soviet sporting machine disbanding her career stalled, she followed Asiate to Spain, where her career was revitalized.

STEVE REDGRAVE

At the age of 34, Britain's Steve Redgrave became only the fourth Olympian in the modern games to win four gold medals in four consecutive Olympiads when he triumphed in the coxless pairs.

Before the race in Atlanta began, Redgrave wiped his hands on his white towel and maintained the quiet confidence that has marked his career.

At the race's start, he and his partner Matthew Pinsent burst out to a lead that they never gave up. Pinsent seemed to crack a slight smile on the water as the other boats fell behind.

The historic victory was not achieved easily. The Australian pair of David Weightman and Robert Scott closed to within a second by the race's end, while Redgrave and Pinsent lost steam. But time ran out.

Crossing the finish line first, Redgrave's arms collapsed on his oars. He was too spent to look up at the crowd. But Pinsent raised a strong fist to the spectators. Since dropping out of school at the age of 16, the sport has been Redgrave's trade. He was a member of the coxed fours who won Olympic gold in Los Angeles in 1984 and in 1988 at the coxless pairs with Andrew Holmes, with whom he also took the bronze at the coxed pairs.

In 1989 he took up bobsledding and was a member of the crew that won the British four-man championship that year. But any thoughts of ambitions in the Winter Olympics were put on hold as he picked up the oars again for Barcelona 1992, where he equaled the all-time record with a third Olympic gold, at the coxed pairs with Pinsent and cox Garry Herbert.

After making history in Atlanta, his first words were: "If you see me anywhere near a boat, shoot me."

Redgrave will be in Sydney attempting to add an unprecedented fifth Olympic gold to his collection.

LEFT: *America's Gail Devers (foreground), narrowly defeats Jamaica's Merlene Ottey to win gold in the 100 m final.* Mike Powell

ABOVE: *Alexei Nemov of Russia on the parallel bar.* Simon Bruty

PREVIOUS PAGE: *Aline Stoica of Romania displays her agility in the individual rhythmic gymnastics component.* David Cannon

TOP: *Allen Johnson of the USA crashes his way to gold in the 110 m hurdles.* Tony Duffy

ABOVE: *Musician Ray Charles performs at the Atlanta summer games.* Mathew Stockman

RIGHT: *Anna Lindberg of Sweden in the women's 3 m springboard finals.* Simon Bruty

ABOVE: *Diving practice at dusk.* Mike Hewitt

OPPOSITE PAGE: *Antonio Ali of Great Britain.* Allsport

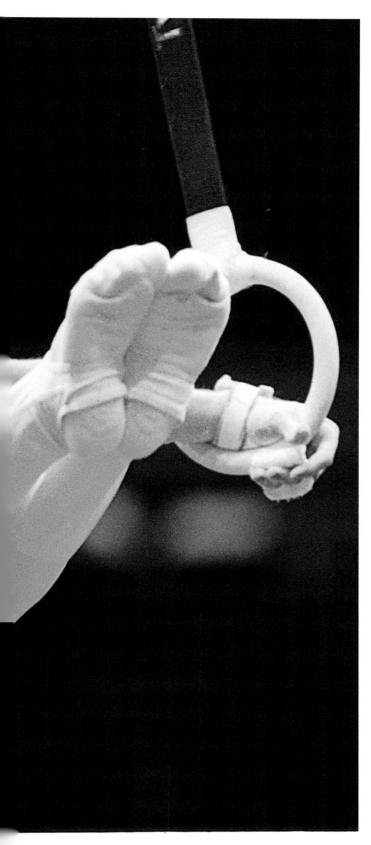

ABOVE LEFT: Yuri Chechi of Italy takes gold on the rings. Mike Powell

ABOVE RIGHT: America's Gail Devers celebrates her gold in the 100 m final. Gray Mortimore

ATLANTA 1996
JULY 19 -AUGUST 4

PARTICIPANTS: 10,310 / MEN: 6,797 WOMEN: 3,513
COUNTRIES: 197
SPORTS: 26 EVENTS: 271
FINAL TORCHBEARER: MUHAMMAD ALI

MEDALS TABLE

PLACE	COUNTRY	GOLD	SILVER	BRONZE
1	USA	44	32	25
2	Russia	26	21	16
3	Germany	20	18	27
4	China	16	22	12
5	France	15	7	15

OUTSTANDING ATHLETES

PLACE	NAME (NATIONALITY)	DISCIPLINE	GOLD	SILVER	BRONZE
1	Amy van Dyken (USA)	Swimming	4		
2	Michelle Smith (IRL)	Swimming	3		1
3	Alexander Popov (RUS)	Swimming	2	2	
	Gary Hall Jr. (USA)	Swimming	2	2	
	Alexei Nemov (RUS)	Gymnastics	2	1	3

ATHLETICS — MEN

EVENT	GOLD		SILVER		BRONZE	
100 m	Donovan Bailey (CAN)	9.84	Frankie Fredericks (NAM)	9.89	Ato Boldon (TRI)	9.90
200 m	Michael Johnson (USA)	19.32	Frankie Fredericks (NAM)	19.68	Ato Boldon (TRI)	19.80
400 m	Michael Johnson (USA)	43.49	Roger Black (GBR)	44.41	Davis Kamoga (UGA)	44.53
800 m	Vebjorn Rodal (NOR)	1:42.58	Hezekiel Sepeng (RSA)	1:42.74	Fred Onyancha (KEN)	1:42.79
1,500 m	Noureddine Morceli (ALG)	3:35.78	Fermin Cacho (ESP)	3:36.40	Stephen Kipkorir (KEN)	3:36.72
5,000 m	Venuste Nyongabo (BUR)	13:07.96	Paul Bitok (KEN)	13:08.16	Khalid Boulami (MAR)	13:08.37
10,000 m	Haile Gebrselassie (ETH)	27:07.34	Paul Tergat (KEN)	27:08.17	Salah Hissou (MAR)	27:24.67
Marathon	Josiah Thugwane (RSA)	2:12.36	Lee Bong-Ju (KOR)	2:12.39	Eric Wainaina (KEN)	2:12.44
110 m Hurdles	Allen Johnson (USA)	12.95	Mark Crear (USA)	13.09	Florian Schwarthoff (GER)	13.17
400 m Hurdles	Derrick Adkins (USA)	47.55	Samuel Matete (ZAM)	47.78	Calvin Davis (USA)	47.96
3,000 m Steeplechase	Joseph Keter (KEN)	8:07.12	Moses Kiptanui (KEN)	8:08.33	Alessandro Lambruschini (ITA)	8:11.28
4x100 m	Canada	37.69	USA	38.05	Brazil	38.41
4x400 m	USA	2:55.99	Great Britain	2:56.60	Jamaica	2:59.42
20 km Walk	Jefferson Perez (ECU)	1:20:07	Ilja Markow (RUS)	1:20:16	Bernardo Segura (MEX)	1:20:23
50 km Walk	Robert Korzeniowski (POL)	3:43:30	Mikhail Shchennikov (RUS)	3:43:46	Valentin Massana (ESP)	3:44:19
High Jump	Charles Austin (USA)	7'10.25"	Artur Partyka (POL)	7'9.5"	Steve Smith (GBR)	7'8.5"
Pole Vault	Jean Galfione (FRA)	19'5.25"	Igor Trandenkow (UKR)	19'5.25"	Andrei Tiwonchik (GER)	19'5.25"
Long Jump	Carl Lewis (USA)	27'10.75"	James Beckford (JAM)	27'2.5"	Joe Greene (USA)	27'0.5"
Triple Jump	Kenny Harrison (USA)	59'4.25"	Jonathan Edwards (GBR)	58'8"	Yoelvis Quesada (CUB)	57'2.75"
Shot	Randy Barnes (USA)	70'11.25"	John Godina (USA)	68'2.5"	Oleksandr Bagach (UKR)	68'1"
Discus	Lars Riedel (GER)	227'8"	Vladimir Dubrovchik (BLR)	218'6"	Vassili Kaptyukh (BLR)	215'10"
Javelin	Jan Zelezny (CZE)	289'3"	Steve Backley (GBR)	286'10"	Seppo Raty (FIN)	285'4"
Hammer	Balazs Kiss (HUN)	266'6"	Lance Deal (USA)	266'2"	Oleksiy Krykun (UKR)	262'6"
Decathlon	Dan O'Brien (USA)	8,824	Frank Busemann (GER)	8,706	Tomas Dvorak (CZE)	8,664

ABOVE: Canada's Donovan Bailey leaps with joy after setting a world record in the 100 m final. Gray Mortimore

OPPOSITE PAGE
TOP: Hicham El-Guerroj of Morocco tumbles in the 1,500 m final. Mike Hewitt
BELOW: Norway's Vebjoan Rodal, a gold medalist in the 800 m final. Mike Powell

ATHLETICS — WOMEN

EVENT	GOLD		SILVER		BRONZE	
100 m	Gail Devers (USA)	10.94	Merlene Ottey (JAM)	10.94	Gwen Torrence (USA)	10.96
200 m	Marie-José Perec (FRA)	22.12	Merlene Ottey (JAM)	22.24	Mary Onyali (NGR)	22.38
400 m	Marie-José Perec (FRA)	48.25	Cathy Freeman (AUS)	48.63	Falilat Ogunkoya (NGR)	49.10
800 m	Svetlana Masterkova (RUS)	1:57 73	Ana Quirot (CUB)	1:58.11	Maria Mutola (MOZ)	1:58.71
1,500 m	Svetlana Masterkova (RUS)	4:00.83	Gabriela Szabo (ROM)	4:01.54	Theresia Kiesel (AUT)	4:03.02
5,000 m	Wang Junxia (CHN)	14:59.88	Pauline Konga (KEN)	15:03.49	Roberta Brunet (ITA)	15:07.52
10,000 m	Fernanda Ribeiro (POR)	31:01.63	Wang Junxia (CHN)	31:02.58	Gete Wami (ETH)	31:06.65
Marathon	Fatuma Roba (ETH)	2:26:05	Valentina Yegorova (RUS)	2:28:05	Yuko Arimori (JPN)	2:28:39
100 m Hurdles	Lyudmila Engquist (SWE)	12.58	Brigita Bukovec (SLO)	12:59	Patricia Girard (FRA)	12:65
400 m Hurdles	Deon Hemmings (JAM)	52:82	Kim Batten (USA)	53:08	Tonja Buford-Bailey (USA)	53:22
4x100 m	USA	41.95	Bahamas	42.14	Jamaica	42.24
4x400 m	USA	3:20.91	Nigeria	3:21.04	Germany	3:21.14
10 km Walk	Yelena Nikolayeva (RUS)	41:49	Elisabeta Perrone (ITA)	42:12	Gao Hongmiao (CHN)	42:19
High Jump	Stefka Kostadinova (BUL)	6'8.75"	Niki Bakogianni (GRE)	6'8"	Inga Babakova (UKR)	6'7"
Long Jump	Chioma Anjunwa (NGR)	23'4.5"	Fiona May (ITA)	23'0.5"	Jackie Joyner-Kersee (USA)	22'11.75"
Triple Jump	Inessa Kravets (UKR)	50'3.5"	Inna Lisovskaya (RUS)	49'1.75"	Sarka Kasparkova (CZE)	49'1.75"
Shot	Astrid Kumbernuss (GER)	67'5.5"	Sun Xinmei (CHN)	65'2.75"	Irina Khudorozhkina (RUS)	63'6"
Discus	Ilike Wyludda (GER)	228'6"	Natalya Sadova (RUS)	218'1"	Ellina Zvereva (BLR)	215'4"
Javelin	Heli Rantanen(NOR)	222'11"	Louise McPaul (AUS)	215'0"	Trine Hattestad (NOR)	213'2"
Heptathlon	Ghada Shouaa (SYR)	6780	Natasha Sazonovich (BLR)	6563	Denise Lewis (GBR)	6489

SWIMMING — WOMEN

EVENT	GOLD		SILVER		BRONZE	
50 m Freestyle	Amy van Dyken (USA)	24.87	Le Jingyi (CHN)	24.90	Sandra Volker (GER)	25.14
100 m Freestyle	Le Jingyi (CHN)	54.50	Sandra Volker (GER)	54.88	Angel Martino (USA)	54.93
200 m Freestyle	Claudia Poll (CRC)	1:58.16	Franziska van Almsick (GER)	1:58.57	Dagmar Hase (GER)	1:59.56
400 m Freestyle	Michelle Smith (IRL)	4:07.25	Dagmar Hase (GER)	4:08.30	Kirsten Vlieghuis (NED)	4:08.70
800 m Freestyle	Brooke Bennett (USA)	8:27.89	Dagmar Hase (GER)	8:29.91	Kirsten Vlieghuis (NED)	8:30.84
100 m Backstroke	Beth Botsford (USA)	1:01.19	Whitney Hedgepeth (USA)	1:01.47	Marianne Kriel (RSA)	1:02.12
200 m Backstroke	Krisztina Egerszegi (HUN)	2:07.83	Whitney Hedgepeth (USA)	2:11.98	Cathleen Rund (GER)	2:12.06
100 m Breaststroke	Penelope Heyns (RSA)	1:07.73	Amanda Beard (USA)	1:08.09	Samantha Reilly (AUS)	1:09.18
200 m Breaststroke	Penelope Heyns (RSA)	2:25.41	Amanda Beard (USA)	2:25.75	Agnes Kovacs (HUN)	2:26.57
100 m Butterfly	Amy van Dyken (USA)	59.13	Liu Limin (CHN)	59.14	Angel Martino (USA)	59.23
200 m Butterfly	Susan O'Neill (AUS)	2:07.76	PetriaThomas (AUS)	2:09.82	Michelle Smith (IRL)	2:09.91
200 m Medley	Michelle Smith (IRL)	2:13.93	Marianne Limpert (CAN)	2:14.35	Lin Li (CHN)	2:14.74
400 m Medley	Michelle Smith (IRL)	4:39.18	Allison Wagner (USA)	4:42.03	Krisztina Egerszegy (HUN)	4:42.53
4x100 m Freestyle	USA	3:39.29	China	3:40.40	Germany	3:41 48
4x200 m Freestyle	USA	7:59.87	Germany	8:01.55	Australia	8:05.47
4x100 m Medley	USA	4:02.88	Australia	4:05.08	China	4:07.34
Springboard Diving	Mingxia Fu (CHN)	547.68	Irina Laschko (RUS)	512.19	Annie Pelletier (CAN)	509.64
Highboard Diving	Mingxia Fu (CHN)	521.58	Annika Walter (GER)	479.22	Mary Ellen Clark (USA)	472.95

SWIMMING — MEN

EVENT	GOLD		SILVER		BRONZE	
50 m Freestyle	Alexander Popov (RUS)	22.13	Gary Hall Jr. (USA)	22.26	Fernando Scherer (BRA)	22.29
100 m Freestyle	Alexander Popov (RUS)	48.74	Gary Hall Jr. (USA)	48.81	Gustavo Borges (BRA)	49.02
200 m Freestyle	Danyon Loader (NZL)	1:47.63	Gustavo Borges (BRA)	1:48.08	Daniel Kowalski (AUS)	1:48.25
400 m Freestyle	Danyon Loader (NZL)	3:47.97	Paul Palmer (GBR)	3:49.00	Daniel Kowalski (AUS)	3:52.15
1,500 m Freestyle	Kieren Perkins (AUS)	14:56.40	Daniel Kowalski (AUS)	15:02.43	Graeme Smith (GBR)	15:02.48
100 m Backstroke	Jeff Rouse (USA)	54.10	Rodolfo Cabrera (CUB)	54.98	Neisser Belit (CUB)	55.02
200 m Backstroke	Brad Bridgewater (USA)	1:58.54	Tripp Schwenk (USA)	1:58.99	Emanuele Merisi (ITA)	1:59.18
100 m Breaststroke	Frederick Deburghgraeve (BEL)	1:00.65	Jeremy Linn (USA)	1:00.77	Mark Warnecke (GER)	1:01.33
200 m Breaststroke	Norbert Rozsa (HUN)	2:12.57	Karoly Guttler (HUN)	2:13.03	Alexei Korneyev (RUS)	2:13.17
100 m Butterfly	Denis Pankratov (RUS)	52.27	Scott Miller (AUS)	52.53	Vladislav Kulikov (RUS)	53.13
200 m Butterfy	Denis Pankratov (RUS)	1:56.51	Matt Malchow (USA)	1:57.44	Scott Miller (AUS)	1:57.48
200 m Medley	Attila Czene (HUN)	1:59.91	Jani Sievenen (FIN)	2:00.13	Curtis Myden (CAN)	2:01.13
400 m Medley	Tonl Dolan (USA)	4:14.90	Eric Namesnik (USA)	4:15.25	Curtis Myden (CAN)	4:16.28
4x100 m Freestyle	USA	3:15.41	Russia	3:17.06	Germany	3:17.20
4x200 m Freestyle	USA	7:14.84	Sweden	7:17.56	Germany	7:17.71
4x100 m Medley	USA	3:34.84	Russia	3:37.55	Australia	3:39.56
Springboard Diving	Ni Xiong (CHN)	701.46	Yu Zhuocheng (CHN)	690.93	Mark Lenzi (USA)	686.49
Highboard Diving	Dmitri Sautin (RUS)	692.34	Jan Hempel (GER)	663.27	Hailiang Xiao (CHN)	658.20
Water Polo	Spain		Croatia		Italy	

SYNCHRONIZED SWIMMING

GOLD		SILVER		BRONZE	
USA	99.720	Canada	98.367	Japan	97.753

470

TOP: *Yugoslavia's Dejan Bodiroga (left) and America's Shaquille O'Neal (right) collide in the USA/Yugoslavia basketball finals.* Rick Stewart
ABOVE: *America's Justin Huish takes gold in the archery.* Rick Stewart

OPPOSITE PAGE: *American tennis star, Andre Agassi took gold in the male singles' tennis final.* Gary M. Prior

BOXING

EVENT	GOLD	SILVER	BRONZE
Light-Flyweight (-106 lb)	Daniel Petrov (BUL)	Mansueto Valesco (PHI)	Oleg Kurukhin (UKR) / Rafael Lozano (ESP)
Flyweight (-112 lb)	Maikro Romero (CUB)	Bulat Dzumadikov (KAZ)	Albert Pakeyev (RUS) / Zoltan Lunka (GER)
Bantamweight (-119 lb)	Istvan Kovacs (HUN)	Arnoldo Mesa (CUB)	Raimkul Malakhbekov (RUS) / Khadpo Vichairachanun (THA)
Featherweight (-125 lb)	Somluck Kamsing (THA)	Serafim Todorov (BUL)	Pablo Chacon (ARG) / Floyd Mayweather (USA)
Lightweight (-132 lb)	Hocine Soltani (ALG)	Tontcho Tontchev (BUL)	Terrance Cauthen (USA) / Leonard Doroftei (ROM)
Light-Welterweight (-140 lb)	Hector Vinent (CUB)	Oktay Urkal (GER)	Bolat Niyazymbetov (KAZ) / Fathi Missaoui (TUN)
Welterweight (-147 lb)	Oleg Saitov (RUS)	Juan Hernandez (CUB)	Marian Simion (ROM) / Daniel Santos (PUR)
Light-Middleweight (-156 lb)	David Reid (USA)	Alfredo Duvergel (CUB)	Karim Tulaganov (UZB) / Esmouhan Ibraimov (KAZ)
Middleweight (-165 lb)	Ariel Hernandez (CUB)	Malik Beyleroglu (TUR)	Mohamed Bahari (ALG) / Roshii Wells (USA)
Light-Heavyweight (-178 lb)	Vasili Jirov (KAZ)	Lee Seung-Bae (KOR)	AntonioTarver (USA) / Thomas Ulrich (GER)
Heavyweight (-201 lb)	Felix Savon (CUB)	David Defiagbon (CAN)	Nates Jones (USA) / Luan Krasniqui (GER)
Super-Heavyweight (+201 lb)	Vladimir Klichko (UKR)	Paea Wolfgram (TGA)	Alexei Lezin (RUS) / Duncan Dokwari (NGR)

JUDO — MEN

EVENT	GOLD	SILVER	BRONZE
Super-Lightweight (-132 lb)	Tadahiro Nomura (JPN)	Girolamo Giovanazzo (ITA)	Doripalam Narmandakh (MGL) / Richard Trautmann (GER)
Half-Lightweight (-143 lb)	Udo Quellmalz (GER)	Yukimasa Nakamura (JPN)	Israel Hernandez Plana (CUB) / Henrique Guimares (BRA)
Lightweight (-156.5 lb)	Kenzo Nakamura (JPN))	Kwak Dae-Sung (KOR)	James Pedro (USA) / Christophe Gagliano (FRA)
Light-Middlleweight (-172 lb)	Djamel Bouras (FRA)	Toshihiko Koga (JPN))	Soso Liparteliani (GEO) / Cho In-Chul (KOR)
Middleweight (-189.5 lb)	Jeon Ki-Young (KOR)	Armen Bagdasarov (UZB)	Marko Spittka (GER) / Mark Huizinga (NED)
Light-Heavyweight (- 209 lb)	Pawel Nastula (POL)	Kim Min-Soo (KOR)	Stephane Traineau (FRA) / Miguel Fernandez (BRA)
Heavyweight (+209 lb)	David Douillet (FRA)	Ernesto Perez (ESP)	Harry van Barneveld (BEL) / Frank Moeller (GER)

JUDO — WOMEN

EVENT	GOLD	SILVER	BRONZE
Super-Lightweight (-106 lb)	Kye Sun (PRK)	Ryoko Tamura (JPN)	Amarilis Savon Carmenaty (CUB)
			Yolanda Soler (ESP)
Half-Lightweight (-114 lb)	Marie-Claire Restoux (FRA)	Hyun Sook-Hee (KOR)	Legna Verdecia (CUB)
			Noriko Sugawara (JPN)
Lightweight (-123 lb)	Driulis Gonzalez Morales (CUB)	Jung Sun-Yong (KOR)	Isabel Fernandez (ESP)
			Liu Chuang (CHN)
Light-Middleweight (-134.5 lb)	Yuko Emoto (JPN)	Gella Van De Caveye (BEL)	Jenny Gal (NED)
			Jung Sung-Sook (KOR)
Middlleweight (-145.5 lb)	Cho Min-Sun (KOR)	Aneta Szczepanska (POL)	Claudia Zwiers (NED)
			Xianbo Wang (CHN)
Light-Heavyweight (-158.5 lb)	Ulla Werbrouck (HUN)	Yoko Tanabe (JPN)	Yelena Scapin (ITA)
			Diadenis Luna (CUB)
Heavyweight (+158.5 lb)	Sun Fu-Ming (CHN)	Estela Rodriguez Villanueva (CUB)	Johanna Hagn (GER)
			Christine Cicot (FRA)

FENCING — MEN

EVENT	GOLD	SILVER	BRONZE
Individual Foil	Alessandro Puccini (ITA)	Lionel Plumenail (FRA)	Frank Boidin (FRA)
Team Foil	Russia	Poland	Cuba
Individual Épée	Alexander Beketov (RUS)	Ivan Trevejo Perez (CUB)	Geza Imre (HUN)
Team Épée	Italy	Russia	France
Individual Saber	Sergei Podnyakov (RUS)	Stanislav Sharikov (RUS)	Damien Touya (FRA)
Team Saber	Russia	Hungary	Italy

FENCING — WOMEN

EVENT	GOLD	SILVER	BRONZE
Individual Foil	Laura Badea (ROM)	Valentin Vezzali (ITA)	Giovanna Trillini (ITA)
Team Foil	Italy	Romania	Germany
Individual Épée	Laura Flessel (FRA)	Valerie Barlois (FRA)	Gyorgyi Horvathne-Szalay (HUN)
Team Épée	France	Italy	Russia

Boxing great Muhammad Ali — who won gold in Rome — gets a medal to replace the one he threw away after being refused service at a restaurant, on the basis of his color, in America during the 1960s. Jed Jacobsohn

A close-up of the medals handed out in Atlanta. Stephen Dunn

WEIGHTLIFTING

EVENT	GOLD	SILVER	BRONZE
Flyweight	Halil Mutlu (TUR)	Zhang Xiangsen (CHN)	Sevdalin Minchev (BUL)
Bantamweight	Tang Ningsheng (CHN)	Leonidas Sabanis (GRE)	Nikolay Pechalov (BUL)
Featherweight	Naim Süleymanoglu (TUR)	Valerios Leonidis (GRE)	Jiangang Xiao (CHN)
Lightweight	Zhang Xugang (CHN)	Kim Myong-Nam (PRK)	Attila Feri (HUN)
Middleweight	Pablo Lara (CUB)	Yoto Yotov (BUL)	Jon Chol-Ho (PRK)
Light-Heavyweight	Pyrros Dimas (GRE)	Marc Huster (GER)	Andrzej Cofalik (POL)
Middle-Heavyweight	Alexei Petrov (RUS)	Leonidas Kokas (GRE)	Oliver Caruso (GER)
First Heavyweight	Akakidei Khakiashvilis (GRE)	Anatoli Khrapaty (KAZ)	Denis Gotfrid (UKR)
Second Heavyweight	Timur Taimassov (UKR)	Sergey Syrtsov (RUS)	Nicu Vlad (ROM)
Super-Heavyweight	Andrej Chemerkin (RUS)	Ronny Weller (GER)	Stefan Botev (AUS)

WEIGHTLIFTING WEIGHTS

FLYWEIGHT	-119 lb	BANTAMWEIGHT	-130 lb	FEATHERWEIGHT	-141 lb
LIGHTWEIGHT	-154 lb	MIDDLEWEIGHT	-167.5 lb	LIGHT-HEAVYWEIGHT	-183 lb
MIDDLE-HEAVYWEIGHT	-205 lb	FIRST-HEAVYWEIGHT	-218 lb	SECOND-HEAVYWEIGHT	- 238 lb
SUPER-HEAVYWEIGHT	+238 lb				

GRECO-ROMAN WRESTLING

EVENT	GOLD	SILVER	BRONZE
Light-Flyweight (- 1 05.5 lb)	Sim Kwon-Ho (KOR)	Aleksandr Pavlov (BLR)	Zafar Gulyov (RUS)
Flyweight (-114.5 lb)	Arman Nazaryan (ARM)	Brandon Paulson (USA)	Andrei Kalashnikov (UKR)
Bantamweight (-125.5 lb)	Yovei Melnichenko (KAZ)	Denis Hall (USA)	Cheng Zetian (CHN)
Featherweight (-136.5 lb)	Wlodzimierz Zawadzki (POL)	Juan Delis (CUB)	Akif Pirim (TUR)
Lightweight (-149.5 lb)	Ryzsard Wolny (POL)	Ghani Yalouz (FRA)	Aleksandr Tretyakov (RUS)
Welterweight (-163 lb)	Feliberto Aguilera (CUB)	Marko Asell (FIN)	Jozef Tracz (POL)
Middlleweight (-180.5 lb)	Hamza Yerlikaya (TUR)	Thomas Zander (GER)	Valeri Tsilent (BLR)
Light-Heavyweight (-198 lb)	Vyachetslav Oleynik (UKR)	Jacek Fafinski (POL)	Maik Bullman (GER)
Heavyweight (-220.5 lb)	Andreas Wronski (POL)	Sergei Lishtvan (BLR)	Mikael Ljungberg (SWE)
Super-Heavyweight (-286 lb)	Alexander Karelin (RUS)	Matt Ghaffari (USA)	Sergei Moureiko (MDA)

FREESTYLE WRESTLING

EVENT	GOLD	SILVER	BRONZE
Light-Flyweight (-105.5 lb)	Kim Il (PRK)	Armen Mkrchyan (ARM)	Alexis Vila (CUB)
Flyweight (-114.5 lb)	Valentin Jordanov (BUL)	Namig Abdullaeyev (AZE)	Maulen Mamirov (KAZ)
Bantamweight (-125.5 lb)	Kendall Cross (USA)	Giga Sissaouri (CAN)	Ri Yong-Sam (PRK)
Featherweight (-136.5 lb)	Thomas Brands (USA)	Jang Jae-Sung (KOR)	Elbrus Tedeyev (UKR)
Lightweight (-149.5 lb)	Vadim Bogiyev (RUS)	Townsend Saunders (USA)	Zaza Zazirov (UKR)
Welterweight (-163 lb)	Buvaisa Saityev (RUS)	Park Jang-Soon (KOR)	Taykuo Ota (JPN)
Middleweight (-180.5 lb)	Khadshimurad Magomedov (RUS)	Yang Hyun-Mo (KOR)	Amir Khadem Azghadi (IRN)
Light-Heavyweight (-198 lb)	Rasul Khadem Azghadi (IRN)	Maharbeg Chadartsev (RUS)	Eldari Kurtanidze (GEO)
Heavyweight (-220 lb)	Kurt Angle (USA)	Abbas Jadidi (IRN)	Arwat Sabejew (GER)
Super-Heavyweight (-286 lb)	Mahmut Demir (TUR)	Alexei Medvedev (BUL)	Bruce Baumgartner (USA)

MODERN PENTATHLON

EVENT	GOLD		SILVER		BRONZE	
Individual	Alexander Parygin (KAZ)	5,551	Eduard Zanovka (RUS)	5,530	Jano Martinek (HUN)	5,501

CANOE SLALOM — WOMEN

EVENT	GOLD		SILVER		BRONZE	
Kayak 1	Stepanka Hilgertova (CZE)	169.49	Dana Chladek (USA)	169.49	Myriam Fox-Jerusalmi (FRA)	171.00

ROWING — WOMEN

EVENT	GOLD		SILVER		BRONZE	
Single Sculls	Yekaterina Khodotovich (BLR)	7:32.21	Silken Laumann (CAN)	7:35.15	Trine Hansen (DEN)	7:37.20
Double Sculls	Canada	6:56.84	China	6:58.35	Netherlands	6:58.72
Coxless Pairs	Australia	7:01.39	USA	7:01.78	France	7:03.82
Quadruple Sculls	Germany	6:27.44	Ukraine	6:30.36	Canada	6:30.38
Eights	Romania	6:19.73	Canada	6:24.05	Belarus	6:24.44
Lightweight Double Sculls	Romania	7:12.78	USA	7:14.65	Australia	7:16.56

ROWING — MEN

EVENT	GOLD		SILVER		BRONZE	
Single Sculls	Xeno Mueller (SUI)	6:44.85	Derek Porter (CAN)	6:47.45	Thomas Lange (GER)	6:47.72
Double Sculls	Italy	6:16.98	Norway	6:18.42	France	6:19.85
Coxless Pairs	Great Britain	6:20.09	Australia	6:21.02	France	6:22.15
Quadruple Sculls	Germany	5:56.93	USA	5:59.10	Australia	6:01.65
Coxless Fours	Australia	6:06.37	France	6:07.03	Great Britain	6:07.28
Eights	Netherlands	5:42.74	Germany	5:44.58	Russia	5:45.77
Lightweight Double Sculls	Switzerland	6:23.27	Netherlands	6:26.48	Australia	6:26.69
Lightweight Coxless Fours	Denmark	6:09.58	Canada	6:10.13	USA	6:12.29

YACHTING — OPEN

EVENT	GOLD		SILVER		BRONZE	
Star	Brazil	25	Sweden	29	Australia	32
Tornado	Spain	30	Australia	42	Brazil	43
Soling	Germany		Russia		USA	
Laser	Robert Scheidt (BRA)	26	Ben Ainslie (GBR)	37	Per Moberg (NOR)	46

CANOE SLALOM — MEN

EVENT	GOLD		SILVER		BRONZE	
Kayak 1	Oliver Fix (GER)	141.22	Andraz Vehovar (SLO)	141.65	Thomas Becker (GER)	142.79
Canadian 1	Michal Martikan (SVK)	151.03	Lukas Pollert (CZE)	151.17	Patrice Estanguet (FRA)	152.84
Canadian 2	France	158.82	Czech Republic	160.16	Germany	163.72

CANOEING — WOMEN

EVENT	GOLD		SILVER		BRONZE	
500 m Kayak Singles K1	Rita Koban (HUN)	1:47.65	Caroline Brunet (CAN)	1:47.89	Josefa Idem (ITA)	1:48.73
500 m Kayak Pairs K2	Sweden	1:39.32	Germany	1:39.68	Australia	1:40.64
500 m Kayak Fours K4	Germany	1:31.07	Switzerland	1:32.70	Sweden	1:32.91

CANOEING — MEN

EVENT	GOLD		SILVER		BRONZE	
500 m Kayak Singles K1	Antonio Rossi (ITA)	1:37.42	Knut Holmann (NOR)	1:38.33	Piotr Markiewicz (POL)	1:38.61
1,000 m Kayak Singles K1	Knut Holmann (NOR)	3:25.78	Beniamino Bonomi (ITA)	3:27.07	Clint Robinson (AUS)	3:29.71
500 m Kayak Pairs K2	Germany	1:28.69	Italy	1:28.72	Australia	1:29.40
1,000 m Kayak Pairs K2	Italy	3:09.19	Germany	3:10.51	Bulgaria	3:11.20
1,000 m Kayak Fours K4	Germany	2:51.52	Hungary	2:53.18	Russia	2:55.99
500 m Canadian Singles C1	Martin Doktor (CZE)	1:49.93	Slavomir Knazovicky (SLO)	1:50.51	Imre Pulai (ITA)	1:50.75
1000 m Canadian Singles C1	Martin Doktor (CZE)	3:54.41	Ivan Klementyev (LAT)	3:54.95	Gyorgy Zala (HUN)	3:56.36
500 m Canadian Pairs C2	Hungary	1:40.42	Moldova	1:40.45	Romania	1:41.33
1,000 m Canadian Pairs C2	Germany	3:31.87	Romania	3:32.29	Hungary	3:32.51

YACHTING — MEN

EVENT	GOLD		SILVER		BRONZE	
Finn	Mateusz Kusnierexvicz (POL)	32	Sebastian Godefroid (BEL)	45	Roy Heiner (NED)	50
470	Ukraine	40	Great Britain	61	Portugal	62
Mistral Sailboard	Nikolas Kaklamanakis (GRE)	17	Carlos Espinola (ARG)	19	Gal Fridman (ISR)	21

YACHTING — WOMEN

EVENT	GOLD		SILVER		BRONZE	
Europe	Kristine Roug (DEN)	24	Margit Matthijsse (NED)	30	Courtney Becker-Dey (USA)	39
470	Spain	25	Japan	36	Ukraine	38
Mistral Sailboard	Lai-Shan Lee (HKG)	16	Barbara Kendall (NZL)	24	Alessandra Sensini (ITA)	28

SHOOTING — MEN

EVENT	GOLD		SILVER		BRONZE	
Small-Bore Rifle (Prone)	Christian Klees (GER)	704.8	Sergei Belyayev (KAZ)	703.3	Jozef Gonci (SLO)	701.9
Small-Bore Rifle (3 Positions)	Jean-Pierre Amat (FRA)	1273.9	Sergei Belyayev (KAZ)	1272.3	Wolfram Waibel (AUT)	1269.6
Rapid-Fire Pistol	Ralf Schumann (GER)	698.0	Emil Milev (BUL)	692.1	Vladimir Vochmianin (KAZ)	691.5
Free Pistol (50 m)	Boris Kokorev (RUS)	666.4	Igor Basinski (BLR)	662.0	Roberto Di Donna (ITA)	661.8
Running GameTarget	Ling Yang (CHN)	685.8	Xiao Jun (CHN)	679.8	Miroslav Janus (CZE)	678.4
Air Pistol	Roberto Di Donna (ITA)	684.2	Wang Yifu (CHN)	684.1	Taniu Kiryakov (BUL)	683.8
Skeet Shooting	Ennio Falco (ITA)	149	Miroslav Rzepkowski (POL)	148	Andrea Benelli (ITA)	147
Trap Shooting	Michael Diamond (AUS)	149	Josh Lakatos (USA)	147	Lance Bade (USA)	147
Double Trap Shooting	Russell Mark (AUS)	189	Albano Pera (ITA)	183	Zhang Bing (CHN)	183
Air Rifle	Artem Khadzhibekov (RUS)	695.7	Wolfram Waibel (AUT)	695.2	Jean-Pierre Amat (FRA)	693.1

ABOVE LEFT: Mexico's synchronized swimming team. David Leah

ABOVE RIGHT: Russia's Yanina Batyrchina won silver in rhythmic gymnastics. Pascal Rondeau

SHOOTING — WOMEN

EVENT	GOLD		SILVER		BRONZE	
Sports Pistol	Li Duihong (CHN)	687.9	Diana Yorgova (BUL)	684.8	Marina Logvinenko (RUS)	684.2
Small-Bore Rifle (3 Positions)	Alexandra Ivosev (YUG)	686.1	Irina Gerasimenok (POL)	680.1	Renata Mauer (POL)	679.8
Air Rifle	Renata Mauer (POL)	497.6	Petra Horneber (GER)	497.4	Alexandra Ivosev (YUG)	497.2
Air Pistol	Olga Klochneva (RUS)	490.1	Marina Logvinenko (RUS)	488.5	Maria Grusdeva (BUL)	488.5
Double Trap Shooting	Kim Rhode (USA)	141	Susanne Keirmayer (GER)	139	Deserie Huddleston (AUS)	139

ARCHERY — MEN

EVENT	GOLD	SILVER	BRONZE
Individual	Justin Huish (USA)	Magnus Petersson (SWE)	Oh Kyun-Moon (KOR)
Team	USA	South Korea	Italy

ARCHERY — WOMEN

EVENT	GOLD	SILVER	BRONZE
Individual	Kim Kyung-Wook (KOR)	He Ying (CHN)	Olena Sadovnycha (UKR)
Team	South Korea	Germany	Poland

CYCLING — WOMEN

EVENT	GOLD		SILVER		BRONZE	
Road Race	Jeannie Longo-Ciprelli (FRA)	2:36:13	Imelda Chiappa (USA)	2:36:38	Clara Hughes (CAN)	2:36:44
Time Trial	Zulfia Zabirova (RUS)	36:40	Jeannie Longo-Ciprelli (FRA)	37:00	Clara Hughes (CAN)	37:13
Sprint	Felicia Ballanger (FRA)		Michelle Ferris (AUS)		Ingrid Haringa (NED)	
3,000 m Individual Pursuit	Antonella Bellutti (ITA)	3:33.595	Marion Clignet (FRA)	3:38.571	Judith Arnt (GER)	3:38.744
Individual Points Race	Nathalie Lancien (FRA)	24	Ingrid Haringa (NED)	23	Lucy Tyler-Sharman (AUS)	17
Cross-Country	Paola Pezzo (ITA)	1:50:51	Alison Sydor (CAN)	1:51:58	Susan DiMattei (USA)	1:52:36

OVERLEAF: America's David Robinson goes for the dunk on the way to victory over Angola. Mike Powell

CYCLING — MEN

EVENT	GOLD		SILVER		BRONZE	
Road Race	Pascal Richard (SUI)	4:53:56	Ralf Sorensen (DEN)	4:53:56	Max Sciandri (GBR)	4:53:58
Road TimeTrial	Miguel Indurain (ESP)	1:04.05	Abraham Olano (ESP)	1:04.17	Chris Boardman (GBR)	1:04.36
Sprint	Jens Fiedler (GER)		Marthy Nothstein (USA)		Curtis Harnett (CAN)	
1,000 m Time Trial	Florian Rousseau (FRA)	1:02.712	Erin Hartwell (USA)	1:02.940	Takandu Jumonji (JPN)	1:03.261
4,000 m Individual Pursuit	Andrea Collinelli (ITA)	4:20.893	Philippe Ermenault (FRA)	4:22.714	Bradley McGee (AUS)	4:26.121
4,000 m Team Pursuit	France	4:05.930	Russia	4:07.730	Australia	
Individual Points Race	Silvio Martinello (ITA)	37	Brian Walton (CAN)	29	Stuart O'Grady (AUS)	25
Cross-Country	Bart Brentjens (NED)	2:17:38	Thomas Frischknecht (SUI)	2:20:14	Miguel Martinez (FRA)	2:20:26

EQUESTRIANISM

EVENT	GOLD		SILVER		BRONZE	
Three-Day Event	Blyth Tait (NZL)	56.8	Sally Clark (NZL)	60.4	Kerry Millikin (USA)	73.7
Three-Day Event Team	Australia	203.85	USA	261.10	New Zealand	268.55
Grand Prix (Dressage)	Isabell Werth (GER)	235.09	Anky van Grunsven (NED)	233.02	Sven Rothenberger (NED)	224.94
Grand Prix (Dressage) Team	Germany	5553	Netherlands	5437	USA	5309
Grand Prix (Jumping)	Ulrich Kirchhoff (GER)	1.00	Willi Melliger (SUI)	4.00	Alexandra Ledermann (FRA)	4.00
Grand Prix (Jumping) Team	Germany	1.75	USA	12.00	Brazil	17.25

TABLE TENNIS — MEN

	GOLD	SILVER	BRONZE
Singles	Liu Guoliang CHN)	Wang Tao (CHN)	Joerg Rosskoff (GER)
Doubles	China	China	South Korea

TABLE TENNIS — WOMEN

	GOLD	SILVER	BRONZE
Single	Deng Yaping (CHN)	Chen Jung (TPE)	Qiao Hong (CHN)
Doubles	China	China	South Korea

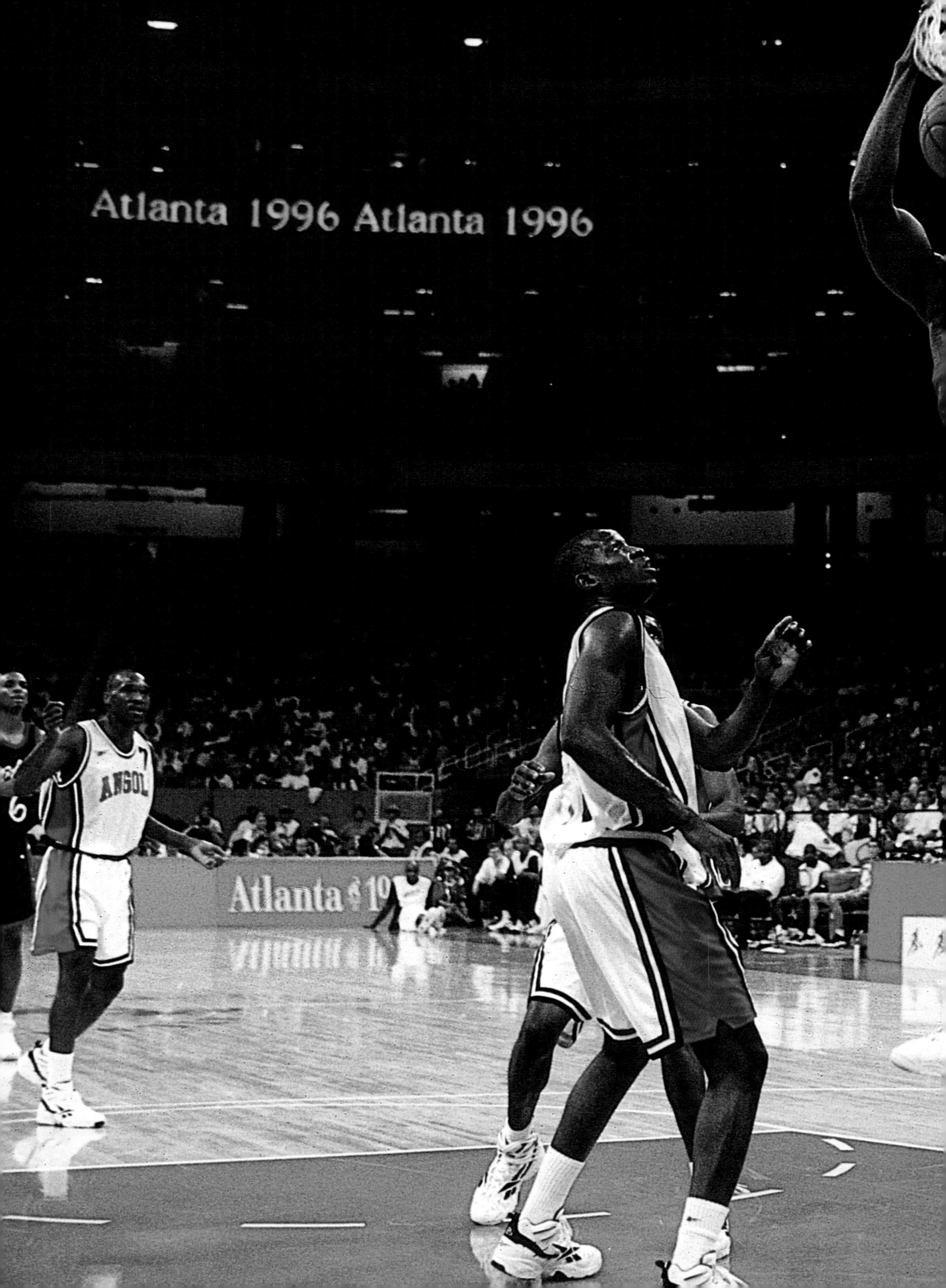
Atlanta 1996 Atlanta 1996
ANGOL
Atlanta

GYMNASTICS — MEN

EVENT	GOLD		SILVER		BRONZE	
Individual Combined Exercises	Li Xiaoshuang (CHN)	58.423	Alexei Nemov (RUS)	58.374	Vitali Sherbo (BLR)	58.197
Team	Russia	576.778	China	575.539	Ukraine	571.541
Parallel Bars	Rustam Sharipov (UKR)	9.837	Jair Lynch (USA)	9.825	Vitali Sherbo (BLR)	9.800
Floor	Ioannis Melissanidis (GRE)	9.950	Li Xiaoshuang (CHN)	9.837	Alexei Nemov (RUS)	9.800
Horse Vault	Alexei Nemov (RUS)	9.787	Yeo Hong-Chul (KOR)	9.756	Vitali Sherbo (BLR)	9.724
Horizontal Bar	Andreas Wecker (GER)	9.850	Krasimir Dounev (BUL)	9.825	Vitali Sherbo (BLR)	9.800
					Fan Bin (CHN)	9.800
					Alexei Nemov (RUS)	9.800
Rings	Yuri Chechi (ITA)	9.887	Szilveszter Csollany (HUN)	9.812	Dan Burnica (ROM)	9.812
Pommel Horse	Li Donghua (SUI)	9.875	Marius Urzica (ROM)	9.825	Alexei Nemov (RUS)	9.787

GYMNASTICS — WOMEN

EVENT	GOLD		SILVER		BRONZE	
Individual Combined Exercises	Lilia Podkopayeva (UKR)	39.255	Gina Gogean (ROM)	39.075	Lavinia Milosivici (ROM)	39.067
					Simona Amanar (ROM)	39.067
Team	USA	389.225	Russia	388.404	Romania	388.246
Floor	Lilia Podkopayeva (UKR)	9.887	Simona Amanar (ROM)	9.850	Dominique Dawes (USA)	9.837
Horse Vault	Simona Amanar (ROM)	9.825	Mo Huilan (CHN)	9.768	Gina Gogean (ROM)	9.750
Beam	Shannon Miller (USA)	9.862	Lilia Podkopayeva (UKR)	9.825	Gina Gogean (ROM)	9.787
Asymmetrical Bars	Svetlana Chorkina (RUS)	9.850	Wengji Bi (CHN)	9.837		
			Amy Chow (USA)	9.837		
Rhythmic Individual	Yekaterina Serebryanskaya (UKR)	39.683	Yanina Batyrchina (RUS)	39.382	Yelena Vitrichenko (UKR)	39.331
Rhythmic Team	Spain	38.933	Bulgaria	38.866	Russia	38.365

TENNIS — MEN

	GOLD	SILVER	BRONZE
Singles	Andre Agassi (USA)	Sergi Bruguera (ESP)	Leander Paes (IND)
Doubles	Mark Woodforde/Todd Woodbridge (AUS)	Tim Henman/Neil Broad (GBR)	Marc-Kevin Goellner/David Prinosil (GER)

TENNIS — WOMEN

	GOLD	SILVER	BRONZE
Single	Lindsay Davenport (USA)	Arantxa Sanchez-Vicario (ESP)	Jana Novotna (CZE)
Doubles	Gigi Fernandez / Mary Jo Fernandez (USA)	Jana Novotna / Helena Sukova (CZE)	Conchita Maranez / Arantxa Sanchez Vicario (ESP)

HANDBALL — WOMEN

GOLD	SILVER	BRONZE
Denmark	South Korea	Hungary

HOCKEY — MEN

GOLD	SILVER	BRONZE
Netherlands	Spain	Australia

HOCKEY — WOMEN

GOLD	SILVER	BRONZE
Australia	South Korea	Netherlands

VOLLEYBALL — MEN

GOLD	SILVER	BRONZE
Netherlands	Italy	Yugoslavia

VOLLEYBALL — WOMEN

GOLD	SILVER	BRONZE
Cuba	China	Brazil

BASKETBALL — MEN

GOLD	SILVER	BRONZE
USA	Yugoslavia	Lithuania

BASKETBALL — WOMEN

GOLD	SILVER	BRONZE
USA	Brazil	Australia

SOCCER — MEN

GOLD	SILVER	BRONZE
Nigeria	Argentina	Brazil

SOCCER — WOMEN

GOLD	SILVER	BRONZE
USA	China	Norway

HANDBALL — MEN

GOLD	SILVER	BRONZE
Croatia	Sweden	Spain

BEACH VOLLEYBALL

	GOLD	SILVER	BRONZE
Men's Pairs	USA	USA	Canada
Women's Pairs	Brazil	Brazil	Australia

BADMINTON — MEN

	GOLD	SILVER	BRONZE
Single	Poul-Erik Hoyer-Larsen (DEN)	Jiong Dong (CHN)	Rashid Sidek (MAS)
Doubles	Indonesia	Malaysia	Indonesia

BADMINTON — WOMEN

	GOLD	SILVER	BRONZE
Singles	Bang Soo-Hyun (KOR)	Mia Audina (INA)	Susi Susanti (INA)
Doubles	China	South Korea	China
Mixed Doubles	South Korea	South Korea	China

BASEBALL

GOLD	SILVER	BRONZE
Cuba	Japan	USA

SOFTBALL

GOLD	SILVER	BRONZE
USA	China	Australia

THE MILLENNIUM
GAMES

INTRODUCTION

The Millennium Games

It sprawls across a huge area 10 miles west of Sydney ... a $433 million monument to the Summer Games of 2000. Its arches rise 190 feet from the floor of Sydney Olympic Park, a cluster of 14 sports venues connected by pristine brick walkways. Here will be the soul of the games. Hills have been built and made grassy, endangered frogs have been saved. The stadium's official name is Stadium-Australia, but everyone calls it the Olympic Stadium.

It is here the future of the Olympic movement will be determined because, just as in Moscow 20 years earlier, the modern games are at a crossroads.

After the disasters of Atlanta and the cash-for-vote scandals which have dogged the movement in the preparations for the first Olympics of the new millennium, the International Olympic Committee desperately needs a 21st century pick-me-up to ensure they do not go the same way as the ancient games.

Sydney is promising to deliver. A vibrant, outdoorsy community, Sydney is already touting 2000 as the "Athletes' Games" because the city's air quality and average daytime temperatures (61 degrees to 68 degrees in late September) should be optimal for athletic performance.

Organizers are already promising that no Atlanta-style transportation problems will surface in their city. For one thing, there will be fewer spectators: Current estimates are that 6.1 million tickets will be sold

In Sydney, most athletes and members of the press will be able to walk from their lodgings to the venues. Besides the main stadium, the Sydney Olympic Park will contain the Olympic Village, the Officials Village, the Media Village, the Main Press Center, the International Broadcast Center and 15 of the 27 Olympic sports venues — all within a circle two miles in diameter.

Since the city is set on a harbor, ferries will be used to supplement ground transportation. Most importantly, Sydney's existing public transportation system, unlike Atlanta's MARTA, is designed to handle the kinds of numbers Australia's largest city (3.74 million in the metropolitan area) will see during the games.

It is all in keeping with Sydney's boast that the 2000 games will be the greenest in history.

The main facilities have been built on a once-disused industrial brown-field known as Homebush Bay. Formerly home to a government-run slaughterhouse, brick pit, rubbish dump and armaments store, as well as to private chemical companies, the land and the adjacent wetlands and river system had been thoroughly degraded by decades of environmental assault.

Sydney also hopes that planning will help it avoid the technological glitches that plagued Info '96, the IBM system that was supposed to distribute Atlanta competition results and athletes' biographical information instantaneously but was so slow that people began referring to it as Info '97.

Also, unlike Atlanta, the government has a huge financial stake in the success of the games. Indeed, the government of New South Wales, of which Sydney is the capital, has underwritten the cost of venue construction – estimated at $1.2 billion ($840 million US) – in exchange for which taxpayers have been guaranteed 90 per cent of the profits.

Ultimately, though, it is the athletes which make the games. If they continue to perform as they did throughout the 20th century, then the future of the Olympic games should be secure well into the 21st century.

RONALDO DA COSTA

For a decade, the world marathon record resisted all challenges from some of the finest distance runners of the ages. Then in Berlin in 1998 the little-known Brazilian Ronaldo da Costa covered 42.195 kilometers in 2hr 6min 05sec, slashing 45 seconds off the previous mark.

Da Costa is running's rags-to-riches story. Just as generations of boxers fought their way out of the slums of New York's Bronx and London's East End, so da Costa has run away from the poverty of the Brazilian favela. One of 12 children, he grew up the son of a farm laborer in Descoberto, 110 kilometers north of Rio de Janeiro, in the same district where footballer Pele was born.

Tests conducted on da Costa using machinery that was developed for the US space program, and is now used on jet fighter pilots in the Brazilian air force, have shown the little man to be a freak of nature.

He has a resting pulse of just 45 beats per minute (the average is 60) and in da Costa this hardly rises even after prolonged, demanding running. Blood tests have shown an ability for steady, high-paced running which the scientists in Rio had never before encountered.

Such is da Costa's celebrity in Brazil — where he is known as the second most famous Ronaldo, in deference to the international soccer striker — that he is unable to train in his own country.

CATHY FREEMAN

Cathy Freeman became a national figure in Australia in 1994 when she waved the Aboriginal flag after winning Commonwealth Games gold medals in the 200 and 400 meters in Victoria, Canada. Australia's Commonwealth Games chief Arthur Tunstall was widely rebuked for criticizing Freeman's gesture, but the pair later made a television commercial together.

Conservatively, Freeman, the 1998 Australian Personality of the Year, is worth about $1.1 million a year and the pressure on her to perform well in Sydney will be immense, especially after finishing second in the 1996 Atlanta 400 meters and winning the world title in Athens a year later.

Disaster threatened to ruin her plans in 1998 when a serious Achilles injury sidelined her. But she

has battled back and is set to be the most familiar face during the Sydney games, staring down everywhere from billboards.

She knows that without a gold medal all the money will not mean so much. "Sure I've experienced success," she says, "but true success to me is an Olympic gold medal."

As an an Aboriginal, Freeman has found herself at the center of disputes between political parties who believe that athletes from ethnic communities should boycott the games because of Australia's past treatment of them.

But she has made it clear that nothing will divert her from her plan to win the gold medal in Sydney. And if she wins, will she carry the Aboriginal flag?

"If I'm allowed to, I will. If I'm not, I won't."

HAILE GEBRSELASSIE

Haile Gebrselassie, the 1996 Olympic 10,000 meters champion, is to distance running what Ronaldo is to football or Michael Jordan to basketball. The Ethiopian redefines the outer limits almost every time he steps on the track and is a prolific world record breaker.

Gebrselassie has been called a "genetic phenomenon." He runs with seemingly effortless grace, his head barely moving as he strides like a sprinter on the balls of his feet. For a distance runner, he possesses an enormously powerful chest and long legs.

Gebrselassie has a keen sense of athletics' history and wants to win the 5,000 and 10,000 meters in Sydney to be ranked alongside Miruts Yifter, his compatriot who did the double in Moscow in 1980.

"I want to run better in Sydney than I did in Atlanta two years ago," said Gebrselassie. "I got one in Atlanta, I would like two in Sydney — like Miruts Yifter did in Moscow, when I stole my father's radio so I could listen to the commentary. I dream for that. Our people are poor. When we get something from somewhere, our people will be very happy."

Gebrselassie is already fantastically rich in one of the poorest countries on the map but is careful not to flaunt his status. He has a lucrative five-year shoe contract with Adidas worth $2.5 million and has done a TV commercial for Pepsi-Cola in East Africa. Between endorsements and fees for running in meets, he earns as much as $1.5 million each summer.

MAURICE GREENE

Americans believe that 24-year-old Maurice Greene is the man to step into Carl Lewis's shoes. At the Athens Grand Prix in 1999, he broke Donovan Bailey's world 100 meters record set during the Atlanta Olympics three years earlier when he ran a phenomenal 9.79 — five-hundredths of a second faster than the Canadian.

Greene seems to have a sparkle in his eyes which Lewis had in his heyday. It indicates a belief that he can become the first American to cross the line first in an Olympic 100 meters since Lewis in 1984. (Lewis retained his title in 1988 but only after Ben Johnson was disqualified.)

When he won his World Championship crown on the same Athens track in 1997, his coach John Smith described him as "a diamond in the rough." Now the rough edges have been smoothed away and Greene is predicting he will put US sprinting back on top.

Born in Kansas City, Greene never attended a four-year college like many American athletes. He started running when he was eight years old and remained in Kansas City with his high school trainer,

Al Hobson, until 1996 when his father drove him to Los Angeles to work with Smith, the former world 440-yard record holder.

Now he promises to seek victories at both 100 and 200 meters in Sydney to live up to the number plate on his Mercedes: MO GOLD.

American track athlete Maurice Green. Mike Powell

HICHAM EL GUERROUJ

The Millennium Games

Algeria's Nouredinne Morceli, the defending 1,500 meters champion, is poised to be knocked off his throne by the new Prince of the Desert Hicham El Guerrouj. The Moroccan's coronation as the world's finest middle-distance runner of his generation might have taken place in Atlanta in 1996 if he had not tripped on Morceli's heel after moving up to challenge him at the start of the last lap, allowing his rival to claim the title.

El Guerrouj showed what might have been a few weeks later at the Grand Prix final in Milan by ending Morceli's four-year, 45-race winning streak at 1,500 meters and the mile. Then, in 1997, he succeeded Morceli as World Champion and a year later broke his world record in the 1,500 meters, setting new figures of 3min 26.0sec. In Rome, in July 1999 he broke the world record for the mile, which had been standing for six years, completing it in 3:43.13.

Aziz Daouda, the technical director of the Moroccan federation, already rates El Guerrouj higher than Said Aouita — a North African treasure after a career that included world records and Olympic titles.

Yet El Guerrouj, who will turn 26 during the Sydney games, may not ever have taken up running if it had not been for his mother. He wanted to be a goalkeeper but she got fed up washing his dirty kit and he turned to the track!

Hicham El Guerrouj of Morocco is hoping to avenge his heartbreaking tumble in Atlanta with a 1,500m victory in Sydney. Mike Cooper

GRANT HACKETT

The Millennium Games

Grant Hackett's clash with Kieren Perkins over 1,500 meters in Sydney has had the Australian public agog with anticipation for more than two years.

While Perkins, the dual Olympic 1,500 meter champion, was taking a year off after his Atlanta triumph, Hackett came from seemingly nowhere to take his place atop the podium.

Hackett's first Australian team was the 1997 world short course (25 meters pool) swimming championships in Gothenburg, Sweden, where he won his first international 1,500 meters title as well as being part of the winning 4x200 meters relay team and third in the 400 meters freestyle.

He followed that up with a win in the 1,500 meters at the Pan Pacific Championships in Fukuoka, Japan. Then he cemented his place as the new world distance king with victory in the 1,500 meters at at the 1998 World Championships in Perth.

As Perkins struggled to get back into form in his pet event, claiming only bronze in the Kuala Lumpur Commonwealth Games final, Hackett produced his best ever performance to clock 14min 50.92sec.

The Gold Coast university student has beaten Perkins in the past two years when the swimming superstar has been far from his peak. Hackett wants the opportunity to race him on equal terms in Sydney.

"It's nice to beat Kieren Perkins — but to beat him at his best would be a lot better," he says. "Having Kieren swimming fast is good for the sport and also for me. It keeps me on my toes the whole time."

MIA HAMM

The Millennium Games

Mia Hamm makes commercials with Michael Jordan, was chosen one of the world's 50 most beautiful people and is the greatest goal-scorer in soccer history. Her autobiography was released in 1999, explaining how she has won a World Cup and Olympic gold medal.

She is considered the most marketable female athlete in America and has a building named after her at Nike headquarters — as does Jordan.

The 27-year-old Hamm should be in her prime in Sydney when she leads the US women's soccer team. If soccer repeats its performance at the 1996 Olympics, before the largest crowds ever to watch the sport, women's soccer could take another giant leap forward.

Hamm represents the future of the sport. Another outstanding performance in the Olympics could catapult her even higher up toward Jordan's scale. She is already the most well-known soccer player in the United States, ahead of even male players like Kasey Keller who play in the English Premiership.

Not only is Hamm one of the world's fastest players but her accuracy with either foot is remarkable. She has a feel for positioning and such quick acceleration that it is startling when she is not the first one to a free ball.

LORETTA HARROP

The Millennium Games

Loretta Harrop is looking forward to the 2000 Olympics in her native Sydney. The women's triathlon is the first event on the program in a country which worships the outdoor life and relishes each of the individual sports of swimming, cycling and running that make up the triathlon.

Harrop, a former butterfly swimmer who turned to the triathlon after missing out on the Australian national team for the 1994 Commonwealth Games, will be propelled to the status of national icon if she triumphs.

The former Cavendish Road High student, who represented Queensland at volleyball, netball and swimming, did not creep up on triathlon's big names. She arrived in spectacular style, determined to go all the way to the top. An ITU race in Sydney in October 1997 kick-started Harrop's professional career by finishing second to World Champion Emma Carney.

It removed any doubts and convinced her she could compete and beat the best. She has carved out a reputation as a street fighter. She has devoted a herself to improving her running which was "embarrassing" when she started out.

The person least surprised by Harrop's stunning improvement this season has been her father, Russell. "She's a gutsy little girl for her size," he says. "She's always been very, very determined, whether it was at swimming, playing netball, or karate. She's never satisfied. She always wants to do better, nothing beats her."

A gold medal in Sydney would take some topping though.

Hometown favorite, Loretta Harrop, originally a swimmer, will compete in the triathlon. Phil Cole

RAYMOND HECHT

Raymond Hecht hopes to fulfil the potential in Sydney which he first showed as a teenager in 1987 when he was ranked among the top juniors in the world and tipped for greatness.

Then injury intervened and his career went into a downward spiral. The German pulled himself out of it and was unlucky to miss a medal in the 1996 Atlanta games when he finished fourth.

But the javelin is such a technical event that anything could happen in Sydney. As befits a man who is a trained mechanic, Hecht loves tinkering with his technique in an attempt to make everything go smoothly.

"There is nothing better than watching the spear leave your hand and soar onwards and upwards," he says. "When it lands beyond 90 meters, it is a specially sweet moment. "

One bizarre claim to fame for Hecht is that he must be the only javelin thrower in history to have set a national record in a snowstorm. It happened at Essenbach in February 1994 when he threw 90.06 meters. Almost immediately afterwards the meeting was abandoned because of a blizzard!

Hecht's personal best of 92.60 meters was set at Oslo in 1995 and ranked him Number One in the world for that year. "That was a very special moment — but finishing fourth in Atlanta was a horrible feeling," he said.

"I believe I can win the gold medal in Sydney and then I will retire a happy man."

MARION JONES

The transformation of Marion Jones from college basketball player to the most successful female track and field athlete in Olympic history could be the story of the Sydney games.

The American is planning to chase gold medals in the 100 meters, 200 meters, long jump, 4x100 meters relay, and 4x400 meters relay — which would eclipse even the four victories of the Holland's Fanny Blankers-Koen in London in 1948.

Track historians see another Wilma Rudolph, the 1960 Olympic triple gold medal sprinter, or Florence Griffith Joyner, who also won three golds in 1988. Others look to the future and see Jones traveling at speeds and jumping distances never attained before by a woman.

"If she stays on track she's going to be one of the greatest females ever to put a pair of shoes on," says John Smith, who coached France's Marie-Jose Perec to the Olympic 200 and 400 meters titles.

Her feats are already pretty extraordinary and

Trevor Graham, Jones's coach, believes the 24-year-old can some day break the world record in three events — the women's 100 meters, 200 meters and long jump.

Jones was an outstanding teenage runner who, at the age of 15, produced times of 11.14sec and 22.58sec for 100 and 200 meters respectively for her Californian high school. She could have gone to the 1992 Barcelona Olympics but instead took up a basketball scholarship at North Carolina University, only returning to the track in time for the 1997 season.

RIGHT: America's Marion Jones. Jamie McDonald

WILSON KIPKETER

At the Atlanta games in 1996, the world's top 800 meters runner, Wilson Kipketer, was kept out because he was in the process of switching his citizenship from Kenya to Denmark. Few doubt he would have won the gold medal.

Since then he has become a citizen of his adopted Scandinavian homeland, won two world titles at his specialist event, and, in 1997, reduced in two stages the world 800 meters record down to its present mark of 1min 41.11sec.

"I was not able to compete in the Atlanta Olympics and so this is one title I want to win," said Kipketer. "And I want to win it for Denmark because the country has helped me enormously and opened its door wide to me."

Kipketer, a former schoolboy at the famous St. Patrick's College, left Kenya in 1990 to study engineering in Copenhagen, fell in love with a Danish girl and Denmark and has never left. His decision to take out Danish citizenship attracted fierce criticism in the place of his birth and it was the Kenyan government which blocked him receiving his new passport in time to run in Atlanta.

During 1996 and 1997, Kipketer was unbeaten and seemingly unbeatable. But he was hit by a bout of malaria during a visit to Kenya in 1998 and is not the dominant force he once was. But if justice is served, he will win the gold medal in Sydney denied to him in Atlanta.

SIMON LESSING

Simon Lessing, resident in England for just one month of his life, is Britain's biggest hope of a gold medal in Sydney. Lessing, whose mother was born in Britain, spent the first 18 years of his life in Cape Town and Durban, stopped a month in London, then moved to France.

The triathlete, a nephew of the famous writer Doris Lessing, has won a record four world titles and is heavily tipped to strike gold in Sydney when the sport makes it debut on the Olympic program.

Lessing, World Champion in each of the past two Olympic years, must see off a phalanx of highly-rated Australians, inspired towards excellence by the prospect of Olympic glory on home soil.

His strongest weapon is his running. He is helped by Thierry Brusseau, an 8min 22sec steeplechaser and French Olympian, who trains with and advises Lessing just outside Salon de Provence, in southern France, where the Briton lives.

A former South African champion, he fled the country of his birth before the sporting ban was lifted to concentrate on his triathlon career and to avoid having to do national service. While never having lived in the UK, his parents moved back to Scotland in 1998 and you can bet that British fans will not be slow to hail his success if he wins in Sydney.

Simon Lessing represents Great Britain. Phil Cole

502

DENISE LEWIS

One of the few success stories of the British expedition to Atlanta in 1996 was that of Denise Lewis, who proved herself one of the greatest all-round female athletes in the world with a bronze medal in the heptathlon. Come Sydney, the vivacious athlete will be the favorite to emulate the gold medal won by Mary Peters at Munich in 1972.

Lewis, from Wolverhampton, first came to prominence after winning the Commonwealth Games gold in Victoria in 1994. It in was there that she beat the defending champion and overwhelming favorite Jane Flemming by eight points. She has since gone on to regain her Commonwealth title, in Kuala Lumpur in 1998, and also lift the European crown, in Budapest.

Not since Daley Thompson's days has Britain been able to boast such a successful athlete. "I can't say one person inspired me," says Lewis. "Not even Daley when he was at his best. I just moved into it."

While Lewis the athlete has made outstanding progress during the last few years, Lewis the model has also made a striking impression. As one of the most memorable pin-ups in the Olympic fund-raising calendar put together by Sharron Davies, Lewis, who has also featured in an Adidas poster campaign, has the looks to maximize the commercial possibilities her talent has given her.

Denise Lewis of Great Britain will compete in the heptathlon. Alex Livesey

TEGLA LOROUPE

When Tegla Loroupe returned to Kenya after winning the New York City Marathon in 1994, a party was organized and the villagers presented her parents with nine cattle, 16 sheep, and some land. Yet it was the words of the women in her tribe she still values the most.

"You did a good job," they told her. "You showed that we are like the men, we can do things. We are not useless."

Male athletes have made Kenya synonymous with success in long-distance running, but women are discouraged from competing beyond the age of 16 when they are expected to start a family.

Loroupe will start as the favorite for the Olympic marathon title after setting a new world record of 2hr 20min 47sec in Rotterdam in 1998.

At 4 foot 11 inches and 85 pounds, and with feet so tiny that even children's running shoes are too big for her, Loroupe is the smallest world-class marathon runner — and probably the toughest.

One of seven children from the town of Kapenguria on the Ugandan border, about 400 miles from Nairobi, Loroupe began running for the same reason most Kenyan youngsters do: to avoid being late for school. "If you were late they beat you," she said.

She is a member of the Bokot tribe, nomads who once drove their cattle across the plains of Kenya. As a child, speed work took second place to ranch work. "It was good training for me," she says. "I often used to chase the cattle herd for up to 12 miles. I didn't know I was training."

FIU MINGXIA

RIGHT: After winning Olympic gold in 1992 and 1996, China's Fiu Mingxia retired. She returns to competition in Sydney. Tony Duffy

PREVIOUS PAGE: An aerial view of Olympic construction in Sydney. Nick Wilson

Fu Mingxia riveted the Olympics when she became a champion at all of 13. The Chinese woman won gold medals in 1992 and 1996, then retired at 19, tired of diving and ready for college. Now she back is aiming for the Sydney games.

From the 12-year-old who became the youngest diving world champion in 1991, Fu has grown into a confident 21-year-old with gold tints in her black hair and who is ready to captivate the Australian public.

On the springboard in Barcelona, she was all compact, controlled, muscular grace. Fu won the springboard and platform at the Atlanta Olympics in 1996, the first woman in 36 years to do so.

Spotted at age 10 and brought to Beijing from her home in Hubei province, Fu endured eight or nine hours of training a day. When she retired after Atlanta, she said she was exhausted. She enrolled at Beijing's Qinghua University and gained a lot of weight.

"I didn't want to put on a swimming costume," she said. "I didn't really miss it."

Then the realization that history beckoned brought her back. In Sydney, where she will again aim for the platform-springboard double, Fu could become the first diver to take five Olympic golds.

She has likened her return to diving to learning how to bicycle. Fu says: "When you first start, you're all wobbly, but the more you ride, the smoother you become. That's the feeling."

DOMINIQUE MOCEANU

Dominique Moceanu stood on the podium in Atlanta, a gold medal around her neck, a wide grin on her small face, the world seemingly before her.

At 14, she already was one of the best US gymnasts ever. And with her cute, Nadia Comaneci-like looks, bubbly personality, and endearing story of Romanian parents, she was a marketing dream.

But reality has a funny way of rewriting fairy tales, and Moceanu's pretty story is no different. Since Atlanta, her life has been ripped apart by money, ambition and family differences that not even love is strong enough to overcome.

Her money has disappeared and her father, Dumitru — who was accused of inquiring about hiring a hit man to kill her coach and a close friend —

was at one time forbidden from coming near her. Victory in Sydney would be one of the most emotional moments of the games.

Moceanu was enrolled in classes as a toddler and shortly after her tenth birthday she started training with renowned coach Bela Karolyi, who'd already led Comaneci and Mary Lou Retton to gold.

With the Olympics just a year away, Moceanu mania went into full swing. She made the cover of *Vanity Fair* and even published her autobiography.

She did not win any individual medals in Atlanta, but when the Magnificent Seven became the first US women's team to win gold, the spotlight grew brighter and the money poured in. That is when the problems in Moceanu's life, so carefully covered up over the years, began to show.

LEFT: America's Dominique Moceneau, hopes to repeat her team's Atlanta gold medal performance. Doug Pensinger

IAN THORPE

Ian Thorpe, nicknamed the "human thorpedo" after his Perth world title triumph in 1998, appears on target to sink his rivals again at the Olympics.

The Australian schoolboy at the age of only 15 stamped himself as Australia's youngest ever male world swimming champion in Perth, mowing down Queensland's Grant Hackett to win the 400 meters freestyle in 3min 46.29sec.

Eight months later, he swam within an agonizing one-hundredth of a second of the world 200 meters freestyle record at the Kuala Lumpur Commonwealth Games and was just 0.55sec outside Kieren Perkins' world 400 meters record days later. He was also part of Australia's world record beating 4x200 meters

freestyle relay team in Malaysia, where he won four gold medals.

Thorpe broke his first solo world record at the Australian short-course titles just after the Commonwealth Games, clocking 3min 39.82sec over 400 meters and wiping out the previous record held by New Zealand's Olympic champion Danyon Loader. It earned him the accolade of Swimmer of the Year in 1998.

Thorpe, who propels himself through the water with size 16 feet, hopes to contest the 100, 200 and 400 meters freestyle events in Sydney. He has had no trouble catching the eye of sponsors after Perth and is one of the most sought after athletes in Australia.

GABRIELA SZABO

Hailing from Dracula's Transylvania, tiny Gabriela Szabo looks so pale you fear she may have been a victim of the mythical brute. But when the 23-year-old lines up for the 5,000 meters in Sydney, she will be the one hoping to put the bite on the rest of the world.

The Romanian has been an outstanding distance runner since her teenage days, claiming the 1991 European 3,000 meters title and the world junior crown the following year.

Szabo is proof that looks can be deceptive. Standing barely five feet tall, it appears one puff of wind could blow her over. Yet she is set dominate the world of women's distance running into the new millennium. She is already in the record books for winning the world title in Athens in 1997 and completing the 1,500-3,000 meters double at the 1999 world indoor championships.

The only blot on her record is failing to make the 1996 Olympic 5,000 meters final. But the little girl who departed the stadium in tears returned a few days later with a new core of steel to claim an unexpected silver in the 1,500 meters.

"She looks like a tiny doll but she has the heart of a great athlete," says Doina Melinte, Romania's 1984 Olympic 800 meters champion.

Szabo is blessed with two things that any great distance runner must have: endurance and the ability to finish very fast. She has the range to be a world beater at every distance between 1,500 meters and 10,000 meters, and eventually even the marathon.

Tiny Gabriela Szabo of Romania is medalist hopeful in the 5,000 m.Clive Brunskill

MARK TODD

Mark Todd is one of the most respected names in eventing and universally acclaimed by fellow riders as one of the greatest horsemen in the world. But Sydney will be his swansong. Afterwards, Todd plans to retire and return to his farm in New Zealand with his wife Carolyn and their two children, James and Lauren.

Born and raised in Cambridge, New Zealand, Todd started life as a farmer. But after the 1978 World Championships in Lexington, Kentucky, he moved to England to concentrate on eventing – the first New Zealand eventer to do so, although all their top riders have now followed suit.

Todd had Moscow 1980 in his sights as first

Olympics but was disappointed due to boycott. But he won the individual gold gold medal at Los Angeles four years later on a tiny horse called Charisma, which he had brought over from New Zealand and had been told would never be more than a Pony Club pony!

Following his victory, Todd was voted most eligible bachelor in New Zealand and appeared on "This Is Your Life."

He retained his title in Seoul four years later but was denied the opportunity of a hat-trick in Barcelona when his horse Greylag went lame on the eve of the cross-country section and he had to withdraw.

Remarkably, history repeated itself in Atlanta in 1996 when Todd's horse Kayem also suffered injury.

DEBBIE WATSON

No one could begrudge the Australian women's water polo team their time in the Olympic spotlight. The event only makes its Olympic debut in Sydney — a full century after men's water polo first appeared on the program at the 1900 Paris Games — because of the persistence of the players.

The Aussies, the World Cup silver medalists, even donned their cossies to picket leading world swimming officials during a visit to Australia before they eventually relented and made some space on the games program in 1997. The chance to compete at an Olympics was enough to convince former national team captain Debbie Watson to stay in the sport until 2000.

Water polo can have few better or more entertaining spokespeople than Watson as it battles for recognition and publicity with many other relatively "minor" sports.

She is genuinely grateful that with Australia gaining an automatic place on the draw as the host nation she will be able to make her Olympic dream come true in a sport she describes as "a combination of wrestling, rugby, synchronized swimming, and survival swimming all whilst looking incredibly innocent."

The team will be preparing for Sydney almost as full-time athletes. "So we can actually afford bread and water and condensed milk and all that sort of stuff now," jokes Watson.

LIST OF ABBREVIATIONS

AHO   Netherlands Antilles
ALG   Algeria
ANG   Angola
ANT   Antigua
ARG   Argentina
AUS   Australia
AUT   Austria
AZE   Azerbaijan
BAH   Bahamas
BAR   Barbados
BEL   Belgium
BER   Bermuda
BIZ   Belarus
BOL   Bolivia
BRN   Bahrain
BRU   Brunei
BUL   Bulgaria
CAN   Canada
CAY   Cayman Islands
CHA   Chad
CHI   Chile
CHN   China
COL   Colombia
COM   Comoros
CPV   Cape Verde
CRC   Costa Rica
CRO   Croatia
CUB   Cuba
CYP   Cyprus
CZE   Czech Republic
DEN   Denmark
DMA   Dominica
DOM   Dominican Republic
ECU   Ecuador
ESA   El Salvador
ESP   Spain
EST   Estonia
ETH   Ethiopia
EUN   Commonwealth of Independent States
      (used after the breakup of the old
      Soviet Union)
FIN   Finland
FRA   France
FRG   Germany (West)
GAM   Gambia
GBR   Great Britain
GDR   Germany (East)
GER   Germany (as a combined team)
GHA   Ghana
GRE   Greece

GUA   Guatemala
GUI   Guinea
GUM   Guam
GUY   Guyana
HAI   Haiti
HKG   Hong Kong
HUN   Hungary
INA   Indonesia
IND   India
IOP   Independent Olympic
      Participants
IRL   Ireland
IRN   Iran
IRQ   Iraq
ISL   Iceland
ISR   Israel
JAM   Jamaica
JOR   Jordan
KAZ   Kazakhstan
KEN   Kenya
KOR   Korea
KSA   Kingdom of Saudi Arabia
KUW   Kuwait
LAT   Latvia
LBA   Libya
LBR   Liberia
LCA   Saint Lucia
LIT   Liechtenstein
LTU   Lithuania
LUX   Luxembourg
MAD   Madagascar
MAL   Malaysia
MAR   Morocco
MAW   Malawi
MOZ   Mozambique
MRI   Mauritius
MTN   Mauritania
NAM   Namibia
NCA   Nicaragua
NED   Netherlands
NEP   Nepal
NGR   Nigeria
NIG   Niger
NOR   Norway
NZL   New Zealand
OMA   Oman
PAK   Pakistan
PAN   Panama
PAR   Paraguay
PER   Peru

PHI   Philippines
POL   Poland
POR   Portugal
PRK   Democratic People's Republic of
      Korea
QAT   Qatar
ROM   Romania
RSA   South Africa
RUS   Russian Federation
RWA   Rwanda
SAF   South Africa
SER   Serbia
SIN   Singapore
SLE   Sierra Leone
SLO   Slovenia
SOL   Solomon Islands
SRI   Sri Lanka
SUD   Sudan
SUI   Switzerland
SVK   Slovakia
SWE   Sweden
SWZ   Swaziland
SYR   Syria
TAN   Tanzania
TCH   Czechoslovakia
THA   Thailand
TJK   Tajikistan
TKM   Turkmenistan
TPE   Taipei (formerly
      Formosa/Taiwan)
TRI   Trinidad and Tobago
TUN   Tunisia
TUR   Turkey
UAE   United Arab Emirates
UKR   Ukraine
URS   Soviet Union
URU   Uruguay
UZB   Uzbekistan
VAN   Vanuatu
VEN   Venezuela
VIE   Vietnam
VIN   St Vincent and the Grenadines
VOL   Upper Volta
YEM   Yemen
YUG   Yugoslavia
ZAI   Zaire
ZAM   Zambia
ZIM   Zimbabwe